SILVIE

SILVIA GROHS-MARTIN

WELCOME RAIN / PUBLISHERS
New York

SILVIE by Silvia Grohs-Martin
Copyright © 2000 by Silvia Grohs-Martin.
All rights reserved.
Printed in the United States of America.

Silvia would like to thank Kati Meister, Janet Keller
of the Shoah Foundation, Iris Rainer Dart,
Sandra McDonald, Patti Kenner and Jutta Sayles
for their friendship and support.

Direct any inquiries to
Welcome Rain Publishers LLC,
225 West 35th Street, Suite 1100,
New York, NY 10001.

CIP data available from the Publisher.

ISBN 1-56649-150-9
Manufactured in the United States of America
by BLAZE I.P.I.

First Edition: July 2000
1 3 5 7 9 10 8 6 4 2

⤚Contents

INTRODUCTION 1

PART ONE A MAKE-BELIEVE WORLD
One 5
Two 25
Three 40
Four 58
Five 76
Six 92
Seven .108

PART TWO BOUNDLESS BORDERS,
UNENDING JOURNEY
Eight .125
Nine 136
Ten 154
Eleven .181
Twelve .198
Thirteen 212

PART THREE AND ALL THE GODS WENT
TO FIND ANOTHER WORLD
Fourteen 227
Fifteen .246
Sixteen .259

Contents

Seventeen 271

Eighteen 288

Nineteen 302

PART FOUR   TWENTY KILOMETERS TO LÜBECK

Twenty 327

CASUALITY COUNT 350

EPILOGUE 351

INDEX 357

❧ Introduction

It was a wonderful day. Perhaps the Dutch people of Amsterdam had made special arrangements with the weather god. It was absolutely perfect, and the tourists were impressed. The quaint city with its narrow cobblestone streets was cluttered with vacationers, most of whom were taking pictures of each other. Enormous crowds gathered at the boat stands, impatiently waiting for rides through the picturesque canals. Less ambitious groups invading the outdoor coffeehouses, happily soaked in the late August sun, while buzzing waiters, their sweat dripping into every drink, did their best to accommodate the thirsty wanderers.

I watched this carefree display thinking how much everything had changed. I lived here once, and somehow I had always known that one day I would return.

I left Amsterdam in the early spring of 1943. This was now August 1964. More than twenty-one years had passed. Not only years, but lifetimes. In these lifetimes I had lived in America, globe-trotted across the earth — never staying anywhere very long, never really knowing why.

I do know now.

I have returned to Amsterdam because this is where my theater is — the glorious, magnificently grand Schouwburg where as an actress I spent the most joyous and the most devastating days of my life. Built in 1891, it served for half a century as the showcase for every international artist, including the great Sarah Bernhardt.

During the German occupation of Amsterdam, in the early spring of 1941, all Jews were banned from public places. Chosen as a specific Jewish theater, the Schouwburg had become the last and only outlet for social and cultural activity.

By October 1942, the "Final Solution" of the Jewish problem — deportation to concentration camps — abruptly brought down the curtain. Overnight, the Schouwburg became a detention center and transit depot. Through massive raids, Jews were dumped there; and other performing artists and I, forcibly detained, were put to the dismaying task of guarding our own audiences. For many Jews, this theater was their last place of residence.

What happened there has haunted me — has never let me go.

On that sunny August day as I let the city's playful mood engulf me, walking alongside strangers through old familiar streets, I saw my own reflection in a mirror — forty-five years looked back at me. And, as I looked back on those forty-five years, I suddenly realized I no longer could escape reliving my life, telling my story, and that of this theater.

PART ONE

A
Make-
Believe
World

⌐ ONE

I WAS BORN IN VIENNA, AUSTRIA, and given the name of Silvie. I grew up with lots of Viennese waltzes, the sensuous aroma of chestnut trees in bloom, and a taste for the good life. Viennese people have a reputation for being extremely charming, and I did my best to live up to it. Vaccinated with romantic nostalgia, I am the product of a make-believe world, heir to a peculiar, bittersweet culture.

My immediate family were my parents; an older sister, Kate; a twin sister, Elly; and our stone-deaf grandmother. My upper-middle-class Hungarian mother was all woman, including her Hungarian temperament. She was a perfect lady. Mama had a great deal of flair, and was quite enchanting, at least that's what Papa said. I was told that I looked exactly like her. We both had flaming red hair, the same delicate features, and very fair, almost transparent skin. Mama's eyes were grayish-blue; mine, grass green, and she assured me that having grass green eyes was very special. My sister Kate claims that when the doctors took their first look at me, they immediately informed my distressed parents that I would never survive: "Too sickly, too frail, too tiny."

Our family occupied a lovely apartment on the fourth floor of an elegant old house, right in the heart of Vienna, with many large rooms, lots of big windows, mysterious, long hallways, and a spectacular view. From the bedroom windows, we could see most of the city and a huge flowering church garden. From the dining-room windows, we saw the Blue Danube Canal which, as every Viennese will tell you, was never blue.

I don't recall the first years of my life at all. Since there is nothing stored in my memory bank, I have earnestly considered the possibility that I was born at the age of four. At four, awareness struck me like lightning. An extraordinary thing happened: I became a full-fledged actress, and quickly jumped from imitating grown-ups in Mama's clothes onto the professional stage. My appearances ranged from comedies to tragedies, none of which I understood, but, oh how I adored the applause and all that magic.

I was fifteen when my biggest break came. A major German film company offered me a starring role in a movie, to be shot on location in Berlin. Mama was to come with me. It was all arranged. Our suitcases were packed; we had said our good-byes and were waiting for the taxi when the phone rang. The caller asked us to please drop by and pick up some last-minute changes in my contract. Mama asked me to go. I was to meet the telephone voice in his suite at the Grand Hotel. When I got there, a heavyset, cigar-puffing man waited for me at the door. Instead of an introduction or "Please come in," he hit me with a bombshell. My contract was canceled! Not the film — me.

Why? Because I was a Jew!

I bit my lips until they bled. A skinny man, with horn-rimmed glasses, brought me a glass of water. I couldn't swallow. He mumbled that my agent had been instructed to tell me why. The fat movie mogul was merciless. Not only did he tear my contract up, but he also felt compelled to give me a full account of my ancestry. "You are a Jew, your mother is a Jew, and you have a non-Aryan grandmother." It wasn't a statement, it was an accusation. I said nothing; just choked back my tears and left.

Mama was waiting for me in front of our building, taxi, luggage and all. "Send him away, we're not going anywhere!"

In our apartment, I threw myself on my bed and beat the feather pillows with my fists. It did not bring me any satisfaction or release. The moment Mama walked in, I blurted it all out: "They've taken the part away from me because we're Jews and because Grandma is not an Aryan!" I didn't even know what that meant.

Mama's color changed from pale to pink and then to paper white. She was stupefied. A mechanical headshake was all she could manage.

I screamed, "Tell me *why?* Why was my biggest chance just blown to bits?"

"Nonsense," she uttered. "It 's all nonsense."

"Why don't you tell them that? I bet that's gonna make them change their mind!"

Mama paced back and forth, then stopped short in front of me. "You want an answer? I don't have one." Then she said that things were a little rough in Germany, but that there was no reason to believe they would affect us here.

"What things? Why is it rough in Germany, and what has it to do with me?"

"Nothing, that's just my point. Rumors! I've been hearing them for years. Just didn't want to believe they were true."

"What rumors?"

"That they don't want Jews in Germany."

"Why not? Have we done something?"

"Of course not!"

"Who the hell are 'they'?"

"Nazis! A small group of fascist, power-hungry fanatics who stir up anti-Semitism to cover up their crimes."

"What crimes?"

"Plundering. Stealing from the Jews, persecuting the Jews, and blaming it on the Jews."

"But they're not doing this here?"

"No, they're out to get the German Jews, not us."

"Then why won't they let me do the movie? I'm not German."

"Because you can't! They'll cancel our visa. People are trying to get out of there, not in."

"That's rotten, really rotten. Why didn't you tell me all this before?"

"Tell you what? That the new Nazi Party is nothing but a blown-up hoax and will fizzle out before your next birthday? Nobody believes they can last. The whole world is laughing at them."

"Are the Jews in Germany laughing?"

"No."

"Why don't they fight back, or leave?"

"I don't know. I guess some of them fight, but they have no weapons. And some of them left."

"What about the others?"

"They stay because that is their homeland, just as Austria is ours . . . It isn't easy to start all over in a strange land."

Mama was not as good an actress as she pretended to be. I know she tried her best to be calm, but even her casual, "There will be other movies," and, "I'm am sure it's all for the best," did not convince me.

While most Viennese fox-trotted through the carnival season and waltzed from one ball to the next, I sat home brooding. How could I be Jewish when I had never even seen the inside of a synagogue? True, we had religious education in school, at least to some degree, for every denomination. But it was not compulsory, and I went only twice. The Bible could have interested me, I loved those ancient stories, but learning Hebrew and reading sentences from right to left was not for me. Small wonder I knew nothing about Judaism or my religion. But now many questions kept popping up in my head. Questions I should have asked long ago.

"Mama, you put Daddy in a Jewish cemetery."

"Yes."

"Did you have to?"

"Of course not. It was the right thing to do."

"Why?"

"Because we're Jewish."

"Do Jews believe in God?"

"Yes, they do."

"Then why don't you? You said there is no God. I heard you say it."

"I had my reasons."

"Because of Papa? Because he went to sleep when he was still so young?"

"Yes!"

"Perhaps God doesn' t like Jews."

"Don't say that! Don't you ever say that."

"He sure doesn't care much about the ones in Germany!"

"Stop it. Don't you get all crazy because of what's happening in another country. You're blowing it all out of proportion."

"No, I'm not. I lost my movie role because of it."

"Just as well. They're barbarians over there. It could never happen here. Not in Austria. We are a civilized nation."

Mama did not enjoy the conversation. She pleaded with me to forget about it. "An actress should only be an actress. Leave politics and religion to others."

"Henny is Jewish. Stella Birnbaum is Jewish. I know because they told me so."

"Can't you talk about anything else?"

"They're my friends, and they're nice girls, aren't they?"

"Yes, they are nice and come from good families."

"I want to know why Stella always eats up our ham when she comes to visit. She says it's because of her parents. You know what I think? I think they're stingy. They just don't want to spend the money. Of course, her poor mother lost all her hair and now she has to wear a wig."

Mama seemed amused. She even laughed. "I can't believe this. Didn't they teach you anything in your religion classes?"

"Not about Stella's mother, they never even mentioned her."

I was laughing, too, just because Mama was. And then I told her that she knew very well I did not attend those "right-to-left" reading exercises, but had been playing football instead. Mama gave me a one-minute lesson about Jews: We were assimilated modern Jews, but the Birnbaums were Orthodox and still observed the old laws and traditions; one had to do with a woman not being allowed to show her hair, and so on.

"And that's why Stella eats our ham?"

Mama, in a much better mood, suggested I should ask a rabbi, kissed me and left.

As the days pushed forward, my ugly silver screen experience was blotted out. Mama had always done whatever possible to further my career. Not that she was a pushy stage mother, but she was convinced that some day I'd be a great actress. On a day-to-day basis, Mama's efforts to channel my intractable temperament must have been exhausting. At the theater, however, I was as disciplined and conscientious as any pro. Consumed by my desire to be the very best, I spent much time backstage, always watching, listening, and learning. I cannot recall a single moment when I did not succumb to the electrifying magnetism of the theater.

Mama got me a one-year contract at a marvelous theater, the New Vienna Playhouse — large, sparkling with elegance and splendor. It had two galleries and lush blue velvet loges.

The man whose know-how held it all together was Dr. Leo Strauss, a direct descendant of Oskar and Johann Strauss, Vienna's very own musical geniuses, the undisputed emperors of the Viennese waltz.

It was a great honor to be Dr. Strauss's protégée. He watched over me as though I were his test-tube baby — artistically, that is. I owe him much. Until he took me under his wing, the roles I had gotten were distinguished by their diversity, not by the artistry of my performances. I had played a pixie in a magic show, a flower girl in an operetta, and a landbaron's daughter who got drowned in a lake. The little son in *Medea* was the only part I never liked. Too gruesome. My stage mother, quite insane, killed herself on stage, with a knife, right in front of me and the other kid who played my brother.

What I hated most about the role was that they cut my hair and put thick brown makeup all over my legs, arms and face. The preparations took over an hour. When I finally got to go on, I didn't have a single line. At one point, Medea pulled her "little sons" so close, hugging us with such passion, that she almost cracked my ribs. Mother Medea was very fat; she had to wear a corset. Smothered in her opulence, I kept hitting my nose on that stiff whalebone.

It was my good fortune that I did get to work with some of the truly great actors. They taught me, without the benefit of a drama coach, the most valuable lesson of all: Always believe in the character you portray, for if you don't, the audience won't either. Throughout my young acting years, I benefited greatly from the Golden Era of the theater. The gala nights were sensational. But so was every night. The audiences were charged. The performers were charged. Nothing was ever routine, no matter how often one played the part.

I had gotten my first starring role when I was not yet eleven years old, in a comedy, *A Clever Lad*. I had wanted to stop everyone on the street and tell them about it. Mama, for the first time since Papa went to sleep, was really excited and happy. My co-star was Karl Kneidiger, and he was a legend. I had all the funny lines, and this seasoned, grand old actor taught me how to upstage other actors and the importance of timing.

"Upstaging," Karl Kneidiger said, "you use only when some pompous ass tries to steal your lines, or cuts into the laughs you're getting."

I was on stage all through the play. I had the first word and the last! (Mama called it typecasting.) As the streetwise little boy in *A Clever Lad*, I took my first solo curtain call. There I was, on that big stage, four feet tall, taking a bow all by myself. The curtain opened and closed, opened and closed, and I kept bowing and bowing, feeling ten feet tall. When the lights came on, the audience stood up and cheered: "Bravo! Bravo!" and I felt as though the whole world were applauding me. Dr. Strauss had given my family the best seats in the house, and I could see my deaf grandmother looking as stately as an empress, applauding and waving to the audience as though it were her grandchild's coronation. I know it was her night, too.

In September 1937, upcoming social events rated more space in the Viennese newspapers than the hellbound situation in Germany. To the best of my knowledge, no one paid much attention to it. Austria had its own political headache, and whatever chess game was being played out behind the governmental democratic doors, it was kept top secret. Not so in Germany. Germany was littered with propaganda, and all those nice folks over there swallowed it up. Thanks to enormous sums of external industrial money and internal ballyhoo, the little Austrian paper-hanger and his two-legged bloodhounds had grown into a mighty dragon.

"Heil Hitler!" The Third Reich was born.

In my country, the charming Austrians kept on singing and drinking and were ever so merry. I was busier than a bee: almost nightly, I appeared in a play or sang chansons in three different cabarets, lovely chansons by talented young songwriters written especially for me. And after the performances, I studied for the then compulsory Actors State Exam. It seemed that suddenly too many youngsters wanted to achieve great fame as actors. Thus, the state exam was instituted, with rather stiff requirements. One had to study for at least two years at drama school — preferably with Max Reinhardt, or Professor Wieland, or at the Academy.

One had to know twenty plays and twenty roles, and, hopefully, remember all of them. Twelve classics and eight modern roles. Also, European literature, and all the where's and when's about the playwrights. No theater could engage you without your having passed the exam. And if the examining board decided that the aspiring newcomer did not weigh heavy on the talent scale, he, or she, never got another chance. Less than five percent passed.

Stage experience or no, I loathed tests and exams. Also, I was a bit leery about the classics, which definitely were not my forte. On my crucial day, Professor Wieland took me aside, and in a voice that sounded very much like cut glass, told me that his lifelong reputation and that of his school rested on my shoulders. It was not exactly what I wanted to hear.

But then, this sweet, stately, white-haired man gave me some advice which I have remembered all my life: "Look straight at them. Forget that you have seen them as King Lear and Faust. Think of those great men sitting on a toilet with their pants down. And just before you start your scene, say to yourself, 'You down there, kiss my ass!'" It shocked me, but was he ever right ... everyone looks ridiculous with their pants down.

My state exam took place in the Burg Theater, which in itself is reason enough to faint. Even the walls there echo the words of Julius Caesar, Hamlet and Othello spoken a thousand times by the lord-actors of this manor.

When my name was being called, I took a long, deep breath and put those sacred cows on the toilet before I reached the footlights. There they were, first row center, the Barrymores of Europe.

I passed! Received my diploma, and with it, a friendly reminder to pay my theater guild dues. Thank you, Professor Wieland, not only for your splendid coaching but for your wonderful advice. Through many precarious situations, this bit of psychology has served me well.

Early in 1938, a big show was planned for Switzerland, and the producer was looking for a girl who could sing, act, and also be the principal acrobat in a dance trio. It was one of those thrown-in-the-air by one guy and hopefully caught-by-the-other routines. After several instructions and rehearsals, the other two-thirds of the trio decided I would do just fine. Mama signed the contract, and I got what I wanted: top billing. The duo came from the circus, and after they had trained and worked with me, I felt I could have joined Ringling Brothers myself. I flew through the air with the greatest of ease, a Jewish actress without a trapeze. Except for the start and finish, I never got to see the stage at all. Strictly a stay-up-there-girl routine. Five or six hours a day I sweated a few more of my meager pounds off, and naturally, was black and blue from top to bottom.

What I remember most, before the first train of the morning rolled out of the station and carried me away, was Mama standing on the platform, waving good-bye. I knew her eyes would follow the cold steel rails long after the train had lumbered down the tracks. "See you in six weeks," I shouted over the low, steady rumble, but she had vanished in the morning mist.

It was March 12, 1938, when I crossed the border into Switzerland, and the Germans marched into Austria. Because of this eruption, my six weeks on the road turned into twenty-six globe-trotting years.

⌒

THE SHOW I ORIGINALLY LEFT with was a smash. Critics professed that we had brought them, perhaps for the last time, the loveliness and joyful heartbeat of Vienna. "Now trampled and violated by the lunacy of Hitler," one of them wrote. "One wonders, will Vienna ever sing again?"

For the next two years, my home was wherever friendly authorities gave me permission to stay and work. Except for reading tea leaves and sleeping in tents, my life very much resembled that of a Gypsy. I moved around a lot, slept in fleabags and bridal suites, worked in large theaters and smoke-filled dives, in small cabarets and very fancy supper clubs. No matter where I appeared, the critics never let me down. One of Zurich's most respected critics compared me to a princess out of a fairy-tale book. "A voice like a tiny golden violin, childlike, and yet disturbingly exciting, with a growing intensity that demands attention." With every good review, I celebrated my triumphant success, and it never dawned on me that already my life had been fragmented. Yet my passport was a sure indicator. It was full of short-term visas: entered–left–entered–left.

When the Nazis came to Austria to show my hospitable countrymen how to get rid of those "lousy Jews," most of the population welcomed the new regime. Austria had always been anti-Semitic, but never in a demonstrative way. It was just there, like a wart — the prejudicial birthmark of a nation. No one I knew had been subjected to it, but then I never had more than a bird's-eye view. And the lovers of wine, women and song thought nothing of dragging old men through the streets and kicking their faces in until they pleaded for mercy. The women were beaten and called "whores, filthy Jewish whores."

Swastika Heil! Swastika Heil!

Unfortunately, history has never recorded the truth about the people of my country. Satan's armies did not invade. It was a simple matter of "annexation."

There must have been some among those good Christians who did object. But none too loudly, for there was no resistance. The majority willingly became constituents of the new order — whether for profit or power matters little. Yet a lot of Jews slipped through their ghoulish fingers, at least in the first eight or nine months. It wasn't too difficult then. Buying one's way out by bribing a helpful Austrian official was most useful, if one had the winning ticket in the freedom lottery: a visa! Many ended up in Shanghai.

It's hard to imagine Vienna *Gemütlichkeit* at the seaport in eastern China. However, under the circumstances, that probably was the best place to be. No need for a visa there. They let you in and let you stay. The lovely Viennese waltzes could still be heard in Zurich, Paris, Brussels, and I dare say even in Shanghai. But in my city, Vienna, they played something quite different: One, two, three, march . . . one, two, three, march.

Mama could not write about any of it. But every new arrival brought us another earful of bad news difficult to digest, because in spite of anti-Semitism, it was a puzzling paradox. Austrians hated Germans, have always hated them. There is absolutely no correlation between the two nations' characteristics and lifestyles. It is only the similarity of language which often mistakenly has put them in the same category. How then could Austrians embrace those shouting, stampeding Germans? As painful as it may be, I have come to believe that there is an appalling flaw in the character of the lovable Austrian. It is my firm and irrevocable conviction that beneath his layers of charm lives a coward.

More and more artists, stuck in Vienna, needed contracts to get out. My producer sent many fake ones, and in isolated cases, it did help. But not enough. There was so little we could do. We ourselves lived abroad from one work permit to the next. In between, we sat in crummy police offices requesting one more extension — and one more, and one more.

More than a year before I left, my sister Kate had become Mrs. Julius Polese. They lived in our apartment with Mama. Julius, a Catholic, much older than Kate, had a big position with Canadian Pacific, something to do with railroads, hotels and travel.

The producer-director of the show in Switzerland was Mr. Otto Dürer, a most inventive man. After about seventy percent of our original cast had left, he sold all the spectacular costumes and sets. He picked up new talent and put a revue together, a type of cabaret entertainment that could perform in large theaters or small places. Sometimes there were more of us on stage than in the audience, which was bad for our pocketbook, but we ourselves had more fun.

Dürer came from a very distinguished and wealthy family, with lots of titles and lots of money. But now Dürer, just like the rest of us, was only a Jew. He wanted to protect me from those male wolves howling at my door. Unfortunately, he was an insanely jealous man. For almost three years, I kept running away from him. Whenever possible, I tried to get away to Budapest — and Ferry. Ferry was the stabilizing force in my life. Except for Papa, I never felt that safe with anyone.

⌐

I FIRST MET FERRY when I was five. We met at Wörtersee, a beautiful summer resort in Austria where my parents had always rented a villa. The grown-ups had great fun there, but for small frys like myself, there wasn't much to do. The manicured lawns, stretching for miles around the big lake, had that unmistakable don't-step-on-me look, and the flowers, much too neatly planted, stood arrayed like little soldiers waiting to be counted, not picked.

On the last day of vacation, a much acclaimed dinner at the hotel left a lasting impression on me, while my first encounter with a Hungarian relative left a lasting impression on him. We often ate at the hotel, but that night was different. A special table was reserved for us. Starched tablecloth, starched napkins. I was wearing a starched dress and could hardly sit down. It was a starchy affair.

The musicians played schmaltzy songs, and in true Viennese tradition everyone hummed along. The highlight of the evening was eagerly awaited. My eyes, fixed on the French doors, expected an Oriental king (I'd read about one in some fairy tale) with dazzling gifts for everyone. Instead, the kitchen door swung open, and through it marched a tall, fat man in a white uniform, white gloves, and a tremendous white hat, also starched. Instead of gifts, he carried a huge pot, which he carefully placed in front of my father.

The Oriental King (whom the grown-ups called chef de cuisine) reached into the boiling pot, and with artistic skill took out a steaming, horrid-looking bright red thing, with frightful claws, many legs, long antennae, and beady eyes. Everyone applauded. To me, the creature looked like a ghastly red spider. I saw it crawling toward me, and convinced that its large pincers were trying to nip me, I ran. Long after my legs had stopped running, my heart still raced ahead of me. Upset and angry, I sat down in the cool don't-step-on-me grass, feeling extremely sorry for myself. The fact that I later learned the thing was a lobster, imported from who knows where, thus worthy of this ceremonial attention, did nothing to alter my opinion of it. I'm sure the lobster shared my view.

I was alone. There was no one around; nothing moved, not even a lost butterfly. I was beginning to feel miserable all over again, when I spotted something shiny behind a tree. Approaching with great caution, I discovered to my immense delight that it was a brand-new bike. I would borrow it and go for a ride. Except for two major problems, it was a splendid idea: the bike was much too big, and it was a boy's bicycle. I solved one problem by taking off my starchy dress; but unfortunately, the bike's size couldn't be changed. No matter. I was determined to make it. After much maneuvering,

I took a firm grip of the handlebars, and from then on it was all up to the bike, since my feet could not reach the pedals.

The bike and I went down the wide serpentine driveway all the way to the village. Well, almost all the way. Suddenly, a tall boy stood in the middle of the road, waving and yelling, "Stop! Stop!" A split second later, a collision ended my search for the brakes. The boy got knocked down, with the bicycle on top of him and me on top of the bike. I escaped with some minor cuts and bruises, the bike was bent out of shape, and the cursing stranger had a broken arm. After we got ourselves disentangled, people from the hotel and the village came running. We must have been quite a sight: me, almost naked, except for panties, patent leather shoes, and the lovely blue satin ribbon dangling sadly from my hair; he, three times my size, moaning and rattling on and on in a foreign language while pointing accusingly at me. When my parents reached us, Mama took one look at me and fainted. I took one look at the crowd and wished to be back at the lobster table.

I didn't learn till the next day that the boy I had run down (that's what he claimed), was my fourteen-year-old cousin from Budapest. His name was Ference — Ferry, for short — and naturally, it was his bike. He was on his way to summer camp, and upon specific request from his mother had stopped to meet us. I regret that there was neither summer nor camp for him. Ferry was taken to a hospital, and then, with bike, shipped back to Budapest. After this innocent little disaster, the close relationship between our mothers suffered a temporary setback. Ferry refused to come within a hundred miles of me. It took six years before I saw him again — at which time I broke one of his skis.

My first trip to Budapest when I was seventeen was Mama's gift to me for winning bouts with a broken leg and then rheumatic fever. Budapest was marvelous, except that there were too many relatives. I was passed around as though I were the only salt shaker on a large dining table. Often I heard them talk about my second cousin, Ferry. I kind of had the feeling that he was considered a good catch. At twenty-six, an architect and builder, he ran the family business. He had been sent an invitation to the family reunion at the Gellert Hotel, the finest in Budapest, at which I would be the guest of honor. He could not possibly refuse such an invitation.

Three dozen long-stemmed white carnations and a polite note, "Sorry, but urgent business forces me to leave town," arrived instead. I thought, "He still remembers, that's why he won't come!" Of course, the elders didn't know about our unfriendly past encounters, but they were surely disappointed. I was disappointed, too. And if I broke his arm and ruined his bike when I was only five, and broke his ski racing on our newly-waxed floors when I was eleven, that was all his fault anyway.

Then, a couple of days before the reunion, Ferry phoned. He didn't have to leave town after all, and could he please still attend. Naturally, I immediately attacked my wardrobe — all four dresses — and chose my new, not hand-me-down, cornflower blue lamé dress. I did need some practice with those high-heeled shoes, but it was worth it. I fully intended to dazzle him.

At the Gellert, Ferry sat directly across from me. I recognized him at once. No, I sensed that it was he. There was a lot of conversation going on among the relatives. Ferry said nothing; his instant attraction for me was written all over his face — he made no attempt to hide it, to the dismay of my unmarried cousins. His expression was a mixture of perplexed surprise and enchanted fascination. While the chatterboxes chattered all around us, he spoke to me through his eyes. Forest green they were, large and striking. Ferry was good-looking in an unassuming way. Broad-shouldered, tanned, and very sporty. Perhaps a little shy. Not quite at home in groups like this, but so refreshing.

Whatever days were left, we spent together. We raced through the countryside on his motorbike, smelling the orchards heavy with fruit. Or up to the vineyards, through fields of grapes growing on woody vines. In his car we drove to his cabin on the river for swimming and boating and picnics in the sun. Dinners at quaint, romantic places where violins played Gypsy music and afterward we danced the night away. It was a strange romance. We needed to see each other all the time, and yet he never touched me. I felt that he was someone very special. But at seventeen, I was neither wise enough nor old enough to realize how truly extraordinary he really was. Not until it was much too late did I fully come to know the boundless inner beauty of this man. He was the brother I never had, the friend who would have stood by me forever, the lover who could have made me proud to be a woman. He would have been the husband who could have made a marriage last — even with me.

I would never be that young again, nor that innocently happy.

Ferry's mother, Aunt Shari, wanted him to go to America, but he refused to go. She asked whether I knew that Ferry and his younger brother, Anatol, were not of the Jewish faith: she had had them converted at birth, to what I don't know. She told me a lot of things Ferry didn't. That he wanted to marry me, but felt he had no right to take me away from my career. Also, he was afraid that I wasn't ready to settle down, that being his wife would not be enough. Too young! "Do tell him to learn English. He will if you ask him to." Frankly, I didn't understand why she wanted them to leave Budapest. They had such a good life there, and they weren't even Jewish.

On one of my trips to Budapest, I got myself a contract to sing and dance solo at the Moulin Rouge, without the help of Otto Dürer. I only accepted it to be near Ferry. The Moulin Rouge was a copy of the Parisian famous nightclub, though not quite as grand, but lots of good international acts, and many fans and feathery-dressed ladies who danced a little and drank a lot — mostly with rich and tired businessmen. On the surface, all glitter and glamour. But only half a flight up were the *chambres separées*, well known all over Europe. That's where the real intimate shows took place. There, older, rich married men met for a brief hour with young and poor little chorus girls, or with their mistresses. Everything was handled most discreetly: the champagne, the caviar and the lovemaking on the satin couch. I'd never even been inside a place like this.

When it came to signing the contract, which was mailed to Mama, she crossed out the small print; the line where it said that every female performer had to mingle. Clever Mama.

My contract was for four weeks with option, but would not take effect until several months later. Which meant I had to leave Ferry again. I never left because I really wanted to. It was those Hungarian visa-givers who made it so tough to stay. Ferry kept looking for those in charge to buy me another week or two. Sometimes he found them; sometimes he didn't. Then it was back to Switzerland again, and Otto. More cabarets, more letters from Ferry, and more people fleeing Vienna. All looking for the same thing: a place where being a Jew was not a crime.

When it was time for me to begin my engagement at the Moulin Rouge, I came back to Budapest. Mama had signed papers declaring me legally of age. Now, even though I was not I could negotiate and sign my own contracts. Though I was happy to be back with Ferry, I was not happy with the Moulin Rouge engagement. I didn't like all that false glitter. Men kept undressing me with their eyes, champagne corks popped while I was singing, and already after my first number, the maitre d' wanted me to mingle. I showed him my contract with the crossed-out clause. Of course he argued. But it was signed by both parties, and there was nothing he could do.

Each time I left Ferry, it became harder for us to say good-bye, and more uncertain when we would see each other again.

While in Switzerland, I got a contract to work with the famous Princess Operetta Theater in The Hague, Holland. The season started at the end of September 1938. For the first time since I had left Vienna, I stayed in one place long enough to remember where bathroom and kitchen were. The Hague was lovely; so was the theater, and the apartment I had rented.

Kate's husband Julius managed to get transferred to Rotterdam. They were now living in The Hague, and Julius commuted. I finally got Mama out of Vienna: "Permission to visit her daughter." When Mama left Vienna, she gave the house key to the concierge, and all our furniture with it. She knew that she would never sleep in Papa's bed again. Having to leave her home and Papa's grave was very hard on her. Mama could never really free herself of Vienna. She suffered from a very common disease: homesickness. Not me. The more I found out about my countrymen, the less I cared about ever going back. I cut this whole country out of my life just like an abscess, drained out the pus and never shed a tear. I don't know whose idea it was, but we applied for emigration visas to the United States. We weren't the first ones. The quota was full, and we had to wait.

The popularity of those operetta productions was unbelievable. There wasn't a town in Holland where we were not known and loved. The reception was always fantastic, and the theaters sold out months ahead.

Hugo Helm, who owned the Princess Operetta Theater, was the real brainchild. A prince of a man, this little old ugly German Jew had the mind of a genius and the heart of a giant. I've never met a kinder man. Unfortunately, he was the victim of a severe heart ailment — love. In his case, quite fatal. The love in his life was a tall, blond, blue-eyed Brünnhilde. A German Aryan. They lived together, for many years, so I was told. She wore the finest furs and the most expensive diamonds. Naturally, he trusted her completely.

I was given great parts and should have been content, yet I was not. A month before the season ended, I asked Director Helm to please release me from my contract. He could have held me to it, but he did not. He told me that I could always come back, could count on him if ever I should need anything at all. My first bit of security for more than a year, and I threw it right out the window.

I managed to get another show in Switzerland, and Mama came with me. After a couple of months, Mama had to return to Holland (visa expired). She moved in with Kate and Julius: there they would wait for me — and our emigration papers.

I finished whatever shows were still booked, and then took off for Budapest again. It was to be my last visit there. After the first two weeks, the Hungarian busybodies gave me only one more extension on my visa. Ferry frantically tried to buy me more time. No luck. After four weeks, they kept my passport. They granted me three more days, assuring Ferry that I could count on their personal farewell and on their helping me board the train.

I usually stayed at Ferry's home. Ferry and I had spent the last evening as though a thousand more were ours yet to share. We both tried not to bring up the subject of parting again. He watched me pack, and then we said goodnight. We said goodnight a dozen times or more.

There was a knock on my door. Ferry. He wanted to know, did I want some fruit? I joined him in the parlor with only my white satin nightgown on. I did not think of tempting him, only that there should be no door between us, not ever, and certainly not these last few hours. He had placed my chair directly opposite his. Our legs touched while we kept eating slices of fruit which neither of us really wanted. I felt he was wrestling with himself. He kept glancing at the couch and quickly back at me again. We stuffed pieces of melon into each other's mouths, and laughed, not too convincingly. We told each other funny stories which somehow missed being funny. And then the plate was empty.

Ferry took a deep breath and blurted out that he was stupid because he had not allowed himself to do what his feelings kept telling him to do. Holding them back was driving him crazy, but, "It's better this way," he said; "the other way would have been even more unbearable. Neither of us would have had a moment's peace."

He struggled with every word. There was a battle going on between his heart and his head. I knew it, and did nothing.

The clock went *tick-tock,* and he stroked my hair. *Tick-tock.* His hands caressed my face. And then the night whispered to me, "I've got to go now. I gave you all the time I had. You didn't use it." We should have loved each other then till we could love no more. Why didn't we? Why didn't I reach out?

The next morning, he took me to the station in a taxi; my head rested on his shoulder, his face was buried in my hair. He held my hands so firmly, and yet so gently. As the porter took my luggage, Ferry asked whether I was really going to America. I told him that I didn't know. Maybe I would, maybe I wouldn't . . . Three Hungarians looking like the three stooges were already waiting. Ferry ripped the passport out of the bald-headed one's hands and shouted something that couldn't have been nice in any language. My passport was given to the conductor, who had to keep it until the next border. We only had a minute or so left.

My arms clasped Ferry's through the open window. He looked upset. The train pulled out, and he ran with it, yelling, "No good here anymore, no good! Meet you in Switzerland for skiing in March. Will you come? I'll write to you where!"

"Yes, yes, yes!" And then the locomotive puffed its black smoke into the air; his fingers slipped out of my hand. Someone shut the window.

Romania: Border control. I got my passport back.

Yugoslavia: Border control. They wanted to see my passport.

Italy: Border control. *Passaporto, prego, Signora.* Another stamp, another country.

Switzerland, France, Luxemburg: Control, control, transit visas, permission to travel through.

Belgium: Permission to stay and work. For a while.

The Germans were in Czechoslovakia, and had just crushed Poland.

Otto Dürer was waiting in Antwerp and had signed a lease on a theater.

For my birthday, Ferry sent me a dozen long-stemmed cardinal red roses and the wish that I could stay as lovely and innocent as I had been with him. "For this," he wrote, "is what's so beautiful about you. I am afraid that other men don't look at you that way. And even though I long for you more than I ever dared to let you know, I will not do anything about it. Not until we're certain where our lives are headed, and we can be together without having to say good-bye again. I will see you in March and hope that times will be much better then. I don't quite understand all that is happening in Germany, in your country, and in others. I know that you don't either. Be careful! Yours, Ferry." I still have all his letters.

Five months until March: It's longer than eternity. What if my American papers come through before that? I'll wait. The visa is good for a year. Ferry and I can go to the States together.

There was a theater again, a stage, and I did my thing — different things for different shows. I played in Antwerp, Brussels, and at large hotels on the Belgian coast that were open all year round.

Meanwhile, the long arm of divine injustice kept spreading like a contagious disease, and Adolf, the mighty Godfather, kept his promise and put a contract out on every Jew. It kept the Nazis busy, and the business of murder booming. While the small countries of Europe were gobbled up with Germany's tremendous appetite, England kept drinking tea. The United States, still nurturing a hangover from the big depression and already reveling in its new prosperity, was much too far away to see the murky waters in which whole nations were drowning.

And I, like most of my contemporaries, kept on singing my songs through cities of drifting hope, not understanding anything. For more than two years now, fate kept steering me away from danger. As Hitler "liberated" Austria, I was on my way to Switzerland. Not too much later, thanks to a bad case of laryngitis, my engagement in Prague was postponed. I danced in some other country just as the master race charged into Czechoslovakia.

And now Belgium. The fates were still smiling here. I was still smiling. Each time I thought about my date with Ferry, my heart turned somersaults. I thought and dreamed about it, but never made it to the Swiss mountains. Instead, my watchdog producer decided that we should get the hell out of Belgium, too. I didn't want to. I wanted Switzerland. But that country no longer listened to the plight of thousands and had closed its doors. Only its banks, already swelling with an abundance of obscene wealth, opened their impregnable vaults to the world's war promoters. Stolen treasures and blood money were well guarded there.

The results of this immoral neutrality for me were surprisingly simple: I had run out of countries to run to.

Holland was the only place left. No borders to cross except into Holland. My family was there, and if I wanted to become a full-fledged emigrant, and one day greet the Statue of Liberty, it had to be from Holland. I actually arrived in The Hague by taxi — all the way from Brussels. It may have been a first. I missed the Storm troopers by two days, or rather, they missed me.

Mama, Kate and Julius had moved to the seashore resort of Scheveningen near The Hague, and I got my old apartment back in The Hague. My twin, Elly, was in London.

In the weeks that followed, I looked for an escape hatch, but there was none. My mind went on a crazy merry-go-round until the extraordinary, paralyzing truth hit me: I was trapped in a city that was still free. The parks and places I had known so well had suddenly become closed circles, a labyrinth that led nowhere at all. I lived right at the corner of a square. Its most attractive features were lots of pretty trees and many friendly dogs. It was a neighborhood of respectable and quiet folks. The only friends I had close by were a comedian, Walter, and a famous tenor, Kurt Preger, living in sin with a quite lovely, not-so-famous singer, Ruth. Together, we listened to the ever-changing rumors bouncing back and forth like Ping-Pong balls. The news broadcasts, quite different from the unofficial rumors, kept telling us that we had nothing to worry about. Somehow, it wasn't very comforting, especially not after the first bombs had already dropped. While people dashed from their homes, running into the streets and into each other, the voices on the radio still insisted that everything was under control. My street definitely was not. The square, filling rapidly with unruly citizens, resembled more and more a colony of angry ants whose queen had fled.

Around the corner, only a block away, were soldiers' barracks. I never saw anyone in there before, but now they were obviously occupied. Some pale-faced, soft-looking youngsters were lurking about, pretending to be soldiers. While the city was experiencing its first major confusion, they were still learning how to march.

Holland is a flat country. Large bodies of water flowing from the sea into the canals make it a land of bridges and dams. Any attempt to defend it is, at best, suicide. Even so, the Dutch fought. Out of its hopelessly ill-equipped army, a handful of incredibly courageous men emerged. Against insurmountable odds, these few blew up bridges, opened the dams, and gave their lives in a desperate struggle, trying to stop the inevitable. Perhaps it was the innocence of these peace-loving people which must bear the responsibility for their totally obsolete military strategy. Or they might have known all along that any resistance was hopeless, yet fought in spite of it.

The simple logic of the Dutch, at least according to the newscasts, was that with no more bridges left and most of the command points underwater, Hitler's armies could not march in. In a sinister way, they were right.

There was very little marching. When the Storm troopers got tired of playing games, they simply summoned five hundred bombers, flattened Rotterdam completely, and then proceeded with the invasion without any further interference.

The siege began on May 10, 1940, and lasted five days. My recollection of those dark hours is mostly sketchy and out of focus. The memories recorded are only flashes of scrambled scenes resembling blurred slides seen rapidly through a faulty projector. It left me muddled and disoriented.

After it was all over and the city of Rotterdam had been wiped from the face of the earth, a strange stillness settled over the country. It was inexplicably quiet. For a while, nothing moved: the streets empty, the houses bolted, and the windows tightly shut looking like implanted glass eyes — cold and livid. Behind locked doors, a nation held its breath.

With Walter, Kurt and Ruth, I spent the days in paralyzing silence, choking on fear yet riddled with anger and despair. At night, walking the corridors of sleeplessness, I heard the land itself cry.

↬ Two

ENGLAND — We must get to England! It sounded rather far-fetched, but in fact the coast was always cluttered with fishing boats. All we needed was one fisherman willing to take us across. On clear days, the cliffs of Dover could be seen from the pier, rising out of the ocean like an oasis in a watery desert. The initial shock of the past few days had worn off, and in its place, an immeasurable desire for survival took over. Intuitively, we sensed that probably for the last time, we still could govern our own destiny. This was exciting.

A new vigor surged through us, mixed with a sheepish pleasure that the four of us, Walter and Kurt, Ruth and I, were about to outsmart the tyrannical huntsmen. There were no elaborate plans made — no plans at all. From The Hague the only logical place from which to depart for England was Scheveningen. That and leaving the very next day was all we knew.

All that night, the stars had tried to peek through the clouds, but the thick, gray blanket in the sky just lay fat and swollen, allowing neither moon nor stars to be seen. With the break of dawn, a fine drizzle came down, a mistlike moisture accompanied by the timid light of a new day.

Kurt had spent the last few hours before our departure trying to calm Ruth, who had tearfully decided not to come with us. Walter, our chamber comedian, had a similar surprise for us. The little funny man exclaimed that he did not wish to look for his destiny, but rather have destiny come look for him. And so it came about that Kurt and I would set out for Scheveningen alone. England seemed never closer, nor was it ever farther away.

On the morning of May 20, 1940, Kurt and I began our impromptu flight to freedom. It was still drizzling, and the clouds never quite went away. Not wanting to arouse suspicion, we dressed casually and traveled light. A toothbrush, a comb, and some money stuffed in our pockets. Even so, we must have been conspicuous. A rather odd couple: Kurt was at least six feet two and and weighed over two hundred fifty pounds. It took four large steps of mine to keep up with one of his. The golden-voiced tenor was only in his late twenties, but looked much older. Not quite five foot three, weighing no more than a hunded pounds, I still looked like a child.

For over two hours, walking through the haze of dawn, we followed the tracks of the tram, and never met a soul. The enemy was nowhere to be seen. Friends were nowhere to be seen. It was an eerie expedition. As we arrived at the beach, we found this otherwise buzzing place had also surrendered its paradisiacal days to the elements of force. There was no sign of life anywhere. The fog was thick and chilly. We stood around, stared into the dusky waters, and waited. Hoping for one man, one boat to take us to Dover. After our legs had gotten stiff, we sat down on a bench and waited some more.

A dreary afternoon faded in and out. Twilight came, and still we waited. We were tired and lonely. Neither of us knew what to do. We left the bench and trodded aimlessly along the promenade into the soundless night. My legs had gone to sleep, my clothes were clammy and my stomach very empty. We did not complain. Whatever thoughts we had, whatever doubts unnerved us, we didn't let the other know. Stubborn and silent, we kept on walking, mile after mile after mile.

Suddenly, Kurt grabbed my arm. "Listen," he whispered, "someone's coming."

I felt faint. Footsteps came toward us, unhurried and steady.

"It's only one," he voiced breathlessly, "it can't be a stinking German, they wouldn't dare to walk alone."

A heartbeat later, a glaring flashlight hit our faces and a thundering man's voice released an alarming avalanche of curses. "You scared the shit out of me!" A swearing Dutchman. He wasn't much taller than me, wore a heavy raincoat and rubber boots. His complexion was ruddy and weather-beaten. The hands were working hands, rough and full of calluses. He could have been a construction worker, a bricklayer. Or a fisherman? He unloaded a truckful of appalling words, spitting them out like decayed teeth, while his flashlight examined every inch of us. Once he was satisfied that we represented no danger, only a startling intrusion on his lone night walk, his tone became much friendlier. "Hey, big guy, what you doing here with that kid?"

"Turn the damn light off," Kurt hissed.

He did. The three of us moved closer together in a mutual gesture of trust. We asked if he was a fisherman, and he said, "Yes."

This little word instantly erased the crippling day we had just waded through, those dreadful hours when even the seagulls seemed to ignore our very existence. We told the man why we were here, that we were Jews and needed help. The fisherman listened intently, but appeared extremely nervous. He looked at us long and hard, measuring each word, and then let out a stinging "*No!*"

We begged, offered money. I cried, but it was of no use.

Kurt grew wild with frustration. He didn't give up. "Why not? Why won't you take us?"

Unexpectedly, the fisherman raised his arms and pointed straight across to where the ocean was. He yelled: "You want to know why not? You want to know what's out there? My brother is out there. That's what! Yesterday, my only brother took my boat and filled it full of people just like you and now they're all dead! I got no brother, and got no boat. I can't help you." His nose was dripping, he sobbed without restraint.

"Oh, my God, my God," we kept repeating it, not knowing what else to say.

"Mines everywhere — nothing but mines. I saw the whole thing right from down there, it all just blew up, and then there was fire, lots of fire, even the water was burning. He was only thirty, my brother, only thirty — "

The rain kept falling. The poor man seemed to relive the tragedy over and over again; his arms kept punching the air as if he were hitting the enemy. Mines: how could that be? We had never even thought of mines. What in heaven's name did we think of? Our somber friend interrupted his shadow-boxing long enough to inform us that we had come too late. He and his buddies did help quite a few get across in the first couple of days after the invasion; there were no mines then. When they were put there, he didn't know. He had just come from his brother's wife, and she understood nothing. His brother left four little children who wanted to know when their father was coming back.

"Go home," the fisherman muttered. "I can't help you, just go." I wanted to scream. I wanted to run away. I wanted to do anything but watch the fisherman clutch his new sorrow with the resignation of a condemned man. "He hurts," I thought, "he hurts so much, and I don't know what to do about it." The night on the pier with the fisherman stayed with me for a long time. A casualty of war — he was not a soldier. His brother blown to bits for wanting to save the lives of strangers. How many little ones in villages and towns were asking, "When is my father coming back?"

⤚

AFTER THE INCIDENT IN SCHEVENINGEN, our little group dispersed. Kurt returned to his girlfriend, at least for a short while, and I moved in with my family. From then on, contact between us was practically nil. Not that we didn't want to see each other, but The Hague and Scheveningen had become two separate cities, and communication was increasingly difficult. These kinds of abrupt changes in one's immediate circle of friends grew more and more common and were quite typical of the strange times in which we lived. It was only because of these circumstances that I was not aware of how my friends had gotten through the Rise and Fall of the Third Reich. Not until it was long over.

Kurt never gave up trying to get out, and one day his efforts were rewarded. He made it to Switzerland with the help of the Dutch underground. There, he sang his heart out before a stoic audience and died several years later, a "natural" death. He'd suffered a heart attack right in his dressing room between the second and third act of *Madame Butterfly*.

The fate of crying Ruth is almost a Cinderella story. Tall, blond, and blue-eyed, she managed to "buy" some Aryan blood just in the nick of time. It not only saved her very fair skin but did wonders for her career. Walter's destiny did come looking for him, and took him away. One day, some neighbors say, he left the house and just disappeared. The comedian exchanged his comfortable, airy apartment for a dingy, damp and dim-lit attic. While the rest of the world was killing each other off, Walter sat out the war alone. For more than two years, he did not see a human face. Food was pushed through an ingenious tiny trapdoor by the people who had hidden him. Heavy wooden boards kept out the enemy, if not the thunder of war.

Not until many years later, not until a scarred and trampled Europe began to lick its final wounds, holding its battered face, cursing, up to God, did I see Walter again. At last, he too received the blessings that come with peace. His outer appearance hadn't really changed too much, except for an increasing nervous twitching followed by some weird convulsions. But he survived. He was to never again work as a comedian. Instead, the little man surrounded himself with philosophical books. He never married and remained a loner. Whenever anyone asked him what he did during the war, he'd simply say: "I sat on a chair in an attic."

I WISHED I KNEW HOW TO EXPLAIN my sudden appearance at my family's home at 3:00 a.m. What plausible reason could I give for knocking at their door at such an hour? My escape to nowhere had left me discomposed and exhausted. I could still hear the fisherman crying and in my mind the North Sea was still burning. How could I get into the house? Ringing the doorbell was out of the question — it would have awakened the whole neighborhood. I knocked, waited, and knocked again. Nothing! I should have gone back with Kurt. I sat down on the stoop, made myself very small and fell asleep.

The next morning a neighbor notified my family that "a little girl" was sleeping in the doorway. Shocked but relieved, Mama had Julius carry me in and put me to bed. I did not awaken till late afternoon. Before Mama had a chance to bombard me with questions, I told her that I had come because I thought it wiser for all of us to be together. I had walked because it was safer . . . Naturally, I had to leave my clothes behind. And, naturally, I'd gotten lost! I never mentioned England, fishermen, or mines.

Scheveningen was hardly recognizable. Just like an empty movie set. The hotels, restaurants and coffee shops closed — no customers. The beach chairs stayed in the storage rooms. Only the sand, baking lazily in the sun, did not seem to mind the eerie silence.

By now, the chance of emigrating to America was less than zero. I had all the time in the world to continue my English lessons but understandably, no desire. Mama admitted that these were troubling times; Julius thought that they were of historical significance. Instead of English lessons, Julius gave me an up-to-date account of the present situation brought about by the kingpins in charge, the governing bodies. The news on the political horizon was less than rosy. In September 1938 the great English statesman, Neville Chamberlain, had signed the Munich Pact, and from that moment on, the dye was cast. While humbly asking Hitler for "peace with honor" he almost sold out England to the demagogue. Chamberlain got neither peace nor honor. A year later, Churchill was appointed First Lord of the Admiralty, and Britain and France declared war on the Third Reich. That was the good news! The bad news was that there was not a single English or French man in Germany, but the Germans were everywhere. So far, they didn't even bother to declare war, and that was scary. "Nevertheless," said my wise brother-in-law reassuringly, "England is getting stronger and the United States will also help."

When? That he couldn't say. Neither could the British Broadcasting Company, whose crystal ball was cloudy. While we were marking time and fabricating hope, the American ambassador to London, Mr. Joseph Kennedy, advised President Roosevelt to "Stay out of it!" Italy had declared war on Albania. Russia had taken a bite out of Poland. Germany already had taken everything else. The voices on the radio never shut up. The BBC was circumspect, but the hateful master race, having control of the Dutch airwaves, kept blasting their "Sieg Heil!" into my ears until my head was splitting. I still had not seen a single one of them, yet I had come to think of them as rats — not humans — rats wearing swastikas and infesting Europe with the plague.

The walls inside the apartment kept closing in on me. I had to get away. Somewhere, anywhere where I could breathe. My family was up in arms about my wanting to get out. Again and again, they warned me about the danger "out there." But I just couldn't sit around and wait wait wait — so I ran to the sea. Walking along the shore, the air felt so good . . . so reassuring . . . free . . .

I walked along the pier. No one at the pier. No one at the beach. It belonged to me, for now. I let my thoughts roam with the wind in search of last summer's holiday magic. Oh how good it had been then!

↩

EVACUATION! The waiting was over. It had begun, the first official order of the Nazis. On lampposts, stores, on walls and doors, the signs were posted: Evacuation.

Jews first!

When? At dawn.

Where? The main square.

What may we take with us? One suitcase and one bag.

Julius had gotten my belongings from The Hague just in time for me to leave them behind now. When we got to the square, a lot of people were already assembled there. The families stuck close together but were immediately separated. We would be sent to different places.

Where to? Inland.

Where inland? No one knew.

For how long? No one knew.

Kate and Julius were still sitting on their suitcases when, in the late after-noon, a bus pulled away bearing Mama and me. It took many months be-fore we found out that Kate and Julius had been sent to a place called Vught in the south of Holland, close to Hertogenbosch. They had large detention centers there which later on became prisoner-of-war camps for Dutch sol-diers and other enemies of the Reich, among them Christians who had hid-den Jews and the Jews they had hidden.

Mama and I got "railroaded" to Enschede, geographically only one whis-pering "Sieg Heil!" away from the German border — too close for comfort. If one could have lured Hitler into this godforsaken place, he would have killed himself much sooner. For some reason, the people seemed to be under constant sedation; they all looked like sleepwalkers.

I spent six days among these zombies trying to find out who was in charge. I discovered it was a nice little Jewish zombie whose only ambition in life was to sleep through the war, undetected and undisturbed. When I told him I was an actress and that this place was ill-suited for my artistic temperament and would he please give me permission to put up my tent somewhere else, he replied, his voice a hazy fog, "You mean, you're not happy here?"

I guess I tired him out, for he gave me a piece of paper stating that I could travel to Utrecht and "temporarily" settle there. Mama had to stay behind. Five or six months later, when I finally got her out, her only reference to this insipid place was one deep sigh and a meaningful "Oy!"

Utrecht is as inland as one can get in Holland. Not overly exciting but pleasant — known for its university, a fantastic theater, now closed, and for generally being cultural. Thanks to my touring with the operettas, I knew it well.

The man in charge at Enschede had told me to report at once to the Jew-ish Committee, where I would be taken care of. These understaffed, over-worked organizers had their hands full trying to cope with too many new arrivals, all of them needing a place to stay. Their headquarters were in two small rooms on the second floor of an old house better known as the Rumor Factory. The Dutch Jews of Utrecht were most gracious. They not only opened their homes to us, but even gave us pocket money. In order to save us embarrassment, they sent it to the committee, and the committee handed it out. I met a lot of colleagues there. We talked showbiz, exchanged stories and laughed with a heavy heart.

I was given a nice home to stay in belonging to a young couple, Greta and Gus and their lovely baby, Bibi. My hosts were rather straitlaced and conservative. Not much humor; but then, there wasn't all that much to laugh about. Like most Dutch, they spoke several languages. They had seen me on stage many times and liked my work. However, that did not save me from the ordeal of having to speak Dutch. They insisted, "You live in our country, you speak our language."

At the Rumor Factory, one had to wait for hours in the noisy, cramped room before receiving attention. Everyone came because they didn't have much else to do. It was the best guessing and speculation center, the best word-of-mouth newsstand in town: "The butcher told me . . . I don't know where my brother is . . . I heard from a very reliable source that we'll be sent home soon . . ." Where is "home"?

Twice a week my colleagues and I met in a coffeehouse, had one cup of coffee, two glasses of water, and a whiff of the pastry. Out of this wild social life, the idea of trying to practice our profession again was born. We asked permission from the committee, but they gave us practically no help. "You have no work permit, and we can't get involved, so be careful." So, very carefully, we canvassed the city, trying to find a benevolent restaurant owner with a small banquet hall and a large, generous heart. Very carefully, we weeded out the unsuitable owners with stingy hearts till we found the right spot.

We opened our clandestine "Cabaret International" and played to empty chairs. How much more careful can one be? Advertising was out. Selling tickets was out. We were left, therefore, with an audience of other equally broke colleagues and an occasional diner looking for the washroom. The Cabaret International folded, or rather, it never got off the ground. However, it did give me the necessary incentive to try something else.

Through my hostess, Greta, I had met quite a few women, and it became obvious that the ladies of Utrecht could use help in losing some of their potato-and-gravy pounds. I was certain that gymnastics would be the answer, and talked it over with Greta, who agreed that it was a fine idea. Then I phoned the Jewish Committee and told them they could keep my allowance in exchange for a tambourine. I found a vacant basement which was as drafty as it was large, but cheap. What it lacked in natural light, it made up in exposed electrical wires. I bought some cracked mirrors at the flea market, turned the promotional work over to Greta (she knew everyone), and then anxiously waited for the gravy-lovers to rush to my basement.

My first class had one student. Since I only charged a minimal fee for maximum limbering up, I was sure that in no time at all I would need larger facilities. After a few weeks, I had ten ladies with a hundred sore muscles among them. Their bulges decreased and they were ever so grateful, but they did not bring me any other gravy-lovers. I kept the exercise classes going, which kept me in excellent shape but not my financial status. It just wasn't enough.

Of course, it was a hiatus existence and I knew it. My life was without substance. I functioned fairly well, though, mostly in a state of dazed numbness. Nothing was really good and nothing was really bad. It was all meaningless. A kind of involuntary drifting that could go on and on or stop altogether.

An interesting phenomenon was the Dutch in Utrecht who stuck to their daily routine with unyielding obstinacy as though the bogeymen were on another planet, not practically in their backyard. They were indeed as well informed as one could be, yet peace had reigned in the Netherlands for a hundred years and anti-Semitism did not exist. Race propaganda fell flat on its face here. The Jews in Holland were shoemakers, tailors, teachers and factory workers, not just bankers and industrialists. The thought that the merchants of death were after the Dutch Jew too never entered their minds.

My hosts were a perfect example of this almost touching naivete. In Copenhagen, the horror brigade had already gotten drunk on power and Danish beer, had plundered Oslo and praised the Führer. Yet, in the home of Greta and Gus, we still had dinner at six. While the Storm troopers marched into Paris and through the Champs-Elysées with their "Sieg Heils," we had our *copje tea,* as always, at eight. France had capitulated. The Germans drank French cognac and raped French women, but Greta, as always, poured our *glasje melk.* Even with darkness creeping over the town and just before we said *welte rusten,* Gus took *dat lieve hondje nog evente wandelen,* that dear doggy for a walk.

⌒

No mail from Ferry. I write and write, but who knows whether my letters even reach him. I don't dare mention my situation, and as I weigh each word before I put it down, I feel as though my pen is writing on eggshell, not paper. There is also the uncertainty about my return address. Do I really have one? His last letter reached me in Scheveningen. I guess his others are there, too. Nobody is forwarding anything. Mama is still in Enschede, and I haven't the foggiest idea where Kate and Julius are. Ah well! At least my education has improved. Thanks to Hitler and my hosts, I now speak Dutch fluently.

Another birthday. It's been a seesaw year. This time no long-stemmed roses from Ferry, not even a note. I miss him so much! Greta insists on giving me a party, though I'd much rather forget about it. What is there to celebrate? All week long she's been baking up a storm. The house smells of long ago — of butter cookies and chocolate cake. It smells of my childhood . . . of our kitchen in Vienna. Greta invited some of my colleagues and my gym class students. I shake a lot of hands and say a lot of thank-you's.

Then, Greta sheepishly informs me that a special guest has just arrived, and he is my real birthday present. Standing in the hallway, he is real all right, but for the life of me, I can't consider him a present: Otto Dürer, the producer. He has marvelous news for me. If I wish, I can move to Amsterdam and work there. He has leased another theater and has all the necessary papers. The Dutch police chief gave the okay. Otto had no trouble finding me. The Evacuation Committee referred him to Enschede, and they gave him my address in Utrecht. Very accommodating. I do hate the thought of him bailing me out. Of course, his motives are strictly selfish, but so is my decision to go with him. Otto says that everyone in Amsterdam is working and having a good time. What do I have to lose? I'm not any safer here. Everyone in Europe must register with the police, not only foreigners but everyone. Which means that the Germans know where we are anyhow. Where we are and what we do. They can grab us here, they can grab us there . . . they can grab us anywhere.

AMSTERDAM — What a pleasant change! I can't believe the Nazis are here too. It looks so normal. I love it — all of it! The parks, the flowers and the hours spent in the Rijksmuseum with more Rembrandts and other works of old masters than I have ever seen. In the Concertgebouw they are still playing symphonies, not marches. The entire city is quaint and picturesque. The coffeehouses and restaurants are full, the commercial districts crowded with shoppers. What a lively place compared to Enschede and surburban Utrecht. Five months since the invasion, and the victors haven't even burned a synagogue yet.

There are other encouraging signs. The German Jews who arrived here right after Hitler's rage began are all back in business — textile, fur, diamond and steel — and doing extremely well. Great artists are here too, enough to fill a dozen stages. A pessimist might say there is something weird about this life-as-usual routine, but I'm not one of those. Why give myself a headache trying to figure it out? I have rehearsals to think about, and how to get Mama out of Enschede. I also must let Ferry know that I now have a permanent address.

The theater Otto has leased is about ten minutes from the center of town on the Plantage Middenlaan, no. 4. It is named the Beatrix, after one of Queen Wilhelmina's granddaughters. Directly opposite is an old Catholic orphanage and, just a block away, the Population Registry: National Identification Center. The Zoo is also there, and a few doors from the Beatrix is another much larger theater — the Hollandsche Schouwburg, or Dutch Theater. The well-established Nelson Revue plays there, and they do have a head start on us. We are doing fairly well, but are not sold out. On good days the theater is half full; on bad days we blame it on the weather. The Nelson Revue isn't sold out either, but they blame it on us.

Hallelujah, Mama can come to Amsterdam! The Dutch police chief, after listening to my humble plea, took affirmative action at once. When I first went to see him, I had no idea he was part of the Resistance. Many here are aware that a well-organized, strong underground movement is doing all sorts of things to make the Germans nervous. There is even speculation that some of them have high positions, with access to vital information. Who are these men and women? Most likely they came from every walk of life, from upper echelon to average citizen. Whether specially trained in espionage and sabotage, whether deciphering codes or intercepting secret documents, their common goal is saving lives. They are my heroes!

The German invasion brought us an Austrian governor, Seyss Inquart, the Wehrmacht, the Brown Shirts, the Black Shirts, the *Sturm Abteilung* S.A. — the Storm troopers — the S.S. Gestapo, and who knows what else. They each had their separate headquarters so they could clearly define who had authority over whom. The military defense was in the hands of Herr Christianson, who was responsible for the invasion.

Our Gestapo chief was Blumenthal. A Jew could get arrested just for having such a name. Cold-blooded, sadistic monsters like Blumenthal played a major part in Hitler's heinous reign of terror, and sadly enough, there was also the Dutch Nazi Party, the NSP. It was quite an education, except that by the time I knew the difference, it was too late to make a difference.

I've just seen my first "Heil Hitler" German — he'd been found floating in one of the canals, very dead. Someone in the indomitable Resistance could not resist supplying this Brown Shirt with a permanent furlough. The canals in Amsterdam are an ideal place for drowning, and there have been others. In the fog, the Resistance waits to grab the Nazis and shove them in. Now, according to the grapevine, the Germans may no longer step out alone after dark. They do still carouse, but only in groups, getting drunk in nightspots, visiting the whores in the red light district, and staggering, with a little help from the Resistance, into the wet trap. The next morning they're fished out, also in groups. Heil!

I move into a nice hotel which I can't afford, but what the hell, it makes me feel very grown-up living alone without supervision, at least until Mama arrives. I finally find out where Kate and Julius are. They are all right, but Julius has lost his job with Canadian Pacific. His office in Rotterdam, like the city, no longer exists.

Herbert Nelson of the Nelson Revue came to see me, to find out whether my professional talent would be an asset to their company. He is eight years older than I, looks like a diplomat, is sophisticated, witty and a perfect gentleman. I like the lyrics he writes, his smile and his clear blue eyes. And when the Nelsons ask me to leave Otto Dürer's show, I quickly say yes.

Herbert and I fancied each other. In the first week of January 1941, while riding in the last car of a tram, Herbert said, "I have no money and no future, will you marry me?" And I, enthralled by his offering me absolutely nothing, said, "Yes." Herbert wanted to get married immediately, but when we applied for the marriage license, we were told that "immediately" was already too late. Herbert's father was one hundred percent Jewish and his mother a pure Aryan, which made my betrothed enough of a Jew to louse up his life too, and enough of an Aryan to prevent a marriage to me. So, the wedding was off, but the engagement was on. Herbert's parents didn't care, but Mama was a bit disappointed that she couldn't cry at my wedding.

Herbert and I lived together for a short while, and when we found a larger apartment, Mama moved in with us. My husband-to-be was not only an extraordinarily talented young man, he was also the son of Rudolf Nelson, the great artistic aristocrat. Rudolf Nelson composed the songs sophisticated audiences wanted to hear, and it made him rich and famous. The Nelsons came from Berlin. A keyboard virtuoso, Rudolf played his music for Emperor Kaiser Wilhelm and other European nobles. Rudolf Nelson was a star and a starmaker. He created the intimate cabaret and owned his own theater in Berlin. Except for Marlene Dietrich, his shining stars are forgotten; yet they were the mirror of an era which did reflect a dazzling way of life with all its splendor and no regrets.

When Rudolf Nelson left Berlin in 1933, he took with him his wife Kate Erlholz, Herbert, and several beautiful women. Heading straight for Amsterdam, he at once continued his glamorous cabaret revues in the Duschinski Theater. He did not understand politics. Rudolf Nelson never even considered emigration, nor that he was an emigrant. To him, his stay in Amsterdam was only a temporary geographical change of scenery, and with all the German Jews there, he still had many fans. Every afternoon he sat at the Caffee Schiller on the Rembrandt Plein, surrounded by his faithful, and held court. Not once did he allow reality to infiltrate his world. His language was music and music was his religion. The last thing he ever considered was that he was also a Jew.

Did I love Herbert? I must have. He was a loving, lovable man. Not my great passion, but I did feel a deep affection for him. We were friends, truly friends, and he never let me down.

What about Ferry? Had I forgotten him already? Not a chance. I could no more forget him than I could forget breathing. One can love two men — at least I could. I knew that most of Ferry's letters had gotten lost, and when after almost a year I heard from him again, my world already had become very small. Budapest and Ferry were many million miles away, and his letters the faint echo of a distant past. I lived inside a tiny circle: within this circle were only Mama, Herbert, and the Nelson Revue at the Hollandsche Schouwburg.

⤶

I HAD A LOVE AFFAIR with every inch of this theater. The walls, the seats, the footlights and the drafty backstage. I could not imagine ever leaving it — my dressing room was home to me. It wasn't fancy, just a mirror, a makeup table, and a chair, but it was mine. My theater — I'd come to think of it as such — was beautiful. How often its interior had been redone, I don't know. It certainly was in mint condition. The indirect lighting under-neath the marble panels gave it an almost modern look, a lovely contrast to the garnet red carpets and comfortable seats. Even in the last row of the sec-ond balcony every whisper could be heard, and without a single pillar to ob-struct the view, one could see every smile.

Audiences breathing in its atmosphere and warmth enjoyed chatting in the foyer, using the wide staircases leading to the balconies, the decorative lounges, and the subdued elegance. And what a stage! Large, deep and equipped to mount any production. There was a third floor too, with office space and room for sets and costume storage. The dressing rooms were all on the same level as the stage, no steps to climb. As with most theaters, a long, narrow alley led from the street to the stage door. Unlike most, it had its own charming little courtyard.

The Schouwburg's exterior was structurally strong and solid. Impressive hand-carved white stone arches with ornamental leaves and laurels framed the black-lacquered entrance doors, accentuating the glowing glass bowl lights above. Slender columns with deep rims, and jutted steplike squares and triangles, gave it a symmetrical blend of form and shape.

The Schouwburg's legend began in the summer of 1891, when Amster-damers, strolling through the Plantage Middenlaan, noticed a board being nailed to the front of a large wooden house. The house belonged to the es-tate of the deceased Mr. Westerman, founder of the Zoo. Written on the board was the announcement of a new operetta theater under the direction of Mr. Keef and Mr. Buderman. This unexpected news surprised everyone and caused a great deal of controversy. Only a few steps away there were already two operetta theaters, neither doing well; why add another one? But the very ambitious young architect Bombach argued that they were out-dated, dilapidated and unsafe. He insisted that he would build the Schouw-burg better, stronger and superior to those in other world capitals. The architect's perseverance paid off. Capacious, seating approximately seven hundred and fifty people, with twenty-eight emergency exits and enough water outlets to turn the whole neighborhood into a sea in case of fire — he built the Schouwburg using only Dutch workers and Dutch money. On May 5, 1892, with great festivities and even greater national pride, the Schouwburg opened. Generous Bombach gave his theater to the city of Amsterdam.

At the premiere, jubilant voices shouted: "This temple will stand forever! Whatever else may fall or vanish, the Schouwburg will not!"

Theater companies from all over the continent came to play there, the biggest and the best. Over the years, having become sort of a national monument, its name, fittingly, was changed to Hollandsche Schouwburg — Dutch Theater. The languages spoken on stage, however, and its repertoire were manifold: light operas and comedies, Greek tragedies, even the famous Russian Blauer Vogel cabaret of Berlin, played at the Schouwburg. And when, shortly before her death in 1923, the great Sarah Bernhardt gave her moving farewell performance on this stage, it deserved no less than to be called a temple of art.

The temple's glory lasted for half a century, its history much longer. In 1941, it became the Joodsche Schouwburg — Jewish Theater. And even with war raging outside its heavy doors, and with the ratty eyes of the enemy watching it day and night, Jews through many seasons of uncertainty still sang their songs of hope in there.

⤳ THREE

SOMEWHERE IN AMSTERDAM, in newspaper morgues, faded articles about the Jewish Theater are collecting dust. In city archives, classified records and statistics are also collecting dust. Tourists might wander through the Anne Frank House and notice a couple of theater programs on display. The captions read: JOODSCHE SCHOUWBURG; the dates October 1941 — seventeen months after the German invasion.

The recorded history of this theater and its staggering changes provides, at best, an indistinct, peripheral tracing of events spread sparsely over twenty-two years. But buried underneath the statistics, and layered by the webs of time, the phenomenal story of the Joodsche Schouwburg has never been told: the story of a theater and of human entrapment.

Perhaps you would care to journey back to 1941 with me? I very much want to unlock the doors of this once proud temple, and have you step inside. I lend you my eyes and ears so you can see what I have seen and hear what I have heard. I can't lend you my heart, for it is still bleeding; nor my soul, which is too badly scarred, but free. Still, you will witness a happening like no other, in a theater like no other. You'll see it as a sanctuary, with celebrating spirits, joyful and happy. You'll see it as a cage, with thousands trapped inside its wailing walls. But do not cry, for far too many cups of sorrow have spilled in there already. There isn't room for anymore.

Don't leave. It isn't over yet. You've come this far; do stay with me, stay till the end. And now that I've given you a preview, loaned you my eyes and ears, please take your seat and watch the curtain rise . . . and fall . . .

The year 1941 was a good one for Yugoslavian wine, Russian caviar — and Jewish actors living in Amsterdam. In the spring, the Third Reich added Yugoslavia to its menu and nibbled on Russia — no longer their friendly ally — but did not rob the Schouwburg of its tasty gourmet dishes. On the contrary, we in our theater prospered. Not only did we inherit many more seasoned actors, but lots of money, thanks to de Herr Van Leer, a wealthy graphic industrialist and well-known patron of the arts. The Van Leer Foundation sent many grants our way. Van Leer made only one request: half of the ensemble had to be Dutch. The executive director of the foundation was not a Dutchman, but Dr. J. Levie, a German Jew. The third-floor office was his business headquarters, and he did a most admirable job, not only as administrator but as an arbitrator for Rudolf Nelson and the newly hired Dutch star, Henriette Davids. Both Rudolf and Henriette wanted to be head of production and each disliked the other intensely. Henriette spurned Nelson because he was a social snob and a German. He found her distastefully common and her broad slapstick humor unfit for his sophisticated cabaret. Even with a world in chaos, these two could think of nothing else but top billing and production rank.

Henriette had tremendous mass appeal. She came from the streets of Amsterdam and knew what the common man wanted to hear and what made him laugh. Dear Henriette was a comical music hall queen, snappy, as much of a tyrant as Nelson, and as tough. She was not even five feet tall, with short fat legs and crippled feet. When Henriette smiled, two rows of gray stubs appeared. But that wasn't all. Once, when I barged into her dressing room unannounced, I made the unpleasant discovery that she was completely bald. Henriette wore wigs. Not for the same reason as Stella's mother — she wasn't Orthodox, just bald. All the same, Henriette needed no one's sympathy. She was rich and famous. Immensely talented in her own way, she used her preposterous physique as a tool.

While patient Dr. Levie tried to negotiate a truce between those two old stars inside the Schouwburg, outside, the Nazis had sent their underlings with large posters all over town. On newspaper stands, at public buildings, museums, parks, and in little cafés, their latest order was being affixed to everything that didn't move. For those who could not read German, or cared not to, loudspeakers blasted through every street:

↬

EFFECTIVE IMMEDIATELY!

JEWS currently employed in any field of entertainment must be terminated at once!

JEWS are forbidden to attend theaters, concerts or movies!

WARNING:
Anyone defying this order will be arrested!

↬

The news reached our theater while rehearsal was in full swing. I was working on a new dramatic song, "The Saga of the Unknown Soldier," with its timely lyrics: "What did you fight for . . . what did you die for . . . nobody gives a damn . . . nobody knows your name . . ." and much too absorbed to hear my colleagues' protests and curses. Someone pushed me away from the piano and shouted into my ear, "We're finished!" It took a couple of minutes before it sifted through my brain that something more dramatic than "The Saga of the Unknown Soldier" was taking place.

Finally, Dr. Levie went on stage and asked us to be calm. "Pull yourselves together!" He told us to just stay put and wait for him. It was about noon when he left. Though we didn't talk about it anymore, no doubt we all had the same thought: *What are we going to do?*

It was early evening when Dr. Levie returned. "I have good news. The Germans have given permission to let us keep the Hollandsche Schouwburg. From now on, this will be a Jewish theater, and you'll be playing for Jewish audiences only. Do you understand? We did it. It's ours!"

Out of nowhere, bottles of champagne and glasses appeared. We popped the corks, poured the wine, raised the glasses toasting each other and the Schouwburg, "Lachaim!" We hugged and kissed, drank the champagne, sang, danced, and shouted, "Lachaim! Lachaim!"

We never asked, nor were we told, how Dr. Levie had managed to pull it off. Had he used the prestigious Van Leer Foundation as a diplomatic weapon, or had he found other channels? Reassurance was all we needed. Was it really true? It was.

Later, with considerably less emotion, I thought about all this. It occurred to me that the Germans might have had their own reasons for letting us keep our theater. As far as I could figure, it had little to do with Dr. Levie or the foundation, but a whole lot to do with the Schouwburg's location. Somehow, the Nazis chose to believe that our temple stood right in the middle of the Jewish ghetto. Since mostly Jewish actors played there, and several Jewish shopkeepers had settled there long ago, why not keep us all together over there? "Over there" was a ten-minute tram ride from the center of town, away from the clean, nice people. A perfect ghetto, except there was none — nowhere in Amsterdam, and certainly not on the Plantage Middenlaan. Not with the Catholic orphanage right across from us and the animals in the Zoo, unless those lovely giraffes and monkeys were also Jews. One thing I knew, just a few doors down the street, in the tavern belonging to good churchgoing Dutch folks, kosher drinks were never served.

Ironically, it was the Germans' decision about our theater that ended the enmity between Rudolf Nelson and Henriette. They put away their boxing gloves, shook hands for the first time, and blithely agreed to share top billing as heads of production. Mazeltov!

All summer long, a stream of artists keep knocking on Dr. Levie's door. Thanks to the Germans, we now have half of the symphony orchestra, their soloists and conductor, in our theater, as well as ballerinas, choreographers, and the best set and costume designers. There is no limit to the sort of entertainment we can provide. No limit to the stars illuminating our stage. We're making magic — magic for our audiences! They come to us with such enthusiasm, it is they who keep us on a constant high. No matter the season, our public turns our stage into a botanical garden. I take my curtain call amid a sea of flowers, inhaling the scent. And once back in my dressing room, I read the little notes attached: "Thank you for making dark days brighter. . . . As long as we have you and the Schouwburg, we shall not despair. . . ."

All our performances are sold out. If our theater were three times as large, there still would not be an empty seat. The range of productions is enormous, thanks to Dr. Levie's faultless coordination. Our public goes overboard with gifts for us. The textile merchants shower us with exquisite material for gowns; the furriers with furs; and thanks to the leather manufacturers, an ample supply of handmade shoes and bags comes our way. Even my under-wear is especially made for me — crêpe de chine, satin, and silk. I don't need to buy a thing. It's a crazy paradox, but I can't help feeling very rich. I only re-gret that I don't get to do more dramatic scenes. I'm not given much serious material to play. A poignant chanson or two, a quiet lullabye, but nothing too sad or heavy. Dr. Levie says there's enough of that outside the Schouwburg. In here, it's happy hours only, no political innuendos.

A tall, skinny Nazi has come to watch us every night, sitting in the first loge, stage left, listening to every word. We have many Dutch songs and skits in our shows which he can't understand. Night after night he sits there stiff as a board, without expression. It must be his fault that our scripts are being censored now. All of a sudden each word we utter has to be sanctioned by their intelligentsia: "blond," "blue-eyed," "gorgeous" are blacked out. Jews, so say the master race, are never blondes, cannot be blue-eyed, and are not per-mitted to be gorgeous. We laugh about this foolishness; we laugh about Henriette Davids who, anonymously, has sent her blond wigs to the Ger-mans. Of course it's a nuisance. But as long as it doesn't stop the press — Jewish newspaper only — from singing our praises, or our public from launching their own word-of-mouth publicity, who cares?

We are in such demand that by October a whole string of tickets are being sold on the black market. I don't know who sells them, but I do know who buys them: our non-Jewish friends. On the black market the price for an evening at the Schouwburg is sky-high, but our friends don't mind. We do not keep the money. It all is channeled to the underground or to some needy Jewish families. Naturally, we are thrilled about these clandestine vis-its, thrilled that these good people have not forsaken us.

Of course, the rumor factories are flourishing here, too. Whether in cof-feehouses or at the homes of friends, there are always those who know something that others don't. Just when I've made up my mind not to listen to any of it, the Germans announce that the Führer wants radios. Ours! All Jews must turn them in. Now I can't listen to the BBC anymore. I could go to my neighbors; they asked me to — but it is risky for them and me.

A couple of weeks later, still in October, the Germans issue an astonishing declaration: Austria has become Germany and the Austrians Germans!

It means good-bye passport; it means that a German one will be issued instead — for those with Aryan blood. I and the other foreign Jews are de-clared non-desirables, which automatically makes us lose our citizenship too. Frankly, I don't give a damn. I lost my country long ago. But Mama is mad. She now insists that she is Hungarian, as if anybody cared. Herbert also has to turn his passport in, but he gets it back. Rudolf Nelson doesn't and his wife does. It is obvious that the Nazis are still very mixed up about mixed marriages, which is why I don't know about my sister Kate and her Catholic husband.

We, the undesirables, are stuck with an identification card with a picture and a big fat "J" for Jew on it. The Department of Interior likes the name Sarah so much that it has generously given it to all Jewish women; it's printed on every female ID card, lest we forget. Sarah is my name . . . and my native country is now listed as Germany, not Austria, which makes me an undesirable German instead of an undesirable Austrian. Is that better? They say we must carry the JEW card with us at all times. Some of the refugees call it a bad omen and talk about dark clouds beginning to gather. I wonder — the climate is definitely changing. Lately, there is a chill in the air. A Hitler chill . . .

December used to be one of my favorite months. Not these days. The future is so frightfully uncertain — a dark, sealed book with a swastika on it. I would like to take time out for nostalgia, be quiet for a while and reminisce, think of Papa, of Ferry. I don't want to forget all that was good in my yesteryears. But I cannot. There is much going on!

↬

HITLER HAS DECLARED WAR on the United States. There is other world news, too: Pearl Harbor! Somewhere, at the other end of the globe, on a beautiful island where palm trees shade the white-heat days, where tropical fruit and bright-hued flowers grow, the Japanese have sunk a lot of ships and killed so many American boys. I thought that the Japanese were gentle people who liked living in ricepaper houses surrounded by tranquil lilypond gardens and bonsai trees.

It seems a bit vain and callous to worry about our jewelry at a time when the Americans are mourning their sons. But ever since the radio incident, we've had to give some thought to our valuables. Should we hide them? Naturally, we don't want to lose anything. Also, there is the possibility of a food shortage, in which case, we'll need something to barter with. I don't want some black marketeer making a bundle on my pretty baubles. Everything Mama owns is an heirloom or a gift from Papa — she'll never part with them.

A week before Christmas, the clever Nazis solve the problem for us. Rich and festive is their festive season, thanks to the nice Jews, who have made such a sizable contribution. Sizable, but not complete. Much stays hidden, and what we dare not hide, we entrust to friends. My voluntary sacrifice is peanuts, but Aryan Margit, from across the street, with her heart of gold, will keep my pretties for me. Only for a while — only till the Americans come. It can't be too much longer, can it?

↩

ANOTHER WARNING, another restriction:

JEWS are barred from restaurants, coffeehouses, and libraries!

They are cutting into our *Lebensraum* — our space, our freedom of movement.

The churchbells ring out the old year and ring in the new, and Dr. Levie delivers a New Year's message to our public. The Joodsche Schouwburg will no longer be heated. Our coal rations have gone up in smoke.

I convince myself that Dutch winters are not so bad. Somehow, I believe that the Schouwburg will protect us. Her roof is like a mother's blanket, large enough to keep all her children warm. I don't know whether architect Bombach is still alive, but I am certain that he has built the Joodsche Schouwburg for us.

The winter fog is dark and gloomy, the streets dimly lit. I take long walks and let the moisture cleanse my face. Sometimes, I stop, look at the frosted sky, and wait — wait for the American planes to come. I want to be there when they land. I want to be the first one to say, "Thank you!" — in English, of course. But they don't come. What are they waiting for? Whenever I pass a coffeehouse, I press my face against the window and stare at the people sitting inside. Are they so different from me? My feet are wet. I'd like to go in, have hot chocolate, and rest a while. Maybe next year. Maybe next year that skinny Nazi in our theater will no longer be there. Maybe a handsome American will have taken his place and be smiling at me.

↩

JANUARY 1942:

It's hard to find a taxi these days, and the trams don't run that often anymore. It's spooky waiting in the dark and riding home through the dead of night. Mama always worries. I tell her not to. I keep telling her that all through the month of January, till one snowy morning she doesn't have to worry about my riding the tram anymore.

JEWS may no longer use public transportation!

JEW! JEW! JEW! I must have heard and read the word five thousand times or more in these last few months alone. Are we that important? Every restriction sounds like a screaming threat. There is this voice which keeps on yelling the same contemptible warnings over and over again. It sounds like a poisonous needle has gotten stuck on a record. No more public transportation one day, and a strict curfew the next.

Now, the matinees are moved up to noon, the evening curtain rises at six, the performances finish earlier, but we reach our homes much later. We have to walk through the pitchy darkness.

↩

FEBRUARY:

We, the undesirables, may no longer mix with the desirables. We may not visit their homes, nor they ours. We may not even talk or say hello if we pass each other on the street. The Dutch Jews still don't want to believe that all the "May Nots" include them too, and our Aryan friends ignore the Germans' blackmail altogether. They keep coming to our theater, even though it means having to borrow a Jewish ID card. It is no longer just the shows that bring them to us, but a strong pledge of solidarity, an unspoken reaffirmation of friendship. Never once have I peeked through the curtain without seeing familiar non-Jewish faces.

Our industrial and manufacturing comrades are no longer working for themselves. The Third Reich has sent inspectors to inspect them and their merchandise. The plants and factories now have Nazis strutting about. It's a profitable enterprise for the Germans. They keep the goods, and the Jews do the work. It's called "appropriation." What could be more appropriate? It's being said that a lot of the old masters from the Rijksmuseum have also been "appropriated."

↩

MARCH:

The war of nerves continues, and they are using the amplifiers again.

Jewish sculptors and painters are forbidden to exhibit their work in public galleries. The artists lose their space in public galleries, their clients, but not their sense of humor. A full-page ad appears in our weekly paper: "LOST: walls to hang my paintings. LOST: space to display my sculptures." Dr. Levie takes out another ad, "FOUND: Jewish walls to hang your paintings. FOUND: Jewish space to display your sculptures. Come to the Joodsche Schouwburg."

We have an art gallery! Now we are a real cultural center — symphonies, concerts, operettas, cabaret, ballet, art exhibits. Is that all? No, our people also need a place where they can meet. Where else can they go since everywhere is off limits — except to the Joodsche Schouwburg?

The first-floor lounge becomes a coffeehouse and, through the only doors still open to them, our faithful patrons rush in. We post a sign in the lobby: "Social Club — Jewish members only — daily 10 a.m.–1 p.m. and 3 p.m.–5 p.m." Dressed in their Sunday best, crowds of exhilarated people fill the staircases waiting for available tables.

⤶

APRIL:

April Fool's Day is here, but the Hitler boys are not fooling.

JEWS are forbidden to be married at the City Hall. Where can they go now that the synagogues are closed, the Torah hidden, and the rabbi without his temple? Only to the Joodsche Schouwburg. We have a small anteroom right next to the Social Club, a perfect place for a wedding chapel. While we're rehearsing, while lights are being checked, tags put on new paintings, carpets vacuumed, and seats dusted, many a blushing bride and groom exchanges vows: ". . . for richer, for poorer, in sickness and in health."

⤶

MAY:

Spring is here. I made it through the winter without catching pneumonia. My dressing room is full of yellow daffodils. Not exactly my favorite color, but the Germans seem to like it. The poisonous record needle is blaring again.

JEWS: All Jews must wear the yellow Star of David.

Jews caught without it will be arrested. It must be conspicuous. It must be sewn onto the clothing on the left side above the chest, only a few inches away from the heart. I have a drawer full of these yellow patches, these Stars of David, but I can't get myself to tell the seamstress to sew them on. Mama curses in Hungarian. Herbert keeps shaking his head, and Rudolf Nelson still hasn't tuned in to what's going on.

They are no longer taking just a radio or a pretty ring. They're labeling us, robbing us of our dignity. I feel like I'm tied to a post in a marketplace with everyone pointing their fingers and shouting, "She is a Jew . . . she is a Jew . . . Don't touch her, she has leprosy." I won't wear it, I won't. I hate them!

Dr. Levie says, don't rock the boat. Don't do anything that may cause us to lose the Schouwburg. Keep calm. Dear Dr. Levie. All he's worried about is our theater. Anything to save it. "Wear the yellow star," he pleads. "Wear it!"

I'm listening to the afternoon concert with my pockets full of yellow cloth. I keep remembering that I didn't even know I was Jewish till I was seven, and then it didn't mean a thing to me. To this day, I haven't seen the inside of a synagogue. Hitler is making me a Jew.

We are to have a run-through before the evening show. I'm in a lousy mood, and Henriette Davids is late for rehearsal. That makes me feel a little better. There won't be time to bring those patches to the seamstress. The others keep looking at their watches, a sure sign that they are worried. Henriette is never late. Maybe she got herself arrested: she has such a sharp tongue and speaks her mind quite openly.

Thirty minutes later, roaring with laughter, she waddles in. "You've got to see this! All the Amsterdamers are wearing the star. No, not the Jews, the others. I've seen two pregnant ladies with it pinned to their big tummies, and a poodle flaunting it on his tail!" Henriette is giddy with excitement; she slaps her thighs, cheers, and leaps about. I think she is going to have a seizure. "Come quick," she cries. She motions us to the door, and already her crippled little feet are tramping ahead of us.

Before Henriette has reached the corner, her unshapely arms are flying up and down and she is shouting at the top of her lungs, "*Ik hou van jau . . . Ik hou van jau . . .*" I love you . . . I love you. She must mean her country and all those brave Dutch folk. Wherever I look, people are wearing the Star of David. They're singing and dancing in the streets as though this was the still unforeseen D-Day. These strangers have turned our humiliation into a celebration. The Germans must be furious. They will retaliate, I'm sure they will. But nothing happens, no arrests.

That evening, our orchestra plays the Dutch national anthem, and then the *Hatikvah,* the Jewish national anthem. It's the first time, and the audience goes wild. They dance in the aisles, clap their hands and sing, sing with the might of an untamed river. Soulful, fiery, passionate. It gives me goosebumps. I don't think this theater has ever witnessed such jubilation.

It takes quite a while before it is all quiet again, before Dr. Levie can speak. Composed and dignified, he thanks the people of Amsterdam for their support and says that we are lucky to be here and not in Germany, where no one has lifted a finger to help the Jews.

The brave Dutch have worn the yellow star for just one day, but they have made their statement, and I for one shall always remember their grand gesture. Now they have taken it off; we have put it on — and everything is back to normal.

Amsterdam is lovely in May. My eyes feast on the myriad flowers. I love this mild and gentle season. Garden furniture awaits the outdoor patrons who still can frequent coffeehouses. The street vendors have shed their winter clothes and are selling fresh eel and herring as they have done since they were boys, as their fathers did before them, as has been their custom for centuries. One could almost believe that the evil ones are no longer here. I like to sit on a bench in the park with the sun on my back. I like watching the blossoms open and reach for the light, like tiny baby fingers. But these warm, bright moments pass too quickly, fade into a gauzy mist, while the black breath of the enemy whips away the vestal spring.

↞

NOW WE MUST WEAR the Star of David on stage as well. We must wear it on our costumes, evening gowns, on dinner jackets, negligées and ballerina tutus.

↞

SUMMER 1942

JEWS: May Not Sit in Parks

JEWS: May Not Stand Together on Streets

JEWS: May Not Congregate in Houses

JEWS: May Not! May Not! May Not! *Achtung . . . Warnung . . . Verboten.*

I'm wearing a chain around my neck and it is choking me, but such is life in the forbidden city now. What would I do without the Schouwburg?

↞

KATE IS HERE; she's gotten a one-day pass and wants to see a doctor. Kate isn't ill, but there is no sparkle in her eyes, no color in her face. Mama says she is having a trying time in that Godforsaken place they have sent her to. Her living quarters are cramped, and she doesn't even have a kitchen. She has to cover the bathtub with a board and put a heating plate with two burners on it if she wants to cook. I'm sure she is miserable and lonely, and I don't even know what she and Julius are living on. Yet, with all these uncertainties, Kate wants a baby. That's why she came.

Kate is glad she can visit with us, but I can sense that she is battling a lot of anxieties. It's all those doctors she has been seeing without results. After returning from yet another specialist, she looks even worse. Kate is crying. Strange, I've never seen her cry before. I try to think of something that might cheer her up. Then it comes to me . . . Fannie, of course.

"Hey, Kate, how would you like to meet a terrific psychic? She lays cards, but not for money, and only when the spirits move her. Her name is Fannie, and she is a real nice lady."

Kate looks at me as though I'd just invented Fannie, but I can see my sister is perking up. Quickly, I pick up this encouraging sign and talk about the psychic's powers. Naturally, I don't tell her everything. I wouldn't dare, not in her depressed frame of mind. I don't tell her that when Fannie gave me a reading a year ago, my future looked pretty shitty. Her prediction was that I'd be going on a long, long trip, wouldn't come back for ever so long, and while away, unimaginable, ghastly things would happen to me. And even though she swore I'd come out all right in the end, she'd gotten all upset and ill. I kept thinking, no wonder she doesn't ask for money; such foretelling would make an onion cry. The worst thing was that Fannie believed everything she told me. The best thing was, I didn't. How could I be taking a long trip when I wasn't allowed to leave town? How could something terrible happen to me somewhere else when I was stuck here? I didn't want to hurt her feelings then, but I was certain that she had used the wrong cards.

The only reason I thought of Fannie was that last year during my reading, she had said Kate would give birth to a son within two years. She didn't even know that I had a sister, yet she kept repeating, "The one who lives in Holland, not the other one who lives somewhere else." I had asked Herbert whether he might have shown her some photographs of us, but he said no.

So, I thought, what the hell, considering all odds, she might be half right. Right about Kate, wrong about me. Funny, at the time of her prediction, I had no idea that Kate wanted a child. Wishing makes one believe almost anything, and my down-in-the-dumps sister wanted to believe, wanted this psychic to tell her what the doctors could not.

After I had introduced them, I waited in the salon, keeping my fingers crossed. When I saw my sister again, I knew Fannie had done right by her. The cards still said the same. A son next year. In her little, faraway voice, Fannie said to Kate, "Be happy," and Kate, who never before believed in that sort of thing either, was.

Back to Vught she went, bringing Julius a whole lot of smiles, a whole lot of straw hopes. Watching her go, I thought how Hitler had changed my beautiful sister into a lonely plain Jane. Hard to imagine her cooking on top of a bathtub, or sitting in a shabby room with black air-raid shades on the windows, and waiting by a drab, dreary light for the son the cards had said was sure to come.

⤺

THE DAYS OF LIGHT are all but gone now, and it is the eve of the year. Already, the trees are dropping their green leaves. The little courtyard behind the stage door is wearing a wilted sepia hedge, and yesterday's summer has burned the lavender morning glories all dead. I wonder whether the Schouwburg's blanket will shield us from the wintertime again.

There is a visitor backstage. A tall, good-looking S.S. man. Out of nowhere he suddenly materialized. He wasn't there when I began my chanson. But somehow, during the last chorus, I feel a pair of eyes on me, and as I glance in the direction of the wings, I see him standing there. He is all eyes, all ears, with a big smile on his polished, repugnant face. I'm not at all sure what to make of it, and for a second there I think I might have imagined him. But when the curtain comes down, I hear him applaud. He plants himself right where I'm about to exit.

I can't go the other way: the stage crew is busy with preparations for the next scene. I have no choice but to walk directly toward him, and with less than a foot between us, the S.S. man salutes me. I don't know what to make of that either. Each time I take another bow, he smiles, nodding his skull-head cap approvingly. I finish with my last curtsy, and as I pass the black, leather-coated uniform, he says, *"Entschuldigen Sie bitte, ich hoffe dass ich Sie nicht nervös gemacht habe?"* — Forgive me, I hope I didn't make you nervous? Stupefied but polite, I answer, *"Überhaupt nicht."* Not at all. He salutes again and tiptoes to the other side, and I, with heart in my mouth, race to my dressing room, where I'd like to stay till the war is over.

Ten minutes later, on my way to the stage, I see him walking noiselessly behind the backdrop. He doesn't touch a thing, but seems extremely interested in the theater's layout. Some of my colleagues have noticed him too and are as dumbfounded as I. As I wait for my cue, I find myself staring at him. He looks as though someone had poured him into his medal-studded uniform, as though his salute and smile were part of the costume. He is making a special effort to be as unobtrusive as possible. Just before the finale, I hear the squeak of his shiny boots, like tiny mice, outside my dressing room, and then the sudden *thump* of a door.

He is gone. Gone into October's half-lit evening. I don't know who he is, why he came, what he wants or when he'll materialize again. After the show we all debate the purpose of this uninvited visitor. Some say he may have wanted to check whether something illegal is going on behind the fireproof "Iron Curtain" — something that blond, wooden Nazi in the loge might have missed. Like an underground printing press, or explosives. Not here. Not in this temple, our last outpost and citadel.

SHE WAS THE REINCARNATION OF VENUS, this girl who sat in the window, played her guitar and sang with the voice of a nightingale. Her almond-shaped gray eyes were forever laughing, her puck nose like the petal of a thirsty flower and her ruby lips the promise of sweet wine. Hers was the curved sensuous body that every man desired. Hers were the days, the hours, the minutes that came from the fields where happiness grows. And she was my best friend: Margit.

Margit lived right across from me on the Maasstraat in Amsterdam Zuid (south), and I had seen her sitting on the windowsill with her guitar and listened to her singing for many months before we met. It seemed that everyone except me knew her. Women would say, "Well, that's Margit," as though they couldn't conceive of anyone not knowing her.

Each time I opened my window, there she was, the beautiful nightingale. Each time I left for the theater, she chirped, "Have a nice day."

Margit's twenty-two-year-old past had been spent mostly in the circus. She was born in a pink candy-striped wagon to parents she doesn't remember. She had traveled all over Europe with her troupe — they were her family and she their good-luck charm. She was weaned by a sword-swallowing lady who later on tried to teach her her trade. But Margit wanted to ride the white stallions, learn how to swing from trapeze to trapeze, and to toe-dance on the high wire. She climbed the rope to reach the trapeze before she was nine. She balanced on the high wire, with her red sequin leotard, before she knew that boys weren't girls. And she was still a little tot when first she mounted the proud stallions, when first she rode the Barbary horses with the graceful skill of a champion. The world of the circus, she always said, is a wonderful world for a child to grow up in. Utilitarianism is the only religion there, and camaraderie the language everyone speaks.

The very first time a friend brought her to our home, I looked at her radiant face and wondered whether she ever was sad. But? Margit had found her nirvana in the sawdust tents of the circus, and her reservoir of "perfect blessedness" never ran dry. Life to her was one big adventure. Life was love, and love the soul of mankind — the force that ruled her existence, the magic carpet she lay on and the emblem she nobly wore.

Margit lived with some invisible Dutch folks who had taken her under their invisible wings when her circus, also bruised by the war, had to close. She hadn't worked for a long time. When there wasn't enough food for the animals anymore, and not enough safe roads left to travel on, but a pretty good chance that she and her candy-striped wagon would end up in a German army camp, the tents came down. The animals were in some zoo now, at least most of them, her adopted family scattered all over the European continent, at least most of them (some did end up in army camps). And she, being fluent in Dutch and the ways to a Dutchman's heart, ended up here.

She was engaged to the nondescript son of her guardians, which I guess was better than being pursued by concupiscent soldiers. I don't think she ever planned on marrying him. She may have gotten engaged to please his virtuous parents, not wanting to defame their cardinal law. I met this innocuous Dutch boy only once. He was as dull as dishwater, and had as much humor as a Greek tragedy. But he loved her and was extremely protective of her.

What did she think about the Nazi hell-raisers? About the persecution of Jews? About the restrictions which even restricted their own restrictions. She laughed. "They will not harm you. I know those Germans are a little crazy right now, but it won't last. If they would only realize that holding a woman is so much better than holding a gun, the war would be over in no time." I must have looked slightly puzzled, not knowing how to take her startling solution of how to end a war, for Margit winked at me and then cheerfully chirped, "It's true."

Perhaps she only said it to amuse me. But then again, who knows? She never gave me a rundown of the men who had walked up to her small room on the top floor, of the arms that had held her, or who her lovers were. Yet I could always tell when she had had "one of those nights." I could see it in her face the next day. Her cheeks would be flushed and her voice had a tremulous resonance as though the echo of it was still with her. And she was even more beautiful — after love. Did her fiancé, under cover of night, also creep up the stairs to her room, lie on the mauve satin sheets under the nocturnal sky of her blue ceiling? I don't think so. Her cheeks were never flushed when he was home.

Margit and I did not talk girl talk. She knew that I was just a novice compared to her, and even though she had more than a year's "head start" on me, it wasn't likely that I could ever match her score. She was much taller than I. She had charming dimples and chestnut brown hair which shone as though a hundred little starlights were hidden in there. Her magnetism sent signals to every man within a hundred miles, so they said. Well, I don't know about that.

I do know that she was a wonderful friend. To know her was to feel the warmth of summer in the midst of a storm, like being pulled out of the darkness into the light. Her radiant joy in all she smelled, tasted, and touched was so complete, so natural, that it was impossible not to be enchanted by her.

Every morning she came with her guitar, settled at the edge of the tub while I was taking my bath, and sang to me. Little poems set to music she had written herself. Songs about love and about her white stallion days. I'd given her my jewelry to keep till after the war; she gave me a book of poems to keep forever. I let her wear my silver fox whenever she went out; she gave me a golden talisman, two filigree hands joined together with the inscription, "Friendship."

Margit brushed off the days of suspended judgment as though they were fluffs of lint. She was not a fighter. "Hate" and "enemy" found no place in her compassionate soul. She never wanted to "slay the beast," as I did. She only wanted to help. It was her unshakable belief in mankind, her loyalty to her friends, which led her down the "unsung hero's" path. When first she started taking chances, it wasn't much more than a game to her. A "so-what-are-they-gonna-do-to-me?" sort of thing, like her visits to our house long after it was forbidden. And she never let a week go by without showing up at the Schouwburg with the Jewish ID card belonging to Toni, my other best friend. She took care of old, frightened Jews who didn't dare to go out anymore. She lit their candles for the Sabbath and ran all over town to find a good, cheap kosher chicken for them. It really wasn't much more than a game — at first.

Not more than five minutes away from our house lived Toni. She was the one who had brought Margit to our home. We were like the Three Musketeers. Ravishing Toni was a genuine social butterfly, now a grounded but undiscouraged jet-setter. Not too long ago she had been dining in Rome, yachting on the French Riviera, the guest of a kilt-wearing duke at his castle in Scotland, and with half a dozen Spanish matadors at her side, had strolled through the Casbah in sunny Algiers. She and Margit had been friends for a long time.

Toni had two great talents. One, she managed never to work a day in her life; and two, she never worried about anything. When the Hitler punks — that's what she called them — put her high-flying gear into idle, she simply parked her dancing slippers and came home to roost.

A long, long time ago, there was this war called World War I, which someone lost and someone won, but even after the guns fell silent and the wounded soldiers' blood had dried, a lot of hungry children still cried. Toni was one of them. Her papa never came back from the battles he so gallantly fought for his Austrian fatherland. (The Germans had sucked the waltzing Austrians into that one, too.) And her mama, so saddened by the loss of her man and the hungry look in her baby's face, sent her to Holland, where a lot of little bodies became stout and sturdy again, a lot of little tummies full.

And that's where Toni found her new foster parents, the Cohens. Child-less themselves, this warm-hearted, middle-aged Jewish couple took this tiny girl with the large, jet black eyes and the thick, raven black hair and made her their own. Toni grew up in Vienna and Amsterdam. She spent the early school years with Mrs. Mausner, her mother; the holidays with her fos-ter parents.

It's most unlikely that Toni's flair and charm stemmed from her mother. In photographs Mrs. Mausner looked unimpressive, sort of permanently down in the dumps. Nor do I think that life with the Cohens emboldened Toni's questful jet-set climb. But rather, the rich debutantes she went to the Swiss finishing schools with opened the world's glamour doors for her. I never met Toni's real mother, but with her foster parents I struck up a nice friendship. Their life was simple. It rotated around the dry goods store they owned and operated, their daily walk to and fro, and, naturally, Toni. Toni's social sphere was not within their comprehension; nevertheless, they would have bought the world for her if she had asked for it. Kind, generous people. Every guilder they had saved was for Toni. Many, many guilders. Mrs. Cohen often said, "We made a good place for Toni so she'll never have to worry."

A couple of months before the Germans raped this country, the Cohens sold their shop. It had nothing to do with foresight, only with the swollen aching feet of Mama Cohen. Forty-five years she stood on a hard cement floor selling her goods, and after forty-five years her feet gave out. Now she was in a wheelchair. On nice weather days Papa Cohen took her for a wheelchair ride around the block. The same one they had walked together for fifty years. That's how long they'd been married. Of course, they didn't understand why war had come to their peaceful land, or why this Hitler man didn't like Jews. But otherwise, they were quite happy. There was much love in their hearts for each other, and a whole universe full for Toni.

Toni cared a great deal about them. She brought a lot of laughter to their old, unstained years. She was a spirited girl, vivacious, and full of fun — as fiery as a thoroughbred racehorse and as streamlined as a high fashion model. When she walked down the street on her *click-click* high heels with her Parisian suits and her radiant smile, she looked more like a fine Spanish señorita or the Italian mistress of a nobleman than a Viennese Jewess waiting for doomsday. But then she never gave doomsday a thought.

Everyone was her friend and she had friends everywhere. How many *affaires de coeur* she confessed to her diary, if she ever kept one, I couldn't even guess. At the time the Nazis began to really make asses of themselves, Toni had no special lover. I'm sure of it because she'd mentioned that she didn't find the climate for amour too favorable. "These days," she said, "sweet words like 'I adore you' are out, and 'Hurry, I must be home before curfew' in. What's a girl to do, turn into a stopwatch?" Why else would she declare that "Love just doesn't bloom too well when all your sweetheart wants from you is food stamps! Got some honey?"

Mama was delighted to have two new daughters, and Herbert became the envy of every man. Three beautiful women at his side; what kind of hardship days are these? Except for sleeping, Margit and Toni practically lived in our home. They thought of Herbert as their brother and Herbert liked this arrangement just fine.

↶ FOUR

The stone in the wall and the wood from the floor
shall cry out whenever injustice is done.
— OLD TESTAMENT

THE CALENDAR MADE no special mention of that day. It wasn't even Friday the thirteenth. I had a ten o'clock rehearsal call, and as I rushed to the theater, I reminded myself that I had to squeeze in a costume fitting, too. It was the morning after that tall S.S. man had visited us backstage . . . It was the morning of the final curtain, for on that morning the Joodsche Schouwburg became the gateway to hell . . .

The moment I stepped inside, I knew that disaster had struck. The stage, devoid of scenery and props, resembled a burglarized house and the ropes, swinging from the high catwalk, a snaring hangman's noose. All the paintings and sculptures were gone. The seats in the orchestra, stalls, and parquet circle had been wrenched out of their foundations and placed sideways along the two walls. The chairs, separated by small passageways, faced each other; five rows one way, five the other. Except for the emergency lights, looking like blood red fireflies, the theater was dipped in darkness. My colleagues hovered ghostlike around the piano barely visible, but I knew who was there: Martin Roman, our musical arranger; Bert van Dongen, Holland's favorite pop singer and my handsome partner; Henriette Davids; Sylvain Poons, Henriette's comic counterpart; and two great old seasoned German stars, Otto Walburg and dynamic Kurt Gerron.

I trudged over to them and halfway there I heard Martin whisper, "He's back! The Nazi who was here yesterday is back. I think he's in your dressing room." Before I could ask why our theater was all torn up, the heavy walk of boots caught my attention. An instant later, I met the steel gray eyes of the doomsman again. He had stopped center stage, right under the hangman's rope. This time he didn't click his heels, did not salute. He stood, legs spread, arms folded behind his back, his chest full of polished medals. His eyes swerved, squinted, then fixed themselves on something only he could see. A wary silence hung over us.

"I am Obersturmführer Aus Der Fünten. This theater has been taken over by the German Command Invasion Forces and will be used as a deportation center for Jews. You will remain here. You will keep the Jews who are brought here in line. You are not to contact your families or friends. You are not to ask or answer questions. You are to carry out the duties I am assigning to you, expediently and without dissent.

"You! You! *You, you, you!* Line up the Jews!

"Keep them away from the doors!

"Keep them away from the stage!

"Keep them in their seats!

"Keep them quiet! Put their effects up here! Dish out the soup! Wash the dishes! Clean the toilets!"

His words, in rapid succession, shot out like cannon balls. He never pointed a finger, but gave the "you" commands with his eyes. I stared at the ceiling above the stage with its exposed catwalk and spotlights, and wished with all my might for it to crash down and bury him. I was still staring when he said, "If you're averse to staying here, you can leave on the first transport tonight."

He marched off. No one spoke.

Hours passed. We sat around trying to digest the indigestible. It was no use: we could find no answers. As I dully viewed the gloomy derangement of our theater, I realized that I was witnessing the death of the Joodsche Schouwburg.

In the early afternoon, the first stream of stampeding victims stormed through the Schouwburg's doors. They came on trucks — hundreds and hundreds of them. Some had nothing but the clothes on their backs. Caught unawares, they had been picked up on the streets. Others, taken from their homes, lugged half their household behind them — lamps, rugs, feather quilts, old candlesticks.

These, here, had been our audience. These were the people we had sung to, danced for, laughed with through oh so many thorny seasons.

Barely an hour after the first casualties had arrived, the abused Schouwburg was a wall-to-wall mess. The raids, ordered by the Germans and carried out by the NSP, Dutch Nazis, had turned into a first-rate witch-hunt. Most of those bounty hunters (five guilders for a Jew) were volunteers. They smoked the Jews out and spat them into the Schouwburg like a gushing rivermouth. It triggered an instant wave of confusion in an atmosphere of total disbelief. We were besieged by never-ending questions: "Why are we here . . . Where are we going . . . When will they tell us . . . ?" A sea of wounded eyes begged us for answers. A chorus of somber voices wanted to know, "What will happen to us?"

"It's going to be all right," we told them. "It's going to be all right . . ." We had sung to them, we had danced for them, we had laughed with them, and now all that was left to do was lie to them.

Amid this chaos, we hauled their luggage, carried the babies, made room for lame old men, and brought water to the thirsting. All through the shouting, the weeping, the pushing, the shoving, we tried to establish some sort of system, some sort of dignified order. It was a hopeless task. Parents kept losing their children, the weak passed out on the stairways, and every time I moved, somebody's hand gripped my arm as though I were a life raft. Each time the bounty hunters dumped another human load into the theater, the hygienic conditions worsened. By evening, the toilets were flooded. The stench crept through the Schouwburg like an open sewer.

There was no food. No warm milk for the babies. No hot soup for the old. No beds for the sick. There was nothing but defeated hope. As night sieved through the doors, 1,037 men, women, and children climbed onto the trucks and vanished in the hostile night.

It was about two in the morning when the last good-bye had faded out. I was numb. Insensible to grief. Insensible even to exhaustion — despite my feet being swollen, my stomach empty, and my eyes red and blurry from the smoke and the stinking, stagnant air. I stood amid the residue that those who'd gone had left behind. A scarf, a hat, a cigarette case with the inscription: "All my love." Gloves, a pair of slippers, a baby rattle and countless other things. Souvenirs. All from the bag of tricks that fate bestowed on them.

There is this twilight region that one can drift to and float on for a while, where consciousness and unconsciousness are all the same. Sort of a self-induced anesthesia. It dulls the senses, kills the pain, and yet, one still knows all that's happened. I think that twilight came to me after the trucks had wheeled away and the Schouwburg fell silent once more. For an unmarked time, the solitude of nothingness sustained me. But then this wretched day rose up again and flashed before me as if it were a sound camera with automatic shutters. It clicked on images, brought back echoes, zoomed in on faces, recorded voices. Voices and faces I had known so well.

The Moskowitzes — Olga and Sam — were the first friends I had stumbled on. It was a mournful hello. They carried only one little suitcase, a testimony to a life of running and hiding. Their beat-up valise had traveled with Olga since first the Russian Cossacks had burned down the house of her parents in Kiev where she was born. Her childhood had been a constant flight from persecution. From the Russian pogroms to the Polish pogroms, and after that, Germany. When Olga married Sam, he made her promise on their wedding night that she would leave her travel bag and all her sad, old memories behind. But she could not. It was her link to the past and the warning voice of the future. She never went to sleep without first checking whether it was still under her bed. Only she knew what was in it. Olga was Mama's friend. They had met at Mr. Moskowitz's shop when Mama brought some clothes there for alteration. He wore hornrims, was a slender, quiet German tailor of Polish descent. She was a dumpy, deep-voiced chatterbox with a funny, chipmunk face. Their home was a miniature Grand Central Station for emigrants. Olga collected all the strays.

Back in Frankfurt, they had owned a big house and many stores. Here, only a tiny shop and a modest home. In 1933, when some Hitler boys broke Sam's nose and looted his stores, he suffered a heart attack and never fully recovered. Still, he worked all the time. Luckily, their two sons were in England. They went there to study and stayed. Now they were flying for the RAF and each time Olga talked about them, her Russian eyes sparkled. When first she saw me in the Schouwburg, she thought that the bounty hunters had caught me too and started to cry. I really had trouble convincing her that this wasn't so, that I was "free." Only last week she had brought borscht and a new teakettle just because ours didn't whistle anymore. She always brought, gave, and did for others.

Now they were here. And her little suitcase was going to travel once more. "Sam is tired," she said. "I don't think he's going to make it. He was home resting when they came. They pushed him. What for? Such big lugs pushing my sweet old Sam. Did you know they're getting money for us? Those lugs were bragging that the German Nazis are paying them five guilders for every Jew they catch. That's all I'm worth? Five guilders." Her Yiddish accent came through, and with it the tragic humor so typical of wise old Jews.

Olga looked at the mass confusion, let out a horrendous sigh, and fell into a chair. "Look," she cried. "Look what they've done to your beautiful theater! Look at all those poor people! Some inheritance our forefathers have left us. Two thousand years of misery. I'm telling you, it's enough. Such *meshugas*. Silvi, be careful. Don't let the swines get you." She glanced at her crouched husband. "You think you could find a blanket for my Sam? He doesn't look well, does he? Oy, what a job they've given you! A fine actress like you. Letting you do their dirty work. Such a shame. Go . . . go! Get me a blanket, and go help the others." She embraced me and whispered, "Your mama, you'll take care of your mama?"

"Yes, I will."

"Bless you, my child, bless you." And then she motioned for me to leave. As I walked away, I saw her put her arms around Sam. She cradled him like a child.

The Moskowitzes were not the only ones I knew who were caught that day. There also was my hairdresser, Bonnie Sterkenberg, and her husband, George. They greeted me with a big smile and a hug. Both had sailed through the bitter years of occupation with spunk, humor, and unbeaten optimism. Both believed in a just God and trusted Him. They believed that man, on the whole, was good, and that evil could not rule the world, for it brought no rewards, but goodness did. They believed that they had been rewarded all of their lives, for happiness had been with them always. George was young, attractive, a diamond cutter and an ardent joke collector. Bonnie was young, attractive, a hairstylist and pregnant.

"We'll be back before the baby is born," George said with unyielding conviction, "Whatever place they send us to, we'll be useful. Everybody needs a hairdresser, and Bonnie is the best. And if they don't want me to cut diamonds, I'll cut something else."

They had brought two large suitcases. I wondered which of them was full of diapers. They sat out the hours in patient acceptance. In patient acceptance they climbed on the trucks . . . I never saw them again.

The raids continued that cold October. For four more days and four more nights we waded through the flood of people that poured into the Schouwburg. There were no guards inside. It was all up to us. Out on the street, two rangy NSP brutes fought off an anxious, angry crowd with passionate obscenities, fisticuffs and boot kicks.

⤙

ON THE SECOND DAY OF DOOM, I spotted Margit in the street crowd. The bounty hunters had just unloaded their latest catch when, through the open door, I caught a glimpse of her. I shouted her name and she shouted back, "Are you all right? I brought you a change of clothing and food. Catch!" She hurled a large paper bag through the air, but before I could catch it, the towering NSP man had snatched it away and kicked it into the crowd of gathering sympathizers. Then he spun around, grabbed me, and flung me, like a javelin, into the packed Schouwburg. It happened faster than a flash of light. I landed on top of several people who got knocked down with me. The man next to me was bleeding. A thin red line stretched from his left temple down to his eyelid. I saw him wipe the blood off with a fine white handkerchief. He seemed more startled than hurt. I felt a strong urge to cry, a slight pain in my left hip, and an overwhelming desire to strangle that NSP bastard.

Most of the people I'd collided with were pretty nice about it. Not all, though. There was this sour-looking girl who kept yelling that I had broken her glasses and she couldn't see a thing without them. She was furious. "You knocked me over! How could you be so stupid?" A bearded young man tried to explain that I did not initiate this, but she didn't seem the least bit interested.

Otto Walburg was backstage. He looked awful, all pale and drawn. The dear man wanted to know how long this madness was going to last. I surely had no answers. He kept saying that he couldn't handle this nightmare and that he was going to leave, no matter what. His breath seemed to be stuck in his throat. He was wheezing. That night, just before another thousand or more were stowed on the trucks and herded away again, Otto Walburg suffered a heart attack. The tormenting irony was that Walburg survived the attack, but after only a few days at home, two NSP brutes broke down his door and whisked him away. This he did not survive.

My hip was bruised. Nothing serious, but it hurt. Tomorrow I'll be black and blue, I told myself. It suddenly struck me how ominous "tomorrow" had become. Not something I could really think about in this bedeviled here and now. I did think though of Margit. If I could just have talked to her. At least she knew about the raids. I guess everyone did. What else did everyone know? Did they know about the demoralizing conditions in here? Or how many Jews the Nazis had slated expendable? Was it to be *all* of us, or just a few thousand? My God. "Just" a few thousand. It's inconceivable!

⌐

ON THE THIRD DAY OF DOOM, stacks of dishes and large tin drums with soup arrived. Our people carried them to the first floor, and I was told by an exhausted Kurt Gerron that I had kitchen duty. Up there in our former wedding chapel, now soup kitchen, I saw a tall, lean man stooped over the drums: another friend, my special friend and personal physician, Dr. Peters. Instead of a doctor's coat he wore an apron; instead of a stethoscope, he held a ladle. Dr. Peters dealt out the soup as if it were a therapeutic tonic. He was a true healer, not only of ailing bodies but of melancholy spirits, too. His infinite compassion had salvaged many a wounded soul.

We dealt the soup to anyone who wanted it. The lines were long — the hands holding the plates, the hands of friends, hands of brothers. I heard a lot of timid thank-you's, and many please-help-me's. Hours passed. The soup was gone, but the lines did not cease. Even after we had told them there was nothing left, they still waited. Waited, till day succumbed to night, till through the foggy darkness the baleful trucks rolled in . . . and then they waited no more.

In the small sink of our coffeehouse, we rinsed off the dishes — and washed away the traces of a thousand more Jews.

Dr. Peters had not gotten picked up, nor had he been involuntarily detained, as I had. He was here at his own request. He had asked and received permission from the Germans to care for the sick in the Schouwburg. They had given him a "temporarily exempt from labor transport" pass. In the weeks to come, this code name "stay of execution" paper became the most-sought-after black market commodity. For some unexplained reason, in spite of the paper forgers printing false identification cards by the gross, this specific paper was hard to come by. Dr. Peters's was the first one the Germans ever issued, and for a while it was worth a king's ransom.

There wasn't really a lot he could do for the sick. Not in this whirlpool of dismayed confusion. But, if he had not been there, had never seen their faces, nor breathed the Schouwburg's convulsive climate of fear, he might not have become a smuggler of Jews. What had begun as a one-man crusade that bitter night in the theater has over the decades grown into a mighty underground network. A far-reaching one — far beyond his master-minding the first illegal flight of Jews to Israel through the secret corridors of Europe. I have no details of his other rescue missions or the weapons he used in the war for survival. I do know, though, that his work is not finished. And because it isn't over yet, because he is still out there fighting the never-ending battle against the Hitler heirs, I dare not reveal his true name. Let me just say, if not for him, a lot more Jews would have been slaughtered.

Not till twenty-two years later, not till extensive research for my book compelled me to peel away the layers of the past with all its scabs, did I pick up his trail again. A trail of awesome whispers that led me straight to this intrepid man. I found his friendship door wide open, with many old thoughts of the past flowing through. And I found him to be wise and a man with a purpose, a man of perception, vision and valor. A man of high morals and quiet strength. Still healing and caring. We shared wine, music and ripe summer days — but not his secrets.

⸺

ON THE FOURTH DAY OF DOOM, no irate or curious citizen could get near the Schouwburg anymore. The street was blocked off. Only the trucks, delivering their five-guilder goods, came and went. Inside the somber warehouse the lack of air and sanitation had reached its heaving climax. Young men kept carrying bodies back and forth in search of unspoiled space. There were moments when I wanted to pass out and truly wondered why I didn't.

By noon, we had our first suicide. A man's broken body was lying in the alley. A third-floor window was his way out. I didn't see him jump; others did. I only heard the screaming. People kept rushing to the fatal window, kept calling to him, holding their arms out as though they still could reach him, as though they wanted him to hold on. As though he could, or would have wanted to . . . How small he looked from way up there. Like a crumpled piece of cloth. Dr. Peters had pushed up the stairs behind me. "We must make sure," he said, and so we went back down to see for ourselves.

It wasn't a cloth. It was a man. His head was sharply tilted to one side, his face distorted as if in pain, and his eyes had the look of a hunted animal, one that could run no more. Dr. Peters tried to find a heartbeat, but there was none; he gently closed the stranger's eyes and covered him with his coat. The shoes and one hand stuck out. Nice black shoes with neatly tied shoelaces and a nicely manicured, ringless hand. There was nothing unusual about this man — except that he had killed himself. I wish he could have come to rest in the cool green grass of a meadow. Not in an alley, not on hard stones. Too wretched a death. Too cold a deathbed.

The bounty hunters' latest tour de force brought truckloads of older people. Most of them carried little more than their old age. They were not given any time to pack. Among them was a man dressed in a World War I uniform. He wore medals instead of an overcoat, and a shiny sword instead of a cane. Naturally, he caused quite a stir. Once, he had been a brave soldier, had earned the rank of lieutenant colonel and been honored by his fatherland. For loyal services rendered he had been given two rewards, the Iron Cross and a steel plate for his shot-up head. With these credentials as his calling card, he asked to see the officer in charge so he could request the immediate release of himself and his wife. We told him that Operation Schouwburg was not a military maneuver. Still he persisted. He spoke in a thin, diluted voice as if he were still lying in the trenches afraid the enemy might hear him.

At no time did he accept the fact that the Germany he loved was no more, that it had long forgotten those who once had fought for it. Nor that the land he still called home, the land that once had produced Goethe, Heine, Schiller, Bach, Beethoven and Brahms, was now producing a nation of racists. He was a man out of step with time. His wife tried her best to stop her husband's pathetic exhibition. "Fati," she said indulgently, "why don't you sit and rest a while? You look all tuckered out."

"I will, Mother, I will, as soon as I have spoken to the commander here. Then we'll go home." He gave her an affectionate peck on the cheek and marched off.

"What do you think he does at home?" she asked me. "He writes letters to his old comrades. He writes them but he never mails them. Then he goes and buys newspapers and never reads them. You should see his room. Pictures of the Kaiser, photographs of his army days, his student diplomas, and his grandmother's old furniture. A junkyard. He likes to pretend. He pretends that everything is as it was, that Germany is still great and that the Nazis don't exist. I say to him, who took away your house and your business? Who wouldn't let your son become a professor at the university? Who broke Laura's heart? You don't remember? I ask. Such a nice boy, you said, sure, his *goyem* papa got him a fat job with the Nazis so he can sit on his *toches* and won't have to fight. One day he loves Laura, and the next, the nice boy doesn't want to know us anymore. Nazis! You say there are no Nazis, okay!" There is a pause. I feel I should say something but I can't think of anything she doesn't already know. Her round, brown button eyes pan quickly across the crowd. "I'd better find my soldierman before he makes everyone enlist in the 1914 war."

ON THE FIFTH DAY OF DOOM, the bounty hunters unloaded an entire convalescence home. Some couldn't walk, others couldn't stand, and all of them needed water and blankets. We carried the weakest ones into the orchestra pit and laid them down. The floor was icy cold. No fire to keep them warm; yet they did not complain. After we had "placed" them, we moved into a corner and commiserated. How many roles we had already played in this, the Schouwburg's last and greatest drama.

While we pooled our individual experiences, I learned that not everyone in my group had followed Aus Der Fünten's orders. Henriette Davids, for instance, disclosed that she no longer hauled luggage. She had found a better way to help: Henriette had unpacked her humor trunk and played the clown for her sad but loyal audience. Her eyes were puffy, swollen, but her audience saw only her funny face and heard only her droll jokes. She'd sprinkled laughter on every fearful minute, for laughter was her trade.

Sylvain Poons had tried at first to follow Aus Der Fünten's verbal script, which had him name-tag people and effects. Sylvain tried, but much too countless were the numbers, too jumbled and confusing the mounting nameless mass, and so he threw the tags away, caring instead for what he cared most about, the children. He showed them magic tricks and told them tales with happy endings. He gave piggyback rides to little ones with big tears in their eyes, and prayed with them: "Now I lay me down to sleep, I pray the Lord my soul to keep, if I should die . . ." Humorous Sylvain with his middle-age spread and his mock moonface looked done in, old and broken, a sad comic.

And my pretty leading man Bert wasn't pretty anymore. His face was full of grimy sweat, and he needed a drink. He'd never gone that long without booze. Bert had carried bedding, carpets, rocking chairs and tons of books. Now he couldn't lift a pin anymore. Bert had never known sorrow before or seen despair at such close range, but he did not fold. Bravely, he tackled the overflowing toilets and his sobriety. Poor Bert. What a time to be sober!

Our happy-go-lucky music man Martin freely admitted that he'd never even attempted to carry out the order to "keep them away from the stage!" Martin was still too much in a daze to discharge the oppressive duties he was to perform. All he was really sure of was that he had played the piano, had given impromptu recitals for *les misérables*. Except for his music, Martin had never been serious about anything. Unlike many of his countrymen, he did not stick around when the Hitler menace ravaged Berlin. He had fled.

There we were, the six of us, huddled in a corner like thieves, trying to make sense of it all. Still trying to understand why our Schouwburg had not protected us, why we no longer could protect the Schouwburg. Wet-eyed and weary were my comrades and I, shaken and numb. Even sparkling Kurt Gerron had lost his luster. Kurt and Otto Walburg, now in some hospital fighting for his life, were contemporaries, and I had often heard the two talk about their days in Berlin. Their recollections were like an afterimage of their colorful life. Each had his own favorite story. Walburg's was always his notorious acting debut in Oscar Wilde's *Picture of Dorian Gray*. The new-comer had only one line: "Dinner is served."

"Well," Walburg said, "we all have to start somewhere."

Kurt Gerron would review the exciting events of his impressive career, like the sensational *Threepenny Opera* premiere back in 1928 in which Lotte Lenya became an overnight celebrity. Kurt was never quite sure how often he had played it, but it was well over a thousand times. He did the original recording, played in it on the screen, and he kept playing it and playing it in other theaters until Hitler had it banned. The night it closed, some Nazi punks surprised them with a cartload of squashy tomatoes and rotten eggs. Their aim was pretty good, and they doused everyone on stage. Kurt, with egg on his face, ran for the nearest toilet, but Lotte Lenya and her husband Weill were in there; so he bravely returned to face the music. But the curtain was already down; the public screamed and fled; and to the best of his blurred knowledge, the cast and Nazis beat each other up.

Now, in the Schouwburg's dying hours, Kurt was in charge of the lost-and-found. Another losing battle. "Find me a hiding place," the lost souls had begged of him. "You must know one place where we can be safe." And he had bowed his head in sorrow, for he knew of no secret corners, no hidden panels, knew of no way to save even a few. In the shadowy half-light my mighty friend and comrade in grief stood trembling and deposed. He wasn't mighty anymore.

"Are you the custodians of this place?" an elderly woman with raisin eyes and an old cocker spaniel face had inquired.

"I guess we are now," we replied. "Last week we were actors."

"Last week," the crinkled voice continued, "I had a warm bath and a soft bed. Where am I, anyway?"

"You're in a theater."

"You don't say. What did you play here, comedies?"

"Yes, mostly."

"Say, this wouldn't be the Joodsche Shouwburg, would it?"

"It would."

"I do declare. For two years I've been wanting to come here, but I've been bedridden. My doctor kept saying, wait till you're better, so I waited. Now I'm here. You think it means I'm better? Hey, Rosa," she called to a curled-up body leaning against a cue box, "we've got orchestra seats!"

It was pouring outside. Heaven only knows how many drenched and shivering people had teemed into the Schouwburg. Their belongings were soaked. Lobby, seats and carpets wet through and through. There were dark, ugly stains on the red carpets and upholstered chairs — like infectious blood. One more dilemma, one more health hazard. With practically no ventilation and inadequate sanitary facilities, an influenza epidemic was virtually unavoidable.

More are coming. Always more. They keep on bringing them in. None of those rain-pelted groups was brought straight from their homes to us. Their captors had first driven them in the open trucks all over town.

How long he had been sitting there so unobtrusively and shyly I cannot say. How long his eyes had followed me around, I do not know. I must have passed by him before. Director Hugo Helm! I never dreamed he'd end up here too. More than three years ago, when I left his Princess Operetta Theater in The Hague, he was a most successful, happy man.

"Director Helm," I blurted out, "what in the world are you doing here! When did you move to Amsterdam? How are you?" I was only too keenly aware how inane this greeting must have sounded, but what was I to say? I kneeled before him and looked into his wise old rumpled face. "Are you all right?"

"I am fine, child," he unemphatically replied, unbuttoning his water-logged raincoat. "Don't look so flustered, I am quite well." He was as cordial as he had always been, demure and composed, but too damn calm for this trying situation. His inertness perturbed me.

"What are you doing here?" I echoed.

He smiled a wispy smile, then slowly eyed the lumped-together sea of faces. "What are they doing here?"

I inhaled the dankness of his clothes and smelled the damp smutch of his shoes. "God damn it," I thought, "why didn't he stay in The Hague?" "Why didn't you stay in The Hague! It's safer there, isn't it?"

"Not for me, Silvie, not for me."

There was no sadness in his voice, no bitterness or indignation. Nothing. His aloof detachment amid such grimness stumped me. Strange, but he was not part of the tense consternation at all. Almost as though only his body was still here while he himself had already passed on, with no one to mourn him.

"Were the Nazis after you in The Hague?"

"No."

"Does anyone know where you are?"

"No."

"Shouldn't I try to get a message to someone?"

"No."

"But don't you have someone waiting for you?"

"No one."

No one . . . No one . . . He sounded like the echo of a forgotten soul. Friend to so many, had he no friend left? Sure he did. But not the one he had counted on.

Come into my parlor, said the spider to the fly, and the dumb fly did. Hugo Helm's spider was his longtime girlfriend Brünnhilde. She was a clever spider, for she had known exactly when to spin her crafty web. "Fly," she'd cooed seductively one day. "I think that the Nazis will take your theater away; you better turn the legal ownership over to me."

And since it made such good sense, he did. Not too much later, thinking only of him, she had him put his other holdings in her name too. Why not? he thought. Had she not been his cherished companion, who had so enriched his winterbound days, and had she not stuck by him through all the fat, fat, diamond-dazzling years? Whom else should he have trusted if not her? Should he have questioned her probity? Of course not! It never entered his mind. Actually, once Brünnhilde had control of his wealth, she proved to be quite charitable. She didn't eat her mate like other black widow spiders do, she just threw him out.

The loss of his fortune meant little to him, and he could have dealt with the loss of his lady love too, but not her betrayal.

Everyone who had known Hugo Helm liked and respected him. His proficiency and gentlemanly ways won him high praise. He could have found refuge with his peers and with those who refused to trade humanity for a sack of gold. But his self-esteem was crushed. He was ashamed to see his friends, and afraid to see the Nazis. Disillusioned, he hid in dark doorways and never knocked on a friendly door. He roamed the streets till, unintentionally, he found himself on the road to Amsterdam . . . Highways, back roads, fields, small villages, dim railroad depots. In the end it made no difference which way he went, all roads were the same, sooner or later they all led to the Joodsche Schouwburg. Hugo Helm got picked up before he'd reached the inner city. I think he was glad that he had been caught, for he was sapless, extinguished and burned out. His road had ended — the wandering Jew need wander no more.

Hugo Helm was not a garrulous man. He had no desire to wistfully recount the saddening prelude that had led to his arrest. No matter how many hows, whens and whys I asked, I got only philosophical quotes, hints and innuendos from him. He really said very little. What he himself so desperately needed to erase, I retraced, retrieved, and put into my memory file.

I had held his hands. I had rubbed his fingers, wanting them to feel warmth again. I had seen his sparkless eyes bid me farewell. A long and melancholic farewell . . . He seemed the saddest man in the universe.

From then on, I avoided any personal encounter with those I knew. Whatever mishap had brought them here, however bravely they took it in stride; sooner or later they all asked the same question — "Can you get me out?" Even Director Helm. But he was only jesting. The others weren't. He'd said, "I'm glad that you can't. You see, I have nowhere to go." He had wanted me to help the two young, frightened lovers who were seated across from him. Two youngsters he didn't even know. "Just like Romeo and Juliet," my old director had mumbled, "born in the wrong century too."

When the merciless hours had wiped out the day, and a rain-soaked night came to collect its haul again, I stood at the door. As the unblest ones marched into the moonless depths, I stood at the door. I had not said good-bye to anyone. I had not hugged a baby, kissed a friend or put my arm around a weeping brother. I just stood at the door.

It is always so still after they've gone. I am wrapped in coldness, like my theater, which is dying bit by bit.

"Are you the custodians of this place?" the old woman in the orchestra pit had asked, and we had said, "I guess we are now." This place, as she called it, the Joodsche Schouwburg, is no longer a place or a theater; it is a tomb where good men's utopian hopes lie buried . . . And I am one of the custodians.

❧

ON THE SIXTH DAY OF DOOM, the Jewish Committee took over, and we were told to leave. Mr. Asscher (formerly president of Amsterdam's large diamond center) and Mr. De Cohen (formerly president of something equally important), both now heading the committee, had finally sent some volunteers to relieve us — with the sanction of the Germans, naturally.

While I sat sluggish in a chair, one of those volunteers came up to me and told me to go home. And I, benumbed and heavy-eyed, got up and left. Walked out. After five agonizing days and nights, a simple "Go home" was it.

The rain had stopped. A chilly morning had paved the streets with a wintry frost. The air was as cold as death. The streets as silent as a graveyard. Torpid and faint, I tramped along. "Soon it's going to start all over again," I thought. "The raids, the daily hunts, the human shame. Well, I am out of it. I don't want Mama and Herbert asking me a whole lot of questions when I get back. I don't want to talk about it now. I may never want to talk about it."

Mothers always know when their child has returned. Always! No one had told her I'd been released; yet she knew. I saw her standing in the hallway, Mama and Herbert. "I'm back," I voiced, sounding like a ventriloquist. Their arms around me, we walked into the living room. The fire in the fireplace was lit, but the flat was cold. Mama sighed, said that I was thin, so thin, and something about chicken soup and a hot bath. Herbert talked about coal rations getting sparser, a definite food shortage, and Mama Nelson not feeling too well.

I said nothing at all. Just quickly embraced them and went to my room. I felt empty. Like my bloodless, blurred face in the mirror. For a long while I sat on my bed and stroked the clean white sheets. And then my eyes shut out the world around me, closed. I went to sleep. When nature had replenished my depleted energies, I awoke. The hands on my watch showed seven o' clock — whether it was day or night, which day or night, I couldn't tell . . .

Mothers also know when their child awakens. Mama came to tell me that dinner was ready. Did I want her to bring me a tray, or did I feel up to eating in the dining room where Toni and Margit were waiting for me? It's been their sixth visit to our home. The sixth night of the sixth day of doom . . .

I rushed to greet them, and many hugs later I ate the leftover spindly shanks of a chicken and then took a warm bath in a very cold bathroom. On the surface, nothing much had changed. Mama still talked about the Hungarian baker who had promised her sugar and flour, and Herbert still combed the city in search of the milk and honey that once had so enriched this land. Toni was still not afraid of the Hitler punks, and Margit still played her guitar and her, "so-what-they-gonna-do-to-me?" game, just like before. Only the stakes had gotten higher, the risks much greater, and it wasn't a game anymore. But Margit informed me, almost immediately, that she now planned to hide Jews in her place. Of course I tried talking her out of it, which got me nowhere at all. Her mind was made up. No matter how loud the warning drums, she heard only the voice of her own conscience, the only one she listened to. Dear Margit . . . dear playful, white-soul friend . . .

The next morning, Margit insisted on showing me her hiding place. With ill-concealed skepticism, I went with her. Where, I kept asking myself, does one hide in a room not much larger than a doll's house? Margit's where, of all places, was her closet. Except for, "You must be kidding," I couldn't think of anything to say. But what did it matter? She would have paid me no mind anyhow. The moment we had reached her snuggery, she wanted me to do my own investigating. It made me feel extremely foolish; yet I did it. Because I knew she was expecting it, I gave it a good going-over. I went through her clothes, I rummaged around, made a mess of her otherwise neatly arranged wardrobe — and found nothing.

My friend was triumphant. She truly savored this moment. One black market vodka later, Margit disclosed her secret. She had built a doggy door into the back wall of her closet. This ingenious contraption, cleverly concealed by removable shelves and cluttered with shoes, led to a closed-off empty corner, once part of a now seemingly inaccessible attic. Even after she had explained it to me, I still couldn't find the trigger whose secret release would expose the hiding place. There's no denying that I was impressed and convinced if I had not found it, no one would. Least of all the headhunters, who definitely weren't smart enough to even imagine something like this.

Caught up in Margit's excitement and my own curiosity, I tried the doggy door and got immediately stuck in it. It was frightfully small — one could barely squeeze through. After many tries, I managed to wiggle myself in. There I discovered that the empty space behind it was as low as it was narrow. I assumed a pretzel position, experienced the alarming sensation of having been locked into a mini-vault, and hurriedly wiggled myself out again.

"That's really something," I managed with strained enthusiasm, while shuddering at the thought of ever having to use it myself. I did have another black market vodka before I let Margit know that I had felt extremely claustrophobic and worried about the air supply. But Margit wasn't a bit concerned. She was fully convinced that the pin-sized holes she had drilled into the wall were more than sufficient. Moreover, declared my friend, the success did not depend on the amount of oxygen or the size of the doggy door, since no one was meant to stay in there too long anyhow. I sure was relieved to hear that.

Margit's ace in the hole, as she liked to refer to it, was really the location of her room. Top floor — sixty-four stairs to climb before one reached her door. Old and squeaky wooden stairs. Allotting time — sixty-four steps worth of time. Surely, anyone stowed away in her doll's house could get into the mini-vault by then. There would be warning signals, too. If the ringing of the downstairs bell or the slammng of the front door didn't give Hitler's errand boys away, their stamping boots certainly would.

As for the Jews who could not make it through the doggy door, Margit would have the women — never more than two — lie in bed faking illness, and the men, never more than one, in bed with her locked in passionate embrace . . . and most likely not faking at all.

Her place was not a permanent solution; one hardly could sit out the war up there. Still, for an undisclosed period of time, many a chased one would find temporary refuge in Margit's room at the top.

Less than a month had passed since the Schouwburg's fall, and whoever had thought that it couldn't get worse was badly mistaken. The raids not only continued but intensified. At first the five-guilder-a-Jew hunters had taken their victims from the streets. But nowadays, very few Jews still dared to venture out, and so the hunters were making house calls. Whenever possible, the Dutch Resistance let us know about the raids. Sometimes a brave courier — or the grapevine — would bring us the bad tidings. But no matter how we found out about it, the bottom line was always the same: Disappear, get lost!

And then the Jews tried to get lost, flurried and fled to another part of town where they were safe for a day or two, or even a week. And my theater stood empty then for a day or two, or even a week. Other times the signals had gotten crossed, were intercepted, or came too late, and then the headhunters had a well-heeled day. They scooped up the Jews, trucked them away — collecting their blood money . . . And then my theater stood chockful again for a day or two, or even a week.

It was a hell of a winter, this brutal 1942–43. Morale fell, black marketeering rose. Those who had stocked up on food, cigarettes, toiletries, firewood or coal and sold it, either got caught or very rich. Those who bought it either got caught or very poor. Those who did neither stayed hungry and cold. It was indeed a hell of a winter, this brutal 1942–43.

FIVE

THE FURNISHINGS IN MR. STERN'S DINING ROOM had been quickly moved to the attic to make room for sewing machines — twenty-four, to be exact. The Germans had loaned them to Mr. Stern so he too could do his bit for the war effort. The fact that they belonged to him in the first place was paradoxical but hardly surprising. Not that I felt one way or the other about Mr. Stern and his sewing machines, except that for a few weeks there we shared a mutual interest: neckties! The kind men wear in uniform — German uniforms.

Mr. Stern had been looking for experienced seamstresses, which prompted Toni, who knew him well, to suggest that he hire me. He said no; and when she suggested her idea to me, I also said no. In the end, we both changed our minds. He, because of his fondness for Toni, and I, because of the timely "temporarily exempt from labor transport" paper which came with the job. Nothing else could have induced me to leave my home at 6:00 a.m. and face the drudgery of stitching that began punctually at seven. I loathed every moment of the ridiculous charade. Nevertheless, having this precious document in my pocket did make me feel a whole lot safer. And this new experience did teach me a thing or two, none of which had anything to do with sewing. I willingly admit that I and the sewing machines never got along. My needle got stuck, zigzagged around, or broke altogether. Whatever fabric I managed to rescue bore absolutely no resemblance to a necktie.

All in all, this idiotic job lasted barely five weeks. Stern did not fire me. The Germans fired Mr. Stern. Perhaps he made too many neckties or not enough. Perhaps they found a better use for Stern's machines. All I know is that on one of those miserable mornings, a pompous Nazi came, shut down the atelier, and took my "temporarily exempt" paper away.

As for Mr. Stern, well, if his luck didn't run out, he may have outlasted the Nazis. Frankly, I didn't much like him at first. His nervous mannerisms made me nervous. Also, he definitely looked a bit queer. Stern always wore the same old spectacles, the same silly grin and the same subservient expression. His clothes were equally odd. One could never tell whether his rumpled suits were too large or whether he had recently shrunk. Naturally, I thought him a boot-licking fool. Worse — I suspected him of being a collaborator. Not someone I liked to admit to knowing at all.

Much later, I learned that he was neither. Stern only played the fool to fool the enemy. In truth, he was a brilliant trickster, a crafty, clever Jew . . . Someone worth having known.

Our paths never crossed again, and if it hadn't been for Toni's foster papa, Mr. Cohen, who'd known Stern all his life, I still would think him a nincompoop. From old photographs, however, tucked away in Toni's foster parents' memory drawers, old and faded like the days of their youth, and from the lips of Papa Cohen himself, "Gimme a listen and I tell you a *soy a Geschichte* [such a story]," I got to know the real Marcus Stern — the Marcus Stern who began his career in the tiny back room of a run-down store where he designed and sold taffeta- and lace-embroidered petticoats for brides and less maidenly ladies.

The ladies must have fancied his work and him a whole lot, so says Papa Cohen, because they paid him many compliments and much, much money. He expanded, bought a huge building, refurbished it, put in office suites, elegant showrooms, and brand-new machines. When, a few years later, Anne, the beautiful model he had married, bore him two beautiful little models, all his dreams had come true. Marcus Stern loved his work, his family, his Queen and the land of tulips and windmills that had been so good to him. His land!

War came. The Nazis came. Oppression came. But Marcus Stern kept his factory going. Friends fled. His neighbors fled. The rabbi of his synagogue fled. But Marcus Stern kept his factory going. Only after many moons, and with no end to the war in sight, did he decide to sell his business. It was no longer doing well, but it still was worth a heck of a lot. Why let the Nazis steal it?

"Time to sell," he said to his wife over breakfast one morning as the first leaves of autumn colored the trees. And she agreed.

"I can't get any new fabrics and my best customers have canceled their orders," he sighed, disheartened. "I must find a buyer and sell, sell quickly," Marcus told his spouse one late afternoon as the last leaves of autumn fell to the ground. And she nodded her pretty head.

"I haven't had one decent offer. No one will give me a guilder for it. It's worth a fortune. Why can't I find any takers?" he asked his wife as the blue cold of winter rolled over the earth. And she said nothing . . .

Papa Cohen never understood why his boyhood friend did not close the business and just walk away from it. "What a tenacious Jew!" he would exclaim with sudden emotion, and then, "I guess he couldn't let go."

Every day Stern would go to the factory, wander through the empty plant and wait. Even on Sunday. Wait for an offer, a taker. Papa Cohen no longer remembered when he came. Only that early one morning, the "taker" walked in. Inspector Bull was his name and shit was what he offered Mr. Stern for his building, the equipment and the last dozen silk negligées. Inspector Bull was, the old man recalls, a man of breathtaking action. He immediately declared everything, including Stern, property of the Third Reich, and before poor Marcus could wipe the sweat from his brow, a brand-new operation — the slam-bang production of parachutes — was ready to roll.

Papa Cohen insisted that his friend was more concerned about the destination of the parachutes than his own fate. That, he'd say, was in God's hand.

As to the planned assembly-line production that was to operate with meteoric speed, it apparently ran into a lot of trouble. Cause of the problem was Stern's fine lingerie machines, which simply couldn't handle the heavy cloth used for the sky umbrellas. Result: their time schedule went down the toilet. Thus, the "taker" in charge of chuting them out by the thousands had to cool his heels and wait till one of his underlings could steal heavier machines elsewhere.

To Stern, the fact that the sewing machines were now useless to Bull was a heaven-sent sign that all was not yet lost. Armed with nothing but his wits and a great deal of chutzpah, the nervous, bespectacled little man with the rumpled suits pleaded with Bull to lend him his machines so that they, and he, could do other jobs for the good Inspector. Bull agreed. It actually made ridiculously good sense: Marcus Stern knew everything about materials and fabrics; Bull knew absolutely nothing. Besides, every Nazi liked having a little Jew in his pocket.

And so it came to pass that Inspector Bull and Marcus Stern entered into a strange alliance, or as Papa Cohen pointed out, a chess game. No need to guess who played the king and who the pawn.

A footnote: Toni never joined Stern's charming sewing circle or any other "temporarily exempt from labor transport" job opportunity. She really was opposed to working. Instead, not too much later, she had a strange someone duplicate Margit's ID card with her picture on it. Now there were two Margit Heinrichs.

There was a time when a Jew in Amsterdam was harder to find than a needle in a haystack. Either they had already been rounded up, or they had escaped much earlier, were hidden, or had false papers. It's hard to believe that any of those spurious ID carriers would have been mad enough to risk detection for the sake of a stroll in the park or a foolish visit to a dress shop. Hard to imagine, but that's precisely what my two best friends, Toni and Margit, did. Not that one stayed at home while the other gallivanted about. They both stepped out together. Walked hand-in-hand down Nazi lane together. Tweedledum and Tweedledee, both the one and both the other. Whatever made them think that two of the same IDs were better than none?

Long before my friends had done their silliest best to get themselves into a whole lot of trouble, I already had my silliest best behind me. My escapades were just as *verboten* as theirs were. Everything was. But my stepping out was strictly business, and I always went out alone, and without any papers. My silliness began with Piet. Piet was a bedridden young invalid — polio, I think. Piet had, from where I don't know, lots of cigarettes he didn't smoke and a horrendous sweet tooth, but no sweets. The old Hungarian baker, hidden behind his empty shelves, had lots of sweets he didn't want, but no cigarettes he did want. Herbert knew the invalid, Mama knew the baker, and that's how I, who didn't know the invalid or the baker, wound up pedaling my neighbor's bike through the slushy streets of Amsterdam. One oilskin-covered cart of cigarettes for the baker, one cart of sweets for the invalid. To and fro, to and fro. For arranging this moving swap meet, Herbert got a sack of coal, Mama sugar and flour, and I leg cramps from pedaling so hard.

I vividly remember each one of these illegal cycling trips. There were Germans racing by me in their cars, splashing me. There were puddles, pot-holes and the dreadful paddy wagons crossing right in front of me. My dozen or so deliveries stopped when the invalid ran out of cigarettes, the baker out of sweets and when my neighbor wanted his bicycle back. I never thought of it as black marketeering — only as a trade between friends — which, retrospectively, wasn't worth risking my neck for, either.

THE DOORBELL RANG ABOUT NOON. Two short rings, staccato-like. Herbert, expecting delivery of a dozen eggs as payment for a song he'd been commissioned to write, opened the door, and two larger-than-life bounty hunters walked in. There hadn't been any raids for more than a week now, and none were expected that day. The grapevine's forecast had been calm and fair, a good day to spend with family and friends, if one still had any.

Our home was rarely without people. Friends kept dropping in long after it was *verboten*. It was no different the day the bounty hunters showed up. There were seven of us at home: three Jews, one half Jew or half Aryan, and three pure Aryans. A very mixed crowd and a very *verboten* gathering. Thus, definitely not a good day. The Dutch NSP pair had planted them-selves smack in front of the open living-room door. It was Robert, our friend and landlord, an Aryan, who stood up first. Without delay he asked them, in what I thought was a most defiant tone, what they wanted. He didn't wait for them to answer, just let them know that this was his house and their presence here was most unwelcome. He showed them his obvi-ously impressive ID and demanded they leave his home. As I had feared, his bravery was wasted: they didn't budge. Robert then tried to explain that his sister Martha, who was also present, wasn't at all well and not strong enough to handle any excitement. Martha, a piano-teaching spinster, was about to give a little recital. He asked his silent sister to just go ahead and play. Dear Martha, however, remained glued to her chair without a peep or gesture except for her trembling hands pulling at her skirt. I wasn't any bet-ter off than Martha — I too was glued to my chair. Not my eyes and ears, though; they, quite independently of the rest of me, remained sharp and clear. I did see Herbert heading for the piano while nervously clearing his throat, heard Margit strum the strings of her guitar, and heard Mama's, "Oh God."

The NSP pair, rugged individuals both of them, had not moved an inch. I had noticed the older of the two holding a white sheet of paper in his right hand, which looked like a list of names. It was just that, and mine was on it, and impassively he called it out. He kept repeating and repeating it as though it was the only one he could read, the only name on that list. The other much younger one never said anything at all. He kept blowing smoke rings into the air.

My mind, muddled and confused, thought only crazy thoughts of how to escape. Ironically, though, as the moments passed, it was the repetitious sameness of that bounty hunter's voice calling my name that cleared my head. I suddenly realized that neither of them knew which one of the four women was me, or whether I was there at all. What if I kept quiet? What if the others were to say that they knew nothing of my whereabouts, that I had left, moved out, was gone, just gone? Would they believe it? Whatever this was all about, one thing was clear. This was not one of their five-guilder-a-Jew roundups. What were they really after?

Ultimately, it was the sobering fear that these two, fed up with waiting, would arrest all of us, which spooked me into raising my hand and confessing my name. A moment later, the older man broke the suspense by telling me that I was under arrest and had to come with them. "Now!" he shouted, crossing my name off the list.

I looked at Herbert, whose face was whiter than the sheets I'd slept on. Margit's guitar went still and just before the men whizzed me out of the room, Mama let one more "Oh God" escape. In the entry hall I grabbed my coat and with the men on my heels ran weak-kneed out of the house.

Down on the street, their open truck was waiting. I climbed on and we drove off. Along the way to where I didn't know then, we stopped a dozen times or so. Each time before they rang another doorbell, I saw them looking at that list. Whomever they were looking for, they found. I knew none of the others. We nodded to each other but did not speak.

I did not think that I would see it again; I did not think that I could bear to see it again. Oh, my beloved theater! They sent me back to you. Not as the rising star you once illuminated with your floods of light, not as the nightingale who in your chiming echo found her sweet songs sounding sweeter yet. Not as the caretaker of your sacred halls, your grand past, nor as a witness to your cruel rape and desecration. I'm the victim now. Like those before me, those still to come.

The warped irony of having been dumped of all places into my own theater lamed my mind. I walked along the Wall with keen awareness of my
surroundings but no awareness of my own self. Drawn to the stage, I took a
seat quite near it. How naked it was — like a barren strip of uninhabited
earth left behind by a dismembered world. They had changed the routine
since I'd been here last. Now the belongings were piled up in the foyer, and a
German soldier boy was standing guard. Most of the rows were still empty.
Only a few people had been brought in yet.

Around 2:00 p.m. more people came, then more and still more. So many
little ones among them. Who knows whether my lame mind would have
moved from its mental wheelchair if my ears had not again and again picked
up bits of conversation about that list. What kind of list was it? And why was
my name on it? I thought of asking a Jewish volunteer about it; but still too
traumatized by my arrest to make a conscious effort, I let it slide. I'll find out
soon enough, I told myself — soon enough.

In the early evening, I noticed a man studying me. Thirtyish, of medium
height and pleasant features, he was a bit too well dressed for such an un-
happy occasion — English tweed and that sort of thing He'd given me a
smile which I, without a clue of what to make of it, halfheartedly returned.
After brushing by me a couple of times, he sat down next to me and without
as much as a hello quickly whispered that he knew who I was and had come
to help me.

His name was Lou. He was a volunteer working with the Jewish Committee, just like the ones who had taken over the bitter duties of my colleagues
and me. Lou's real job, however, was snatching Jewish VIP's out of Nazi
clutches. He knew about this list, and others, and all the names on it. Names
of Jewish scholars, scientists, doctors, teachers and artists. Names synony-
mous with every fiber of Jewish intellect and culture which the Nazis were
determined to destroy and the Jewish leaders determined to save. Lou had
hinted that for some time now some kind of deal between the Germans and
the Jewish leaders was in the works. Sort of a trade-off. The terms: Safety for
those on the lists in exchange for the still-hidden, vast Jewish fortunes.
Whether anything would come of it, he didn't know.

"Meanwhile, we'll do what we can," he said, "warn whom we can, and if
that doesn't work, we'll try to get them out of here one by one. You see," he
added with a wistful smile, "the tragic joke is that we both have the same
lists. Worse, we gave it to them. We had to. They were ready to burn every

house down. Anyway, don't worry, I won't let them catch you. Not tonight. Just do as I tell you and you'll be fine. I promise it."

He'd given me no chance to let whatever he had told me sink in. Most of it whiffed by me like a breathless wind. Only after he'd gotten up and walked away did his undisguised disclosures slowly begin to register in my brain. Of course, it crossed my mind that he could be a crackpot with a sick sense of humor instead of a man risking his all to save one more Jew, but I just didn't believe it.

The instructions he had left me with were much too detailed and much too carefully planned to be a hoax. I was to get rid of my yellow star, take off my makeup and hide my shoulder-length red hair with a scarf. The key word was inconspicuousness. Once I no longer could be recognized, I was to find a seat in the last row, close to the foyer, with a clear view of the staircase. There I was to sit down, speak to no one, and most important, not leave my place until I heard from him again, no matter who might ask me to do so.

This was it — for now. Lou would not contact me again until 11:00 p.m. At eleven, he'd be standing at the bottom of the staircase and signal further instructions to me from there. "Keep your eyes fixed on the staircase," he had stressed over and over.

Six o'clock: I had five hours till eleven. Five hours to take my makeup off, but nothing to take it off with. No cleansing cream, no soap and water; and no comb or mirror either. As for the yellow star, I would have loved to tear it off my coat, but I could not. Could not do any of the things Lou wanted me to do. It was my hasty exit from home that had made me leave even my handbag behind. I brought nothing but myself. Now here I was with only the naked stage between me and my dressing room. The naked stage . . .

I must have dozed off. What woke me was the subconscious feeling of someone having dropped something into my lap — I might have been drowsy and a bit blurry-eyed, still, there it was: a paper bag with everything I needed for the masquerade. Thick bobby pins for my thick hair, scissors, a soapy washcloth and a big, black, shoddy shawl. From that moment on, I had no doubt that Lou was who he said he was and that my life could not have been in better or more trustworthy hands.

I diligently followed Lou's instructions. Washed off my makeup, hid my hair under the shoddy shawl and then cut off the hateful yellow star. Still, the hours stretching endlessly before me caused me a great deal of anxiety.

83

Should I stay where I was and wait for the jitters to pass? Or should I go and look for the seat Lou wanted me to find? Perhaps time would pass faster there. The woman next to me was praying. I envied her her faith. I had none. She too was alone here. Alone with her God. I used to pray a lot when I was little, before Papa went to sleep . . . I haven't prayed since.

There was a long line waiting outside the rest rooms; a long line waiting for soup. The rest of the downtrodden just waited. I couldn't find an empty seat. The minutes crawled with snail-like speed into the hours, one hour as lingering as the next. All evening long I stood and watched the weak ones give in to sorrow and weeping. All evening long I stood and watched the stout ones spark their spirits with the embers of hope.

A little past ten, I found an unused folding chair. Over the heads of others I carried it to where I was to station myself and sat down. It felt good not having to stand anymore. I was tired but unable to relax. All I could think of was that I knew no more now about Lou's mysterious plan for my getaway than I had known five hour-hands ago.

At ten-thirty, I started surveying the stairwell. Access from the lobby to the staircase was still roped off. I tried remembering what time on those earlier nights the hunters from hell had come to pick up their catch of the day. Which hour was the witching hour? I so wanted to pin down the very minute, but could not. My head went fuzzy just thinking of it.

Zero hour came seven minutes after eleven, and just like the rerun of an old movie, I'd seen it all before: the confusion, the fear, the defiance and the resignation. Once the Schouwburg's doors opened these nights, they would not close again till the theater stood empty.

Lou was standing on the third step of the staircase when our eyes made contact. Perhaps he didn't want to risk drawing attention to himself, for a second after our first silent communiqué, he stooped down, which made it virtually impossible for me to read his signals. When standing on my toes and lifting my head as high as I could didn't solve the problem, I climbed on my chair. From there, as I looked over a sea of faces, I saw him frantically waving at me. He gestured to get to him fast.

Getting off my chair was easy; the rest was not. I had to fight my way through the jostling crowd, being thrust forward and backward at the same time. Just when I thought I'd never make it, I felt Lou take hold of my arm. He pulled me away from the door, away from the people with their uncharted future. Lou kept shoving me toward the rope. In one sweep he flung me over, hustled me up the stairs, past the lounge, up another flight, and another, never letting go of my hand.

Reaching the hallway on the third floor, we stopped running. We were both out of breath. Facing each other, we stood — I still in a bit of a whirl, he smiling slightly. I would have liked to relish the moment and ask Lou a whole lot of questions, beginning with why me and what now, but I sensed I'd get no answers.

Lou kept assuring me that all was well, that I was safe, at least for tonight. I'd be spending the night right here in my theater. "Just make sure you're gone before daybreak, and whatever you do, don't come back down again. Don't do anything but stay put. You must. Otherwise, I cannot guarantee your safety."

Once I had managed to make my getaway, Lou's strong advice was for me to go home and stay there a few days. He figured that with my name now off the list, home would be the last place they'd be looking for me. Besides, how were they to know that I wasn't on tonight's transport? Granted, there was no guarantee that by some unlucky coincidence they wouldn't find out I was still around. Perhaps not straightaway — but what about later? Later did not worry Lou in the least. He'd already taken care of that. Lou had gotten me a job at the Catholic orphanage across the street from the theater. Mother Superior was expecting me. I wouldn't be paid any money, but I'd be getting that precious temporary exemption document. Lou assured me that I could trust Mother Superior, that she knew all about me and understood. About the job itself and whether it would involve my teaching the children singing and dancing or perhaps making up stories they themselves could act out, he had no idea. "Whatever it takes," he said, "you'll do."

Lou had to leave. "I got to get back before I'm missed," he said a bit reluctantly. "You'll be fine. Just try to relax and take it easy." As he walked me down the hall, he asked me whether I remembered Dr. Levie's office. "You'll be spending the night there." He then said that the window behind the desk was my way out. With this astonishing announcement, he took away the shawl, the one I had found in my lap, remarking that tomorrow someone else might be needing it.

I had a strange reaction to all this: a feeling that this was only the beginning. That once I started to hide and to run, I would have to keep on hiding and running, keep on using disguises and props like this shawl if I wanted to make it. Disguises and props. Is this what it takes to make it through? Disguises and props and windows to climb out of, and a man like Lou. Quite suddenly, I felt very sad. Perhaps he saw the *Weltschmerz* in my eyes, for he took my hands in his, held them firm, and in a warm, tender tone said, "Don't be sad and don't despair. One day you'll come back here, not to hide and climb out of windows but to sing again, and I shall send you beautiful flowers — and this shawl — to keep. You'll remember me then, won't you?" His lips softly touched mine, and for a fleeting moment he held me in his arms. In this moment, the stranger I was never to see again became my most intimate friend.

We kept walking down the hallway toward Dr. Levie's private office, when suddenly I saw a German soldier, the same one who had been standing guard in the foyer when the headhunters first brought me in. While I held on to Lou, he greeted the soldier with a friendly, "Good evening, Resnick [I think that was his name]. Have you gotten over your cold?"

Resnick muttered that he was feeling much better and then discreetly walked away. I was dumbfounded. Lou kept whispering, "Don't panic, don't panic," and then he explained that his group, under the auspices of the Jewish Committee, had bought the German soldier and that Resnick was now working for them. Soldier Resnick's job was, at least for tonight, to take care of me. Lou went on to say that Dr. Levie's office was now Resnick's quarters and that's where I'd be spending the night. Inside. With the soldier, recruit of both the Germans and the Jews, standing watch outside my door.

"Sleep," Lou stressed. "You must get some sleep. If you can't sleep, then try to rest. Resnick will look after you and wake you before dawn."

Lou then opened the door, led me inside, and pointed to the window, "Take a good look. Remember it's your only way out." He whispered a quick "God bless," and was gone.

I knew the room, knew it well. Once this had been Dr. Levie's sanctuary. Every piece of furniture in it then had come from his home. The large mahogany desk by the window with the matching swivel chair, the tobacco-leaf leather fauteuil. The beautiful ivory silk screen with the white marble lamp base and the burnt umber chaise lounge with the thick arabesque-design Persian rug. All so very distinguished and comfortable. I believe that most of Dr. Levie's thinking and planning for us and the Schouwburg was done right here in this room. Time after time, between breaks, I would run up just to look at the pictures he had on the walls. Photos of us — his actors — taken during rehearsals and gala first-night curtain calls, pictures full of flowers and smiles.

It sure looked different now. The room was as sparsely furnished as a monk's cell. It had only a wooden kitchen table and a chair, an old wastepaper basket, one broken lampstand with a soiled, jaundiced shade and one small bed. No rug on the floor and not a single photograph anywhere. A large painting of the Führer in his favorite "Sieg Heil" position hung right over the bed.

There I was, with nothing but the night before me and not a living soul nearby except that German soldier who, thanks to his bribable heart, was going to look after me for another six hours.

He hadn't been wearing the uniform of a Nazi. I really couldn't tell what military outfit he belonged to or whether he had any rank at all. Most likely just an ordinary corporal or a private moonlighting as a bodyguard for Jews. His austere quarters were much too unembellished to house a medal-studded Nazi.

Nevertheless, I found it stressful just the same. Sleep . . . rest? In this German soldier's bed, with Hitler's picture right above? I'd seen his eyes, those piercing, crazed eyes looking so fiendishly alive. Oh, how I wished that there was some other way to get me through this night. Something just a little less frightening, a little less bizarre. There was nothing to read. Not even one of their nauseating propaganda leaflets, or a news sheet reporting the latest lies of their victorious conquests. No radio, either.

It struck me how absurd and ludicrous the situation was. First, the Germans paid the Dutch NSP five guilders for each Jew they caught. Next, the Jews paid the Germans, the Resnicks of their fatherland, ten times that much for just one Jew and just one night of protection. Finally, on a much larger scale, and true to their diabolic principle, the Nazis, who had plundered and robbed Jews all over Europe, were financing their war against the Jews with what they'd stolen from the Jews. Maybe one day I might even laugh about this tragicomedy. One day maybe . . . not now . . .

I had unlocked the window, opened and closed it several times, to make sure that it worked, and then locked it again. I had reached out, reached into the moonless night searching to find the roof outside. The ridge was lower than the window ledge and more than an arm's length away. No real problem as long as the roof was flat. Most roofs in Amsterdam were.

My stomach was growling. I realized that I had forgotten to eat the sand-wich Lou had slipped into the brown bag. I was beginning to get a terrible headache, a chronic disease of the war. I couldn't afford to get weak now. The only thing I could think of was to ask Soldier Resnick for something to eat. Lou hadn't said that I shouldn't talk to him. When I opened the door, just wide enough to alert his attention, I got no response. So I opened it wider and then all the way. Still nothing. I finally stepped out into the hall-way, only to find it as empty and silent as the rest of this dead quiet theater. No sign of Soldier Resnick. He was gone, and I was alone.

I did not panic. Just quickly went back inside and shut the door. My head was throbbing. Could he have forgotten about me? Or gotten bored and gone somewhere to have himself a drink or two? Not likely. There was a curfew for the military, too. Except I didn't have any idea what time they had to be tucked in. Certainly much later than us. It really didn't matter all that much. If I didn't fall asleep, I wouldn't have to worry about him waking me before dawn. And I just never, absolutely never, could sleep in the same room with the Führer, on an empty stomach, too. There was no need for me to look at my watch to know that dawn was still a million nights away. I did wish I could have stopped the church clock bells from striking in the night. It makes for a lonely sound, as though there may never be another night. What good are bells anyway — do those already asleep need to know what time it is?

The little paranoid voice inside me kept questioning: What if you get out through the window but cannot see because the fog is too thick? What if there isn't any fog and you can see everything out there, but everything out there can see *you*? What if the roof of the next building is not flat, but steep or doesn't connect to any other roof? What if you slip or fall or get lost? What if you do not slip, or fall, or get lost, but cannot find an open window to get into another house? What if you find an open window but land in someone's room instead of a back staircase? And what if this room is full of Germans?

There was a knock at the door. Lightheaded and a bit nauseous, I was un-able to decide whether to head for the window or the door. I did neither. When I heard it being opened, I turned, and there he was: Soldier Resnick. In one hand he carried a canteen and in the other a small, paper-wrapped carton. Without a word he walked to the table, put it all down, unwrapped it, and took out a piece of sausage and a slice of bread. He poured coffee from the canteen into his flasklike cup and motioned for me to sit down and eat. He had not looked at me, or spoken one word. While I muttered a thank-you, sat down and ate, he looked out the window. After I had finished, I thanked him again, which he acknowledged with a slight nod. He then left the window and went to his army bed, looking down as if he were debating his next move. A few seconds later, he pulled the tucked-under blankets loose. I watched him turn back the blankets, prop up the pillows and smooth the sheets.

It wasn't till he had taken off his tie and started unbuttoning his uniform that my gratitude turned to chilly panic — Rape! It was the one thing I hadn't thought of at all. How could I not have? "I'm Jewish," I cried, as if he didn't know, as if those magic words would save me. I made a dash for the door, but he was faster. He swung me around, and as we looked at each other for the first time, I saw that he was more scared than I.

I don't know how long we stood like this. I only remember thinking: *He's just a boy! A boy who in all likelihood will get himself killed before he ever gets to be a man.* Soldier Resnick, somebody's son . . . somebody's brother . . . somebody's friend. Not mine. We were enemies because his Führer had ordered him to hate Jews.

Soldier Resnick buttoned up his uniform, put on his tie, moved away from me, and, pointing to his bed, said, *"Hab keine Angst"* — Don't be afraid. Then he marched to the door, switched off the light, and left. I was spent with fatigue. In the dark I groped my way to the bed, crawled in, and with Adolf's picture above me, fell asleep.

The night was barely on the wane when the soldier knocked on the door. I opened my eyes, saw Adolf's picture and immediately got up. I scudded to the window, opened it, and with the first flicker of dawn swung myself over the ledge and out.

The roof was flat, but the gravel beneath my feet made my footsteps sound like gnashing teeth. It slowed me down. The weather, and my sense of direction, were one and the same — poor! The dirty sky hung over me as though it had not decided yet whether to swallow me up, drown me in rain, or blow the clouds away and let a bit of winter sun shine through. I could see well enough to know where I was going, except that I did not know where to go. I walked and walked every which way, forward and backward, leaping from roof to roof, around and around in circles like on a merry-go-round.

The windows I saw on those spreading rooftops were not inviting. All the latches were bolted. All the black air-raid shades drawn. I tried them all. My hands, stiff and raw from the cold, kept pressing against their frames, but they refused to yield. I had come far, too far to turn back. Besides, what would I be turning back to? Moreover, daylight already had chased away the dawn, and I had to find some way to get off these much too visible rooftops.

After countless frustrating leaps, I finally spotted a group of smaller houses. The moment I detected one with a very low rooftop, I jumped. It seemed a long way down, but a safe landing was the least of my worries. I had lost a lot of time but accomplished very little. No unlocked window. Ultimately, I did resort to something a little more drastic: with the heel of my shoe I smashed the first accessible window, put my sleeve-covered hand through and released the latch from the inside. The broken glass clattered to the ground with the loudness of a thousand windblown chimes. Once inside, I found the staircase and raced down to the front door. It was locked — three different locks but not one key! My noisy break-in had awakened the dogs in the neighborhood. Their barking and howling, mixed with the high-pitched meows of some meddlesome cats, drowned out the distant sirens.

This house, however, was silent and empty. I walked from room to room. It did not look as though its occupants had left it in a hurry. Everything seemed in its place, but missing human scent and touch. Once this must have been a home filled with music — a magnificent grand piano stood in the living room with a bust of Mozart on it next to a picture of a bride and groom cutting their wedding cake. In the dining room the antique, hand-crafted grandfather clock was also silent. Only the menorah on the mantel over the fireplace revealed that this had been the house of Jews. I had a strange reaction — uneasy, almost guilty — as if I'd broken into their lives, not their house. Whoever they were, they were gone.

I made my exit through the study window that led into the backyard, relieved to be back on the ground again, though I was still a long way from being home free.

Amsterdam has twice as many backyards attached to other backyards as it has connecting roofs. The only way to tell where one home ends and the other begins is by their fences. I saw every size, color, style and height. But what I didn't see were the little gates I had expected casually to walk through. There was nothing casual about any of it. Besides, with the entire canine population howling like a pack of wolves by now, it was no longer a question of when the first window would open or how many heads would be peeking through the curtains, only who would first be calling the police.

Jumping over the fourth fence, I landed in a prickly hedge. It knocked me out, putting an end to this hurdle race. When I came to, I felt the wet tongue of an Irish setter licking my face, while two hefty female arms were trying to unprickle me. The owner of those hefty arms was in a quandary whether to curse or comfort me or just turn me over to the police.

With the woman's help, I struggled to my feet. I'm convinced that my pitiful appearance did more to touch her heart than any explanation I could have possibly come up with. She took me into her house, let me use the bathroom, administered first aid to my scratched face and hands, and made me tea. She then asked whether I wanted to stay a while. I shook my head, thanked her, and left through the front door.

Outside, Ping-Pong–sized hailstones and an ill-willed wind slapped my face, making it difficult to read the street names. The city was awake now. People trickled through the streets in a part of town I hardly knew. I didn't dare ask for directions, just slogged on alone. Slogged through squares, parks and over bridges, many miles. I truly don't know how I got back again. But I did . . . Somehow, I made it home.

∽ Six

THE BUILDING THAT HOUSED THE ORPHANAGE had seen many centuries and many orphaned youngsters come and go. It was hoary with age, its walls and ceilings cracked, the stone tiles in the flooring worn and bleached. Old radiators, steamless and rusty, stood idle. Stairs, burdened by the weight of antiquity and neglect, had lost their luster and smoothness. Long, narrow windows, their glass mouths mulishly shut, sneered at the world outside. It was not a friendly house.

I had come to see Mother Superior three days after my flight over the rooftoops and was greeted by her with open hostility. She wasted no time in letting me know how little she thought of my profession and those engaged in it. In her opinion, an actress was either a whore or a rich man's mistress — but never anyone who did an honest day's work. She had expected me all right, but did not think that I, at best a pampered theater person, deserved shelter in her undefiled orphanage.

She was a stern one, this gruff, white-haired matron, stern, but impressive. Vigorous, decisive and strong. A figure of authority in every sense of the word. Even with me standing up — she never offered me a chair — and her sitting behind an enormous desk, she towered over me.

Religious objects were strangely absent from her sanctum: no crucifixes or statuettes of the Virgin Mary. Mother Superior herself did not wear a habit, but a blue and white–striped uniform with starched collar and cuffs.

The only religious symbol, dangling from the celibate lady's neck, was an ornamental silver cross.

My interview with her was a one-sided affair. She talked, and I kept my mouth shut. In her brusque but frank manner, Mother Superior told me that as a devout Christian she could do no less than help those who'd suffered the agony of persecution, no matter who they were. As superintendent of the orphanage, however, she said her charges had to come first. Furthermore, I mustn't expect favors or any special treatment, for the only stars she admired were up in heaven. After a string of ungracious comments about my "misguided, unchaste" life, she switched to the sour facts that dealt with work.

She instructed me to return early the next morning — unless of course I'd changed my mind — bring a nurse's uniform, a "decent pair of shoes," and the right attitude. Before she dismissed me, she handed me the "temporarily exempt from labor transport" paper, remarking that this would only buy me time, not salvation. Mother Superior suggested prayer.

I had the uniform she wanted and "decent" shoes to match at home in my theater wardrobe. I had costumes for every occasion, costumes I had never thought I'd need to play my way out of a labor transport. I remember thinking that this orphanage bit, like Mr. Stern's sewing circle, wouldn't last very long .

I started the very next day but was not allowed near the children. Three holy sisters took care of them. I was handed a pail, a brush, and told to scrub floors.

Mother Superior rarely left her office; yet I knew that she was watching me. I'm absolutely certain that she waited for me to give up. She had not bothered to mention when I first came to her what job this was going to be. Not in a donkey's year would I have equated the fostering of orphans with such a demeaning chore. I was furious with her for being so rough on me. For making my difficult existence more difficult instead of easier. For wanting to teach me humility. Me, a star.

The children? I never caught more than a glimpse of them. By the time I reported for work in the morning, they already had left for school, and by the time they returned, I was still scrubbing the chlorine-reeking soapsuds into the unrelenting stones. I never even knew for how many this dismal place was home. I guess the youngsters were treated all right; just the same I did feel sorry for them. Could be that I remembered the way it was when Papa died and I became an orphan. I felt so lost and lonely then. I wished that these children here could have know my papa. He used to help support an orphanage like this and all the kids there called him their fairy godfather. He would take them to the amusement park, buy them ice cream and soda pops, candies and toys, pay for their rides on the carousels or the big Ferris wheel. My twin and I didn't get to go along; we weren't old enough then, but Kate was. She never tired of telling us how happy he'd made those poor children. Maybe it wasn't just the rides and the candy which put a bit of starlight into their eyes; maybe it was because for one day a week he was their papa too.

My determination to stick it out despite sore knees and chapped hands paid off. Mother Superior, finally admitting that I showed primacy of will, promoted me from ordinary charwoman to nurse. Sister Agnes was to be my instructor. Sister Agnes, in charge of prayers and props, was very obliging but as pious as can be. Sister Agnes, whose face was riddled with smallpox scars, was a true believer: serving the Lord Jesus was all she lived for. Her only shortcoming was her forgetfulness. Tizzy, timid Sister Agnes could never remember what she was supposed to do, or had wanted to say. She herself was quite embarrassed about her absentmindedness.

After I'd been there for about three weeks, Sister Agnes disappeared. Or rather, she didn't come back after she and the other sisters had dropped the children off at school. Neither did the other sisters or the children. I wasn't all that worried at first, thinking that they might have had to stay longer because of some after school function, but when by late afternoon they still hadn't returned, I began to feel a little uneasy. I couldn't imagine what could have happened to them. Not sure what to do, but wanting to do something, I went in search of a clue. Investigating the children's lockers, I found them empty. Their few belongings as well as the meager possessions of the sisters were gone.

I didn't wait till my shift was over to talk to Mother Superior. Expecting her to put my mind at ease, I knocked at her door. I knocked many times, but she either wasn't in or chose not to answer. There was a light coming from underneath her door, but I didn't have the guts to go in.

I spent a very restless night at home. The disappearance of the entire orphanage was all I could think about. By morning, having discarded all sorts of theories as unlikely reasons for what might have happened, I came up with one possibility which did make sense: Namely, that all of them had been moved to another orphanage because this one was being shut down. This most realistic probability was also the most depressing one: if I was right, then I would lose my labor transport exemption paper again.

Determined to find out the truth, I went back to the orphanage.

I don't know when the other children came. They must have arrived after I'd already gone home to brood about it. What caught my attention, once inside, was the overloaded coat racks in the hall. Where the drab and skimpy blue-black coats of the orphans used to hang in an orderly and regimented fashion, there now hung heaps of brightly colored children's winter clothes, all bunched together with no regard for size or neatness. Almost as though they had been slated for a last-minute jumble sale.

Mother Superior's door was wide open. She obviously had been waiting for me. She seemed different — perhaps because she had never before offered me a chair, or perhaps because I'd gotten used to seeing her with her elbows firmly planted on her desk. Not that morning: her hands kept shielding her eyes as if some invisible glare blinded her, and her fingers kept rubbing her forehead as though they were trying to rub out the present. We sat like that for unbearably long minutes. When finally she did speak, her hands no longer shielding her eyes, I found she had aged. And her voice sounded tired and strained. Not like her, I thought. She, more than anyone I had had contact with in those last few months, had never shown any sign of being affected by the events taking place all around her. As though her religious chastity belt had insulated her from a world gone mad.

She didn't know that I wasn't told that her children and the sisters were not coming back. Mother Superior had left specific instructions for Sister Agnes to tell me, counting on her for once not to forget. Of course she did forget. "There was no time," Mother Superior exclaimed. "The order came . . . well . . . you know how they are. Yes, everybody has been moved to another orphanage. Don't you worry, though, this one is not being shut down. I pray it never will be. I do want my children back and the sisters." Even Sister Agnes.

Mother Superior had never talked that much to me before. She was doing her best to make me understand the drastic change that had befallen the orphanage in those last twenty-four hours.

A high-ranking Nazi did not think that the Schouwburg, in its present condition, was a proper place for children — not even Jewish ones. He wanted them to be cared for in the right way. He decided the orphanage would be much more suitable. And so the Jewish children picked up with their parents only yesterday, brought to the theater and unloaded there like all the others, were, unlike all the others, separated from their parents and brought to the orphanage.

Mother Superior, who early in the morning had received the swastika-stamped official order, immediately had her wards and sisters moved. She contacted the Germans and the Jewish Committee requesting supplies. The child-loving Nazi was unavailable — not for comments but for supplies — but some of the Dutch underground together with Jewish volunteers raided a warehouse during the night and dropped off their haul at the orphanage, also during the night.

The children stayed with us for a short time only. Never long enough to settle in, never long enough to know them well. Departure night, destination unknown, for them and their parents came always too soon.

If the orphanage was understaffed before, now we were even worse off. We did get three new Jewish girls — and they the labor transport exemption — instead of the sisters. They were not the problem. The problem was that the children's ages varied so much. Feeding alone became an impossible task. In spite of the underground sending us cribs and other infants' needs, babies kept screaming for their mothers' milk. Spoon-fed toddlers crawled non-stop all over the place, and children long out of diapers started to wet their beds again. Since no regular routine was possible, we improvised from hour to hour.

Once in while, when the weather wasn't too nasty, we let the youngsters play in the courtyard, a few stony squares squeezed in between brick and cement buildings. Somehow, it was always dark there. The overlapping roofs drank up all the light. One could barely see a pocket-sized sky.

⤴

HER NAME WAS FRIEDA, and she was only two years old. She had curly red hair, freckles, and blueish-green eyes full of tears. She looked so much like me when I was her age, so tiny and pale. And so terribly frightened. She sobbed when she was brought in, when she was carried up, and she sobbed when she was put into the crib. She was such a pathetic little thing.

I've seen so many children come and go. Too many to remember their faces or names. My heart went out to all of them, but they did not engrave themselves in my mind like Frieda. The thought of her haunted me long after she'd gone. Why did this child touch me so deeply? What was it about this teeny girl — the way her little arms reached out to me? Her frail and trembling body grew quiet only when I held her. She clung to me so intensely. Wouldn't eat unless I fed her. Wouldn't sleep unless I put my head next to hers. Never laughed, never smiled. Just cried, cried such big tears. I felt such pity for her. I knew she didn't stand a chance. Was she not like a candle on a birthday cake, lit with the same joy and anticipation, yet destined to burn brightly for one moment only, and then be extinguished, with so much light still left to shine? Sad little Frieda.

I don't recall when we began working twelve-hour shifts, nor when we received permission to take the children for early afternoon walks. It must have been toward the end of the winter. Mother Superior had requested it, but we never expected that it would be granted. When finally we could walk with them three times around the same four square blocks, my little Frieda was no longer with me. Nor was she with me when I volunteered for the night shift. I had her for such a short time, loved her so much and could do nothing to save her. I could hear her cries long after they had trucked her away. I could hear her in the nursery, on the stairwell, in the hall, and in the somber courtyard when, alone at night, I stepped out for a breath of air . . . as if she was calling me. Pocket-sized Frieda, who never even got to see the pocket-sized sky.

The bomb hit at midnight. I had heard the church bells chime seven times before the explosion lit up the heavens and drowned out the last five chimes of the witching hour. I had just finished my rounds, stopping in the makeshift nursery on the third floor, when the explosion knocked me to the ground. The orphanage shook and trembled; falling plaster and broken glass were everywhere. Smashed window shutters, furiously blowing in the wind, fought the yellow fire tongues that licked their way from the building next door to us.

I was alone that night, alone with seventy-eight children. Nurse Judy, who should have been there with me, did not show up. After I'd stumbled to my feet, I reached for the nearest crib, grabbed one baby, then another, and raced with them to the staircase. I shouted for the older children whose sleeping quarters were across the hall to head for the basement. Most of them had already leaped down the stairs without waiting for my instructions. I made them stick together in groups of five, putting the older ones in charge of the young ones, hold hands so they would feel more secure, and hurry down to the cellar. Up and down the old stairs we ran, some very brave older boys and I. Up and down, carrying babies and toddlers, till the last of the children were safe.

Amsterdam had not been bombed before. There were no other air attacks that night. No planes had been flying over the city, and I had heard no air-raid warning sirens. So why this bomb? And why hit the building next door which, as far as I knew, held nothing more ominous than old furniture belonging to families no longer living there? Some bungling fool, on his way back from hitting military targets, must have dropped this one by mistake. A few days later the rubble next door was cleared away, leaving as eerie reminder broken walls blackened by smoke and covered with soot, looking like beheaded giants in bleak mourning frocks.

Whether they had slipped into the cellar before the bomb had dropped, or immediately after, I don't know. They were just there: three strange men. With all the goings-on, the presence of these men was less important to me than this new predicament with the children. By the time I was fully aware of the three strangers, they already had taken the children from me, bedded them down, comforted and calmed them.

The men were Dutch — tall, muscular, blue-eyed and unshaven, ranging in age from twenty to forty — and spoke with Amsterdam accents. They wore heavy sailor jackets, navy blue woolen caps pulled down low. They were good with the children, and their strong hands knew how to hold the small ones without frightening them. Only one of them held an unlit pipe in his mouth, and only one of them addressed me by name. They, like Lou, knew everything about me. They — three ordinary men with three ordinary names, Jan, Cor and Gus, fighting no ordinary war — had come to recruit me. They, a tiny fraction of the heroic Dutch underground movement, were seeking my help in saving these youngsters.

Even in my foggy state it was quite obvious that they also knew this damp and dim-lit cellar. They had directed my attention to the ancient chest filled with blankets, and to the shoebox full of candles and matches. It's more than likely that they themselves had put them there.

Miraculous how adaptable most of the youngsters were. Eleven-year-old boys took care of six-year-olds, while six-year-old girls became instant mommies. They hugged the toddlers, cuddled the babies and held each other all through the night.

Among the many lessons the terror years had taught me already was never to answer too many questions and to ask even less. Applying this knowledge to the situation at hand, it soon became clear that in relation to the three intruders, I was at a definite disadvantage.

Their presence in the cellar was neither accidental nor had it anything to do with the bomb. They'd come to establish contact with me and would have found me that night, or the next, or the one after that. I had been on their list too, ever since that child-loving Nazi had turned the orphanage into a transitory depot station.

We sat around the sturdy wooden table on not so sturdy kitchen stools, the four of us. I watched the warm, soft candlelight rise out of the darkness like a blue-veiled dancer, feeling proud and humble that these Resistance fighters wanted me to be one of them. Not for a moment, in spite of their warnings of danger, did I consider not joining.

The briefing was detailed and to the point. By the time the blue-veiled candle flame had disappeared, I was as familiar with the operation, and my part in it, as if I'd thought of it myself — theoretically, that is. Except for getting back on the day shift at once, everything else was to remain the same.

Whether Mother Superior knew of the mission, had given it her blessing, or helped wherever she could has remained a secret.

The major objective of the mission was to "lose" as many children as possible before they were sent on transport. If all went according to plan, the children would be getting new identities, and for a while new parents. They'd be sent, through the underground, to towns, villages and farms all over the land, wherever decent folks would open their hearts and doors to them.

My part in it was threefold:

Step one: Back on the day shift, I was to make sure that, weather permitting, the children were taken for their daily walk, and that I was always with them.

Step two: I was to never take the lead but stick like glue to the tail end of the group, to the youngsters in the very last row.

Step three: I could lose four or five children per outing, but at no time anymore. Otherwise, the risk of detection would not only be too great but could jeopardize the entire operation and everyone involved.

↩

ABOUT TWENTY FEET FROM THE SOUTHWEST CORNER, the last corner to turn before reaching the orphanage, set back from the street stood a small house. Because its entrance door, completely concealed by archways, was practically hidden from view, my three Resistance fighters had marked that location as the drop-off point. Gus would be waiting for the children there. Once I had turned them over to him, the most dangerous part of my assignment was finished.

The transfer would have to be made after we'd been around the block twice, before passing the house for the third time. That's when I, with the youngsters in the last row, would have to start slowing down, lag behind, and thus increase the distance between us and the rest of the group. To be completely out of visual range, I'd have to let the others turn the corner first and then whiz the children in the last row off to Gus. If the timing of my three comrades was correct, I had less than fifteen seconds to turn them over to Gus, watch them disappear behind the archways, catch up with the others, and get back to the orphanage together with everyone else.

I had only been out with the children a few times before taking over the night shift. I had no way of knowing whether or not the routine had been changed. I could only hope that it hadn't. Another counsellor and I always took them out in the early afternoon. Whenever we had too many youngsters, we'd divide them into groups. Take out the first group, bring them back, take the next, bring them back, with one of us in front, the other covering the rear. Each day, it had been the same direction, the same four blocks around the square, the same routine, but we never counted the children. Nobody had ever asked us to — nobody cared. And that's what my three Resistance buddies counted on. Not being counted . . . not being missed.

Unfortunately, that still didn't solve the problem of what and when to tell their parents. It was difficult to predict which way was best. We couldn't tell them way ahead of time, because we ourselves didn't know which of the children would be the ones. On the other hand, we couldn't wait till the very last minute or risk asking their parents whether they really wanted us to take their children. After much deliberation, we decided not to ask them at all but just tell them that their offspring had been sent to places where they would be safe and well looked after.

The children wore name tags and so did the adults. It was about the only time this still made sense. This way Gus, once he had the youngsters, could take off their name tags, hand them to Cor or Jan, who then would get them to whoever was working in the Schouwburg on this rescue mission.

Since the outings never lasted past four or four-thirty in the afternoon and the trucks never came till after eleven, there would be plenty of time to find and explain to their parents as much as we could. None of us could even guess what the reaction of the close-knit Jewish families would be.

It was daylight before we parted. The three had helped to bring the children back upstairs, then cleaned up the broken glass and covered the shattered windows with blankets. Before they left, they asked what code name we should use for this operation. I told them to please make it "Frieda." They did not question it, just said that Mission Frieda was going to start the very next day. Gus would be waiting at the drop-off point from 1:00 p.m. on, regardless of weather. In case of any changes or emergencies, I would be contacted.

After they had left, through the front door no less, I went straight to Mother Superior. She was having her morning tea, and from what I could gather, had already taken a good look at the damage next door. Our own she had not yet investigated, waiting first for my report. I told her as much as I could, without betraying my comrades or the mission, which resulted in Nurse Judy's being fired and my being put back on the day shift without having to ask for it.

I'd never realized that Mother Superior did not live at the orphanage. If it hadn't been for the bomb and the sobering realization that at that moment of crisis, she was nowhere about, I would not have ever thought of it. Now, however, coinciding with my own change of shift, the good lady informed me that as of tonight she would be there all the time. Not knowing where she stood on Mission Frieda, I had mixed feelings about her decision to pitch in. She said she would have a bed brought in for sleeping; she wished to take some of the load off me. No matter what she knew or didn't know, the expression on her face, the tone in her voice when addressing me had changed quite drastically, as though she had suddenly acquired respect for me.

There wasn't a soul on the street that morning. The air smelled of last night's singed debris, mixed with the scent of a new spring. I should have gone straight home so as not to worry Mama and Herbert, gotten some badly needed sleep, but I just couldn't leave without at least one rehearsal without the children, all by myself, knowing that the better I acquainted myself with every inch of these four blocks, the safer we'd all be.

The orphanage faced west. Walking clockwise, the way I would with the youngsters, I slowly headed toward the northwest corner. I studied every doorway, looked over my shoulder, looked sideways and straight ahead. Stopped, went on, stopped again, let my eyes wander, but there was nothing to see. This used to be a pretty square, a few tram stops from the heart of the city. Now, it seemed that most of the houses stood empty

The little park around the corner on the north and east sides of the block had never been more than a resting place for tired feet: a few benches to sit on, a few trees for summer shade, and flowers whenever the seasons allowed them to grow. A quiet place for quiet people then, and now. Nothing to worry about. Both the second and the third sides were easy to observe since all the homes were on the same side. The ones on the north were facing the park; the ones on the east faced the Zoo, or rather, the high stone wall surrounding it. The Zoo was closed; it was the time of year, not war, which was the reason for that. I remember telling the youngsters when we passed that the animals were all asleep. Still, the children never could resist a peek through the heavy wrought-iron gate doubly secured with weighty chains. It reached almost to the southeast corner. Standing in front of it, I could not only see both sides of the fourth block and past the house where Gus would be but also all the way to the southwest corner, the last and most critical one.

This street, block four, was wider than the others, almost a boulevard, slightly uphill, and much busier because of the Population Registry, the National Identification Center, which stood in the middle on the south side of the street, spreading over half a block. Like most government buildings, this too was architecturally uninteresting, cheerless and hopelessly big. There, for the first time on that morning, I saw early birds waiting for the registry to open. The archway safety house was directly across from it.

Of all the government buildings I had seen or visited, I wasn't likely to forget this one. More than two years ago, right in there, Herbert and I were refused a marriage license on the grounds that all of me was Jewish, but only half of him was Jewish. I should have asked that nondescript clerk whether he would give us half a license for half a marriage.

I hadn't been that close to the registry for a long time, nor had I thought about the catastrophic effect the business of this building had had on everyone once the Germans moved in. Inside, neatly typed and filed on four- by six-inch index cards, were the particulars of every man, woman and child who lived here: their persuasion, existence, address, all stated in orderly fashion and readily available to the occupying Hitler menace.

Why didn't they burn every last bit of paper? The Belgians did. Only one hair-raising minute before Hitler's army had marched into Brussels and

Antwerp, their king, Leopold III, had ordered all documents and papers destroyed. It didn't save every Jew, but it did give them a lot more time to plan their escape, to hide or live openly with false ID cards. In any case, it took the Third Reich much longer to catch a Belgian than a Dutch Jew.

The ornamental garlands of ivy and pine tree cones that hung from the arches of the small safety house made for a perfect cover, completely hiding the recessed entrance door, which was unlocked. I quickly slipped inside. It was definitely deserted. Perhaps it was the charming cobblestone courtyard, the tiny old-fashioned windows on either side of the house with the small gate at the far end, which made me think of it as a small-scale cloister or rectory. But perhaps it was only its stillness, which made it look like something left over from another time. I didn't investigate the little gate, but wouldn't have been at all surprised to find some sort of connection between it and the cellar at the orphanage.

I spent no more than a couple of minutes there, then crossed the street to examine it from the Population Registry side. To people waiting for the registry to open, my presence there could mean no more than that I was waiting, too. After I had stared across, paced back and forth, then stared again, I decided to let it be. I'd seen enough to know that only someone with a spyglass could make out anything at all, and even then he would have to know what he was looking for. Besides, I had to believe that my three mates had chosen that house for a reason. They probably thought a busy street much safer than a quiet one. Who would bother about children disappearing into a house one barely could see?

I felt eager after my walk-through, anxious to get going, tense and tight like an overwound watch.

Mama and Herbert would certainly be glad to have me home at a normal time again. They'd never liked my being away at night. Pity that I couldn't tell them the truth about last night and the commitment I had made. Not that they wouldn't have approved of it — of course they would have, would have been proud, but also frightfully worried. Why add another fretful minute to those they had endured already.

The heavens were with us the day we kicked off Mission Frieda. The moment I looked out the window and saw the cloudless sea blue sky, I knew it was a good omen. I was wide awake that morning, and bursting with energy. I got myself ready, raced out of the house and rushed to the orphanage at a speed that amazed even me. In hindsight, my haste served no purpose at all. I still had to get through breakfast, lunch and playtime with the children, naptime for the small fry — none of which made time pass any faster.

Also, as of this morning, the two small rooms adjacent to the hallway, once the sanctum of Sister Agnes and another sister, later used as sick rooms, were now holding wall-to-wall cribs, with and without babies and toddlers. Mother Superior, who had insisted on this rearrangement because of its proximity to the cellar in case of another bomb, did not, to my immense relief, insist on us taking them out, too. The child-loving Nazi had decided to have all nursing mothers now in the Schouwburg come one at a time to the orphanage and feed their babies.

I needed to see it only once — watch only one mother leave the Schouwburg alone, cross the deserted street, her eyes fixed on the bolted windows of the orphanage — to know how desperate she was for her baby.

I needed to see it only once — watch only one mother's face, relieved of anguish, joyously holding this suckling little thing in her arms with so much love and devotion — to know that nothing ugly could touch them now.

I needed to see only one baby's smile light up the room, one mother's happy tears wash away her precious one's fears and feel the aura of their peace for the moment, to know that wherever their journey might end, it must end together, for they are one.

Except for my sadness over little Frieda, nothing of my time spent at the orphanage has touched me deeper than this magical oneness of mother and child. I didn't know it then, but in some freaky way it was this mysterious Nazi's whim to let the mothers come which gave Mission Frieda a chance to succeed.

It was two o' clock when we started to line up the children. Because of the unusually nice weather, they all wanted to go. We were short on staff, but not short on children. This meant that I would have more than one group to walk with, more than four or five youngsters to leave with Gus.

In my excitement I hadn't given any thought to which ones would be the lucky ones, nor that I'd be the one having to make that choice. Once conscious of that responsibility, I could no longer look into their trusting, innocent eyes. I buttoned their coats, put on their mittens, tied their scarves, but when it came to deciding, I went to the kitchen. Let someone unknowing and blameless make this decision, not me. I stayed in there till Nurse Louise called to me that the first group was ready to leave.

Luckily, the choosing was done by the youngsters themselves. Most of them wanted to be first. Just like caged birds, set free, they were bursting to get out. Louise, stationed at the door, had a pretty hard time controlling them.

I let them rush by me without counting them, the same band of youngsters who'd been with me the night of the bomb. It gave Louise and her group a head start, which was precisely the way I'd hoped it would be.

The small hands clutching mine belonged to the timid and quiet ones, the ones fate left for me to bring to Gus. I had three boys and two girls. One girl on each side, holding on tight; next to them the boys, ranging between the ages of four and ten. The girl on my left had a runny nose, while the one on my right kept tripping over her shoelaces. She solved the distance problem better than anything I could have come up with.

The first time around, I saw Gus out of the corner of my eye pressed against one of the arches. I gave no sign of acknowledgment, nor did I draw the children's attention to him or the house.

Second time around, as a delaying device, I used the little girl's numerous battles with her shoelaces, which despite her determination to tie them herself always came undone. While the children in front of us kept trying to keep pace with the ones in front of them, chatting back and forth, mine hardly spoke.

It is quite natural that I should remember this first day of Mission Frieda the best: I was very much aware that my emotional circuit was dangerously overloaded. It all came down to wanting to do so much more than I'd been asked to do.

Each time we turned a corner, I got this overwhelming urge to call out to Louise to let the youngsters run, instead of that drawn-out, leisurely walk. I so wanted them to race back to the orphanage, using the minutes saved, like a precious gift of time given us, to save more children.

Third time around, just before the transfer, I kneeled down and tied the little girl's laces for her. By then the first ones had already turned the corner, which made the distance between us and the others more than enough to deliver my children to Gus.

The final step happened faster than I had thought possible. One second I stood with my arms around them telling them that the man standing by the archway of the little house had been sent by their parents to help them get away from the Nazis. Moments later, the children already were with him.

Perhaps it went so easily because two of the boys, remembering Gus from the night in the cellar, also remembered his kindness and trusted him. Whatever the reason, there wasn't a breath of hesitation or doubt from any of them.

Gus nodded at me, the children waved, and off I went without looking back to catch up with the others. I reached the orphanage together with a couple of older boys who wanted to get lost on their own. While Louise, standing in the open doorway, practiced textbook obedience on them, I slipped inside.

Everyone old enough to stand was standing in the hallway. It was impossible to tell which of the children had just gotten back, and which of them belonged to the second group. When it came to lining them up, they all lined up again, including the two wanting to get lost on their own.

Somehow we did get the second group out, leaving Mother Superior in charge of curbing the unruliness of those who had or hadn't yet been out.

This time, the children were fidgety. There were no timid ones in this group. It didn't go quite as smoothly as before. The main obstacle was of course that I couldn't tell Louise anything. She unfortunately wasn't the least bit interested in one more outing and had about as much understanding of the children's unreleased energies and underlying fears as I had of Sister Agnes's piety. The children wanted to change places with one another; Louise expected them to march like little soldiers. In the end, I managed in spite of Louise, and without the previous unrehearsed delaying tactic of the shoelaces, to hand four more over to Gus, though not the ones I had started out with.

The five I had left with were fast walkers who didn't want to traipse behind. The four I wound up with I discovered zealously climbing the iron gate of the Zoo. Four little monkeys wanting to have some innocent fun before being locked up for the night — or worse. Two were tomboys, two real boys, and none of them older than eight or nine.

We did get to go out a third time. Mother Superior had promised the rest a walk before dark. By then Louise was too bushed to march, and the children were overexcited and tired.

This time, my three little girls — twelve, ten and four years of age — never left my side. Like puppy dogs, they stayed close, walking at my pace and stopping whenever I stopped. They missed their parents an awul lot, and that was all they talked about. When it came time to tell them why I had held them back with me, they too immediately understood, except for the four-year-old who no longer remembered Gus. She went with him anyway because the other two did.

I knew that Gus was pleased because of the way he'd nodded at me whenever I'd passed. An okay day. A terrific day — one dozen children saved! If the weather held up, we'd be doing just fine.

And we were doing fine every rain-free afternoon — whether or not the winds were blowing, whether or not the skies were clear. Yes, we did encounter some unforeseen problems along the way. Everything from urgent visits to the bathroom by a couple of my stragglers at a most inopportune time, to a child hitting Louise and being sent back to me when I already had my quota of five, to a little fellow's yelling that he had to see his mommy in the Schouwburg. In general, the children behaved like troupers. As for the adults in the orphanage, none of them ever bothered to find out why there were fewer children for dinner than there had been for lunch.

↬ SEVEN

IN THE LAST WEEK OF APRIL 1943, Mission Frieda came to
an end. One afternoon, when we took the same walk, passing the same
house, Gus wasn't waiting for the children anymore. Neither was Jan or Cor.
I had received no warning, no indication that something had gone wrong or
was about to. Yet his absence was the surest possible sign that it was finished.
I didn't think for a moment that a touch of the flu had kept Gus or his comrades away. Nothing would have, as long as one more child could have been
saved, not unless the choice was no longer his, and he himself was on the run.

I'd known from the start that one day it would stop. I just didn't know
how or when. Having to bring the youngsters all back again, present and accounted for with nobody counting, was painful. Not knowing what had
happened to Gus and the others was even more painful.

How many of the little ones had he taken with him? About a hundred
and thirty or a hundred and forty. Seems that we could have filled about five
classrooms with the children we had saved. But what about the ones we
could not save — how many classrooms, schools and parks would they have
filled?

Preoccupied with the events of the day, I kept on seeing Gus like a mirage
in every doorway I passed while walking home. What would tomorrow be
like without him, without the brave young man I never really knew . . . ?

The old man pushing his flower cart onto the sidewalk was heading
straight for me. It was hard to tell whether he wanted to sell me something,

or run me over. I was no more than a couple of blocks away from the orphanage when, out of nowhere, he had appeared.

On any other day I might have wondered about him and his flowers in this deserted part of town, especially after sundown; but not today. My mind, wrapped around the last few hours, hardly registered him at all. Even my stepping back to let him pass was more of a reflex than a deliberate move. But he brought his wagon to an abrupt halt right where I stood, virtually blocking my path.

A sudden hailstorm in the middle of summer could not have done more to unwrap my thoughts. Before I could make sense of it, I found myself holding the red tulips he'd taken from his cart and placed in my arms. He whispered for me not to come back to the orphanage and not to go home either. This gray-bearded, lanky, middle-aged man with his dusty dark jacket, worn trousers and knee-high rubber boots even looked like bad news. He never finished a sentence, shortened words as though he were a talking telegram: his voice was clearly marked "urgent."

"Glad to have caught you." A word I liked less and less. "Don't come back. They know it all. Friends okay, they're under. You do same."

He picked up his cart, pushed it back to the street, and hustled off.

I stood where I had stood before, staring intently at the scarlet red tulips in my arms, without the slightest clue of what to do next. Whatever else I hadn't sorted out yet, I did recognize, quite soberly, that I had reached another impasse, as well as just how precarious the situation was.

At this point, my options were nil. I thought of perhaps dropping in on some friends living in another part of town, even considered staying for a while to think things out. Unfortunately, these days, unexpected drop-ins caused unexpected heart attacks. Not the sort of thing one did to friends . . .

Since standing till my legs gave out was only going to make me more tired but hardly wiser, I decided, in spite of the warning, to go home. Mainly because of a very important letter the postman hadn't brought yet, a letter we had all so anxiously been waiting for. A letter that could hold the key to safety for me. If ever there was a time when the delivery of mail was more important than next month's food rations, this was it.

The idea was Herbert's. He had become convinced that if I was to be left alone by the Third Reich, I needed more than just temporary protection. Because his chances with one Aryan parent were so much better than mine (no guarantees of course), he concocted a plan in which, if handled in a most delicate way, I could get one of those priceless Aryan parents, too. Since Mama had never been in Holland before, looking for a fake father here wouldn't have worked. Even if they had been selling Aryan fathers on the black market here — they sold just about everything else — names, dates, places and the authentic signature of a magistrate, including all official stamps, had to be legitimate. Secondly, since I didn't trust any of my Austrian countrymen, the only option left was to find one — a father — in Budapest. Sensible solution: have Mama write a true confessions letter to Aunt Shari, in Hungarian no less, asking her to please find the man Mama had had an affair with. The man who had fathered me. Her letter would have to say something like: Papa away with the merchant marine; Mama so lonely went to visit Aunt Shari, met handsome stranger; and so forth.

How to make it all sound perfectly believable without having my virtuous aunt suffer a heart attack just from reading such a letter was not an easy task. Somehow we had to make her understand that these days sexual morality did not save lives, but that one very broke but otherwise trustworthy Hungarian Aryan male just might. Naturally, he would have to be willing to swear in front of a magistrate, or the devil himself, that he was my father. This written charade was necessary because it wasn't unusual to find one's mail being tampered with. Thus, extreme caution was a must.

The first time Herbert talked to Mama about having me declared illegitimate, she slapped his face and walked out. That was right after my sewing job had fizzled out. She simply couldn't get herself to even make-believe that she had betrayed Papa, although she had to realize the necessity for such a lie better than anyone. I don't think infidelity was what was so upsetting to her, but rather the thought of tainting Papa's memory which she had kept alive, untouched and holy.

Mama did finally write to Aunt Shari, but not till after my arrest when, in spite of my successful escape, she realized that for her daughter the light at the end of the tunnel was getting dimmer all the time.

My arrest must have really frightened her. I found her sitting in the dining room one day, tears streaming down her face, composing the letter while mumbling that Papa would turn in his grave if he knew. I wanted to tell her that Papa, still so very much alive to both of us, was not in his grave but with us, the way he'd always been, and that he understood, the way he'd always understood everything. But I didn't tell her that because I knew it wouldn't change the way she felt about it. To Mama, this was the most difficult letter she ever had to write.

The same evening, I wrote to Ferry. Over the years we both had learned to read between the lines; and he more than anyone would know how to go about finding the right candidate. His feelings for me hadn't changed; but even if they had, I knew that he wouldn't let me down, would do everything possible to help me.

That's why I had to go home. I had to find out whether, for a change, some good news was coming my way. Luckily, my aunt and Ferry had gotten our letters and acknowledged that they understood. Ferry was doing everything, trying to find this lost relative for me. It would take a little time and I just had to be patient, wait it out . . . And so I waited.

In Ferry's last letter, which had arrived less than a week ago, he wrote that he had located the "relative" in question and that he was almost certain this was the one. He had to do a bit more checking and would know for sure in a few days. Recalling the flower man's warning, I couldn't help wondering whether I still had a few days. How many are a few?

With the tulips still in my arms, fed up with zigzagging around, trying to shake whoever my fatigued mind imagined might be following me, I reached my street.

↩

THERE'S NEVER BEEN A SINGLE MOMENT when the sight of Margit did not uplift my spirits. That afternoon when I found her waiting for me at the corner — something she'd never done before — I knew that this troublesome day was far from over. She'd been pounding the pavement for over an hour just to make sure that she could get to me before I reached my house.

As she embraced me warmly, she repeated the flower man's warning not to go home. She didn't mention the orphanage, only that Herbert had also been contacted and told for me to stay away. Even though none of them knew what was going on, Mama and Herbert agreed that I should stay at Margit's at least for tonight. And no, the letter we'd been waiting for hadn't come yet. There wasn't any mail today . . . Perhaps tomorrow . . .

Margit had taken the flowers from me, and after a coquettish thank-you for the benefit of any curious passerby, we went on together. With her arm around my shoulder and the last glow of the sinking sun behind us, we walked into her house. The staircase was dark. Most houses like this had their light switches at the bottom as well as the top of every flight. This one had the switches, but no light. Margit had taken all the bulbs out because she said she didn't want "them" to know that we were here.

Sixty-four stairs. After we had reached the first floor, my friend took off her shoes and had me do the same. "Less noise," she whispered.

Sometimes, in a weird but wonderful way, Margit would know what I was thinking. That's when she'd surprise me with an answer to a question I hadn't yet asked. Like just before we had reached her door and I had been wondering why Mama and Herbert hadn't peeked out the window so they could see me walking with Margit and know that I was fine. Before entering the house I had looked across, hoping to catch a glimpse of them, but the windows were closed and the curtains drawn. As if my thoughts had been written on my forehead, Margit muttered, "I told them not to peek, just in case someone's watching." She'd been really whispering. I'm not sure why. No one could hear us up there. She then wanted to know whether this new surge of interest by the Nazis in me personally had something to do with my work at the orphanage. I told her that the orphanage was being shut down and that I wasn't needed anymore. I said nothing about the children I had helped escape, nor Gus or the others. It was hard not telling the truth, not being able to confide in her, or my family, hard on me but safer for them.

We stood, shoes in hands, in the dark hallway — Margit, I'm sure, wondering what my secret was, and I more and more uncertain when or whether I could go home again.

Margit didn't use her key to open the door. She gently knocked three times, listened, then tapped her feet and knocked again. I assumed her latest lover, a lion tamer, was still in there, but when the door opened, instead of her golden-haired gorgeous lion tamer, I saw a tall, slender, golden-haired girl: Rainer.

We had met before. I didn't know much about her, but I liked her. She made me think of Lorelei — a siren of the Rhine in Germanic mythology whose singing lured sailors to shipwrecks. Not because Rainer lured sailors, but because of her thick, shimmering golden hair. She wore it loose and down to her waist, and it shone like fields of ripened maize. Rainer was earthy, completely uninhibited and marvelously funny. She was Margit's age and Amsterdamish through and through — very refreshing.

Inside Margit's room, in the tiny alcove by the window, there was another girl. She sat smoking a cigarette on one of the two chairs that made up the combined living and dining-room set with the table in between. The air-raid shades were drawn. Only the small blue lamp on Margit's miniature dresser was lit. The light bulb underneath the blue lamp shade was blue, and blue were the smoke rings the girl blew up to the blue, blue sky of Margit's painted ceiling. A sapphire room immersed in secrets.

I knew the other girl, too. Her name was Betty, and she and Rainer were best friends. Since Margit was everyone's best friend, it follows that she was their best friend, too. Actually, I thought it odd that Rainer and Betty were so close. They were completely different. Betty was haughty, self-centered. She too was beautiful, but unlike Rainer, Betty's whole life centered on her looks. Rainer's eyes were foxy brown with a touch of beryl green, Betty's large, dove gray and striking. She had a perfect nose, a perfect mouth and teeth, the perfect height and weight and the perfect hairdo. Never a nut brown hair out of place. Her posture, her manners and even the pitch of her voice were perfect. One could throw up, she was that perfect.

I didn't care for her, and I didn't trust her. I never could trust anyone who didn't show some emotions. Cool like a cucumber Betty. She did have a good head on her perfect shoulders, which she undoubtedly used much more than her heart. Her what's-best-for-Betty-attitude might have been quite useful these days; for her, that is.

I was a little surprised that Margit had invited them. If my presence here was to remain strictly *entre nous,* why this coffee klatch?

Time did not pass quickly. The conversation was empty talk. I so wished for this day never to have happened, wished that I could go back to the or-phanage, help more children, help myself. I knew many people who wished all day long, mostly for miracles. But in wartime one should never wish for anything one can't buy on the black market.

Later that evening, Margit produced sandwiches that were almost edible and a bottle of red wine that was almost drinkable. We, who knew Margit well, were very much aware that her own food rations always ended up in someone else's pocket. Margit wholly believed that others needed them more. The evening chattered on. The smoke-filled intimacy of the room left no space for privacy. Curfew, long before nightfall, came and went, and still there we were all together. By then it had become quite clear that Rainer and Betty were also spending the night. I couldn't figure out why. Surely no one was chasing them. Were they even Jewish? I hadn't thought so. "Are you?" I finally asked them straight out. Rainer said instantly, "Yes." Betty had to think about it — Betty never answered any question without first deliberating.

The wine had made me drowsy. Or was it because the window was shut? I couldn't inhale the clear night air with its fragrant scent of spring, could hardly make out the one sitting across from me. At last Margit lit a candle to clear away the smoke. Even so, I only could see the others' silhouettes.

The explosive ring from the doorbell downstairs came way past midnight. It wasn't the noise of the buzzer breaking the silence that scared me out of my wits but that it didn't stop. As though the chiming throat of it had gotten stuck or someone was leaning against it. "A drunk," Margit murmured, breathing much too heavily. "A drunk," echoed Rainer, hardly breathing at all. Betty blew out the candle, turned off the dim blue light, and said nothing. I, my hands pressed against my ears, tried despairingly to shut out the deafening din. My hands were shaking. That's no boozer, I said to myself, it couldn't be. Everyone knew that the swastika bar-crawlers had a curfew too.

I no longer know how long the four of us just sat, listening to the dispassionate bell. At some point Margit whispered, "Wim," Wilhelm, her fiancé. "It must be Wim! He probably forgot his key." I'm not sure about the other two, but I for one did not believe a word of it. If it was Wim, why did Margit whisper? And what was he doing out so late? How much Wim knew about Margit's private war against the evildoers is hard to say. Yet, he must have had, if not real proof, a mounting suspicion. Whether or not he believed in her magnificent sentiment and faith, he'd never let anyone hurt her.

It had stopped! At long last the terrifying din had stopped. The pin-drop silence that followed was numbing. What a long, frightful pause. Is this what it's like before a hurricane hits, before the crust of the earth swallows one up? I never heard the shuffling of feet downstairs, nor any movement coming from the back of the house, nor heels treading to the front door. Neither did the others. Yet, someone had unlocked the entrance door to let those night stalkers in. It wasn't till Margit, tiptoeing to her door, had opened it slightly to listen, that we heard muffled voices. Betty lit her last cigarette, announced that we wouldn't have to wait much longer. For what, she didn't say. Rainer, in one big swallow, gulped down another glass of that awful wine, muttering, "Dreadful, dreadful," leaving it up to us to figure out whether she had meant the wine or the uninvited.

Quite suddenly the muffled voices became frightfully loud and harsh. I couldn't make them out — not how many there were, or whom they belonged to. Whoever was down there kept on yelling, accompanied by a good deal of swearing. The shouting match, in Dutch, went on and on. Even though I hardly understood a word for all their screaming, my instincts told me that there wasn't a single drunken soldier or sailor amongst them. They knew which bell to ring, which house to come to, and whom to look for. They knew the truth which we'd kept hidden from one another.

It was the nerve-racking thump of boots stalking up the creaky stairs that put an end to the guessing game. If Margit's fiancé and his parents had tried to keep the uninvited from reaching our tower — and I'm convinced that they must have — their gallant attempt had not been successful. Yet Wim was not about to give up. Right on their heels he kept on screaming, until I thought for sure his lungs must burst. He told them over and over again that there was nothing but a broken staircase with loose boards and rusty nails up there, and that only he and his frightened parents were living in the house. They hollered back for him to shut up. Dear lovelorn boy. Brave Wilhelm, willing to risk his life to keep Margit from risking hers. I heard them curse the unlit staircase, the narrow steps not made for their big feet. I heard them curse their crummy flashlights for lack of brightness and poor range. I heard them stumble up, up the stairs, closer and closer, and when I didn't hear them anymore, I knew.

Knew the precise moment when the first one had reached the top of the stairs. I'd have known it even if he hadn't stamped his feet like a naughty child, even if Margit hadn't shut the door again. I could smell his breath through the cracks beneath the door, feel the room grow cold with icy fear and still catch the trembling echo of the hunters, their fists pounding the walls outside in search of the door.

"God damn the whole lot. Bastards, getting me out of bed for this!" one blared. "It's darker than hell up here. Hey, Jew, where are you? I'll find you. I'll find you."

The words, now quietly sardonic, made my skin crawl. *Do it already, do it!* my voiceless throat screamed.

"Come on down, what's the matter with you? Are you nuts?" One of the hunters had had enough. He had stayed on the floor below, letting his angry voice bounce up the stairs like exploding cannon balls. From way below, the third one, saying that he was getting sick of chasing Jews every night, bellowed that he was going home.

Then there was Wilhelm's voice repeating again that there wasn't anyone up there and wouldn't he rather come on down and have a drink instead. At the same time the sudden muted noise of thumps and crashes, like someone taking a nose-dive, filled my ears, followed by a thundering, "I think I broke my leg, God damn it!" The rest was drowned in harsh remarks, grunts and groans, and the heavy-footed movement of bodies. Moments later the downstairs door flew open and immediately slammed shut, leaving the four of us too stunned and startled to do or say anything at all. Frozen silhouettes in a frozen blue night.

When, in this frozen moment of time, the pulsating senses, however slowly, began to think, talk, feel and move again, I knew that I could never spend another night like this. Whether here or somewhere else, it wasn't the place but the waiting for footsteps night after night which would drive me stark raving mad. Like a prison without guards, yet under lock and key just the same, shut away from the world, alone or not, I'll surely break away . . .

How strange that I should not have given thought before that I myself might one day have to hide out for a long, long time. The absolute truth is it never occupied my mind. But now, out of the foggy twilight, filled with events I'd never quite understood, surfaced a new awareness and the realization that this was meant to be. How else would I have known that voluntary confinement was not for me?

I left to use the toilet and returned in time to hear Betty say, "That was close," and Rainer's throaty, "I hope the swine broke both of his legs. I just can't understand it. They couldn't have known about us." Which one of us did she mean? I finally got fed up with all that secrecy and said more than likely they had been looking for me. Margit nodded, and turning to Rainer and Betty, insisted they tell me why they had come, when they were leaving, and where they were going from here.

Rainer agreed that they should share their secret. In her bubbly, wisecracking way, she gave me a rundown of their forthcoming venture, talking about it with the enthusiasm and innocence of a child going on her first picnic. Reserved Betty was a bit more serious and naturally more deliberate in her account of it, but equally convinced that this opportunity would not come again. It had been tested, was foolproof and according to her not even

God Himself could talk her out of it. She finished by telling me that if I had any brains, I better get in on it, too.

The mood swing from half an hour ago to the moment when they confided in me was phenomenal. As if an unseen power had ripped away all fear, leaving only optimism and exhilaration. If, in the early evening, someone had told me that before the night was over, I would put my future into Rainer and Betty's hands, I would not have believed it. Yet, sure as fate, I did.

THEY LEFT THE NEXT MORNING, their spirits higher than mountain peaks, and I followed their trail with this brand-new excitement that only brand-new hope can bring. And would have followed them to the end of the world to reach a land not touched by war and persecution. Given my all and everything for that sweet smell of freedom.

It would change the lives of those close to me for a weary, long while, and for all eternity, forever irreversible, it surely changed mine

The real reason for Rainer and Betty's spending the night with Margit was Harry. Without Harry, they wouldn't be leaving. It was Harry, mastermind of a far-reaching Dutch underground, with ties to a Belgium underground, who was going to take them across the border to Belgium. From there, his Belgian counterpart would take them to Switzerland, where their prearranged entry was also assured. And it was Harry they were going to meet at 11:00 a.m. at a tavern located halfway between our street and the central railroad station. Since both girls lived too far away from their first rendezvous, they had thought it best to leave the day before and spend their last night with Margit. Also, they did want to say good-bye to her.

The girls could bring only one small overnight valise, but all the jewels and cash, foreign currency preferred, they could lay their hands on and carry. Furthermore, they each had to pay two thousand guilders to cover travel expenses, their false IDs, and other miscellaneous items. Cash and jewels were to be thought of as a precious survival kit. "If you have nothing to sell or barter with," Harry had told them, "you can't buy anything either."

Naturally, I was anxious to know how they had found out about Harry in the first place and what that ironclad proof they claimed to have was. How did they know that he and the whole deal were really on the up and up? Rainer did not mind my questions at all, but Betty was definitely annoyed.

Did I think that she could be duped that easily? Did I believe that she would hand over her money to just anyone, take such enormous risks because it sounded good? Never.

Then they explained that very close friends of theirs had heard about Harry through other friends who had gone with Harry, and everything had gone just great. After that, their friends went too. They made it safely to Brussels and were already on their way to Switzerland. I naturally asked how they knew that. They knew because Rainer and Betty had received a pre-arranged postcard with the prearranged coded message from their friends, just like they had received from their friends, and their friends before them. For that's how they had worked it out between themselves: Make up a simple code which only the girls and the friends who'd left knew, then wait for their handwritten postcard. If the message is correct, come.

Their friends had given Rainer and Betty Harry's telephone number and his first name only and briefed them regarding the money, jewels and such. The very last thing they had told the girls before escaping was to wait for their postcard before calling Harry. They'd done just that. Three days ago the postcard came, and three days ago, they'd phoned Harry. Betty boasted that they had even gotten two postcards, one from some small Belgian vil-lage and the other from Brussels. As soon they had the first one, they hustled up the money, dug up their own jewels, begged and borrowed a fair bit more from family and friends, and now, understandably nervous, were waiting to leave.

I got more edgy by the minute. Especially after I had seen and read, thanks to Betty's lighter, both cards from their friends. I probably drove them a little crazy asking the same things over and over again, ignoring the fact that they really didn't know very much since they hadn't met Harry yet.

Rainer, who had spoken to him on the phone, said that he wasn't much of a talker. He'd given them the date and where to be when, made sure that they knew about the money and valuables, asked their ages, heights, weights and coloring for their false IDs, and finished their talk with a half-jested warning not to be late. Long before daybreak, the four of us had made up a code for the girls to use when writing to me. And long before their meeting at the tavern, I left Margit's room at the top with Harry's phone number in my pocket and went home.

The news of my wanting to get out of Amsterdam, leave Holland alto-gether, almost three years after the invasion with the neighboring countries also occupied, was met by my family with lukewarm enthusiasm. "Whatever is best for you, *mein Kind,*" Mama said, looking glum. Mama always called me *mein Kind* when forced to rivet her attention on the uncertainties of a new situation. Herbert said nothing, just bit his lip, a sure sign that he was deeply disturbed. I don't know why I thought they would be as happy as I was. I guess Herbert just didn't want me to go anywhere without him, and Mama, well, could be she wondered whether she'd ever see the day when she could stop worrying about her worrisome child.

When Herbert realized that his bleeding lip was neither going to change my mind nor solve anything, he began reminding me how close I was to getting my papers. He also harped on all the running around Ferry must have done, plus all the money he must have paid for my new father. Didn't I think that in view of all this, I ought to wait a bit longer? And what about Mama? Had I forgotten how painful it had been for her?

No, I had not. I knew how much turning this lie into an unorthodox truth had cost her. How guilty she had felt and how this guilt kept torturing her. Yet, in spite of the pain, I'd been envious of her. Envious of her for having been young when there was still so much time for love. Frankly, I felt cheated. Why couldn't I have had the kind of love she and Papa shared? I was thinking of Ferry . . . too many good-byes . . . ends without endings . . . I thought of Herbert, too. Love does not grow when one's life is on constant alert.

We were all talked out. For the moment. I was certain that I wasn't the only one that hadn't gotten any sleep last night. I hadn't intended telling them about the unexpected scare last night and that I'd come within an inch of being hauled away again. I'd much preferred not mentioning that in my panic I couldn't even think about the hiding place inside the closet, the doggy door Margit had built, nor how trapped I had felt. But when, after we had rested, they still left it up in the air, I told them. Remembering that it took my arrest for Mama to go along with the counterfeit father, I knew that nothing short of a detailed account of this scary incident would do the trick. Their opposition melted away. All they asked was my promise to go with whatever came first. I agreed.

Meanwhile, I had to be tucked away somewhere. Stay out of sight completely. It was decided I should spend the days in our first-floor apartment and the nights in our guest rooms on the top third floor. Our landlord Robert and his sister occupied the second.

Both Mama and Herbert avoided referring to my third-floor accommodation as a hiding place. They understood how paranoid the word "hiding" could make me. Actually, it was quite nice up there. The room itself, all white, was bright and airy. It reminded me of where once, in another century, a young girl might have lain and dreamed a young girl's dreams.

Outside the window, facing south, was the roof. A flat roof. I could get out either through the window, which almost reached the floor, or through the door next to the staircase. I'm sure that the accessibility in itself was why I felt better up there than at Margit's. Margit's window was small, and stepping out meant falling three flights to the ground. It didn't connect to any roof; but mine did. A bell which hadn't been used since who knows when, yet was working just fine, would ring upstairs to warn me of strangers. I'm happy to say, it never rang. Except for one time when, in the early morning, I saw three Dutch NSP strutting like happy peacocks across the roof right past my window, I had no unwanted excitement. They never as much as glanced inside. Laughing and chattering like silly adolescents, their roof excursion had had nothing to do with duty or chasing Jews. They must have had some girlfriends or friendly girls some blocks away with whom they'd spent the night. In the crass light of morning, and being off base in more ways than one, these three clowns had evidently sought higher ground.

Herbert nearly dropped the breakfast tray when I told him about it. All in all, though, I spent some surprisingly peaceful times up there. Once in a while I would stay up late, wander into the large closet where my theater costumes were stored. Just counting my gowns, taking inventory of all my gorgeous costumes, satin and silk evening dresses, feather boas and petticoats, hats and ribbons, everything, made me feel that the stage I so loved, with its fancy masquerade, wasn't really that far away. I'll never think of my theater costumes as just things to hide behind. For me, the echo of the plays and tunes, caught in a shoulder strap or velvet fold, will linger on.

I don't know who all made contributions to my bid for freedom, but the money kept rolling in. When those we knew best, and trusted the most, found out what it was for, they also brought their hidden jewels, dollars and pounds for me to take along. "Take it to Switzerland and keep it for us," they said. "That way we'll know that we'll have something left when the war is over. Take it, please, just take it." After a few days, I had the not so small fortunes of at least half a dozen people, not counting Mama and Kate. Mama gave me everything she still had from Papa and Grandma; Herbert's mother,

her exquisite pearls and diamond engagement ring; Kate, who came after Mama had phoned her, entrusted her beautiful ruby bracelet to me.

At a time when lovely picture postcards were almost a thing of the past — who still took vacations? — one arrived. It had a photograph of trees in bloom. I had been holding the card in my hand without daring to look at where it came from or what it said. When after a while I still hadn't read it, Herbert asked whether I was waiting for the blossoms to fall off. Mama, not paying attention to either of us, simply declared that it couldn't be from Budapest, since neither Aunt Shari or Ferry had ever sent picture postcards. She was right.

The caption on the back read: "Springtime at the park in Brussels," and it came from Rainer and Betty. In Rainer's handwriting, signed by both, she wrote, "It took nine days to get here. Weather perfect, not a drop of rain, please write." The code word was "write"; it simply meant come.

After the three of us had read and studied it several times and after numerous "Let's wait for the next card" cautioning pleas from Mama, which I ignored, I phoned Harry. I did not mention my name, I only told him that I was a friend of Rainer and Betty and that they were expecting me. Harry said, "Fine," then wanted to know whether I had the money and valuables ready and whether I was ready. After I said yes, he asked my physical description and told me what to bring: one overnight case, one change of clothing, nightwear, toiletries, and so forth. I knew it by heart, had packed it in my mind a hundred times each day, each night. Also, I had to make it look like I was only going away for the weekend. I knew that, too.

I was going to meet Harry at 11:00 a.m. at the Blue Lantern Café by the waterfront, the day after tomorrow, one week short of three years after the invasion of Holland and ever so many calendar months away from the end of the war. I wasn't quite sure how I felt about our conversation or Harry himself. It wasn't what I had expected, even though I really didn't know what to expect. Perhaps I thought he'd be a little less matter-of-fact and not quite so detached. His unmistakably common dialect as if he himself belonged on the waterfront also threw me. But deep inside, I knew that all that mattered was that the time had come.

The day before I left, we all went a little bit crazy. Beginning with Mama, who insisted on going to the main post office to make absolutely sure that the Hungarian papers weren't lying around somewhere, to landlord Robert who'd wanted to throw a going-away party for me. Margit wanted me to take her guitar, which she said I could either play or hock. In any event, Margit considered it the perfect instrument for deception. She was absolutely convinced that a girl traveling with a guitar would never arouse suspicion. I did not take it. Toni brought a heavy leather case full of rare old coins belonging to her foster parents, unfortunately much too heavy to carry, and gems. By the time afternoon rolled around, with all the riches that had been brought to me spread out on the dining-room table, it looked like a pirate's treasure. I kept wondering where to put it all.

Luckily, Kate came again, and just in time, too. She made little pouches, filled them with gems and skillfully sewed them into the lining of my coat, mostly on the bottom where the hemline was. The money, she sewed into my inside pockets. We had talked about my family and friends also leaving, once I had made it, long before the postcard had arrived, but never got beyond let's wait and see. Now, with actual proof right before their eyes, it suddenly became quite real and astoundingly exciting. Everyone wanted to go. After Herbert had phoned several friends and his parents to tell them that the waiting was over and I'd be "joining the girls," a kind of grapevine frenzy broke loose. Our phone never stopped ringing — friends, their friends, friends of friends, including those in no immediate danger, all wishing me luck. All wanting me to know that they hoped I would write real soon. "Write," the same magic word on another magic card . . .

I had looked back only once, had waved good-bye to the faces in the window, then quickly crossed the street and turned the corner.

Boundless Borders, Unending Journey

∽ EIGHT

IT WAS PRECISELY 10.55 A.M. when I reached the Blue Lantern. The place itself, a mixture of folk coffeehouse and tavern, was quite ordinary, its patrons consisting of a few old beer-drinking card-playing men, checkers players and one gray-haired woman reading a newspaper. I seated myself at the first table, my eyes focused on the entrance, ordered coffee from a limping, uninterested waiter, and waited. Kate had done a superb job of sewing gems and foreign bills into the lining of my coat; still, I felt weighted down and clumsy. I had tried not to let it bother me while walking, had tried to tell myself that my feathery gray woolen coat, cut full and loose, was ideally fitting for the occasion. It did not show any bulges and really wasn't all that heavy. Just knowing what I carried was enough to make me feel self-conscious. The money for Harry, plus a lot more guilders and Belgian francs, I had put into separate envelopes in my outside coat pockets.

The café, situated halfway between my house and the central railroad station, faced one of the many canals Amsterdam is famous for. But in spite of its being a beautiful spring morning, there were no tourist boats riding the waterways through the city. It had taken me fifteen minutes to reach the café, more than enough time to wonder why Harry hadn't asked me for a photograph since every identification card had to have one, and he had not wanted me to carry mine. "Nothing they can trace back to you," he'd cautioned. "You'll get your new one at the Blue Lantern."

At eleven sharp, a man in his early thirties, of medium height, stocky, with reddish-blond hair and a reddish complexion, walked in. Without a moment's hesitation he walked to my table and sat down. Harry! He did not say hello, he didn't nod, just called the waiter and ordered a beer. He then pushed his chair opposite mine, and while looking directly at me asked me for the two thousand guilders. "Under the table," he whispered, putting both elbows on top of the red-checkered tablecloth. I was still reaching for my right-hand pocket when I noticed that Harry's arm had already disappeared from the table top. His broad Amsterdamish speech matched the quickness of his moves.

Harry undoubtedly was a pro. He knew that I'd be asking questions and the questions I'd be asking, quite obviously the very same he had been asked and had answered before. Only the names of the friends one inquired about were different, and Harry, being a pro, remembered them all.

When I quizzed him about Rainer and Betty, he said they were doing great and were eager to see me again. And when I asked whether they were already in Switzerland, Harry's reply was, "Not yet." Both girls were still in Brussels, and while waiting for me, were having a ball. I would be seeing them in a few days.

At one point Harry reached for my hands, held them for a moment, and I thought, what a kind gesture. While I thought of it as a sign of friendship and understanding, he thought of it as the best way to slip me my new ID — after I handed him the envelope with the two thousand guilders under the table, which he made disappear without my ever seeing where it went.

As for the picture on my new fake ID, Harry said that it was a very good likeness of me, matching the description Rainer, Betty and I had given him. I couldn't prove him right or wrong for he wouldn't let me look at it but made me drop it quickly into my purse. He then briefed me on my new identity, using short abrupt sentences: My new name was Gerda Van Raal, my destination Roosendaal, the nearest town to the Belgian border; I was supposedly visiting my grandmother there; my birth place was Groningen, but I had been living in Amsterdam; my profession, student.

After this introduction to my new self, Harry told me that I would be traveling by train and that we'd better head for the station right now. He pushed away his chair, left a handful of change on the table, motioned me to get up, then took my arm, my suitcase and we scurried out.

I had a lot more questions for him, important ones like: How long a trip? My grandmother's name? What about the signature on my new ID? And many more. But Harry just wanted to get to the station. He kept assuring me that once on the train, I could stop worrying altogether. After we had walked a couple of blocks, Harry suggested that I let him hold on to the other money, just in case we were stopped. It never occurred to me to ask why he thought it would be safer with him; I just handed it over, the bulging envelope with all the guilders and francs. It disappeared exactly as fast as the first one. Except this time, at least, I saw where it disappeared to — into the inside pocket of his raincoat.

His arm in mine, not unlike a pair of honeymooning newlyweds, we walked to the station. Passing other couples, a curious thought came to mind. Those others, also walking arm-in-arm, had surely known each other for a time, while I, less than two weeks ago, had no idea that the man at my side existed. A mere twenty minutes ago, I had not yet laid eyes on him. But now this Harry, this stranger, was carrying my suitcase, holding my money, holding my life in his hands.

The station was buzzing. I couldn't remember having ever seen such activity, as though everyone, with or without travel permit, was fleeing the city. Harry dragged me through the noisy crowd all the way to the middle of the platform. He then stopped short in front of a tall, skinny man who was standing next to a nervous-looking group of people who seemed as though they'd much rather be somewhere else. The skinny man came immediately toward us, greeting Harry with a familiar slap on the back, followed by a big sigh of relief, saying how glad he was that we had come in time. Harry then handed me my suitcase, and the two of them disappeared into the crowd.

I stood, my back pressed against the wooden side wall of a kiosk, with my case, but without my travel permit, train ticket, or my money. I was at a complete loss what to do next. After some exasperating lapse in time, a most distinguished-looking silver-haired, older man, part of the group I'd noticed, came to assure me that John — "He's Belgian, you know" — would be back momentarily. "We don't know which train to take either," the elegant gentleman said.

Eventually, they did come back — Harry to wish me luck and fortyish John with his unmistakable Flemish accent to tell me which train to catch and where to get off. After that Harry disappeared again, this time for good.

John, suddenly beside me, pressed two envelopes into my hand, which unfortunately were not the ones with my money, but fortunately did contain my travel permit and ticket. He then whizzed me past the distinguished older man, saying that we had better not risk traveling together and that the train pulling out in front of me was the one I should be on.

John's shout, "We'll be right behind you!" still rang in my ears when I was either pushed or swept up in the turbulent wave of people that stormed the train. I was on it, but not John or the others. It was packed, not a single seat to be had, with hardly enough room to stand up. My suitcase between my legs, I stood as firmly as the circumstances permitted for what seemed to me a very long time.

The locomotive puffed its way through villages and towns, through fields and meadows. It made whistle-stops, rolled in and out of stations, with me just trying to hang on. While I was taking a mental inventory of this situation, I was already bracing myself for the next round of unexpected events. Thus far I had not been able even to glance at my new ID, a chilling realization in view of the mass uniformed war-wagers surrounding me in this railroad car. Then there was my money, by now Harry's money unless he'd given it to John, which, with the Belgian nowhere about, wasn't anything to cheer about either. I had only a few bills, all Dutch, and some change in my purse. Enough for a cup of tea and a sandwich, not enough to get me back home again.

Somewhere along the way the conductor came and asked for my ticket. While clipping my ticket, he had said for me to change. I wasn't able to hear him. Between the noisy rumbling of the train and the clash of voices all around me, his words were drowned out. John, I was certain, had said nothing about changing trains. Even so, I boxed my way to the end of the car where the conductor was. "Where?" I asked again.

"Next stop," he answered with a friendly nod. "Get off the next stop."

It was a very small station. The passengers who'd gotten off with me hurried to the exit sign and one by one dispersed. It seemed that I was the only one here destined for Roosendaal. With my suitcase and my almost empty purse, I sat down on a bench. I sat and I sat.

Once, a train sped through, and for a fast minute there the little station, hooded in black smoke, was filled with the resonant rumble of weighty wheels riding hard on the patient tracks. I could feel the bench and my suitcase, caught up in the vibration, tremble in rhythmical unison.

My eyes were riveted on the shiny buttons on the stationmaster's coat, the only new and shiny thing on the uniform or the man wearing it. "It's late again," his used up voice complained.

"The train to Roosendaal. Is that the one?" I asked, low-voiced and timid.

"All of them. These days it's a miracle if they come at all. They keep rerouting them but never tell me nothing no more. Well, they don't have to. I'm not stupid, I know what's going on. In the last week, only three passenger trains stopped here. I hear it's worse in the big cities. Military, you know. They need them for the military transports, that's what they say." He mumbled something into the stubby bristles of his unshaven face that could have been a prayer. "You know what I wish, little lady," coming closer, he said trustingly, "I wish them military ones a permanent departure, them and them others too! You know what I mean, don't you?"

"Sure do," I concurred, glad for the interruption and conversation. He belched, sighed, shrugged his sagging shoulders, "You'll just have to be patient and hope for the best. We all do." He trudged away.

People came. Most of them were farmers on their way to the city. The women carried baskets, the men burlap sacks. I couldn't help wondering if perhaps one of my children had ended up there. Finally the train, with a thunderous roar, burst into the station, stopped and almost simultaneously, with the wheels still squeaking, started again. Only the farmers, obviously familiar with the routine, were ready.

"Roosendaal?" I asked a burly young man who rushed by me carrying a sack.

"Yes, miss," and off he went to the front of the train. Mindless, I ran after him.

If someone had asked me then what I planned to do once I got there, I would have had no answer. The stationmaster had bellowed his last all-aboard when, still racing after the young man, I felt myself being lifted up and onto one of the railroad cars—John!

I didn't know whether to slap or kiss him. I was both relieved and furious. I felt like crying, but most of all I felt like strangling Harry. John made a serious effort to explain this unfortunate foul-up. The Belgian's vocabulary was full of Flemish slang expressions which made understanding him an undertaking all by itself. To boot, he prided himself on his sense of humor, which consisted of a crowlike chuckle after every few words, meant no doubt to raise my spirits. It did no such thing.

What had happened was that John and the others had missed the train, forcing John to send me solo into the unknown. John's account of it was that the trouble began when, having elbowed his way to the front of a rail-road car, sure that the group was "right behind" him, he had heard one of them shout: "Stop, please stop. My wife is missing!" Just then the train pulled out, without anyone knowing whether or not the missing wife and their eight-month-old baby girl were on it. John claimed that the man started punching him, screaming that his wife could not be on the train. John proudly displayed a bloody lip, allegedly a souvenir from the dis-traught husband, in case I didn't believe him. I actually enjoyed seeing it. Evidently the little woman had never been on her own before, and—said the husband—she was sure to panic.

Trying to interrrupt John, who hadn't chuckled once while telling this story, was totally impossible. He kept giving details, how the husband Bernie carried on about the baby having been cranky all morning and how miser-able and frightened his wife Rebecca had been. More than once Bernie had picked up his bags and made for the exit. Whenever John went after him, Bernie would drop the luggage on John's feet. Mostly, however, he prayed that Rebecca was not on the train. Finally, when asked why he was so paranoid about her, Bernie showed John the tickets — his and hers. He had both. All she had was her new ID, most likely the baby and a couple clean diapers." How far do you think she'll get on two diapers?" Bernie had hissed.

And that was when the silver-haired gentleman's wife made a dash for the ladies' room, and sure enough whom did she find but Rebecca, diapering her baby. At this point in John's story, I would have liked to drop a suitcase on someone's feet.

At best, it was too vivid a reminder of how easy it was for something to go wrong, for everything to go wrong. What was next?

Next was that we did make it all the way to Roosendaal, arriving there in the early evening. Considering that the distance between Amsterdam and Roosendaal is something like seventy-five miles, the journey should have taken about an hour. I'm still amazed that I didn't ask myself what kind of crazy detour we were on. What had happened in the seven hours between Amsterdam and the border town?

Once we were all together with no more trains to catch for a while, John introduced me to the others. Not till then had I seriously thought of them as going my way, too. We shook hands, smiled and wished each other luck. The little mother, Rebecca, oblivious to anything not directly involving husband or baby, was exactly as hubby had said she was: naive, vulnerable, shy and nervous. Slim, with long brown wavy hair and large brown eyes, she had even features, a pale complexion and a pale, childlike voice. I don't believe she ever realized the trouble she had caused. It was instantly clear to me that her husband Bernie had more than one baby to worry about. Except for being extremely high-strung and a chain smoker, he was really quite nice. Their baby, little Erika, was the ultimate proof of how moronic Hitler's race theory was. Erika had what Hitler hailed as the true Aryan look: sun-kissed blond hair, cornflower blue eyes, an impeccable nose, and the cheeks of a cherub. This beautiful doll, who looked as if she was made of the finest bone china, resembled her father, and like him was terribly restless.

Little Erika, needing constant attention, became the focal point of our group. It meant taking turns carrying her and trying to get her to go to sleep. No one had said that we had to, we just did.

There were six of us adults. Bernie, and his wife Rebecca; the De Hartogs — the silver-haired gentleman with his silver-haired wife, who were about the kindest and most gentle people I could have wished to share this strange journey with. And then Millie, a homely spinster, a fourth-grade teacher in her late thirties, average in looks, brains and wit.

John, who had instructed us not to crowd together while walking through town, stuck to me like glue. I didn't mind his carrying my suitcase or his jolly mood, I didn't even mind his sweet-talking drivel, but when he started to grope me, I got mad. He said it was his nature to be affectionate. I told him nature had nothing to do with it and he better mind his own business. He said I was his business, which I took as the perfect opportunity to ask him where Harry and my money were. Amazing how fast his bony fingers let go of my waistline and how quickly his wandering arm got back on course. Physically, he reminded me of a contortionist — double-jointed, lanky, bouncy and elastic — which matched his double talk. After having asked him for the fourth time where Harry and my money were, we actually engaged in a dialogue, sort of.

"Why did Harry skip?"

"Whaa?"

"You heard me. Why did he run out on me?"

"Who?"

"Harry!"

"Why don' you ask him?"

"He isn't here, that's why I'm asking you!"

"He never go more than the station. He work his end, I work mine. You don' need Harry. You got me!"

"Who's got my money?"

"Whaa?"

"My money! Who's got my money?"

"Whaa money? I don' know nothin' of no money."

"I gave him two envelopes full of Dutch and Belgian bills!"

"Why you give him this?"

"He asked me to. He said they were safer with him, that's why!"

"I know nothin' of no money!"

"You're sure?"

"Sure I'm sure, I'm always sure. You stick wit' me, we go dancing tomorrow night in Brussels, jus' you and me."

"What about Rainer and Betty? I want to see them."

"Tomorrow, you see them tomorrow, everything tomorrow! We go dancing, you, me. Everyone go dancing . . . tomorrow!"

This time it was I who thought it best not to pursue things any further. John's biggest advantage over us was his accent. He knew that we had trouble understanding him. Whenever we asked something he didn't care to answer, he'd either play dumb or claim he had told us that already and we were the ones not paying proper attention.

"At least he smiles," Mr. De Hartog would say cheerfully. "Better than having to deal with a grouch. Besides, he's all we've got. I'm sure he's harmless. He just likes to show off a bit. He's Belgian, you know." The nice gentleman kept making this distinction as though it was of crucial importance. His wife called John our saviour.

It was dinnertime for the people of Roosendaal. The stores were already closed, and except for a few men and women sitting around the fountain in the middle of the town square, everyone appeared to be at home. The men, in working clothes, smoked meerschaum pipes; the woman, plump and middle-aged, just sat, looking relaxed and a bit sleepy. Our footsteps echoed on the cobblestones, causing one of the women to tilt her head in a listening position as if she had expected the sound alone to tell her who we were. She stared at me and after me as we passed. It seemed odd that we should be walking through the middle of town instead of sticking to side streets and keeping out of sight. Perhaps it was a shortcut?

The streets scrubbed clean, the houses neat and cozy, gave one the impression of a place forgotten by war. Yet it couldn't possibly be, not that close to the border. Finally, the town lay behind us. John had insisted that we all walk slowly. "Pretend you're tourists," he had said. "Take in the sights. You can't race through the streets like someone's chasing you. Besides, we got lots of time." Then, after a long pause, "We won't cross until midnight anyhow."

This statement got even the kind and patient De Hartogs upset. John answered their anxious queries with, "Don't you worry, it's in the bag."

One of the few things John did tell us was that the border was approximately seven miles from Roosendaal. Whether this meant from the center of town or the outskirts, he kept to himself. Whatever it was, seven miles after such a frazzling day was a long, long way to walk for any of us. We were all exhausted. Still, we walked, on a wide country road with grazing fields filled with cattle on either side as far as the eye could see.

Darkness fell. We walked. A tiny bit of moon shone down on us. We walked. Millie carried the baby. Little Erika woke, cried, fell asleep again. We walked. Later on Mrs. De Hartog carried her, then Bernie, then me.

It was eerie with no one about on that wide and empty road. No one but the cows in the fields and us. After we had walked a long stretch, we stopped to rest. John, handing out candy bars, said we'd get real food later on. I was so hungry I almost ate the paper too. Hungry and weary. Next to me the De Hartogs, his arm around her shoulder, her head resting on his chest, looked pretty beat. "And this is how their golden years begin," I thought, "on a deserted road, running away like thieves in the night . . ."

It was getting chilly. Fog was rolling in, sucking up the fields on either side of the road, blanketing the cows till not even their silhouettes were visible anymore. Only their long, deep-toned moos, sweeping through the air, bore testimony that living things were out there. We moved on. Because of the fog we stuck closer together, drawing comfort from the nearness of each other's footsteps, from the quiet sound of each other's breath.

The wind came, a cold but light and playful wind. At times it blew the fog away letting us see the road ahead and the big sky above. That's when a crescent moon, imbedded in feather pillow clouds, dispelled the darkness for a time. At one point John told us to get off the road and into the ditch below. He slithered like an eel ahead of me, grabbed the baby and then helped me down. Unless one was standing right on the edge of the road, one couldn't see the ditch below, nor the road from the ditch. John wanted me to "stay put," to keep the baby quiet and wait for his signal to move on. Nobody else came down. I told myself that the others were probably holing up at the other side. I also tried to find an explanation of why, after all that time, John now wanted us to stay out of sight, when we hadn't met a soul since we'd left Roosendaal.

It was exasperating having to keep on guessing why our fearless leader did what he did. Under the best of circumstances, a ditch is an awful place to "stay put" in. The earth was damp and muddy from the last rain. No matter how hard I tried to make the baby and myself comfortable, in the dispiriting expectation of a long wait, it was virtually hopeless. The mud stuck to my shoes and coat, and the baby, completely worn out and sensing my tension, screamed her lungs out. I held her close, let her pull my hair and chew my silk scarf. I also tried humming Brahms lullaby, but that didn't work either. It was truly miserable. In a short time my right arm went to sleep, which is more than I can say for baby Erika; she never did. How much time we wasted "staying put" was no more clear to me than why we went down there in the first place.

The signal finally came in the form of a long, high-pitched whistling sound followed by two, long *pssts*, and at last John himself appeared. Lying flat on his stomach, with his lower part on the road above, his upper part hanging down, he looked like he'd been sawed in half by a disgruntled es-capee. He chuckled, which in this position sounded like he was choking up the candy bars.

"It's almost time," he murmured. "Walk a hundred feet but stay down low, then climb up, I'll help you. Don't forget the baby." And his chuckle was back. How could I walk a hundred feet and at the same time stay down? And how the hell am I supposed to know what's a hundred feet? "Count," he called. "*Een, twee, dree.* Stay on your hands and knees."

The height of irony was that it was this ridiculous crawling on all fours, with my coat dragging in the mud, which stopped Erika's crying. I was cer-tain I'd been crawling much more than a hundred feet before I heard John's whispered order to stop. He slithered down, took the baby from me, and was back on the road again in no time at all. Practice, I thought, he must have had a lot of practice doing this. I was the last one up. The others were al-ready back on the road. Facing the direction we had come from, they stood like rooted shadows, silent and motionless. Perhaps with only a few more steps to go before leaving their homeland, they wanted to look back once more, needed to say one more good-bye to all they had to leave behind. I so hoped it was not second thoughts, faintheartedness or regrets, for their sakes as well as mine.

"What I want you to do now," John said, breaking the silence, "is listen to me very carefully and do exactly what I tell you to do." The rooted shadows slowly turned, formed a circle around John, and listened. "What I want you to do is pick up your bags and form a line. One behind the other. When I tell you to start walking, you start walking straight ahead. Not too fast, not too slow, normal like. Don't look up, don't look down, don't look sideways. Just walk. Don't talk, don't do nothin' else but walk."

He then handed the baby to Bernie and told him that he was to be second in line. Mr. De Hartog would be last and I first, behind John. Without a word between us, we lined up. John gave us a quick inspection, glanced at his watch, nodded twice, as if he was counting, said, "Go," and marched off. I followed on his heels, clutching my suitcase, glad I had something to hold on to.

What I remember most about the last twenty feet before crossing that night was recalling how many borders I had crossed already. Same borders, same reason . . .

∽ NINE

IT ROSE OUT OF THE FOG like the backdrop of a stage set, visible only when one was practically on top of it. There it was, no more than an arm's length away from me. The guardhouse. This was it!

The heavy lowered guardrail stretching across the road with its small opening next to the post looked unconnected, as though it were suspended in midair. A soldier stood in front of the guardhouse. He seemed to be expecting us. John motioned for me to stop, but he kept on walking. When he had reached the soldier, he too stopped. The two men, facing each other, either knew one another or knew of each other. I could not hear what was being said, but I did see John take a fat roll of bills from his pocket and hand it to the soldier, who seemed to be expecting it. He shoved the money into his pocket and then opened the rail.

John motioned for us to walk through. For a fraction of a moment, while we passed through one by one, I saw the soldier's face. Young, I thought, quite young. Hardly old enough to shave. The uniform he wore was German. I wondered whether occupied borders were always guarded by occupied forces or whether the Germans didn't trust the Dutch and Belgians enough to let them guard their own borders. The soldier in the guardhouse made me think of Soldier Resnick, who had stood watch for me that night in the theater. He too had taken money, he too had been so very, very young. From now on I'll call every soldier I meet Resnick, and maybe one day I'll meet one who doesn't take money to save Jews.

It was the same road. The same fields and the same moos breaking the silence, just like those on the other side. This guardhouse, and the German soldier, was all that separated the two countries. A bit of a letdown after all we had to go through to get here. Being the first one to cross, I was ahead of the others. After a few steps, I stopped and waited for them to catch up. At that moment the only thing I wished for was a slight shift in geography. Something that would make the border I had just crossed Swiss instead of Belgian. It wasn't that I didn't like the Belgians or was overly fond of the Swiss. On the contrary, it was a simple matter of wanting to leap ahead, of wanting to be where I yet had to go.

The others were hugging each other and John, completely ignoring the fact that this was an occupied country, too. True, rumor had it that life for Jews was supposedly easier here; thanks to their king's quick action in destroying all documents before the invasion, a lot of them were still walking about and working out in the open without a hitch. Their new papers were completely authentic except for a slight change in religion, which understandably had to be a different persuasion. Of course not everyone was that lucky: the Orthodox Jews didn't fare well at all, and then there were those who got turned in by their very best friends.

John had told us that we could get the right kind of papers in Brussels and just stay there instead of going on to Switzerland.

"It's less than a mile," John announced. He had put his arm around my waist again.

"What is?" I asked, trying my best to ignore his hand.

"The house you stay in tonight, that's what. You get good food and good rest there. See, I told you everything okay. Everything in the bag."

Bernie had come to thank me for looking after the baby while we were all stuck in the ditch. The perfect opportunity, we thought, to question this Belgian Don Juan about the reason for that. Bernie demanded an immediate explanation and got it: Patrols. Just as well we didn't know sooner. Every so often, John said, without anyone really knowing why, two uniformed Germans on bikes would show up at the guardhouse. They apparently only appeared when clouds hung low and fog blanketed the earth. They never bothered to shoot the breeze with their comrade standing watch, did not waste time just hanging around. They were on patrol, patrolling the land their Führer had stolen, piercing the darkness in search of . . . what? Us? Someone like us. When they were done, said John, the two of them would disappear again. Because they had never shown up before ten-thirty nor after a quarter to midnight, and because Soldier Resnick had warned John to always stay out of sight during that time, just in case, we had to tough it out in the ditch. John had never met up with them, nor was he anxious to do so, but trusting the guard, he heeded his warning.

John's repeated assurance of "not much farther" finally became reality. We left the seemingly forever road and turned into a winding byway. It wasn't quite as wide or smooth as the one we'd trodden on for those last stressful hours. I could feel pebbly gravel under my feet. It was just an ordinary road leading to a large stone and brick farmhouse.

The woman who opened the door for us was like the land this house stood on — timeless, weather-beaten, a bit cracked and worn, but sturdy, enduring and proud. Earth Mother. Even her thick blackberry hair, pulled back straight and tied in a bun, reminded me of rich, dark, shimmering soil. The kind that makes everything grow. She was big-boned, had broad but pleasant features. Her very large feet stuck out underneath her long, dark frock, barely leaving the floor when she walked, as though they never wanted to lose touch with the ground underfoot and the land she was born on. She did not speak to us, but her face smiled and bade us welcome.

We had entered the kitchen. Though we never got to see any other part of the house, life away from the fields was clearly lived in here. This was home. I'd never been inside a farmhouse, knew absolutely nothing about kitchens; yet this one bewitched me. It was a place that made one instantly feel whole again and safe, a place that made one think of simpler times. Perhaps it was the soothing sound of the crackling fire in the red brick hearth and its flame-colored fire dance that made me feel so warm and glassy calm. Perhaps it was the myrrh of pinecones next to the firewood, the pretty sight of the burnished, glimmering copper pots and skillets on the wall, or the fragrant lavender hyacinths and pungent white-clustered caraways on the windowsills which filled my senses with such peaceful euphoria. If it hadn't been for the irresistible smell of freshly baked bread and the compelling lure of food, I could have drifted off to sleep.

This was a place that had known no changes and didn't want any. A place where the same old handmade table with the same old handmade benches stood as they had always stood. Faded pictures on the walls, just like the seasons, were as much of yesterday as they were of now and tomorrow. Even the complacent-looking folksy man in his squeaky rocking chair by the fire was of yesterday, now and tomorrow. He wore striped overalls over a plaid shirt, smoked a tobacco-stained snuff-colored pipe that matched his tobacco-stained snuff-colored hands. Whether he was Earth Mother's husband, father or brother, I do not know. He was as old as the fields he plowed and as young as the earth he nurtured.

The table, in the middle of the room, had been set for us with Delft dinnerware. Platters with thick slices of succulent ham, mouth-watering sausages, a generous variety of wonderful cheeses the likes of which I hadn't seen or tasted since who knows when. Warm loaves of crusty, delectable bread and two large tureens of steaming hot soup. Homemade. "Fit for a king," as Papa would say.

I ate as though this had been my first meal ever — or last. We all did. Not for a moment did I wonder where all those culinary riches came from. It was hardly a secret that war-wagers always robbed and plundered the cities first. Long after city folk had sold their last possessions for a bit of food, farmers still had a good supply stored away. Their cupboards were rarely bare. Thank heaven for that.

I wrote my first card to Mama and Herbert after I'd eaten a piggish amount of everything twice, with the exception of ham which I had thrice. John had given us the cards before we started the feast, saying that if we wrote them tonight, we could post them first thing in the morning. Of course everyone wrote. Thinking that I best stay clear of any innuendos, I simply borrowed the clever phrase: "Having a wonderful time, wish you were here." Knowing full well that all Mama and Herbert would be waiting to see was the word "write," I naturally emphasized it by underlining it and adding "please!" When it would reach them, nobody knew.

We never really got to stretch out or lie down on anything vaguely resembling a bed. Since there was nothing we could do about it, we unanimously agreed to make the best of it and put our heads on the table, using our coats as pillows. Not too shabby, considering that my head was resting on a fortune; theirs too, probably!

The one who positively lucked out was baby Erika, who got to sleep in a fine cradle-rocker. For warmth, Earth Mother had put her close to the crackling fire in the hearth near the man in his squeaking rocking chair. I watched them for a while. Watched him put out his snuff-colored pipe and place it in his pipe tray. Watched him stroke her tiny fingers with the gentleness of a delicate dove. Watched him watching her so as not to miss a single stir. "He'll watch her all night," I thought.

The kerosene lamps were hardly flickering anymore. They'd been burning most of the night and were done for. So were the dancing flames in the hearth. Just enough left to keep it glowing and warm. Around me the soundless breathing of silent silhouettes, nestled like lovebirds together in pairs, who had entered the kingdom of Morpheus.

The next thing I knew, our witless leader John was blaring out: "Rise and shine." It was 5:00 a.m. I managed to open my eyelids just wide enough to see a dim flashlight shining down at me. "Time to go," John announced in an annoyingly cheerful tone. "Everyone outside waiting for you. You sure get good snooze."

I tried raising my head, tried sitting up straight, I even tried unclenching my hands clutching my coat, but my body refused to move.

"Want to miss the train," John, deliberately flippant, scoffed into my ear. When I didn't respond, he unclenched my hands and pulled my head-resting cushion-coat from under me. My arms dropped down, my head hit the table and instantly like a rubber ball bounced back again, causing my torso to jerk backward, pushing the bench I'd been sitting on away from me. As I struggled onto my feet, I became aware that they were unquestionably still asleep.

With my numb feet dragging as though shackled together, I followed John and his weak flashlight out of the unlit kitchen into the hall. The group, quietly sitting on their bags and cases, seemed not a bit upset that I had kept them waiting, since they themselves could hardly keep their eyes open. There was no talking, no questions asked, no comments made.

I didn't get to sit down again, didn't get to do anything but quickly retrieve my coat, grab my suitcase and go outside. It was pitch dark and piercingly cold.

"Good heavens," a shivering voice called out. "I thought this was supposed to be spring! Are we in Iceland?"

John assured the voice that we were not and that a little nip in the air was just what we needed to help us wake up.

It wasn't till we were back on the winding byway again that one by one they began talking about the farmer and the prodigious woman in the long, dark frock. Everyone was praising their generosity and kindness, saying how wonderful it was just knowing that people like that still existed. The more they talked, the sorrier I felt for having missed thanking them. How very different their lives were from mine. No frills, no extremes. Theirs was a strange, curiously unassailable, yet beautiful world. If only my orphanage children could have come to stay here.

If only my feet wouldn't drag so much. I didn't dare ask John how far to the station, how many trains we'd still have to take, or anything. He'd either lie or tell me the truth. I didn't know which of the two I would have hated more.

On the main road, an amazing surprise was waiting for us. At first, because of the darkness, we couldn't make out what it was. I thought it looked like a huge cloud that had dropped down to earth by mistake and that's what I told my companions. But Bernie said that I must be dreaming, it couldn't be that, for he was sure he'd seen wheels. As it turned out, he was quite right about the wheels — there wrapped in the mantle of night stood an old draft horse harnessed to a wagon full of hay, ready and waiting to take us to the station. What a splendid idea. No more walking, no more lugging our stuff. John, a great one for laughing and for spoiling rare moments of jubilation, told us not to think of it as a joy ride. He said this stretch of road was often more traveled than some major highways; thus we better understand that the mountain-high hay was not for us to sit on but to disappear in.

Suitcase after suitcase was thrown on the wagon with us climbing right after them. In the dark I tried finding my case, tried to orient myself, which with everyone doing the same seemed quite impossible. I spent the first few seconds tumbling, rolling, bouncing and bumping against my companions. Finally, I did get myself under cover of the hay. What a strange sensation! Of course it got into my hair, my face, my neck and sleeves; yet it felt curiously pleasant. Soft, not like a feather bed, but soft like moss. And warm, not like a fur coat, but warm like a comforter. It smelled sweet, not like honeysuckle, but sweet to the senses. Soft, warm and sweet. I lay myself down, curled up and fell asleep.

It is only forty-five miles from the Belgian border to Brussels. Fifteen from where we crossed to the first small town with a railway station, and thirty miles from there to the Gare du Nord, the main terminal in Brussels. Not much of a trip in regard to mileage.

The wagon stopped about twenty feet from the station. We jumped off, collected our things and immediately went about helping one another get rid of the telltale clues we were all covered with. It was morning now. A cloudy, misty, gray and very cold morning, but a new morning.

"We'll be in Brussels before lunch, won't that be nice," said schoolteacher Millie. With her right behind me, we headed for the depot. While passing the wagon, we saw the driver. It was the farmer. Both Millie and I voiced a heartfelt thank-you, but I don't think he heard us. He kept peering over his shoulder. I had barely taken the first step leading to the platform when Millie with unusual animation called to me, "Look, Silvie, look." I spun around just in time to see Bernie lifting his baby daughter up to the farmer, who, with the same tenderness I'd seen last night, held her close while she with wide-open eyes just looked at him. She touched his unshaven face with her tiny hands, smiled and put her little arms around his neck. At that moment, the mist cleared, and a bright blue sky looked down on them. "How lovely!" exclaimed Mrs. De Hartog. "Look at their happy faces. They're good together, aren't they."

At the station John, not quite as bouncy as he'd been last night, reminded us not to forget to mail the cards we'd written. I don't think any of us would have.

I think the place from which we took the train to Brussels was called Kappelin. It was a whistle-stop town. Our train, a relic from better days, must have once been elegant, comfortable, and fast. Now the seats were broken, the once plush cardinal red upholstery faded and torn, with lumpy stuffing and worn-out springs sticking through. Sometimes after a stop, the train would start and then move back instead of ahead, as though it couldn't go forward without going backwards first. Another source of little joy was the brakeman. He used those brakes, or what was left of them, with vengeful disregard, as though he liked listening to the grating of screeching wheels — or was deaf.

For the first few miles, we had the train to ourselves. Then all sorts of people waiting by the roadside began to get on. The train never stopped where they'd been waiting. They either had to run after it or catch it while it moved backwards. In a sick sort of way, it was almost amusing. This time, my fellow escapees and I were traveling in the same railroad car. We sat a couple of rows away from each other or on the opposite side, close enough to belong together, far enough away not to. Fearless John's lack of sleep had finally caught up with him. The moment we were seated he sank down next to me, dropped his head on my shoulder and entered slumberland.

I don't know when I first noticed or felt that someone was staring at me. I tried not to look up, but the stare was so intense, almost hypnotic, that I couldn't help myself. The man stood on the platfom of the railroad car, his eyes never leaving me for an instant. At first I thought that this man was actually trying to pick me up. Never mind that I was obviously not alone, he kept staring just the same. He was cleanshaven, very tall, very blond and self-assured, probably in his early thirties. He wore a light tan trench coat with the belt pulled tight and the collar turned up. After several long seconds when his stare had brought no reaction from me, not outwardly anyway, he boldly resorted to gestures. At first he only winked, followed by head tilts, which clearly meant, come on. When I didn't come, he used both arms to wave me out. While this went on, his eyes, wandering from me to John and back again, kept on blinking as if they were sending a message.

By then my fellow escapees had also noticed the stranger's odd pantomiming and had become visibly nervous. I did my best not to show any reaction, but I was downright scared. What could he want of me? The longer he stood there, the more impossible it became to ignore him. Finally, I awakened John. While nudging him, I told him about the stranger's odd behavior and that I didn't know what to do about it. John, instantly awake, took one good look at the man, jumped up, grabbed me, my suitcase, whistled the others to attention and called out: "Next car. Walk to the next car and keep on going. Now!"

Turning me around, he shoved me in the opposite direction from where the stranger stood. I did not look back. Just kept on walking from one railroad car to the next. I didn't dare run. Didn't dare arouse any of the passengers' attention. Seven cars later, I stopped and waited for whoever was going to follow me.

The train, huffing and puffing with snail-like pace through the outskirts of Brussels, was now inching its way closer and closer to the heart of the city and the grand Gare du Nord, everyone's end of the line. How long had it been since I was last here? A mere three years . . .

"Thank heaven we made it." said Mr. De Hartog, climbing off the train ahead of me.

Amidst the beehive crowd of swarming people flocking in all directions, no one took any notice of us. The tall, blond stranger was nowhere to be seen. I allowed myself a sigh of relief, and elbowed my way to the exit.

"Last one out pays for breakfast," John announced with a misplaced smile. He stood outside the main exit gate, looking tired and tense as he counted his little flock.

The sun had decided to make this a bright, cloudless day. It made the trolley tracks sparkle like silver and the freshly washed streets shimmer. It made everything look purged, pure and beautiful. Not warlike at all. Movement and action, coming and going, was all around us. Hard to accept that this charismatic city was under hostile rule too.

John, in a hurry to get us away from the station, steered us through heavy traffic across to the other side and into a large coffeehouse directly opposite the Gare du Nord. I really hadn't thought that he had been serious about his breakfast talk, but there we were, the six of us plus baby, illegal as hell and badly in need of a bath and fresh clothes, ordering waffles and cream. I never truly understood why John did bring us here. Not for the waffles, I'm sure — with one sort of powder imitating eggs and another sort of powder imitating cream. There weren't too many patrons there that morning, and only a few of them gaped at us. To my mind, though, even a few were too many.

John, whose assurances were wearing a bit thin, nevertheless insisted that this café, primarily frequented by French-speaking citizens stopping for a mid-morning cup of coffee, was, if not kosher, an okay place to be. The more time passed, the more relaxed John became, as though just entering this place had made us immune to danger. As though no trench-coat-clad, blond stranger could set foot in here.

"The bastard is a spy," John hissed, with unmitigated hatred in his voice. "He works for the Nazis. We come from same town, that's how I know him. He knows what I'm doing, and I know what he's doing. That swine been trying to catch me with the Jews *flagrante delicto,* if you know what I mean . . ."

Although we knew exactly what John meant, he felt compelled to go on. At last, slurping the rest of the coffee with the same revulsion on his face as he had expressed for the spy, he ended on the optimistic note, "There's one in every town."

John's disclosure put quite a damper on our upbeat mood, and we became scared all over again. Rebecca began to cry, which inspired baby Erika to throw her glass of powdered milk at the man seated at the next table. The waiter in a flash brought the bill, saying that he needed the table. Personally, I couldn't have been more glad to get out, though none of us knew where we were headed next.

We spent the next hour on three different trams going every which way, perhaps even riding in circles. I didn't recognize a single square or park. Had my memory gone, or the places I'd known?

When we finally got off, we found ourselves in a part of town I knew I hadn't been to before. This was the Villa District of Brussels: the streets were wide and spotless, with lovely linden trees. These gorgeous homes, set back from the sidewalks with their huge front lawns, blooming shrubs and bright-hued flowers, were a feast to the eyes. It made me forget why we had come.

A few minutes later, we followed John down a long flagstoned walkway that led straight to the entrance of a dazzling, azure villa. Halfway there, John told us to wait while he went on without us. Just like children's first time at the Zoo, I thought, watching the expressions of wonderment on the faces of my mates. It wasn't only the enchanting sights that so intrigued us, but more the fact that we were brought here at all. Who would ever have imagined anything that grand?

We could hear John's ringing of the doorbell — or the echo of it, a chimelike, melodious sound like a glockenspiel. Within a short span, some-one opened the door, but only a little. We had no way of knowing who it was, nor could we hear what was being said. Curious, we tiptoed closer and then waited. Eventually the front door did swing open, a little hesitantly, I thought, and we were told to enter by a timid-sounding, trilling female voice. The number on the mailbox read 14; the street the house stood on was the rue Lincoln.

She must have been a ballerina once, this timid-sounding lady with the trilling voice. I never saw her standing still. Her torso, in perfect harmony with the rest of her body, would sway ever so lightly from side to side, like someone under the spell of music. Her fingers, though, gave her away. Like butterfly wings they too, in rapid succession, trembled and fluttered, inde-pendently of her small, pretty hands, showing how uneasy and jittery she really was. She was dainty, had ash-blond hair and blue eyes with a perma-nently startled expression and traces of a *belle visage* hidden under stage makeup. What made me think she was once a dancer was the way her tiny ballet-slippered feet moved about. She did not walk but leaped, little leaps instead of steps, and when she stood she always assumed ballet's first posi-tion. She wore a Shirley Temple hairstyle and she even had the dimples. We guessed a lot but never really found out anything about her, not for certain anyway.

We didn't fare any better with the house itself. This lovely Mediterranean villa was, like its mistress, full of mystery and elegance. The huge white marble entrance hall, large enough for a ballroom, was completely empty. Not one chair or mirror, no chandeliers or sconces and not a single painting on the wall. Two pearly white doors with solid brass doorknobs, on opposite sides of the foyer, were closed, at least to us, as well as everything else in this part of the villa. We used the staircase, also marble, leading to the upstairs rooms only twice — once going up, once going down. The rest of the time we were confined to the upstairs.

Why? Regardless of what language was used, it ended up like all the other questions we'd tried to find an answer to — a mystery. Actually, we didn't really have all of the upstairs to ourselves either, only one wing. The other, consisting of a hallway with numerous doors all locked, was also off limits. Our quarters, three bedrooms with adjoining bathrooms, a most magnifi- cent salon with a good-size dining room (once a library), proved to be as much of a puzzle as whatever else was locked away behind the doors. We quickly realized that absolutely nothing in this house, including our hostess, made any sense. There was, for instance, this grand salon, with its exquisite Louis XIV furnishings, thick Persian rugs, beveled glass mirrors, crystal chandeliers and black marble fireplace, which was ours to hang about in. The bedrooms, in astounding contrast, were austere and without charm. We judged the bathrooms by the availability of hot water. There was very little; we left it for baby Erika and her diapers.

John did not come upstairs with us, saying that he had still too much to do and that he'd see us later. By then we better let him know whether or not we wanted to go on to Switzerland. If so, arrangements for new traveling permits, and new IDs, would have to be made. Therefore, the sooner we de- cided, the sooner we could either leave or settle in. This time, dear John in- formed us, we'd be traveling by car, a German military car with a military driver — another Soldier Resnick? Also, we'd be no ordinary Jews trying to escape, but doctors and nurses en route to a hospital, wearing the proper professional uniforms. John totally dismissed our very valid concern regard- ing the presence of an eight-month-old in our midst, insisting that no one ever had stopped a car with the Geneva cross on it. If this was so, then why new papers? Mr. De Hartog suggested the little one might suddenly have contracted the measels, and we, of course, would have to rush her to a hospital.

At this point the fact that we, between the six of us, barely knew how to administer first aid did not bother me half as much as the unpleasant geographical reality that had to do with Belgium's surrounding borders. There was Holland, which I had just come from: occupied. France: occupied. And West Germany, worse than occupied. The border which did not connect to Belgium was the Swiss one. The others knew that too but chose not to talk about it. What they did talk about was their definite wish to go on to Switzerland because, voiced Mrs. De Hartog, "we must be free, and one can never be really free in a country that isn't free."

Since her sentiments were our sentiments, we told John to go ahead with whatever he needed to do. He said he would, suggesting that we meanwhile settle down, get comfortable and enjoy the luxurious accommodations provided for us, which he truly hoped we appreciated. He then intimated that we'd be looked after by the lovely lady of this villa, whose name he never mentioned and she never revealed. And as long we didn't bother her too much, everything would be just fine. John promised to bring more picture postcards when he returned so we could write home again, and whatever else we wanted. I wanted to see Rainer and Betty. John swore that I'd be seeing them when we went dancing tonight, that he'd make absolutely sure the girls would be there too.

"Where?"

"There."

"Where's there?"

"At the club."

With this profound declaration, he left.

At first, we weren't sure the lovely lady of the villa understood our marvelous French, our Dutch with a Flemish twist, whether she was sworn to silence, or simply lacked the art of conversation. Not that we got to see that much of her anyhow; she made herself scarce. Her looking after us consisted of a dinner gong, used also for lunch and the opening of the connecting door between our salon and dining room. More than once she managed to sneak out and take her little leaps down the stairs before we could catch her. When we did manage to corner her, we had to settle for the beginning of an unresolved smile, a couple of head nods and a one-word answer, no matter the question: *Zeker* — Sure. Could I have another pillow? *Zeker.*

Whenever our questions (when will John be back? where is John?) became too uncomfortable, she would bite her poppy red lipsticked lips, squint her blue eyes, and then do us the honor of saying it twice: *Zeker, zeker.* This led us to not only naming her Madame Zeker but addressing her that way every chance we got. I must confess I have never met anyone less *zeker* than she was.

The garden of the villa in the rue Lincoln was the most beautiful, most color-rich, dreamy I'd ever seen. The parklike grounds, with white stony pathways bordered by rows and rows of pale pink roses, gentle waterlily ponds, darker pink-painted bridges and a waterfall cascading from a sculptured rock, were a sight to behold. A latticed teahouse at one end of the garden was almost completely covered with copper-orange bougainvilleas and cypress trees, much taller than the surrounding stone walls, softly swaying in the midday breeze; there were lilac trees, stirring memories of long ago; tulip trees, full of large, green, tulip-shaped flowers; acacia trees; the glorious white-blossomed dogwood; crepe myrtle, not quite awake yet; and scarlet fragrant verbenias. Also multicolored pinks, lavender sweet alyssum, azaleas, graceful fringed rose pink bleeding hearts, pungent orange-gold nasturtiums, double bicolored larkspur with white eyes and an abundance of gladiola and hibiscus blossoms. And my all-time favorite, next to orchids, night-blooming jasmine. It was like the secret garden. Like Shangri-la.

For us, the door was locked. We could not enter the garden. I spent most of my time at the large bay windows, sitting on the damask window benches, looking out. Whenever I did so, all my momentary worries would disappear.

The loud, sonorous dinner gong echoed through the house at eight. We had spent most of the afternoon exchanging opinions about the villa, Madame Zeker, and why we couldn't possibly reach Switzerland without traveling through France. As it was, we probably would have to get to Liège and Amiens. What we definitely must do was stay clear of Aachen and Saarbrücken. One could practically sneeze into Germany from there. After many hours, we had decided to leave France to whoever was going to be in charge of getting us there, go to our rooms and take a nap.

Millie and I shared one of the bedrooms. I don't like sleeping with someone I do not know intimately, but she had volunteered to take the bed with the lumpy mattress, so I pretended to be pleased with the arrangement. When I discovered my bed was in worse condition than hers, I slept in the salon.

First evening at the dinner table, no sign of Madame Zeker. We didn't know about her elusiveness then. The table was set with fine china, a white linen embroidered tablecloth, matching napkins, a crystal water carafe with water, not wine, and crystal glasses. There was one picture postcard next to each table setting, but no stamps; a basket full of clean diapers for baby, and for Bernie a carton of those dreadful-smelling French cigarettes. We had French garlic bread and *stampôt* — which is the same as ordinary stew. Little Erika did get fresh milk but otherwise no special food, and she attacked the stew with the singlemindedness of a very hungry baby.

We spent the rest of the evening trying to solve a brand-new riddle while waiting for John: How did the food and dinnerware get up to the dining room? None of us believed that dainty trembling Madame Zeker had carried it up. We spent the rest of the evening wondering whether there might be someone else in the house . . . and waiting for John. We spent the rest of the evening discarding the possibility of someone else in the house . . . still waiting for John. Shortly after ten, while searching for secret doors and passageways, we found the answer to the riddle: A dumbwaiter. We stacked everything together and sent it back down with a note that said: "Where is John?"

Around midnight, we summed up the events of the day, took stock of the good, the bad, the unexplainable, and went to bed. I used the sofa to rest my weary head and body. It worked out perfectly. Once my pensive companions had gone to their rooms and all the lights were out, I pulled the air-raid blinds up, opened the windows and let the night air in. Sleep came swiftly, without dreams or nightmares.

Breakfast was announced with knocks on the bedroom doors. No one had heard anyone come before the knocks, or leave afterwards, but the table was set, and waiting for us was steaming hot porridge which only baby Erika cared for. We did not see Madame Zeker again till lunch and then only for some very brief moments. I think she was afraid to talk to us, for all we got, apart from spicy sausages and bread, was her *Zeker, zeker* routine. After she had left, Mr. De Hartog found something scribbled on a piece of paper next to his placemat which said that John would be coming tonight. With no explanation as to why he hadn't shown up yesterday and no forseeable chance of getting any from ruffled Madame, we had a pretty hard time coping with our frustrations. Bernie, not one for holding back his feelings, promised to strangle John, or Madame Zeker, solely depending on who showed up first, the moment either of them appeared. Meanwhile, he wore out the rugs and the floor beneath with pacing and never stopped smoking those vile cigarettes. I, for the sake of my lungs and my own peace of mind, fled to the window where I spent the entire afternoon revisiting my magical garden. Rebecca withdrew with the baby to her bedroom, her first independent and wise decision, while Millie, a compulsive diarist, wrote till her knuckles cracked.

Perhaps patience comes with age; perhaps it takes a lifetime to master. Perhaps it is a gift given to those who meet adversity with dignity and honor. Perhaps it's just another lesson that we who are still young have not yet learned. In our little group only the De Hartogs had the capacity of calm endurance, that certain wisdom which makes for tolerance, and only they had the good sense to show restraint in the face of this aggravating situation. Holding hands, they sat on the other window bench enjoying, like me, the untarnished beauty of this magnificent garden. It made me think of Papa that awesome day when he tried telling me about the true meaning of spring . . .

Just before the last snow melted, when I was six, and the air already had a certain scent of spring, we all went to the Prater — a gigantic amusement park with merry-go-rounds, tunnel rides, lots of cotton candy, and Vienna's famous Ferris wheel. Now the restaurants were closed and the surrounding woods deserted. But Papa had insisted that the outing would do us good, so we went.

Papa had the whole afternoon planned. There was something he wanted his three girls to find. What, he didn't say. Without having the slightest clue, we spread out and started looking. I was cold, and all I really wanted to find was Mama's warm beaver coat. But Papa wouldn't hear of it: "You're not giving up, are you?"

"But, Papa, how can I find something if I don't even know what it is I'm looking for? How do I know it's even here?"

"How do you know it isn't? You haven't even tried!" He suggested we ought to find it together. He led me through a maze of hidden paths, far away from the others. Wherever I looked, I saw nothing but trees. Most of them had no leaves at all, and I thought they too must be cold. Their wrinkled naked branches, like old men's arms, hung motionless with crippled twigs entangled in other twigs, as though some mystic force had spun a web of petrified wood.

It was so still there, as though the whole forest had gone to sleep, or never was awake at all. We walked for a long time, and I told Papa that I was getting tired. We both sat down on a tree stump, and just as I was about to put my head on his shoulder, I saw it.

Underneath patches of soft melting snow, tiny sky-blue flowers stuck their little heads up. Pansies! Beautiful little faces, bright-eyed pansies. No longer tired, I danced around them, while Papa bellowed three big "Hurrays." Ever so careful, not wanting to step on my timid treasure, we both kneeled down, and Papa whispered, "Silvie, you found spring!"

Perhaps I only dreamed this silent forest, or else the awesome beauty of those little flowers amid this eerie background was magic — Papa's magic. I wanted to kiss him, but Papa was preoccupied. I could tell that he was thinking, thinking deep thoughts.

"Papa?" I whispered. "What's wrong?"

"Nothing, baby, nothing is wrong."

"Aren't you happy anymore?"

"Of course I'm happy. I was only wondering whether or not I should tell you that . . . No! I better not. At least not yet. You're only six and a half, you wouldn't understand."

"Yes, I would! Is it a secret?"

"No, baby, not at all."

When at last he spoke, it was with great intensity and immense fervor: "I want to tell you about spring. The kind of spring that knows no season."

"Papa?"

"Just listen to me, please. Silvie, you are a blessed, gifted child, and because of it, you will always find spring. You see, spring is not only the first new flower, the first bloom or blossom. It is so much more. It means seeking and searching for many things, at different times, in different places. Exploring all there is to explore. For only then will you find what you want most in life. It's out there somewhere, just waiting for you. Go after it, no matter what, and if you do, your life will be filled with a thousand springs — even in the coldest winter. Can you understand just a little of it?"

I nodded.

"Never stop looking, and never give up; reach, reach out! It's all I'll ever be able to teach you. It's all you need to remember!"

He looked at me long and deep, as though wanting to plant his words, like prodigious seeds, forever inside me. And even now I can still hear my father's warm, invincible voice: "Silvie, you found spring!" Perhaps I did. For it was through these little flowers that the wonder of nature revealed itself to me. I wish he were with me now . . .

Just before dinner, we all got together once more to discuss the meaning of the scribbled note we had found at lunch. "Coming." It said that John would be coming tonight. What did it really mean? Did it mean that he was coming to visit, to stay, to bring stamps, to bring Rainer and Betty, or our new papers? Coming to take me dancing, coming to take us to Switzerland? "Coming." But when was he coming?

The evening that followed was a step-by-step repeat of the evening before. Except for the dumbwaiter riddle we so ingeniously had solved already, nothing else, including water, *stampôt*, French garlic bread and waiting for John, was any different.

Madame Zeker never showed, and neither did John. We played cards till our eyes got all blurry and then went to bed.

In the morning, Madame Zeker zigzagged around the exquisite pieces of Louis XIV furniture in the salon as if they were flagmarked poles put there for a slalom run. Actually, it was Madame Zeker's way of gracefully balancing a tray of fresh, delicious, still warm croissants. What a lovely treat!

Our mood soared instantly, and the majority of our group was much too grateful to allow Bernie to strangle our unpredictable, truly peculiar Madame Zeker. We thanked her profusely in three languages, which unfortunately did not increase her desire to answer even one of our questions. After she had slalomed out again, we reluctantly agreed that grilling Madame Zeker was absolutely pointless.

"Patience," advised sage Mr. De Hartog. "We must have patience. What else can we do? I'm certain he'll come," he said almost convincingly. "John can't just leave us here. What good would that do?"

Of course he was right. The more we thought about it, the more we realized that leaving us stranded helped no one. Besides, how much *stampôt* can one eat?

It had started to rain in the late morning and didn't stop till early evening. The flowers in my beautiful garden got enough to last them all season. We had to keep the windows shut. We got the fire going in the fireplace, gathered around, talked, played cards, took a couple of catnaps and talked some more. It was a lazy, sleepy sort of day, a twilight sort of day, an in-between sort of day. We had French onion soup for lunch and for dinner, too. Despite everything, we had finally settled in.

He came at night. When everyone was fast asleep, he came. It caused quite a stir, not to mention major confusion. Madame Zeker, who at this unseemly hour woke us with the news, acted as though she positively was bereft of reason. Leaping from room to room, she turned up all the lights, pulled the covers from the beds, hollering without as much as a breath in between, "*Vite! Vite!* He's here! He's here! You must go now! Go, go, go! *Vite! Vite!*" Then, storming down the corridor, she leaped back downstairs.

I have no idea how much time passed before I got my brain going again. I heard my comrades talking and moving about almost immediately after Madame Zeker's last *Vite! Vite!*, their voices tremulous and flustered, their feet unsteadily shuffling around. When the others joined me in the salon, I was still sitting on my sofa bed.

What the hell was going on? Through all that cursing and complaining, my rattled friends kept changing seats, sitting down and getting up as if they were playing musical chairs. I had barely observed that they all looked like passengers on a derailed railroad car when Madame Zeker appeared again, out of breath, sweating and frantic. Her arms kept shooting up in the air, as she continued spitting out *Vite! Vite!* like balls from a pinball machine. There was no doubt that she wanted us out. There was, however, nothing but doubt in everyone's mind about this sudden departure. Should we go or stay?

From the reserved Mr. De Hartog's "We are not going, this is not right. They should have let us know ahead of time" to Bernie's explosive "Bloody mess! How the hell should I know what's right, what's not?" to Rebecca's "I won't go," and Millie's "Don't know," the only sour conclusion unanimously reached was that we should not separate. We would either all go or all stay.

We were just about to put it to a vote when Bernie, pointing directly at me, challenged: "If it were entirely up to you, what would you . . . ?"

"Go! I would go!" My mouth had run away in all that excitement.

There was a moment's pause. "That's it! No more debate," Bernie said with a sigh of relief. "That's it then. We go!" We hurried to our rooms, scrambled for our belongings and scooted downstairs.

⤳ TEN

THE MAN LEANING AGAINST THE OPEN DOOR by the entrance was not John. He was younger, more athletic. With his headful of thick black wavy hair, his strong prominent features and his self-assured manner, he definitely looked the part of a Resistance fighter. He'd instill confidence in the doubters of the group, I thought, while taking a good look at him.

"I'm Max," he said, with the hint of a smile, as I walked through the door. "Hurry, please, we're very late."

I heard him say, "I'm Max," in his sonorous voice, each time one of my comrades passed by him. One by one we stepped into the darkness of the unlit driveway, walked on, until we reached the darkness of the unlit street.

The vehicle parked at the curb, a couple of feet from rue Lincoln no. 14, was not, as John had told us, a German military car. It had no military markings, no swastika and no Geneva cross. I can't be sure about the color. And not until Max — the last one to leave the villa, first to reach the car — shone his flashlight on it could we tell what kind of vehicle it was. The back had two doors which opened in the middle.

"It's a van," announced Bernie.

Max, with one big move, pushed the doors open and then immediately had us climb in. Before we got to take another breath, the door slammed shut, and seconds later we were speeding through the empty streets of Brussels. There was no light inside the van, though I caught a glimpse of the interior from Max's flashlight as we were climbing in. There were two benches on opposite sides, and oddly enough, regular blinds over the side windows which could be opened from the inside. It was eerie to look out and see nothing but darkness while feeling the wheels burning the pavement underneath.

I wondered whether the driver of the van had his lights on, or whether he himself was driving in the dark. We tried to find something resembling doctors' and nurses' coats but there was nothing, nothing at all. My comrades were a bit on edge, mainly because we never seemed to end up with the one we started out with. There was Harry, John, Madame Zeker . . . and now Max. Was he our driver? Was he even still with us?

I, the instant expert, told the group that this was how the underground game was being played. Here today, gone tomorrow. I don't know whom I was trying to convince.

It wasn't exactly a smooth ride. Because of the speed and the many turns, we were thrown around like rag dolls, which all things considered was just as well since it made it impossible to do any real thinking. How long a ride? I was never sure.

The crass lights of giant flashlights streaming through the open blinds hit us like sudden lightning, simultaneously with the bellowing voices of furious men:

"*Hier! Rein fahren!*" — Here! Drive in!

"*Mach schnell! Komm schon! Schnell!*" — Hurry! Come on! Hurry!

Without a moment's hesitation, I took the false ID from my bag, tore it in little pieces, opened the window and tossed it out.

Inside the van, the air had turned to ice. My comrades, glued to the benches, had momentarily stopped breathing.

The van doors flew open and I found myself staring into a pool of blinding lights.

"*Raus! Alle! Raus! Verdammt noch mal, mach schnell!*" — Out! Everyone out! Damn it! Hurry!

I jumped out and into the arms of a uniformed German. He was not pleased. "*Weiter gehn!*" — Keep going! he yelled. The commands, mixed with insulting remarks, continued. Shielding my eyes, I tried to get away from those awful blinding lights.

There were quite a few of the Germans, all doing what they seemed to do best: shouting. My comrades had climbed or fallen off the van and just like me, had kept on walking.

It must have been some kind of station house, or military post, or something of the sort. We entered through a stone arch, on a stony sidewalk surrounded by stone walls. It looked like a fortress. I saw Max leaning against the arch, the same way he had leaned against the doorway of the villa, showing neither surprise nor shock. He watched me walking past him, watched me closely, and didn't say a word. It must have been my preoccupation with him that made me fail to notice that I somehow had gotten separated from the others. I do recall hearing their footsteps behind me, but when I turned to look, they were gone.

I stood alone in what I perceived to be a round courtyard. Perhaps it was no longer than a heartbeat, but in this click of time I could have gotten away. Why didn't I? Why did I stick around, wait till I felt a soldier's heavy hand on my shoulder, wait till I heard him say, *"Marche, marche!"* I had no answer for it then, only much later; and even much, much later, it was mostly conjecture. I think I stayed for two, totally conflicting reasons: One, I wasn't ready to admit that this was not the way to Switzerland. I might have thought what better place for a rendezvous with one's military car and driver than right smack in the middle of a military post. Why couldn't he be one of them and one of us, another Soldier Resnick?

Two, I more than likely reached this conclusion right away: You can't run away if you don't know where you are, because if you don't know where you are, you also don't know where to go.

So, until I felt the soldier's hand, I was standing there wondering what good it was now to have no papers at all. The soldier, "He's Belgian, you know," Mr. De Hartog would have said, for he indeed was that, wore a different uniform from those I'd seen before. Not quite as stiff and starchy. There were other things in his favor, too. He did not shout, he did not push and he didn't speak German — French only.

He took me into a building with countless steps and narrow hallways. Gloomy, stone-cold. We stopped in a small, oval hall with many heavy iron doors. Standing in front of one of them was a unifomed German with lots of stripes and medals on his heroic chest, and *schmisse,* the cuts and slashes that were the facial souvenirs of fencing.

Legs spread, chest out, he screamed: "Jew! Are you a Jew? Where do you come from? Where are you going? Papers — show me your papers! You fled! Of course, you wanted to flee! I'll teach you fleeing!"

His little shouting session, intended to hit like darts from a blowgun, did no such thing. I suspect that my ignorance regarding his rank had a lot to do with my calmness. "Papers!" he fumed again. Obviously expecting me to hand them over, he opened his extended hand, screaming, *"Papers! Papers!"* louder and louder till I actually thought he'd split his vocal cords.

Not knowing who he was gave me the courage to be cool and convincing. I told him that my papers had been stolen and that I was a German actress, stuck in Holland, a country that wasn't all that fond of Germans anymore. Through it all I looked straight at him. My steadiness seemed to puzzle him, my perfect German even more.

Once he saw that his intimidation spiel didn't work, he continued his questions in a much calmer, almost indifferent tone. He wanted to know why, as a German actress returning to Germany, I hadn't been traveling on a military train. His last question gave me the chance to show off my expert knowledge of travel permits. Did he not know, I replied, that military trains were off limits to civilians except by special permit which, these days, took forever to get.

"And is that why you crawl over borders with Jews?" he sneered. It was this remark which made me realize that he had played this scene already with the others in my group, that they had given him their papers and confessed that they were Jews.

His last words to me were not a question but a promise. While his eyes, steel blue and piercing, cut through me, he promised that if he found out I'd lied, he'd send me straight to hell. He clicked his heels, turned and left.

The Belgian soldier who had escorted me to this inhospitable place opened the door we'd been standing at, said, *"Allez vite,"* watched me go in, and immediately shut it again. I could hear the metallic sound of keys, the snapping of the lock and finally the hollow echo of the soldier's footsteps as he marched off.

It wasn't much bigger than a hole in the wall, this badly lit and over-crowded cell. How did I end up in this cage without bars, this prison hidden away from the eyes of the world? What kind of place was this anyway, and who were all those people? They were crowding around me, talking into my ear, but I couldn't understand them. Not their words, only the sounds. It was like the buzzing of bees, or the chatter of old women mixed with the whining and wailing of mourners.

Faces — a blur of faces! Which ones belong to my friends? I need to find and tell them . . . what? The first one I could recognize was Rebecca. She was sitting on one of the two small benches holding the baby. She had put her scarf over the little one's face to protect her from the ugliness. Rebecca looked smaller and more childlike than before. Smaller and frightfully pale. Perhaps it was the light. Everyone looked pale.

Later, I saw Bernie and the others. Bernie was holding his head the way one does when experiencing a giant headache; Millie and the De Hartogs, pressed against a wall, were trying to hold their ground. We were the only ones with suitcases. The others had nothing but the clothes on their backs. Whoever they were, their journey must have been a shorter one. Eventually, I managed to interpret most of the stories floating around, many of which I had heard before in another place, in another country not all that long ago. Picked up on the street, picked up in a park, picked up in a shop . . . picked up, picked up, picked up. For some, this was a return visit. They had gotten picked up, brought here, let go, picked up, brought here, let go.

One of the men even claimed he had been sent away twice and this was his third time around. Once they got him for carrying too many identification cards, then for carrying none and now for frequenting the hangouts of black marketeers. Was he a Jew? That, he said, depended on who was asking and why. He didn't wear the Star of David on his ankle-length, far-too-large coat. Most of the people in here didn't.

As cells go, this one was lacking the barest essentials. It had no cot, no sink to wash in, no water. And instead of a toilet, a bucket. It stood in a separate corner with something vaguely resembling a divider in front of it.

I had finally discovered a corner I could lean against when I was ordered out again. The German with the scarred face was waiting for me. In the palm of his open hand, he held bits of paper. "Look what my men found. Recognize it?" His voice was icy-cold but calm. "Look familiar? Know where they were? Right where you threw them. Didn't make it all the way out the window. Got stuck between the blinds and the window. Didn't think we'd find them, did you? Did you!" His last "Did you!" was deafeningly loud again. He had shoved his hand with the torn papers right under my nose. This latest trouble caught me completely by surprise and stupefied me totally. I just couldn't believe that such a freakish mishap could have happened. Even less believable was that they would go so far as to track down tiny bits of paper. It seemed utterly ludicrous. Who did they think I was, Mata Hari?

BOUNDLESS BORDERS, UNENDING JOURNEY

I was so aghast that I kept shaking my head, shaking and shaking it, which I suddenly realized the German must have interpreted as a complete denial of his accusation. I followed it up by telling him, a bit shakily, that I had absolutely no idea what he was talking about, that he was badly mistaken because it wasn't mine. At the same time I became convinced that if I stuck to my story, there wasn't much he could do, for he could never prove otherwise. Actually, all I did was follow a very strong hunch that at that specific moment admitting the truth would not have been a very smart thing to do.

While I kept protesting my innocence, he kept staring at me as if he was trying to crawl inside my head. Some fearsome seconds later, I watched him put the bits of paper into an envelope and hand them to me. He then made me another promise. He promised that he would investigate me to find out who I really was. The envelope, he said, I was to hand over to the Commander first thing tomorrow. "You better not mess up," he warned, and marched off. The silence he left behind was heavy.

My brain had registered the word "Commander" but not its meaning. "What's he talking about?" I asked the soldier guarding my cell.

"You'll see," he replied with a blank look on his face.

"See what?"

"Never you mind."

This useless exchange, followed only by *"Allez, allez"* while he unlocked the cell, truly confirmed the ambiguity of my situation.

The air inside the cell reeked of sweat and tears. It made me feel nauseous. I reached for my suitcase and took my toilet water out. The soldier, still standing by the door, asked me to give him some of "that stuff" for his girlfriend. He said it wouldn't do me much good where I was going. He wanted my other stuff too, only because I looked like someone with a lot of nice stuff. For two years the toilet water had been standing on my dresser unopened. For two years I had looked at it, touched it, held it, all the while remembering its wonderful scent and the pleasure I had felt wearing it. It was in the clothes I had left behind, in the dressing room of my dead theater, in my bedroom and in every place I had ever been. I hadn't dared use it because I could no longer have replaced it. Two bottles were all I had left. Two precious bottles of Arpège, one toilet water, the other perfume. I had brought both of them with me all the way from home to prison. Does he really think I'll give it to him?

Hell, no! I opened the perfume bottle, turned it upside down and drop by drop let it run down my face, neck, hair, till it was all gone. Then I opened the toilet water, pushed my way to the middle of the cell and poured it all out. If nothing else, it did make for a fine-smelling cell. The soldier's mouth flew open. He said, "What you want to do that for?" and banged the door shut.

My little stunt instantly transformed wet-eyed faces into smiling ones. Some of them even laughed out loud. The women embraced me and then kneeled down, rubbing their hands on the perfume-soaked stone floor. The men shook my hand and said that I was something of a godsend and a very gutsy girl. Because of my newly acquired popularity, I was offered a corner seat on one of the benches, along with several well-meaning comments and predictions concerning my immediate future, none of which were favorable.

The night dragged on. I sat with both hands in the pockets of my coat holding the envelope with the bits of paper in one and the picture post-card without a stamp in the other. Even without my cellmates' gloomy predictions, I knew that I must not let anyone follow me. I must let my family know that my luck had run out and for them to stay put. So I quickly wrote that I had fallen ill and wasn't allowed any visitors. I asked around for a postage stamp but no one had a stamp. At that moment, I would have given the soldier my perfume, toilet water, and whatever else he wanted for one stamp and one mailbox. Too late. The man with the far-too-large coat had told me that all my valuables would be taken away and that I better hide them. I did not tell him that his advice was not exactly news to me, nor that the gems hidden in my coat were much, much safer than I was. He then said that I should try the soldier once more, offer him money for mailing my card. And try I did. But no banging on the cell door made him open it again. Perhaps he wasn't there anymore.

The walls of the prison cell were covered with names — so many there was hardly room for more. Cut in with knives, razor blades, nail files, scissors, or scratched with fingernails, they told a grim story indeed. Whatever their names, each one of them spelled panic and fear, hope forsaken . . . and betrayal. If these walls could talk, what a riveting tale they'd reveal.

Directly above me someone had written, "May tomorrow never come," and next to it I found the names of Rainer and Betty.

It was noon the following day before the cell door opened again. Belgian guards drove the men out first, with lots of pushing, shoving and shouting.

We didn't know what had happened to them till one hour later, when they let us out too. We were rushed out of the building with the countless steps and narrow hallways onto a stone yard with a wide, streetlike driveway. It was full of trucks: empty, medium-sized, uncovered trucks.

The men from my cell and others I hadn't seen before were out there loading heavy wooden crates onto some extra large vehicles. Regardless of their age or physical condition, they were being whipped and kicked indiscriminately. It was hard to watch, hard not to. Their hands were bleeding, their faces full of sweat and inconsolable despair. Even the youngest and strongest among them seemed near exhaustion.

Another hour passed, with us just looking on, before we all were quick-marched onto the waiting trucks. I was the last one climbing onto the last parked truck. I did not count them, nor the people, only the rifle-carrying soldiers riding with us. Two per vehicle.

The trucks raced down the boulevards, out and away from the city, with the speed of an express train. It made those who might have thought of jumping, including me, change their minds in a flash. The people next to me knew which prison we had spent the night in. "Avenue Louise," they said. "Don't you know about Avenue Louise? It's Gestapo headquarters, the most dreaded place in Belgium!" What they didn't know was where or when this high-geared, tearing road race was going to end. I saw them take off their rings, bracelets and watches, their gold chains, everything worth anything at all, and toss them out. They sailed through the air, all glistering and shiny, landing as sparkling specks on the road. They told me to do the same, but I did not, could not get myself to do it. Instead, I threw out the postcard I'd written in the cell, on which I had hurriedly added: "Will the finder of this card please put a stamp on it and mail it." Right then it was much more important than my hidden gems or the watch and gold charm bracelet I wore. All I could think of was to stop my family and friends from following me. I knew it was a long shot, but what else could I do? I watched the card flutter around as if it couldn't make up its mind where to land. "Someone will find it," I kept telling myself, while watching the card disappear. Must find it!

The trucks drove through a huge gatelike entrance and stopped inside a fairly large, cobblestone courtyard. It was surrounded by barracks. Not wooden ones but regular two-story stone houses with the standard open entrances. Someone bellowed, *"Aussteigen!"* Get off. We did. Two arms, belonging to a man in civilian clothes, helped us down. We were told to line up and shut up. Another civilian-clad, extremely good-looking man then proceeded to count us. He stopped in front of every pretty girl, and only after he had given her a gingerly once-over and his special don't-you-worry smile did he move on. He either was very important or thought he was. There was a certain air about him, and he definitely presented a dauntless front. Except for him and the short blond guy who had helped us down, there was no one in the yard. Behind the windows of the barracks, though, I saw faces, many faces. The civilian had not yet finished counting us when a giant German shepherd came charging by. An instant later, another big wolfish dog helter-skeltered through, scaring us half to death. In my fright I bit my lip, shut my eyes and kept them shut until the crack of a whip made me open them again.

The man holding the whips, one in each hand, wore a German uniform with lots of stripes, a couple of medals and an arrogant expression on his cleanshaven, scarless face. Behind him marched a pudgy, pinkish-complexioned, uniformed German with considerably less stripes, no medals and only one, very dominant, ugly scar. The two must have followed the furry beasts out. Before either of them had reached the first person standing at the beginning of the line, the handsome civilian, walking a few steps ahead of them, called out: *"Actung! Gerade stehn! Der Kommandant!"*

I stood at the far end of the second row, watching Commander Fränk and pudgy pink Unterscharführer Boden inspect the new arrivals. With torpedo speed they asked each one, *"Jude . . . Jude . . . Jude?"* I couldn't hear all the answers, but I'm sure they were mostly yes. It went in double-quick time. In spite of the pace, pink Boden got quite a few boot kicks in. When my turn came, though trembling and still clutching the envelope with the torn ID, to my own amazement I managed to utter, *"Nein! Ich bin Mischling!* [half Jewish]!" Commander Fränk asked me for proof. I stammered that it was still in Hungary or on its way to Amsterdam or there already. For the blink of an eye he stared at me, then marched on. The blond guy with the boyish smile then hung a sign around my neck. It was white, with the letter E on it, and next to it the number 4. I was E4.

The realization that I had failed to give the envelope to the Commander hit me the instant he'd gone on to the next person. I knew that I subconciously had blocked it out. I also knew that I could not risk ignoring it altogether. With the envelope in my outstretched hand and my last ounce of nerve, I called after him, "Excuse me, Herr Commandant, I was told to give you this." He turned, walked back to me, took the envelope, and without as much as a glance, handed it to the one with the signs, told him to throw it away, and continued his inspection.

I was a wreck. I must have looked it too, for the blond civilian with the signs — his name was Fritz — asked whether I was feeling ill. He said that I need not be afraid because the E around my neck was my saftey badge. E, my new friend explained, stood for *"Entscheidung"* — Undecided. Meaning that without papers, nobody could prove anything. Not that I was, not that I wasn't, a Jew. According to Fritz, there were quite a few Es here in this camp called Camp Malin. Some of them had been here for as long as ten months, still waiting for their papers and a decision. Just to make conversation, I mentioned that mine would probably take a very long time too; mail these days was so unreliable. But Fritz grinned, whispered, "You don't have to prove nothing to me," and motioned for me to follow him.

The sign above one of the entrances read: *"Aufname Büro,"* Registration Office. We stepped inside. Most of the people I'd spent the night with at Avenue Louise were already there. So was my little group. The office was packed. Everybody wore a sign. Only a few had the E; the rest wore red ones with numbers. High numbers but no letters. "Transport," Fritz disclosed. "Red means transport. They won't be here too much longer." He then brought me a chair, saying I could expect a long wait — long and not the least bit comfortable. He stayed with me till the next *"Achtung! Achtung!"* talking about this and that, answering my many questions. But most of all, he kept reminding me that I too was now a guest of the Third Reich . . .

Fritz had been right. Hours passed before the handsome civilian — they called him Mayer — followed by Commandant Fränk and pink Boden, came to give their welcome speech. Mayer announced that we were now going to be registered and forewarned us not to make false statements and not to lie about anything. He said that they were sure to find out the truth, no matter how long or how deep they had to dig. The next good news was that we had to hand over all our jewels, all our money and everything else of value. "Don't hide anything," he warned with a good deal of ill prophecy in his voice. "You'll never get away with it. They'll find it. I promise you they will. You all will be thoroughly examined." Finally, Mayer condescendingly informed us that we could keep our clothes and the most necessary toilet articles. Then we were told to line up one behind the other and only to speak when spoken to. The reaction was poorly suppressed outrage. But no one really dared speak out loud. Like dumb little sheep, we lined up, shut up, and only spoke when spoken to.

The line moved slowly, and at times it didn't move at all. I couldn't figure out what was taking so long. There was nothing much to look at in this place. Jaundice yellow walls on one side, and on the other, more walls, and in between windows with nothing but a view of the prison yard. That's where everyone's attention was focused. It was no longer empty. All those window faces had come down to stare at us, wave at us, talk to us. I knew that Rainer would be out there, too. Eager to see me and yet afraid. Anxious to find out whether I was all right, though knowing I couldn't be. I hadn't asked Fritz about either girl. I'd see them soon enough, I thought, hear soon enough about their ill-fated journey, their misbegotten flight to freedom.

Much later, amid a swarm of countless people parading in the yard, I saw Rainer. I watched her make her way to the window I'd been standing at, watched her stop, look up and stare at me. She looked like a ghost. Her eyes were full of tears, full of sorrow. Perhaps she had thought I wouldn't really get caught, or that I hadn't even left home. I tried to smile and nod just to make her feel better, but she suddenly turned and ran back into the crowd. She hadn't yet completely disappeared, and I hadn't yet begun to cry, when the Commander's voice, from the far end of the yard, called out: "Where is the actress? I want to speak to the actress. Now!" It didn't register with me. I don't know how many more times he repeated it.

All at once he stood before me. His was a face that revealed no emotion — stiff, unyielding and dispassionate. He spent unnumbered seconds observing me. At last he said, "I know who you are and now you know that I know who you are. So watch out." and marched off. Around me the hushed voices had resumed; their murmurs followed me into the Registration Office.

The girl behind the typewriter wanted my name, address, age, and where I was born. The next one wanted my money and the jewelry I wore. Even my watch. I emptied my pockets, took off my watch and laid it on the table in front of me. It was a quarter to six. We'd been here for almost five hours. Five exhausting hours. The third one wanted what I still had hidden. She was very friendly, in a patronizing sort of way trying to convince me that it would be better if I gave it to her. Safer. "Everyone is concealing something," she whispered. "You'd be surprised what turns up. Just be smart and don't let them find it. They'll do more than just ask for it."

"They" were two tall guards in Belgian uniforms guarding the exit door. One was horse-faced, with a very large mouth and big protruding yellow horse teeth. The other just looked stupid. Neither of them appeared particularly sociable.

"Well," asked the girl. "What's it going to be?" I shook my head. Behind me, they wanted me to move on. I made my way to the two guards and got to the door just in time to see the horse-faced one knock an old woman's hat off. "Perhaps you still got something hidden in there," he mocked.

"No, nothing, I have nothing anymore," the poor woman whimpered. Then, with sniggering pathos and a ridiculous pose, he called out, "Ladies' Department," kicked her in the butt, and shoved that petrified, pitiful woman through the door. I slipped through right behind her before the two guards slapping their thighs and roaring with laughter noticed me.

There was only one man in this room. A middle-aged uniformed German with a swastika armband. He sat behind a wooden table loaded with personal effects. It had everything: scarves, handkerchiefs, cosmetics, paper money, coins and jewelry. "Last chance!" he called, sounding like someone announcing the last bet for the last race of the day. "Let's see what you forgot to give us," he winked me closer, challenging. I thought he looked pretty harmless. "Everybody does, you know," he went on, "they all forget."

"Nothing," I mumbled, feeling tears swelling up.

I told him my watch and charm bracelet had already been taken from me. Of course he didn't believe me. He made me give him both. Made me turn my coat pockets inside out and empty my handbag. He let me keep my hand mirror and comb, but nothing else, not even my lipstick or powder compact, nor the souvenir Margit had given me — a tiny stork carrying two baby dolls in his beak. She gave it to me to bring me luck, a mascot, and it wasn't worth anything, not to anyone else. I pleaded with him to please let me keep something personal, cried and cried, but could not change his mind. He thought it was only my mascot I was crying about, but of course it wasn't. It was everything! He thought it was foolish of me to make such a fuss about fake little baby dolls, when I and he together could make the real thing. It would be his pleasure to help me out and it sure would be fun. His suggestive spate of words only made me cry more. His final remark, before deciding to let me move on, was that he and my mascot — now his mascot — were anxiously awaiting my return.

The next room, a hallway with partitioned-off cubicles along one side, had two more Belgian soldiers minding the store, as tall and as abusive as the others. I stepped right into their manhandling the same poor woman whose hat had gotten knocked off. They kept yelling for her to undress, but she only sobbed. They ripped the buttons from her coat, tore her sleeves and jerked her all over the place. When her aged and terribly frail husband came to her rescue, those blackguard soldiers struck him down. He stayed down, but didn't give up. He threw his arms around the leg of the one nearest him, grabbing with his bony fingers the lower part of the pants and screaming for them to take their filthy paws off his wife. "Adele," he cried out. "Don't go with them! Don't let them!"

While one guard was pushing the woman into a cubicle, the other dragged the old man on the floor through the hall. It was then that the people waiting their turn lost their self-restraint. Trying to get between them, they cursed the soldiers, hollering for them to leave those old people alone. It only made things worse. When the soldier couldn't shake the old man off, he swung his other leg around and kicked this brave, defiant little man in the head. After that, nobody screamed anymore.

The cubicles had neither doors nor curtains — nothing but a hook to hang one's clothes. Privacy, even in the smallest sense, was nonexistent, even though they separated men from women. I really don't know why they bothered. No matter how threatening Mayer's promise of a thorough examination, I don't think anybody truly understood what he was talking about. I certainly did not. Not then and not after I had already seen some of the women completely naked, with their legs spread in a kneebend position, their upper body bent all the way down. They stood motionless like horses in a stall, with everything exposed, their faces to the wall. It was the guards who did the examining, and it wasn't one's health they were examining. When I finally did figure out the contempible reason for it, I got nauseous. How does one deal with such perverted degradation? Several people passing me in the hall swore they would get even with those hired brutes; others just staggered out as though they were drunk. A half-dressed man running past me hissed, "Treasure trove. That's what they think we are!" He was right. A treasure hunt for treasures far more costly than what they had snatched up before, and it was those protesting the most the guards picked on the most. Looks or age did not come into it; resisting did.

I'd taken my clothes off in record time, stood in briefs and bra, feeling raw, skinned and scorched. The woman ahead of me, in the bent-forward position, was just being searched. They had ordered her to hold her position. The more she struggled, the more they strong-armed her. They were still busy with that unfortunate woman when one of them, barely glancing at me, sneered, "Get dressed, scoot." I was out of there in one leap.

Those who had already gone through the examination hung around in the yard. Some looked dazed, others enraged, but they all looked pitiful, limp, and ready to drop. Hardly anyone spoke. What was there to say? Did they find any diamonds.

I had expected to see someone from my group in the yard but I did not, hadn't since we first stood waiting to be registered. I couldn't stop thinking about them, especially the De Hartogs and the baby. What did they do to Rebecca's baby? How did things go for the De Hartogs? How did this gentle man deal with having to leave his wife with those dreadful soldiers? How did this kind and gracious lady handle herself? Perhaps she was lucky . . . like me.

It was already dark when I got my first bite of food and almost night before I was assigned a place to sleep. They put me and three other Es, into the E barracks; the remaining hundred or more were taken to different barracks. The young man who escorted us to the building housing the Es was, like my new friend Fritz, friendly and also a pool of information. But I was beyond hearing or caring. All I longed for was a bed, a pillow, sleep and oblivion for the rest of the century.

We ran into Betty at the bottom of the staircase. She said that she was just coming to fetch me, had of course expected my arrival and was mighty glad to see that I was at least still standing. Furthermore, she wasn't a bit surprised that I had gotten an E. So had she. She didn't wear it, though — one didn't have to.

Betty had managed to land herself a cushy job as a nurse, in what she called "the hospital." She may not have had the proper credentials, but she did wear the proper outfit, and she looked the part. With still not one hair out of place and still not one tiny spot on her lily white uniform, she appeared ridiculously unaffected by the drama being played out all around her.

I asked about Rainer, asked whether I could have a place close to hers so we could cheer each other up. But Betty did not want to discuss her very best friend. She just raised her hand like someone swatting a fly and said, "Forget about her, she's gone a bit cuckoo," and told me to follow her upstairs.

Nurse Betty had used her influence, or so she said, to reserve a good place in the E quarter for me. But I no longer could listen to her or bear to look into her beautiful, perfect, imperturbable face. Without a word I stumbled up the stairs behind her and on her heels into the unlit barracks. The tunnel darkness of the place was comforting. No eyes to stare at me, no tongues to ask questions. The little flashlight in Betty's hand led the way to the accommodation reserved for me. I had to climb up to it. It wasn't a bed and it wasn't a bunk. I didn't know what it was. It felt like wood. Betty left. She said that she had to go and that she would see me in the morning. I found a blanket and a pillow but no sheets.

Though there were no eyes to stare at me, no tongues to ask questions, I could hear them just the same. Hear them breathe. Hear them speak in hushed tones, hear them whisper and sigh. Hear them move, stir and maneuver about, restless and fidgety. I sat with my legs dangling, wakeful, listening, waiting . . . waiting for a brand-new nightmare.

I don't know when Mayer came to bring me another blanket. I don't know why he came, what he said, nor when I laid down, without undressing, and cried myself to sleep. I cried for two weeks and after that I did not cry again for two years. I also got my period that night, ten days early, had it for two weeks, and after that I did not have it again for two years.

I don't think that I paid much attention to life in the camp those first two weeks. I was too busy crying, having cramps, and fighting the demons that had moved into my head. I'd known that they would come if ever I got locked up for an unforseeable length of time. I knew it the night up in Margit's room with Rainer and Betty when suddenly the doorbell rang and we were trapped. I knew then that I could not just wait it out without going mad. It doesn't have to be a cell or a cage; a room can be a prison too, and a prison without bars is still a prison. Did I not leave because of it? The demons come to those who cannot bear to be deprived of freedom, of action or expression, to those who cannot bear to be stripped of their rights and will. There always must be choices. No human being is born to be somebody else's prisoner if he did not commit a crime.

My demons have not only moved into my head but also into my eyes and body. I not only know that the barracks are moving closer to the center of the prison yard but I can actually see it. Each day a few feet closer. No matter what I do or where I am — sitting, standing, walking — my inner eye sees the invisible walls pushing the barracks together till they have swallowed up the yard and crushed the people in it. I know it's going to happen. The pressure around my head and on my chest is immense, and at night I feel myself falling into something much blacker. It's like a cave-in, like being buried alive. I can hear myself scream, but no one else does, and I'm not dreaming. It's of mind, flesh and blood . . . and outside, nothingness.

I shook the demons when I had no tears left to cry, when somehow I sensed that even the worst reality had to be better than drowning in this black hole of madness.

Malin is about fifteen miles northeast of Brussels, at the crossroads between Brussels and Antwerp, and one of the oldest cities in this part of Europe. The city itself, perfectly circular and completely walled in, is where Belgium's world-famous lacemaking originated. When, or for whom, the barracks were built, I did not bother to investigate. I'm sure it wasn't for us.

According to Fritz, there were about eight hundred people in the camp when we arrived. Countdown here is fifteen hundred. It's not exactly a lucky number. It means transport. Where to, no one knows. But at fifteen hundred, the camp is full and needs to be emptied to make room for the next bunch . . . and the next . . . The only ones staying are Es and those performing some sort of a job like the girls in the office, or Fritz, the sign man, or Piet, who took me to the E building that first night. Piet is a watchmaker and is kept around to fix all the watches — the Nazi staff ones, not ours. We don't have them anymore. Piet is Dutch, from Amsterdam, and a fan of mine. He says I have lots of fans here because there are lots of people here from Amsterdam. Most of them, like him, came to Brussels a while back because of its being so much easier than in Holland. They liked it, stayed till they got caught. For some, it was collaborators causing their downfall; for others like Piet himself, an overdose of cocksureness. He openly sold stolen watches on the street. The rest, maybe as many as ninety, are just like me, disconcerted victims of Harry and John's incredible pyramid con game scheme.

Those who live in Belgium can get packages from home or friends: clothing, books, food, toiletries, even makeup and decent bedding. They also can send their dirty laundry home. We from Holland can't get or send anything. And they can get letters. We can't. Writing, however, is difficult for everyone.

For this, one needs special permission. They call this place a "detention camp," which means, I guess, that we are being detained. It sounds so simple, as if it were nothing more than a slight inconvenience.

I must learn who is who in here, who is important and who is not. Mayer is very important. He kind of runs the show for the Nazi brass. Mayer is the Jewish camp boss, acting as liaison between us, pig Boden and Commander Fränk. Mayer is married to a non-Jew, lives in Brussels and spends his weekends with her at home. Some say he doesn't have to be in Malin, that he has volunteered to assure fair treatment for us, whatever that means. Before he became important here, he was important on stage: Mayer is an operatic tenor. His native country is Germany, and he is basically a very decent man. It helps that he is not afraid of the brass, that his voice and physical appearance are impressive and that he seems to have figured out what makes those Third Reich bigwigs tick. It helps him that Commander Fränk has a soft spot for theater folk in general and tenors in particular, and it helps me that Mayer strongly believes in extending professional courtesy to his colleagues. He was helpful from the very first moment, even though his interest in me wasn't always strictly professional.

Mayer, who was never called anything but that by reticent Commander Fränk or his friends, is really a very smart man. Under the protection of the Germans, he officially has much more freedom and a better chance for safety than those in hiding or those with false IDs.

There are ten barracks in the camp, with room for about a hundred and fifty people in each. Two barracks per house, and all of them one flight up. Families may stay together; couples may stay together; everyone may stay together. Must stay together, since the sexes are not being separated. Our captors are extremely generous when it comes to our sleeping arrangements. They obviously believe in togetherness. I guess they are trying to keep mates and impetuous lovers from crossing the hallway at night. Couldn't handle the traffic. Unfortunately, with only one toilet outside in the corridor, the traffic at night is pretty heavy anyway. One toilet for three hundred. There are others, not too far from the E building, but they are meant for daytime use only. Those, about a dozen, are on the ground floor, all in one row and similar to ladies' rooms in a theater or hotel. The problem here is not only are they not ladies' rooms in a theater or hotel and not for ladies only, but that the lower part of the doors are all missing. The more seasoned detainees call it "the guessing room." Guess who is inside. Naturally, this too is a very busy place, and so are the showers next door, which are not so much for taking showers as they are for placing bets. Bookies are doing wonderfully well. They take bets on how long a wait, do the showers work, and is there any hot water? It's not a place for optimists, they almost always lose; pessimists, on the other hand, are thriving.

It's a good thing we spend as much time as we do in the guessing room, waiting to use the toilet, or next door placing a bet on a chance for a shower. There is no other place, no recreation or dining hall to hang around in. Only the yard. On rainy days we are stuck in our barracks within the confines of a three- by six-foot space, which we scoffingly call our pigeonhole. There is so little room that any moving about gets one into the neighbor's pigeonhole, which nobody appreciates. Everyone guards their own space fiercely. There are no lockers for one's effects, no shelves, no place to store anything. We have to improvise as best we can.

Each of the barracks has a *Stubenältester,* a barracks elder (men only), who is chosen by his peers but also must meet the approval of Unterschar-führer Boden which, strictly according to his mood, he sometimes gives and sometimes doesn't. An elder is responsible for all that happens in his barracks, from cleanliness to fights and thievery to making love, which should be done discreetly, and hopefully by mutual consent.

Whether there are benefits to being an elder is debatable. Fritz has been promoted to one and has moved into my barracks. Everybody likes the little guy. He is extremely helpful, has a good sense of humor and is a wizard when it comes to appropriating our own effects for the benefit of those who need it the most — us. He retrieved and returned Herbert's photograph; and my powder compact, mascara and lipstick. It is these small, personal things which suddenly take on immeasurable importance.

It is a major irony that while those hoarders thought they had taken everything from me, including my worthless little stork, I still have my gem-filled coat. How utterly bizarre that after all the tribulations of the last few weeks, the heart-stopping events which haven't quite yet registered, I still have my coat. And while my mind keeps stumbling over pictures that won't erase, like that of naked women with their legs spread wide and ugly jackals in search of diamonds, I still have my gem-filled coat. The only explanation of such a grotesque oversight is that those living in Belgium, those not having tried to flee, would not have had their valuables hidden and that these guards know that. Those in Belgium weren't going anywhere; only the

Dutch were. Besides, they don't really know where any of us come from. I wonder if the Nazi brass itself knows or cares where we are from.

There is, however, the undramatic possibility that nobody had thought of it. A fluke, no doubt, but wouldn't it be just like them to miss what's right in front of them? In any case, it is amusing and enormously intriguing, which doesn't mean that I know what or when I should do something about it. Mama would say, "Time will tell." I'll keep my coat for now and tell no one — forever.

The barracks buildings are all attached and geometrically identical. Four blocklike, equal squares, none larger than the other, none more inviting or in better shape. They have pitched roofs just high enough that one can't see what's on the other side, the part that is outside. For all I know, Camp Malin could be right smack in the middle of the city or in the sticks away from everything and everyone. It really doesn't matter all that much, merely one more thing to wonder about. To the left of the towering gate, which looks suspiciously like the entrance to a dungeon, is the hospital, the guards and Unterscharführer Boden's quarters. To the right is Mayer's one-room ground-floor domain; and above him, occupying the entire first floor, are Commander Fränk's quarters.

I'm told there is a wash kitchen and a real kitchen, right below Rainer's barracks, which I have never seen. Two more places one instantly hears about are the package room and the coal cellar. While being called to the first one is usually a happy event, the latter never is. Apparently getting one's package from home in one piece, with half of it missing, or not getting it at all depends solely on how many knives, sharp nail files or scissors Boden has bothered to look for and found. The cellar — pitch dark, dirty, with room enough for only one person to stand up in — is usually reserved for es-capees, the ones who have tried to escape in the past and are the most likely to try it again. The Nazi brass believes that a few days "in the hole" will ruin their appetite for it. Distressingly, though, someone like Boden, ill-tempered and fantastically perverted, can send one on a solo holiday to the cellar without any special reason.

I did not officially meet the one sleeping next to my pigeonhole till many days later, at first because nobody ever showed till after I had already cried myself to sleep and then because of a very conscious effort on the part of my neighbor not to meet me. The place on my left, adjoining the corner, was unoccupied, which made mine, with only one "bunkie" to deal with, a choice pigeonhole. When I finally got around to asking who my bunkie was, people giggled. All I had to do was point to the unoccupied place on my left, with its neatly stacked fine bedding, towels and perfumed lace handkerchiefs, and the entire barracks broke up with laughter.

And then one day the stranger who slept beside me said, "Good morning. My name is Jean. What is your favorite color?"

"Blue," I blurted out, completely startled and more than a bit amazed. "And green. Definitely green too!"

"Then we'll have blue one week and green the next. Grass green, like your eyes, that will be lovely. But you mustn't cry anymore, and you mustn't be sad," said the one who hadn't wanted to get to know me at all.

Jean sat, legs crossed, facing me, wearing ivory satin pajamas, smelling of jasmine soap and fresh mint tea, and looking exactly like Oscar Wilde's description in *The Picture of Dorian Gray*. I've never seen such an unflawed and beautiful human being. Jean had already had a whole succession of neighbors before I came along. Somehow, it had never worked out. Did others resent him for having taken up those extra spaces or for being different? Did he resent them for begrudging him those extra spaces or for making fun of his difference? Sometimes I think that he put up his investitures as sort of a barrier, a defense against encounters with narrow-minded men and women. Men afraid that sleeping next to him might actually rub off and change them. Women wanting to change him, wanting to convert Jean, with religion the last thing on their minds.

Friendships born in camps are cut from a different cloth. They're woven with a special thread — one that doesn't tear or weaken, for there is much that's woven into it. No past, no future, only the heartbeat of the moment. Because there is no past, no secrets to divulge, there are no lies. Because there is no future, there are no promises to keep. It is like having found another oar to row the life raft with. To keep from drifting too far away from shore. One stroke at the time, together. And soon I too slept on snow white linen sheets, on feather pillows under soft down covers, and soon I too smelled of jasmine soap and fresh mint tea and wore satin pajamas.

Jean got a package every week. His friend sent him the very best that money on the black market could buy. Food, too. The basic and the not so basic, like ordinary bread with real goose pâté de fois gras. Many a time it felt like we were on an island, the two of us. Especially at night's witching wishing hour, when there was no one to disrupt the magic carpet ride we took into the fairyland of dreams. During the daylight hours, we did what all the others did: we hung around. Jean started me on French again, saying that it was the language of music, the language of love.

Mayer came to see me every day. He thought it great that Jean and I were friends. "At least he keeps you in pâté and goodies," he'd say, "and out of harm's way." Jean did indeed, but what about Mayer? He kept inviting me to his room for tea, claiming that we needed to spend some time alone together so he could teach me about camp life. I liked him fine, but I certainly didn't believe that he had camp life on his mind. Neither did Jean. I told him that if I came, Jean would too; after that, Mayer quite suddenly ran out of tea. He didn't hold it against me, though. Jean said that we were lucky to have him at all. Mayer had warned me about Unterscharführer Boden from the start, repeatedly telling me to stay out of sight and to keep a low profile because of that crazed man's obsession with pretty girls. He hated them. I could, quite possibly, have understood if Boden, being so ugly himself, had hated good-looking men, but he didn't. He never gave a damn about them or other women — only the beautiful ones. Those he stalked, cornered, ridiculed, humiliated and tormented in the most obscene and beastly way. It wasn't always easy to stay out of sight, especially since one never knew when or where he was going to show up next.

Boden was in charge of the most uninspiring early morning exercises, with Mayer leading the parade. Fully dressed and with cobblestones under one's feet, it was difficult to think of this as beneficial to one's health. In the beginning I went every morning, found myself a place in the rear and yawned for an hour. Later on, I tried my very best to get out of it, which was by no means an easy task since almost everyone had the same idea. Unless one could get a note from Dr. Braun, the Jewish camp doctor, claiming previous injury, one had to put up with it. Whether or not an injury had actually occurred was of no importance. What was important was Dr. Braun's willingness to say so and Boden's willingness to accept it. Thanks to Mayer's affection for me and Dr. Braun's regard for Mayer, I got my note.

IT WAS BOUND TO HAPPEN. I knew all along no matter how low my profile, Boden would eventually find me. It was a morning like any other, one day more to get through, one day more away from home. I'd been sitting on my satin-covered pigeonhole in the empty E barracks, lipstick and mirror in hand, when I discovered that my powder compact was missing. I searched and searched but couldn't find it. Everyone else had already gone downstairs for their exercises, or so I thought, when I heard Boden's brazen voice thunder through the yard and barracks. "Everybody out! Get your ass down here and line up with the rest, or else. Now! I know there's someone still up there. If you're not out when I count to three, I'll help you down! What the devil kind of place you mongrels think we're running here? A health resort for lazy bums! Get your ass down here or I do it for you!"

It took longer than the count of three for me to decide whether I should hide under the pale blue down cover or go and face the wrath of ill-disposed, fiendish Boden. Afraid to be alone with him, I warily made my way down the stairs and out into the yard. The people from my barracks stood at attention facing Boden, who was facing the entrance and me. As if by silent command, heads turned the instant I'd stepped outside, eyes gaped. I felt like someone stripped naked and put on public display.

"Good morning, milady!" Boden roared mockingly. "How good of you to join us. I do hope we haven't inconvenienced you too much. We've been waiting for you. Your whole barracks has been waiting for you. I've been waiting for you! Just what was it that made milady late this morning? Needed help with your toilette, or what?"

He came very close, so close that I could see the veins on his temple pulsate. His scrutinizing, steel-cold eyes kept going over every inch of me as though he wanted to make absolutely sure that he remembered what I looked like for the next time around. He wanted to know whether I had left my tongue upstairs and just in case I hadn't would I consider telling him today why the hell I was late!

At this point, all I wanted was for it to be over. I was willing to say anything or do anything, anything to make him go away. I was even willing to tell the truth; what difference could it make? "I lost something," I whispered.

"What did you say?" he yelled. "I can't hear you! What's the matter, lost your voice too?"

I said it again, a bit louder, but he wasn't satisfied.

"Lost what?" he screamed. "What did you lose? Your virginity! Is that what? I think she lost her virginity. That's priceless. Shall we go and look for it!" Exulted and roaring with laughter, he was holding his potbelly, clutching it as if he wanted to make sure he wasn't going to lose that.

I timidly told him that it was my powder compact I had lost. For a moment he looked perplexed, not certain what to make of it, whether or not to keep on laughing. I don't think the absurdity of it ever really registered with him. For a second he stood motionless. Then he let go of his belly, crossed his arms over his chest in a challenging stance, shook his head, whistled through his teeth, repeated, "Powder compact, powder compact," as if to assure himself that he'd gotten it right, and called Fritz, our barracks elder.

"The pretty girl here needs some powder," he told him in a deliberately false tone. "Let's help her out and get some for her." The rest of it he whispered into Fritz's ear. I watched Fritz's face as he listened. He looked stunned, embarrassed and ill at ease. His head turned, and he walked away,

Fritz was heading to the other end of the yard where Rainer's barracks and the kitchen was. The people around me kept clearing their throats as one does in awkward situations. After Fritz had disappeared, I lowered my head and fixed my eyes on the rims of the stones in front of me. It was so much better than having to look at Boden's repulsive face. Anything was better than that.

I do not know how much time passed before Fritz returned, only that I didn't lift my eyes again until I heard that dreadful Nazi spit out more of his sarcastic garbage directed solely at me. He boorishly growled that he had made sure it would last me for a while and that he was pleased he'd been able to help me out. It was then that I saw Fritz hand Boden a bulky burlap sack, saw Boden open it, and before I could step out of the way, I got hit in the face with a torrent of flour, followed immediately by a second, bigger load. It burned my eyes and made me cough and choke. When I tried to shield my face, Boden dumped all of it over my head. I was covered with it. My hair was buried in it. I stood, very much aware that nearly a thousand of my fellow prisoners, including the latest arrivals, must have been watching this vile spectacle born of Boden's unconscionably warped mind.

My eyes, though shut, were burning and my mouth, full of white dust, tasted like chalk — and yet I did not think a single thought . . . Not of how degrading this situation was or what to do about it . . . Not even after the great man had left. My mind had slipped into a vault of its own making, locked itself in, to let the pain subside, to give me time to wrestle with my humiliation which, like an open sore, hurt so much more than my stinging eyes.

I took the hand reaching for mine and followed it to where the showers were. It was Maggie's hand. Maggie was Fritz's girlfriend, but more than that, she worked in the kitchen and always remembered her friends. Fritz had gone to fetch her after Boden had had his fun with me. I remember her washing my hair again and again and that she took my clothes and lent me some of hers. She didn't say much, only that she was glad she wasn't beautiful. Maggie was nice-looking, the kind Unterscharführer Boden never bothered with.

Mayer had missed my initiation ceremony. He was in Brussels on an extended weekend furlough, practicing marital bliss. When he heard about it, he got terribly upset, perhaps believing if he had been there, he might have been able to prevent it. Boden would not have listened to him; Boden listened to no one. He hardly paid any attention to Commander Fränk. Mayer said that Fränk and Boden weren't all that fond of one another. Commander Fränk was very reserved. All he wanted was a good report card from Berlin, no Gestapo in his camp, and for everything to run smoothly. Apart from that, I think he did frown on pigs like Boden, did disapprove of their insidious ways. In addition to abusing pretty girls, Boden enormously enjoyed hosing down groups of people just standing around. For this, he used the heavy firehose. Once it was in full swing, he didn't quit until they all had been flung around, knocked over, and at least half a dozen had sustained severe injuries. Screams didn't help. Pleading did not help. There had to be half a dozen broken bones, or worse, plus major confusion before he would have the water turned off. The entire camp yearned for Unterscharführer Boden to get transferred to the front or worse, but it never happened.

I spent much time with Rainer in her barracks. It was the one that housed most of the Dutch — those who'd been living in Belgium and those who had come here the hard and expensive way, like Rainer, Betty, myself and my group. Suckers, all of us, who thought money was the only price one had to pay for freedom and that all those aiding us were doing it for humanitarian reasons only. What a rude awakening! In Rainer's barracks, there were plenty of stories that made the rounds, and they were, except for minor variations, almost identical. Beginning with waterfront Harry, our only contact in Amsterdam, to John, the common man with an uncommon talent for smokescreening the truth, to Mother Earth, the farmer, aloof Madame Zeker, and finally Max. We had all met and relied on the same people. We had walked the same roads, stuck it out in the same ditch, rode the same trains, slept in the same beds, and in the end there was always Max. He'd taken some of them directly to Malin, without first bothering to stop at

Avenue Louise; others had spent the night facing a wall somewhere, waiting to be shot.

What remained constant was Max picking us up at Madame Zeker's and handing us over to the Gestapo. Some people in Rainer's barracks knew Max from before the invasion, others from after. They had belonged to the same temple. On high holidays they had prayed together — prayed for peace and for the safety of all Jews. One of the men claimed that Max had once gotten arrested with a whole lot of other Jews, but while none of the others ever returned, Max had been seen walking the streets again. "I hope he knows God real good," said a woman whose brother had gotten picked up with Max and not heard from since. "I wonder what kind of excuse he'll be giving Him or us when it's over."

Also discussed at great length was the incident on the train with the trench-coat-clad stranger on the platform. Seems that I wasn't the only one who had seen him, nor the only one he had signaled: There had been others before me. Their reaction was no different from mine: they were as scared as I was. The moment they'd confronted John with it, he made them change railroad cars just as he'd done with us, and his explanation as to the identity of the man was word for word what John had told us. As if he had learned it verbatim, rehearsed it, so as not to make a single mistake. But there was one couple in Rainer's barracks who swore that it was precisely the other way around. The couple had talked to the man without John catching on, and he had told them the same thing about John that John had told them — and later us — about him. He had desperately tried to warn them, wanted them to get off the train and just run. Of course they didn't believe him.

The one who showed practically no interest at all was Rainer. She didn't cry much anymore, but she was sad all the time. Most of the people in her barracks had tried to draw her out, but she did not respond. She hardly talked. Whenever Rainer did reply to some sort of suggestion, it usually amounted to not much more than a "what for?" Much of the time she just sat with her legs crossed, looking straight ahead. She had lost quite a bit of weight and had started to look gaunt. Betty, she never mentioned. I knew that she looked forward to seeing me and that she did feel somewhat better with me around. But I couldn't snap her out of it either. The one who had tried the hardest was Rainer's barracks elder, Martin. Martin and his two friends, Heinz and Werner, both barracks elders in other pigeonholes, were the best there were. Super-handsome, super-intelligent, decent and brave. I came to think of their presence as preordained. If not to openly wage war for us, at least to balance the scale between good and evil. Boden's evil, their good.

At some point, Martin and I became lovers. Instant friendship and instantly inseparable, that's how it was. Not only Martin but Heinz and Werner were my friends too, my brothers. Sharing, caring and looking after me. In olden days, the three of them would have been Don Quixotes fighting to right every wrong. Now, arrow-straight in every way, with a strong sense of self-worth and respect for others, they walked tall and unshaken down this troublesome path.

Elders did not have to sleep in the barracks they were in charge of, and most of them didn't. The idea was to have some time to oneself. My three knights had chosen Werner's barracks because it was the least crowded. There we sat then, the four of us — or five with Jean — studying French, telling stories, and cheering each other up.

Whenever I had an especially bad day, for all the reasons in the world, or maybe just a few, and as a result became distant, indifferent and unfeeling, Martin would take me in his arms and say, "Don't let your heart grow cold and don't turn away. You can't make it alone. None of us can. We need to hold each other so we can hold on. But most of all, we need to remember love." Only twenty-five, he was wise beyond his years. It sometimes seemed as if he had been on this earth before, had walked undazzled and unperplexed in some ancient wise man's shoes. He was a constant surprise to me. So were his friends. Physically, Heinz and Werner could have been brothers. Both were blonder than any Swede or German, over six feet tall, and definitely the type that looked as good in bathing trunks as evening clothes, neither of which they wore in the camp.

Until about ten years ago, Heinz and Werner had belonged to the privileged class. As sons of rich Jews, German ones at that, they soon found their privileged childhood replaced by underprivileged teens. They came to Belgium with their parents, settled in Brussels where both continued their higher education. Heinz studied architecture, Werner medicine. They met in a paddy wagon after a raid on their university landed them first in Gestapo headquarters at Avenue Louise and then in Malin.

Martin had gone a similar route a month earlier. He too was German but had come alone to Holland first. His family, he hoped, had made it to England. Martin was born in Westphalia, the major industrial and coal-mining region of Germany. There, his great-grandfather had a soft goods store which later became a department store and later yet the largest one around. It was a thriving family business, which one day would be his. The business and his family, having been there for almost a hundred years, were highly respected. But like so many others, the family was oblivious to the changing climate. One night, someone put a torch to the store, and what had taken four generations to build was gone.

Martin had gotten to Brussels before the vicious raids in Amsterdam had begun and had been able to work there, sort of. His ending up in Malin was the unfortunate result of being in the wrong place at the wrong time: he got caught trading food stamps. No crime, not even under the iron swastika hand. Except that the man he traded with had been under surveillance, suspected of having too much of that good stuff to be legit. Martin knew nothing about it.

↜ Eleven

I T R E A L L Y W O U L D H A V E B E E N S O M E T H I N G to write home about, if they had let us write: Theater — a show — entertainment! Every Sunday afternoon.

When this all started, I don't know, only that most people in the camp were looking forward to it. Evidently they had been doing this all along, except that the last performances had gotten rained out, which meant that I'd never seen one. When Mayer asked me to lend my talent to the next production, I wasn't quite sure how to react. I did have mixed feelings about it, mainly because of Martin, who definitely did not want me to have anything to do with it. There was a bit of a feud going on between the two of them on account of it, with me in the middle. Mayer tried to win me over by assuring me that it would be very professional, which he said was a cinch with all the artists we had in the camp. Real actors, real dancers and singers with real musicians playing real instruments on a real stage.

Since Mayer had suitcases full of great material, it naturally would have to be a great show. When I still hesitated, he came up with little bribes, like double rations, meaning two bowls of watery soup instead of just one and two slices of old bread instead of one, plus not having to get up early in the moming. It didn't sway me. He finally appealed to my sense of fairness and my ego, telling me how much a little entertairment meant to my fans.

What Mayer didn't tell me was that it had not been Mayer himself who had thought of entertainment. It had been Commander Fränk's idea, his brainchild. What Mayer also failed to mention was that, most of the time, Fränk, Boden and the rest of the loyal brigade sat in the first row watching the show. A regular weekly social event for friend and enemy alike. It certainly explains Martin's opposition. Martin did not approve of entertaining Nazis, even though it wasn't just for them, and knew that I didn't either. Mostly though, because of my run-in with Boden, Martin felt that Mayer should not have asked me at all, or should at least have told me whom I'd be singing to. He was right all the way except that Mayer, who also knew how I felt, thought it might ease the tension and get me off the hook with Boden. I told Mayer to positively count me out. He did — for all of two weeks. After that, he came to tell me that I had been ordered to appear or else. "Or else" to me meant a stint in the cellar, but since I had met some very nice people who'd been there and did make it through, I still said no. The next day, Boden's sneering voice came over the loudspeaker announcing the cancelation of all future shows in retaliation for a certain redheaded young actress's refusal to appear. Any complaints were to be directed to the person responsible.

The next step was either to wait for a mob of angry people to do who knows what to me, or tell Mayer, in spite of Martin's objection, that I would go on. I told him that I was ready to perform and to schedule rehearsals. I am not good at rehearsals, which probably out of sheer desperation gave me the idea. If I were to practice clumsiness, sing off-key and do whatever else I could to be so bad that they would never ask me again, who could fault me? And why not? I only said I would go on — I didn't say that I would be good. What could they do to me, cancel my contract?

Mayer was so relieved that he gave me everything I asked for. Mainly time and space to practice alone. Never thought that making a fool of oneself could be such a difficult job. It wasn't until Mayer, one day before the performance, handed me the words to a new song, that I seriously wondered about what kind of audience the song was meant for. Not my fan club, for sure. What he had given me was two pages of the worst trash, filth and obscene smut — a gift from Boden — with a special request, not order, to add it to my regular routine. I don't know who was more sickened by it, Mayer or I. He stuttered his apologies, saying that he had never felt worse in his life, but would I try it anyway. Just to show Boden that I wasn't afraid to play his game. For a short minute we looked at each other, and then we both walked away. I never looked at it again. Crumpled up, I kept it in my coat pocket, wondering whether a man like Boden had ever had a decent thought in his head.

Outside in the courtyard, they had built a real stage. The one thing seldom lacking in a camp are skilled workers. There was an unusual amount of excitement the Sunday of the show. People were pouring into the yard, fighting for a good place. There were no chairs, and everybody had to stand — scrapes and shuffling for a place in front started long before showtime. How can I describe the way I felt that day? I had never deliberately messed up a performance before, but then I had never been in a situation like that either. Martin would not attend, nor would Heinz and Werner. There were others who, also quietly opposed to the whole idea, remained in their barracks. Still, the large majority just wanted to forget for a while and laugh a bit.

I had stayed clear of the stage and anything close to it till it was time for me to go on. Mayer had given me his room to change in and then his arm to lead me to the open stage. I never liked performing in an outdoor theater and even less in broad daylight. Too many distractions to tear away the veil of mystery that hangs between the audience and me. I do not need to see them to know they are there. But on this Sunday I would have to see them, witness their expressions change from happy anticipation to disgruntled disappointment. I'll lose my fan club for sure. Well, better a fan club than one's principles. My time on stage — three songs, a dance and chitchat — was scheduled to last about fifteen minutes.

I lasted about two, perhaps not even that. One look down at the first two rows and I went numb. There, in medal-studded uniforms and spit-polished boots, sat the Gestapo, big shots straight from their headquarters at Avenue Louise, all the way from Brussels. With their prim and proper wives and girlfriends whalebone-stiff and pompous, they all sat on folding chairs staring, with ghoulish curiosity, straight at me. Boden, smack in the middle, had next to him a painted female, while Commander Fränk with his wife, a nervous brunette in a silver fox coat, by his side took up the last chairs of the first row. Also present, to my ultimate dismay, was the Gestapo chief himself, the one with the scarred face, whose men had found my torn fake ID. As big shots go, he was the biggest shot of all.

They'd obviously come at Commander Fränk's invitation, expecting, if not lavish entertainment, to have a good time, a laugh or two and the pleasure of gawking at us. Maybe they did just that before my entrance, and quite possibly after my exit, but not while I was on stage. No one had a good time then, least of all me. If I could have focused my eyes on something or someone else, I would have. But I could not do it. There were too many of them — too many Germans, too many uniforms, too many skull heads on their caps. Too much Gestapo! It threw me completely, so much so that I didn't have to pretend being awful. I was. The moment I opened my mouth, my voice trembled, cracked, got hoarse, and within a few seconds disappeared altogether. While my lips kept on forming soundless words, the musicians kept playing the same introduction over and over. At some point I signaled for them to stop. They did, and that's when one of the Germans called out: "Dance! Dance for us!"

Without remembering a single step, fake or otherwise, and without any music, I began to move. First slow, then wild and frantic. I did leaps and ac-robatics, meaningless pantomime, slithering and sliding across the stage in such an undisciplined and erratic fashion that I don't think anyone knew what was going on. I somehow ended with a split, about the only thing I recalled having choreographed, and stayed down till Mayer came and led me off.

Nightmarish debacle aside, they were convinced that I'd been putting on an act. In any event, they never asked me again . . . That was the good news. The bad news was that they took away my E4 status. This not only meant that I had to give up the nice pigeonhole next to my lovely Jean, the snow white linen sheets, the jasmine soap and morning mint tea; much more worrisome was the reality that came with it. It meant that I now had become fair game for the next transport. I really had no proof that losing my secu-rity E status was the result of what they had interpreted as deliberate blun-dering, but I had no proof that it wasn't. Nobody seemed to be willing to discuss it, no one actually seemed to know. The best anyone could come up with was: It must have come from headquarters in Brussels.

I moved into Werner's barracks, where Heinz and Martin also slept. Their pigeonholes were next to each other, but much to Martin's and my disappointment, there was no space left for me. In fact, there wasn't much left anywhere else either. Martin decided that I should settle in at the far end of the barracks so as not to be bothered by the comings and goings that went on most of the night, the toilet-going traffic. My new pigeonhole was not a corner one; thus, I had a bit less space, and two neighbors instead of one. Neither of their pigeonholes had clean sheets, or even anything vaguely resembling sheets. The pigeonhole to my left looked like someone had dumped a garbage can, and the one to the right had a worn pair of shoes and nothing else. I think it's understandable that I wasn't all that anxious to meet the inhabitants, especially since Martin and I had counted on spending some special time together, some hard to come by privacy.

I saw the messy one right after lunch when he climbed up to his pigeonhole to take a nap. Later in the evening, shortly before lights out, the wornshoe owner showed up too. They weren't the average neighbors, even here. While the first one did little more than totally ignore me, the second one went straight to Werner and told him to get rid of me. He wasn't having me next to him. Martin had had no idea who my bedmates were and had hoped to get one of them to trade places with him, but neither wanted to budge. One would not give up his corner, or his mess; and the other, well, he operated on a different wavelength altogether.

He was a rabbi, an Orthodox one at that. He wore a long black coat, a black broad-brim hat, a prayer shawl and everything else that his traditional getup required, including a long beard and long curled sideburns. What else he wore on his back, or rather under his coat, were his possessions. It wasn't really all that much; still, it made him look baggy, unshapely and a bit farcical. Too much like one of Hitler's nasty caricatures geared to make brainwashed ignoramuses think that's what all Jews look like. The thick, old-fashioned spectacles he wore — hiding his eyes almost completely — his gray untrimmed beard, stooped shoulders and foot-dragging walk, made him look quite old, probably older than he was. I never learned his name or anything about him, nor did I ever speak to him, mainly because he never spoke to me. A very unpleasant rabbi. He never used his other pair of shoes, he just kept them there to let everyone know that this space was taken. He never stopped complaining, broke out in rages, kept throwing my belongings to the ground and, in a most un-Orthodox way, cursed Werner and me.

What the good rabbi did not do was explain to us the real reason for his unprovoked complaints. Quite possibly he expected every Jew to know, which every Jew, of course, didn't. Only after talking to people familiar with Orthodox Judaism did we learn that a man may not sleep next to a woman at the time of her monthly cycle, when, says the Orthodox law, the woman is unclean. Taking into account that the good rabbi never changed his clothes, never removed his coat, never even changed his socks or anything else, sleeping fully clothed always with his back to me, one might wonder who then was unclean. It didn't shake my self-confidence even a bit. Still, it's sort of strange to be sleeping next to a man who absolutely doesn't want to sleep with you. These were distinctly not normal times.

I didn't fare much better with the messy one to my left. The fact that I knew his name was merely due to everyone knowing it, not to any effort on his part. Jonny. Jonny was a scamp. It was hard to think of him sitting around a dinner table with family and friends. It was hard to think of him as ever having had family and friends. He was cute in a fresh, snappy, youthful way. Jonny did not look like a man but like a boy whose head mistakenly had been screwed onto a man's body. He had laughing but watchful big blue eyes, a dimple on his chin, an open smile and a shock of blond hair. He was short, five six, and muscular like a gymnast. Agile and fast. No one really knew Jonny well — he made sure of that. Footloose, self-sufficient, irrepressible and unflinching, he was serious about one thing only, and that was taking real good care of himself. He exercised a lot, slept a lot and ate a lot because, as he'd be quick to declare, "My body needs it." No one knew where his food packages came from, but he got one every week and feasted on it. He shared with no one, not because he was greedy but because he was always hungry. Each week there was a large white handkerchief inside his package which he used to spread the goodies out on. When he was done, he dumped the rest out in my pigeonhole. I could always tell when he'd gotten another food parcel by the crumbs and peels on my side.

Infuriating as he was, it was not easy to be mad at him, especially when one night after curfew, he took off so Martin and I could be alone. "I'm going to get some air," he announced almost convincingly, as though there was any air to be gotten in the cold hallway at night with all windows shut. "I'll be back in an hour. Don't touch my food," and off he went. He left us alone many a night. We never asked him to; he just did. On those nights, and there were more than just a few, I saw no demons, heard not the drums of war and what I felt while in my lover's arms was joy, beautiful love, my heart at ease.

Jonny had quite a reputation to live up to because though well acquainted with the cellar, having been one of the regulars there, he didn't let the damp and dirty darkness of it get to him. He took his lumps steadfastly and unafraid. Twice before, he had escaped but within hours had gotten picked up again. Jonny knew how to get out but not how to stay out. It al-

* Silvia's mother Adrienne
* Silvia's father, Berthold Grohs, and
  Uncle Rudy, 1920.
* Silvia's mother Adrienne, sister Kate,
  Silvia (bottom left), and twin
  sister Elly, 1919.
* Silvia and Elly walking on the
  boardwalk in Scheveningen,
  Holland, 1938.

* Herbert Nelson, Rudolf Nelson and Mrs. Kate
  Nelson, Amsterdam, late 1942.
* Silvia's friend Toni and Martin Roman at the
  piano in Silvia's Amsterdam apartment, c. 1942.
* Bottom: Silvia's 21st birthday party with Herbert
  and friends at her home in Amsterdam, 1939

* Friend, Rudolf Nelson, Silvia and Herbert Nelson, Silvia's former husband and son of Rudolf, late 1942.
* Silvia, Rudolf Nelson, and Fritzi Schadl (one of the performers R. Nelson had brought with him from Berlin to Amsterdam), 1942.
* The three beauties: Margit, Silvia and Toni, Amsterdam 1943.

* Silvia, c. 1946.
* Revue with Scherzer, de Vries.

* Henriette Davids, Silvia and Sylvain Poons
  in "Artis."
* Davids and Poons singing a song from one of their
  most famous films, "De Jantes."

* Otto Wallburg and Herbert Scherzer.
* Right: Martin Roman and Eddie de Jong.
* Paul Godwin.

* Silvia and Herbert Scherzer, singing and dancing. R. Nelson on the piano

* Top left: Silvia and Henriette Davids as
  "The Nelson Sisters," a parody of the
  Andrews Sisters, 1943.
* Left center: Rudolf Nelson with some members
  of his Schouwburg orchestra: Werner Ulmann, Paul
  Godwin, Juan Miguel, Eddie de Jong, and
  Martin Roman.
* Bottom left and center: Scenes from Rudolf Nelson's
  production "Jazz-Teufel."
* Bottom left: Cabaret scenes with Silvia, Otto
  Wallburg, Sylvain Poons, Herbert Scherzer, Ali Muk,
  Lilli Michel, Michel Gobets, and Ellen Schwarz.
* Right: Silvia in "Lucky Star"
* Top Center: Ali Muk, Ellen Schwarz, Silvia, and
  Lilli Michel.

* Finale of "Cheerio" with (from left to right) Robert de Vries,
Michel Gobets, Otto Wallburg, Henrietta Davids, Sylvain
Poons, Silvia, Kurt Lilien, Ellen Schwarz, and Herbert Scherzer.

Beglaubigte Ausfertigung.

Notariatsurkunde.

Vor mir, dem Stellvertreter des Budapester königlichen öffentlichen Notars Dr. Izsó Lukács, vor Dr. Árpád Gedő erschienen am unterfertigten Orte und Tag Karl Hagymási, Privatier, wohnhaft Budapest, VI. Aradi-ucca 41., der seine Personidentität mit seinem, auf seine person bezüglichen Urkunden nachgewiesen hat und gab vor mir die folgende
--------Erklärung,--------
ab, und ersuchte mich um die Aufnahme derselben in einer Notariatsurkunde.

Ich, unterfertigter Karl Hagymási erkläre hiermit, dass ich mit der, im Jahre 1882. in Budapest geborenen Frau Berthold Grohs /Grosz/, geb. Adrienne Lauter – die zurzeit im Amsterdam /Maastraat 140. Zuid/ wohnt – in den Jahren 1917 – 1918. /Tausendneunhundertsiebzehn – Tausendneunhundertachtzehn/ in ständigem Liebesverhältnisse gelebt habe und aus dieser Liebschaft wurde von der Frau Berthold Grohs geb. Adrienne Lauter in Wien am 1. ersten Oktober des Jahre 1918. /Tausendneunhundertachtzehn/ ein Mädchen geboren, die den Vornahme Silvia erhielt. Ich anerkanne daher, dass ich der natürliche Vater der Silvia Grohs bin, die Zurzeit in Belgien. /Nr. R. 4. Sammellager Mechelen, Kaserne Dossin/ lebt, be-

---

ziehungsweise, dass Silvia Grohs meine natürliche Tochter ist,--------

Im Bewusstsein meiner strafrechtlichen Verantwortlichkeit erkläre ich, dass meine Abstammung rein kristliche ist und unter meinen Ahnen kein Einziger, aus jüdischer Abstammung war.--------

Ich bin bereit diese Erklärung vor mehr welchen Behörde auch mit meinem Eid zu bekräftigen.--------

Von dieser Urkunde können beglaubigte Ausfertigungen für Silvia Grohs und deren Budapester Bevollmächtigten, dem Herrn Rechtsanwalt Dr. Áron Gellért /Budapest, VI. Andrássy-ut 10./ in unbeschränkter Zahl ausgefolgt werden.---

Worüber ich königlicher Notarsubstitut diese Urkunde aufnahm, dieselbe der Partei vorlies, worauf sie dieselbe, mit der Äusserung, dass ihre Erklärung richtig in dieser Urkunde aufgenommen wurde und sie dieselbe guthiess, - vor mir eigenhändig unterfertigte.--------

Budapest am 23. dreiundzwanzigsten Juli 1943. Tausendneunhundertdreiundvierzig.--------
Karl Hagymási m. p. Dr. Árpád Gedő m. p. Substitut des Budapester königl. öffent. Notars Dr. Izsó Lukács laut Erlass Nr. 1412/1932. der Budapester königl. Notariatskammer /L.S./ ---

Ich beurkunde, dass diese, dem Herrn Rechtsanwalt Dr. Aron Gellért ausgefolgte beglaubigte Ausfertigung mit der, mit 6 Pengő Stempelgebühr versehen, in meinem Archiv unter Geschäftszahl 1198/1943. aufbewahrten Original - Notariatsurkunde in Allem übereinstimmt.--------

Budapest am 23. dreiundzwanzigsten Juli 1943. Tausendneunhundertdreiundvierzig.--------

---

Dr. Árpád Gedő m. p. Subsitut des Budapester königl. öffentl. Notars Dr. Izsó Lukács laut Erlass Nr 1412/1932. der Budapester königl. Notariatskammer /L.S./ ----------

26/1943. Fordítási sorszám.
Hivatkozással a magyar királyi igazságügyminiszter urnak 1405/1933. VII. I. M. számu rendeletével nyert jogosítványomra, - tanusítom, hogy ez a német fordítás az idefűzött hiteles kiadvány magyar szövegével mindenben összhangzó. - - -
Budapesten, 1943. ezerkilencszáznegyvenhárom évi julius hó 23. huszonharmadik napján. --------
Mit Berufung auf meine, vom königl. ungarischen Justizminister unter Erlass Zahl 1405/1933. VII. I. M. erteilte Berechtigung, beurkunde ich, dass diese deutsche Übersetzung mit dem ungarischen Texte der beigehefteten beglaubigten Ausfertigung in Allem übereinstimmt.--------
Budapest am 23. dreiundzwanzigsten Juli 1943. Tausendneunhundertdreiundvierzig.--------

Substitut des Budapester königl. öffentl. Notars Dr. Izsó Lukács laut Erlass Nr. 1412/1932 der Budapester königl. Notariatskammer. - - -

Zufolge des Auftrages der Deutschen Gesandtschaft in Budapest stempelfrei.

Hivatkozással a budapesti kir. törvényszék elnöke előtt tett eskümre hitelesen bizonyítom, hogy ezen fordítás a hozzáfűzött irattal szó szerint megegyezik.

Mit Berufung auf meinen vor dem Präsidenten des königl. Gerichtshofes in Budapest geleisteten Eid bestätige ich amtlich, dass diese Übersetzung mit dem angehefteten Schriftstück wörtlich übereinstimmt.

Budapest, 1943. den 24. Juli.

Original wird hiermit bescheinigt.

Amsterdam, den 20. September 1943

AMTLICHE DEUTSCHE BERATUNGSSTELLE
IN DEN NIEDERLANDEN
DIENSTSTELLE AMSTERDAM

Im Auftrage

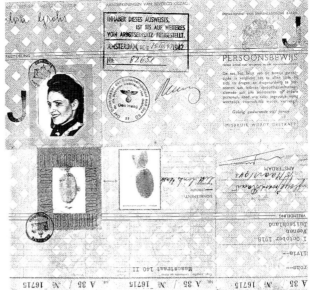

* Silvia's Dutch Jewish ID card, March 1943.
* Scenes of the theater backyard
* The infamous forged letter that tried to establish Silvia as the daughter of an Aryan Hungarian father, in a failed attempt to free her from Malines.

* Inside of the Schouwburg as it looked when Silvia performed there.
* Bottom right: A Holocaust museum now stands on the site of the Shouwburg.

SILVIA GROHS

Silvia Grohs ist in Wien geboren. Sie wurde früh Schauspielerin und war nacheinander am Deutschen Volkstheater, an der Volksoper, im Neuen Wiener Schauspielhaus und im Cabaret «Literatur am Naschmarkt» verpflichtet. Sie spielte zunächst ernste Rollen: Eliza Doolittle in «Pygmalion», das Hannele in «Hanneles Himmelfahrt», die Schlagermizzi in «Liebelei» und die Anni im «Abschiedssouper» von Schnitzler — um nur einige Beispiele zu nennen. Dann ging Silvia als Star einer Wiener Revue auf Tournee in die Schweiz, von wo aus sie als erste Tanzsoubrette an die Fritz Hirsch-Operette in Holland engagiert wurde. Später wechselte sie als Chansonnière und Schauspielerin zur Willy Rosen-Revue über, um dann als Star zur Nelson-Revue zu gehen.

Silvia Grohs ist Schauspielerin, Soubrette und Chansonnière — zur Zeit ist sie die Diseuse der Herbert Nelson-Chansons. In Holland war sie viel fürs Radio tätig; auch hier in der Schweiz hat sie schon vor dem Mikrophon gearbeitet.

Den Krieg hat Silvia Grohs in Holland mitgemacht. Beim Versuch, Verfolgte über die Grenze zu bringen, wurde sie in Brüssel von der Gestapo verhaftet und in Mecheln interniert. Ab 1943 wurde sie von einem Konzentrationslager zum anderen verschickt: sie kam nach Auschwitz und von dort nach Ravensbrück, wo sie drei Monate vor Kriegsschluss in einen unter der Erde gelegenen Bunker gesperrt wurde. Hier wurde sie vom Roten Kreuz befreit. Seither ist sie wieder zusammen mit ihrem Gatten Herbert Nelson tätig.

* A page Silvia saved from Song-Magazin, November/December 1946.
* Silvia's Dutch Jewish ID card, March 1943.
* Announcement for a show at the Hollandsche Schouwburg, 1941.
* Announcement for a show at the Joodsche Schouwburg, 1943.

* Silvia, Amsterdam, 1945.

ways happened during transport, not in the camp itself. There was no getting away from here. Too small a place and not a single open space except for
the enclosed courtyard. No fences to climb, and the only way out was
through the huge, well-guarded gate. Of course we all knew that Jonny
would try again. I often wondered what exactly he was escaping in. He only
wore shorts — white short shorts. I'd seen a couple of shirts and some pants
stuffed in a pillowcase which he kept in his corner but never wore. Then
there was the small matter of shoes. He had sandals but didn't wear them
either. Rain or shine, he went barefoot. He said he could run faster that way.
Run where? Like the rabbi's worn shoes, Jonny's sandals were just standing
around taking up space.

The good rabbi and Jonny had never even exchanged glances. The only
thing the two had in common was me as a bedmate, which didn't thrill
either of them. When Jonny slept, he slept. When the rabbi slept, he snored
or else he prayed. I don't know whether God could hear the rabbi's prayers,
but He definitely could hear him snore.

There's no denying that the pit of my stomach would drop down to my
toes, or turn into knots, whenever the trucks brought new arrivals. At first I
didn't even dare to look for Mama and Herbert, or any of my friends. Instead, I would ask Rainer to do it, but she always claimed that she didn't
know them well enough and wouldn't recognize them. It wasn't true at all.
She knew them all right, but never stopped feeling guilty. Meanwhile, I
drove myself into a frenzy counting the days starting from the date of my
first card, when mailed and possibly received, to the date of the second card,
the stampless and most crucial one. Could anyone have really found and
mailed the second card in time?

I'd finally gotten permission to write home. Yet, no letter, no reply, nothing. Two months had passed since I'd first landed in Malin. I'd watched
spring come and go, a spring without flowers and without the scent of lilacs
caressing the air. A spring that would be hard to remember and impossible
to forget. One afternoon I was called to the guardhouse. Because of my genuine dislike for the two miserable soldiers there, I'd never gone near the forbidding gate. Besides, I hardly needed a reminder to know that I was locked
in and up. As I got within a few feet of it, I saw a wondrous sight.

The gate was wide open. And on the other side, like in a dream, stood Margit — my beautiful, loyal, gallant friend. She smiled that enchanting smile of
hers, which made me feel instantly warm and good. With the exhilaration

of someone just glad to be alive and free, she called to me: "I've brought your papers. Your father's Aryan papers. From Budapest. It's all in here!" In her right hand she held a large manila envelope, which she kept swinging back and forth so I was sure to see it. Then, using a great deal of pathos, Margit began to sing, hamming it up something dreadful. All that was missing was her broken-down guitar. I knew that she was doing this to confuse the guards. She sang a chorus first, then verse, chorus and verse, repeating that very soon I would be free. "Mayer knows, Mayer knows," she twittered, while the guards, totally befuddled, kept clutching their rifles. My heart dancing, I leaped forward, dashed through the gate, and right into Margit's arms.

The reunion did not last very long. I got pulled back almost immediately. The crowd, which had gathered quickly, expressed its amazement and amusement with loud cheers and applause. It ended when Mayer grabbed my arm and whizzed me straight to his room. He sat me down and told me to stay put. He would handle it. His voice was anything but calm. He was anything but calm and I was a long way from comprehending what had really taken place. Mayer said to wait for him and not to budge, no matter what, he'd explain it all later. I heard him lock the door and walk away. The loud, cheering voices in the courtyard had become muffled yet quite orderly, as though they all were one and the same.

I did not budge. All I did was watch the minute hand on his alarm clock mark time. It jerked a little whenever the seconds had gone full circle before it jumped to the next minute and the next. As if it was hard work just to keep going, even for a clock.

Nice room . . . nice man . . . And he didn't even bring me here to sample his brand of tea. When I first came to the camp, he'd promised to write home for me. I honestly never believed he really meant it, thinking it was just another ploy to get me to go to bed with him.

Forty minute-jumps later, Mayer returned, without Margit, without the manila envelope and without my papers. He said she'd gone back to Brussels to try her luck with Erdman, the biggest big shot of them all. Erdman was head of the entire region's occupying forces. I couldn't believe that Margit had actually been here and left again without my having had a chance to talk to her. It made me terribly sad. At least Mayer, trying his best to sound cheerful, could give me a pretty good account of Margit's unprecedented visit. Though it was no substitute for hearing it directly from her, better than not hearing it at all.

Margit had gotten to the camp early in the morning and had told the guards she wished to see the Commander. With a letter of introduction, fake, in her pocket from a so-called party pal in Amsterdam and the long-awaited documents from my brand-new bought and paid for Aryan Hungarian father, Margit had hoped to convince Commander Fränk to set me free immediately. Especially since the envelope also contained a telegram, legit, from the Budapest police chief and a document, legit, from the German Consulate — both corroborating the authenticity of my father's sworn statement. The letter of introduction, requesting that the bearer, Margit Heinrich, German Aryan, be given every courtesy and cooperation, unfortunately did not impress Commander Fränk, mainly because he never read it. He simply refused to see her.

That's when Mayer entered the picture. Commander Fränk told him to just get rid of her. Since Margit was still hanging around in the afternoon, he obviously hadn't. He had tried, but she wasn't about to be gotten rid of. Not Margit. In the hours between her arrival and departure, Margit had been thrown out twice, physically removed by the outside guards, and twice refused an interview with the Commander before Mayer took her to his room. There she told him everything: why she came, how she'd gotten to Malin, and why she had to make absolutely sure that the manila envelope got into the right hands. She just couldn't return home without knowing that. She told him how crucial the papers were, how difficult they'd been to come by and how very long we'd been waiting for them. Mayer didn't even try to pretend that he wasn't smitten by Margit, nor to hide his admiration for her courage and gutsiness. But most of all, I think, it was her selfless dedication, her powerful commitment to her friends that put him in a state of wonder.

As to the journey itself, including the prelude that led to it, it actually was much less of a surprise to me than to Mayer. After all, I knew her. One might even say that it was a typical Margit undertaking. Knowing no fear, she was fearless; knowing no limits, there were no boundaries for her.

The papers from my brand-new Aryan father that Ferry had bought for me arrived three days after I'd left Amsterdam. Mama carried on something awful, cried and cursed Hitler. And Herbert, not too happy about this quirk of fate either, had wracked his brains trying to figure out what to do next. He finally decided to phone Harry to find out where I could be reached. The gods must have been cracking up about that one. Harry's reply was that he'd get back to Herbert as soon as he'd gotten hold of his contacts. Several phone calls and a few days later, Harry told Herbert that I was in transit.

My first card had taken eight days to reach home, but it did change everyone's mood, at least temporarily. Margit told Mayer that she could hear the sighs of relief all the way from my house to hers. They thought it best to wait for a letter from me before doing anything else. They never got one. What they did get instead was the card I'd thrown from the truck, the one that put a stop to Harry and John's treacherous scheme. After twelve days, it came, stamp and all. As to my family's reaction to it, Margit refrained from going into details; she only told Mayer that it wasn't good. Mayer had kept his promise, though. He did write to Mama two weeks after my getting to Malin. It was only a short note to let Mama know where I was and that I was well and safe. Really?

Mayer's note took four weeks. The day it arrived, after talking to Herbert, Margit applied for a travel permit. It never came. So, after weeks of waiting, she left without it on a military train. It follows that Margit, not having a single good reason for being on such a train, got herself arrested. Fortunately, thanks to her German passport, her Aryan grandmother, and her charm and beauty, her escapade didn't end up in catastrophe. Knowing Margit and how men responded to her, I'm not at all astonished that she landed in the arms of a dapper German major with a certain amount of savoir faire and influence. The major was in charge of having all trains at the border thoroughly checked before they moved on. Since he himself only checked pretty girls, not trains, Margit's arrest, carried out by one of his underlings, did not come to the dapper major's attention till many hours later. Meanwhile, my valiant friend had to spend valuable hours in an empty storage room. When, at last, she was brought to him for interrogation, he looked her over and then offered her her freedom in exchange for sharing a bottle of wine and his bed.

Several hours later, he released her from his charitable arms. She called him Karl and he called her his Margit. He gave her a temporary travel permit and a two-man escort to make sure that she could get to her destination and back to him again, and she gave him a false address in Amsterdam.

What Margit didn't tell Mayer, and I didn't find out till after the war, was Mama's unspoken reaction to the predestined card I'd thrown from the truck. While she was reading it, her hair turned white. Her magnificent flaming, golden-red hair turned entirely white . . .

A week after Margit's visit, I received a postcard from her, postmarked Brussels. She wrote that she couldn't get to see Erdman. However, she had managed to latch on to an assistant who'd done some checking for her. He had come back with the incomprehensible news that I was under special investigation. He was adamant about there being a file on me, and in it, amongst other ludicrous accusations, I was charged with imitating Hitler on stage — on stilts at that. Margit also wrote that she personally had put the documents into the right hands and that speedy results were now inevitable. "They're sure to find out that you're completely innocent and will set you free."

At last I knew why the Commander, when I first came to Malin, had said to me, "I know who you are and now you know that I know who you are. So watch out." What else occurred to me was the ironic fact that after all those months of waiting for an Aryan father, I didn't even know his name.

Margit's card did little to cheer me up. I brooded over it all day. At night, right after lights out, Martin and Werner made me come out into the hall with them for a smoke and perking-up talk. Not wanting to get in the way of the nighttime toilet traffic, we sat down on a step close to the top of the staircase. There, dressed in pajamas and nightgown — mine pretty enough for a wedding night — with Martin's raincoat over my shoulders, we smoked our one and only cigarette while discussing yet again the contents of my friend's card.

A few minutes later Jonny, on his way back from the toilet, sat down with us. As usual, he only wore his white short shorts. He wasn't barefoot, though. Jonny wore clogs belonging to the Polish tailor whose pigeonhole was right below Jonny's. He would take them whenever the tailor's passion for garlic and raw onions exceeded what Jonny's nose could tolerate. He'd usually grab them when the good tailor was asleep and didn't return them till the last clove of garlic and the last slice of onion were gone. Till the next time, when it started all over again. Their fights, not always limited to name-calling, were a source of constant annoyance for my friend Werner, barracks elder of this unruly lot. Refereeing was not what he liked doing best, particularly not about onions, to which he himself was allergic. Heinz wasn't with us that night. Some stomach problem had put him in the hospital.

The four of us sat close together, partially because of the cold steps and partially because of Martin and Werner's desire to comfort me. Both had their arms around me, with Jonny, one step higher, directly behind. When Mayer totally unexpectedly shot up the stairs, we were doing nothing more criminal than wondering where we could borrow another cigarette.

In a state that bordered on hysteria, Mayer blurted out: "Boden — Boden is coming! He's in a foul mood and looking for trouble! Get back to your barracks! Hurry — *Move!*"

We hadn't quite gotten to our feet when we saw him. Three steps at a time, he stormed up right on the heels of Mayer, his ugly face a deeper pink with rage. Halfway up, he stopped. Like penetrating X-rays, his cold blue eyes stared at us. "Caught you!" he screamed. "Having a little party, hey! Is that it? A little recreational pawing and smooching before nighty-night. Three guys and one girl! What do you know? We got ourselves a little orgy here. And you thought I wouldn't find out. Stand up! Just what do you think we're running here — a whorehouse?"

He had screamed himself hoarse. His face got puffier and puffier, like an overblown balloon. Without another word, he went past us to the top of the stairs, heading straight for our barracks. He bellowed for everybody to get down to the yard in one minute flat. "As you are!" he coughed. "You're not getting dressed!" With the echo of his voice cracking in our ears, the four of us walked stony-stiff, down the steps and out into the yard.

Torrential rain came down on us as if all the floodgates of heaven had burst open at once. Boden was back in the yard in no time. I noticed that he wore tennis shoes, holding his boots in his right hand. No wonder we didn't hear him coming. He ordered us to march forward to where the first building was and face the wall. Suddenly we were hit with a blazing glare of floodlights. The brightness was horrendous. I was sure that the whole world could see us.

Upstairs a window opened, and the Commander's voice blaring over the swelling sound of the downpour demanded to know what was going on. Boden's unhesitating reply was that he had caught us on the steps making out. "One girl and three men!" he shouted. He went on yelling that since we were still so awake, he thought we might like to do a little exercise. He also told Commander Fränk our barracks number and that two of the men were barracks elders. What a disgrace! While he was busy sounding off, I heard the others from my barracks shuffling out. I tried not to think about what it must have been like for them to be screamed awake, ordered out into the pouring rain without the slightest clue why. Boden, his boots back on and obviously immune to getting soaked, ordered them to line up one behind the other, to keep marching and to keep their traps shut.

I could hear them squishing by us, feel their trembling, feel their fear. "Tomorrow, the Polish tailor is going to kill Jonny," I thought. "Jonny is wearing his clogs and the poor man is sloshing around barefoot. Tomorrow, he'll eat a lot of garlic and onions again . . . after he kills Jonny. Tomorrow, there will be a water shortage in heaven . . . Tomorrow, I'll have pneumonia."

Commander Fränk had had enough. I could hear the upstairs window being shut. Boden called on the two guards to stand behind us while he, with less than a foot in between, planted himself right next to me. "Kneebends!" he commanded. The four of us went down together. He ordered us to hold the position for thirty minutes with our arms stretched out and our heads straight. "The first one to move gets a bucket of water over his head," he hollered, outshouting the rain. "Back straight! Arms straight! Head straight! Back straight! Arms straight! Head straight!" He never stopped. I stood on one end next to Jonny, Werner at the other, with Martin in between. The moment I moved my arms, Martin's raincoat slipped off my shoulders. It left me knee-bending in my sleeveless, low-cut satin nightgown, which clung to my body like snakeskin. I couldn't have felt more naked.

After "hold your position" came the real kneebends, too many to count. Up and down, up and down, with the guards close enough to grab me and Boden close enough to kick me. In the midst of this absurd display, Jonny stepped out of the clogs and without paying the slightest attention to Boden's uninterrupted commands, he nonchalantly tossed them away. He said something like "dumb clogs," and continued with the exercise. I could see him wink and give me a "You're doing fine" nod.

After the kneebends, Boden had us jump! Jump with our legs together, with our legs apart, arms up, arms down, jump up, jump down, up and down, up and down, on and on, on and on.

Next — push-ups! Push up, push down, push up, push down. My lion's mane hair, as Mama always called it, had turned into a red, waterlogged mop. Whipped by the rain, it fell into my face, blinding me, and every time my head went down, I mopped the ground with it. The push-ups continued. The speed increased. Faster and faster still. Boden's commands, spat out with the speed of a run-away train, hit my ears like rapidly exploding firecrackers, thundering and roaring. *"Faster! Faster!"* He'd moved closer, so close that I could smell the wetness of his rain-drenched uniform and leather boots.

Suddenly, as if someone had turned on a light bulb on inside my head, I knew. Knew what this charade was all about. Knew when it would stop. When he would stop. When I gave up. When I couldn't get up anymore. Lay face-down on the rain-soaked stones. When he had booted me into begging for mercy . . . then! Not before!

The non-stop frenzied contest of endurance, a marathon of will, was all that kept me going, that and Jonny's hushed "Hang in there, hang in there" whenever I slowed down. Still, there came a point when I no longer could keep up. My head was spinning and there was this volcano erupting in my ears and chest. I kept gasping for air. It felt like drowning. One of the guards grabbed me by the hair and pulled me up and down, up and down. He used a great deal of force. Pulled me up, pushed me down. After a very, very long time, Mayer came. He was standing next to Boden, shouting for him to stop. "Let them go. Let her go! Enough! You're killing her, I say it's enough! That's no punishment, that's murder!" From the window upstairs, which must have been opened again, the Commander threw a bucket of icewater down, bucket and all. It hit Mayer, Boden and me.

Commander Fränk was furious. "That's it," he roared. "Let them go! Now! At once!" Boden kicked away the bucket, yelled one more "Up!" then ordered us to get out of his sight. "Off, and take your whore with you. Get going before I change my mind!" Once more the guard pulled me up. He then lifted me off the ground, held me up in the air, dangled me back and forth like a puppet on a string and put me down again without ever letting go of my hair. I was desperately trying not to go limp, not to choke while struggling for breath, not to black out.

The next bucket of icewater, no bucket that time, spun me around and off to the side, away from the glaring searchlights. Shaky and wobbly, with no control over my legs, my pounding heartbeat and shortness of breath, I staggered into the darkness. Later on, I found out that both Mayer and Martin half dragged and half carried me into the building where my barracks was. That part is a bit fuzzy, though. I do, however, have a vivid picture of the staircase in my head. The staircase we'd been sitting on when Boden showed up not more than a few hours, a few lifetimes ago. The reason I remembered it so clearly were the steps I yet had to climb. From the top of the staircase, which to me seemed unimaginably high and far away, I could see arms reaching down, beckoning me. I managed a few steps on my own by crawling on all fours, and then I just waited till those reaching arms came close enough to pull me all the way up.

It took a while before my racing heart beat normally again, before my spinning head stopped spinning and I could hear softspoken words, not hollering and shouts. I was carried to my pigeonhole, undressed, dried off, dressed in fresh night clothes and covered with warm blankets. Martin stayed with me most of the night. He didn't want to let go of my hands. He looked terribly sad, and frightened. My gasping had really scared him. He didn't even want to leave me long enough to get himself dried off, till Werner made him change. His handsome face, bent over me, showed the strain of the last hours. I don't know when the others returned, were permitted to creep back into their pigeonholes and steal some leftover sleep from the night. Perhaps they even found a dream or two. I did not find a dream. What I found was someone's arm, in friendship, reaching out to me, heard his whisper, "I'm proud of you." Jonny. He stayed awake to guard my sleep and keep the bogeyman away. Tough little Jonny! I never thought that he'd unlock his heart for me, be my friend.

I awoke the next morning, finding myself alone in the barracks but unable to move. I was too sore and suffering from severe overexertion; muscles I never even knew I had ached like exposed nerves. I made every attempt to dress myself and get off my pigeonhole — slow-motion torture. Yet I did it. I made it down the steps by letting some of my childhood memories lead the way. Memories of those fresh, carefree days when the two of us, Elly my twin and I, pretended that the stairs at our house were not stairs but a very bumpy hill and our fannies not fannies but sleds on which to sled down all five flights. We used to do that whenever we got bored with ordinary banister sliding. It still worked that morning, but it definitely made me wonder why ever we would do this for fun.

The braying voice of Unterscharführer Boden came over the loudspeaker just as I was stepping outside. It forced me to reexamine my decision not only to show my face in public but also to participate in Boden's favorite morning exercises. I had wanted the bastard to know that I was still around, once I had proven to myself that though sore as hell, I was indeed still here. I had wanted to see the expression on his miserable face when he saw me. Somehow I hadn't counted on the extent of his perversity, hadn't figured on his nauseating need to continue the hounding. He blared out the torrid tale of our scandalous deed, releasing a flood of lewd sexual vulgarities. He wasn't a bit shy about who the perpetrators were, with me getting star billing, but also gave a good deal of dishonorable mention to my partners in general and the barracks elders in particular. As for the others in my barracks whom he had marching half the night, certifiable Boden declared that they, most probably, were just waiting their turn with me.

He ended his nasty speech with an abominable pronouncement: As added punishment for us, the sinners, and as a deterrent for all the rest, a two-week long *Packeten Sperre* (no packages) would be enforced. He also suspended our cigarette rations, three cigarettes per week, the latter to remain in effect for an undetermined length of time. The booing and outpouring of unflattering remarks, whether meant for the four of us or him, made me wish that I had never left my barracks.

Hunched over, I crouched my way along the buildings to the other side, where a disgruntled, angry group of people stood waiting for the exercises to begin. I moved into the second row between two women I did not know, relieved that I was wearing my big headscarf.

There was a great deal of tension in the air — tension, fear and exasperation. The ground was still wet, full of puddles, and slippery. I looked for my friends but couldn't see them anywhere. Then the exercises began. Stupid exercises, stupid little moves: head up, head down, lift up and down, shoulders up, shoulders down, lift up and down. I pulled my scarf all the way over my forehead, like a shy peasant girl. Not that I wanted to fool anyone, just testing the water. I saw him first, long before he saw me. He was busy doing what he really knew how to do: inspecting. Walking along the rows with deliberate slowness, he made sure that no one was faking. Unterscharführer Boden no longer conducted those wonderful, invigorating exercises himself; someone else was given this honor. Boden just watched. Watched everything and everyone.

Whatever it was that went through his thin little mind that morning after his insidious speech, and whomever else he was still looking to torment or cut down, he wasn't looking for me. He walked right by me, stopped, kept walking, stopped, and came back. He pushed the one in front of me aside, stared at my face, squinted his eyes, shook his head many times, stared some more and grinned. He'd recognized me. He was visibly stunned, yet without a doubt impressed. "You got guts!" he cackled, amazingly cheerful, his tone reflecting a hefty dose of respect. He then said that I didn't have to stick around in the yard, could take a break, relax, that I was excused. That's what he said, and so I didn't stick around!

Back at the barracks I found Mayer waiting for me. Expecting to find me half dead, he had come to see what he could do to ease the pain. When he didn't find me, he went a bit crazy. He had gone to the hospital thinking that someone might have taken me there, but instead of me he found Werner and Martin. None too chipper but not too much the worse for wear, they were visiting Heinz. Heinz's stomach was fine. When told about last night, Heinz said we should have kept a place reserved for him and that he was sorry to have missed it.

Mayer found a masseur for me: a former boxing champ, heavyweight, right in my barracks. He knew everything about sore muscles and how to treat them effectively. Twice a day he came to my pigeonhole and massaged my aches and pains away. What a champ! Among those who had been forced to night-march in the pouring rain, only a few were sympathetic, the rest boiling mad at us, at Boden and the whole damn mess.

Exactly two weeks from the day of Boden's imposed package ban, the ban was lifted and I was told by Maggie that a package, my first, was waiting for me.

The package room had one window and one door. One very long table: on it, spread out like leftovers from a food fair, sad-looking, moldy and rancid-smelling greetings from home. I guess they'd been there too long. Every one of the parcels had been ripped open, gone through, and thoroughly messed up. Even so, better than nothing at all. Behind the table stood Boden, who hadn't harassed me once since that horrid night. Instead, each time we passed each other, he grinned at me auspiciously. Never having gotten a parcel before, I was at a loss at what to do or say, especially with Boden. The package he held in his hands had not been tampered with at all.

"You must have been a very good girl to get something that nice," he said as he handed it to me. And with a smirk, *"Lass dirs gut schmecken!"* — Enjoy, good appetite!

As I opened my package of crackers and cheese, sausage and soap sent by Jean's friend, I knew then that Boden would never bother me again, that I had won at least a grudging amount of his respect.

✍ TWELVE

HE'D WRESTLED MY SOUP bowl away from me with the desperation of a starving man.

"It's empty!" I hollered. "Can't you see there's nothing left? Give it back!"

But he would not. Holding it close to his chest as if it were an invaluable treasure, he cried out: "No! Please no. I'll take, I'll take. Let me!"

The incident occurred one noon right after mealtime. As I was routinely waiting in line for my turn at the dish-rinse place, the man came, grabbed my bowl, and ran with it all the way to the front, where the dripping water faucet was. Having to wait one's turn every noon and every evening just to clean a battered tin dish and spoon was even more wearisome than having to wait one's turn every noon and every evening just to get whatever it was they were dishing out. Still, no reason to let someone snatch one's meager possessions.

My friends and I hadn't yet decided what, if anything, to do about him when, bowl in hand, he returned. "See," he said, a bit out of breath but joyous. "It's all clean. I only wanted to wash it. Don't want to steal nothing from no one! Nice, eh?"

"Very. Thank you," I replied. He then handed me the bowl, clean and shiny, announcing that he'd be doing our dishes, mine and my friends, from now on every day, twice. Astounded but also amused, we nevertheless told him to forget about it since we didn't have anything to offer in return, least of all food. As it was we rarely had enough ourselves, more than once going to sleep hungry. But the man kept pleading, assuring us that he didn't want no food, or cigarettes, or clothing, wanted nothing at all for it. Repeatedly he kept saying that ours would be the cleanest soup bowls in the camp, and so we let him do it.

The incident itself was indelible not because of what he did or even why but because of who he was. Nobody really knew how long he'd been here. Nobody seemed to remember having seen him before and yet, when asked, he said that he'd been here "All along!" How long that was we never found out.

His name was Joseph. It was the one thing he was sure of. He was proud of it because it was a biblical name. A holy name, which, so he thought, probably meant that he was a little holy, too. Whether Joseph was named after the husband of Mary, mother of Jesus, or the son of Jacob and Rachel, sold into slavery in Egypt, he didn't know either. He might have asked his parents which Joseph they had in mind, but he claimed he never had any. His earliest sketchy memory put him with many other children, in many different places, absurdly referred to as "homes." There, occasionally, people would come and take some of the children to live in a real home. Joseph was never chosen. Not that he wasn't pretty enough, or strong enough, or smart enough, but that those people just forgot about him. He would be standing there and standing there, scrubbed clean, practicing his prettiest smile, which still today looked more like an apology than a smile, but they would walk right past him.

This never changed. Unassuming, timid and shy, the friendless child grew into a solitary man, and with no place to call home, Joseph became a drifter. He always worked, always earned his keep, and kept drifting from town to town looking for someone who'd ask him to stay. But no one ever did. He looked like a blank wall — inconspicuous, almost invisible. Hair and complexion faded tan, like weathered sand. He nearly always kept his head bent low as if he were still a child expecting to be scolded or hit. He was quite tall, too thin, which made his baggy clothes look even baggier, and him smaller and more indistinct. His age, like his birth, was a secret he never bothered to unravel.

He was a simple man. Soul-sick for lack of love, but with no trace of bitterness for those who had abandoned him and a thousand pities for anyone who, like him, was lonely too, he never stopped reaching out. His heart was free of malice, completely trusting and innocent. Joseph liked everyone, and all he wanted was for someone to like him too. Unfortunately, he wasn't good at making friends at all. Even here, where a helping hand was always in short supply, he was being brushed off, ignored. Whatever gave him enough courage to grab my crummy bowl, thus forcing me to notice him, I'll never know. Aggressiveness was not part of his makeup or part of anything he'd ever learned. Perhaps he had reached a turning point, or gotten tired of being looked at without being seen. A friendly hello and a few words of thanks were enough for him. Joseph was like a loyal dog who never left our side. And in these seasons of paradoxical absurdities, amid suppression, forced deprivation and constant fear, he was happy.

Joseph had been caught while passing through a town just as the Germans were hunting down able-bodied men for the loading and unloading of extra heavy equipment — stolen, no doubt. The herculean ones were sent to Germany, the scrubby and scraggly ones like Joseph to Malin, without anyone ever bothering to tell him why, or the kind of place this really was. I do believe that he was still trying to figure that one out.

↩

THE MOOD IN THE CAMP HAD DEFINITELY CHANGED. Something was going on. The atmosphere was different: charged, heavy, like before a storm. And the people were restless and jittery. It must have been someone's remark that there were already more than fifteen hundred of us in here, with the ominous word "transport" added, that had set off the alarm. Everyone was caught up: they disagreed vehemently over who was going to be on it, with predictions ranging from everybody to only some, from letting all the E numbers and staff stay to letting everyone go home, and whatever else they could think of. My friends and I tried not to get sucked into this whirlpool of rumors. Yet the facts, the numbers increasing rapidly with each new arrival, were hard to dismiss.

The only ones paying absolutely no attention to all this were a small group of men aptly called the Flitzers — for flit, fled, flew the coop. Many of the Flitzers, having tried hairbreadth escapes once or twice before, had better things to do than listen to gossip. They were getting ready for the next time — when enough practice and the right kind of luck would pay off, and they wouldn't get caught again. It wasn't their escaping that went wrong; that part had always been successful. They all got a taste of freedom. It just never lasted very long. Sooner or later, mostly sooner, someone would find them, and back to Malin they were sent. There they were stuck into the dreaded coal cellar, staying locked up inside for the same length of time they had managed to be free on the outside.

What this group of men, who often hardly knew each other, had in common was an unyielding persistence — to escape and to teach others willing to take the same risks.

Jonny naturally being one of them keeps insisting that most escapees are never caught. That people have fled by the hundreds and are still out there. Girls, too, many girls. Perhaps he thinks I need a little boost to help me make up my mind. Not so. Neither my friends nor I need any help there. We'd go where Jonny goes, do what he does, wherever it takes us, whatever it takes.

For the first time, now, the ones like Jonny have been made to wear red armbands. I guess the Germans wanted to make sure that everyone knew who they were and what they had done. The Flitzers don't care about it, we don't care about it, nobody cares about it. Rather, it's a great help. At least those wanting to get away knew whom to go to for advice. Red armbands are easy to spot even in a crowd.

I think it's strange that nobody knows where these transports go. The camp is full of rumors, but no one really knows. When I ask Jonny, "Where do they go?" he says that if he had wanted to find out, he wouldn't have fled. He also says, "I better go and practice my flitzing so I won't have to find out."

Jumping — that's what we needed to practice the most because that's what we'll have to do. From a moving train! We also have to practice climbing out and holding on to something while standing outside on those rattling, shaking couplers of the railway car, just in case the doors are locked. We could either jump from the couplers or lower ourselves all the way down, slide under the railway car and lie between the tracks while the train rolls over us — without getting crushed. That one I don't like too much.

Then there is the part which has to do with more manly skills, like breaking the railway doors open, or cutting out a piece of the floorboard or side wall. Nothing too large, just big enough for us to get through. So we can jump!

For that, we need tools. Whether makeshift or the real thing, whether hidden earlier or just smuggled in, suddenly they are quite available. I suspect the flood of packages arriving every day now must account for most of the tools. Oddly enough, Boden, the only one routinely rummaging through them, has lately shown a surprising lack of interest in their contents. He lets the girls from the Registration Office do the rummaging, and they show no interest at all.

We keep practicing: we jump . . . we run . . . we roll . . . we hold on . . . we don't hold on . . . we swing from beam to beam . . . dangle from a rope . . . jump half a flight down . . . jump off the banister . . . balance on the banister. We don't have a moving train to practice on, but we are moving just the same. From every barracks, from every hallway, from pigeonhole to pigeonhole, we're moving. And everyone in the camp knows it . . .

Mayer tells us that Commander Fränk and Unterscharführer Boden have known all along what's going on and find it amusing. Commander Fränk says to Mayer, "Let them think they can get away with it. Keeps them busy." That's why Boden doesn't bother with the packages anymore and lets the girls hand them all out . . . like the Last Supper.

My lovely friend Jean won't be with us when we leap to freedom. It isn't that he doesn't want to or is afraid, but rather he is convinced he won't have to. No transport for him, he says. First, because he still has his E number (still no decision). And second, because of his boyfriend in Brussels, who might have greased some very influential palms in exchange for some very influential promises not to send Jean away. I wish with all my heart that this is so. Still, I think that he should at least prepare himself. But he won't hear of it. Jean trusts his friend. But this is not about his friend . . .

It's etched into my mind like nothing ever before. It's all I've been thinking of. I've never been there, yet I know it, every inch of it. I have never seen a picture of it, but I can see it. Blindfolded or in a moonless pitch-black night, I still can see it. Perhaps a painter might once have thought of painting it, for no reason at all except that it's there. I just can't make out the sound and smell of it. Whenever I try, my mind puts a black piece of crepe over it and then takes me back to wherever I am now — To Malin — to the camp which is a powder keg with the clock still ticking . . .

It's etched into my mind because this is what Jonny has been talking about continuously. He wants us to know every detail of it, know it better than we know anything else, so there won't be any foul-ups. It's a place. A somewhere in Belgium place in the country, where the terrain is hilly and steep, and where trains, huffing and puffing their way uphill, move slower than lame tortoises. It's the now or never jump off the train, leap to freedom place, whose ground I cannot wait to touch. I also know what comes after that. We must run — no — fly! away from there, race down the slope, out of view from the open fields and into the woods. Into the dense, deep dark, thick-growing forest, with higher than mountaintop trees, where the two shotgun-riding soldiers in front and the two in the rear can no longer find us. And where freedom begins . . .

Someone will be waiting for us there. I don't know who it will be, only that they'll be from the Resistance, have done this before and are expecting us. We'll know them by the knapsacks, or their baskets with berries if they are girls. They'll greet us with, "If you're looking for the village, follow us, we know a shortcut." It could be a couple of kids, an old woman or a pair of pretend lovers, but someone will be there and say exactly these words. That someone will drop whoever they find, first at a deserted woodman's shack and go on from there, scouting the woods till all the jumpers are found and safe. After that's taken care of, we'll put up in various underground places, be kept there or moved about.

Those, like Jonny, who already know their way around, or have relatives or friends nearby, are given what they need and sent on their way. And the others, like me, for instance? That, Jonny doesn't know. Again, he didn't stick around long enough to find out. No matter! Especially coming from another country, I'm sure they won't let me just run around loose without any papers. Besides, I won't be alone. I'll be with Martin, Werner, Heinz and servile Joseph, who can't wait for the real games to begin, the "moving-train games," as he calls it.

⤻

A STATUESQUE YOUNG OPERA SINGER by the name of Fritzi has just climbed off the truck, the first one of the latest arrivals. She has her mother, a kitten and no luggage. Some career-minded thieves have literally abducted them from a passenger train on their way home from a concert tour, stealing their money, their papers and all their luggage. After hitchhiking for a while, Fritzi and her mother got a lift from a friendly off-duty taxi driver. Certain that they would want to report the crime, the driver dropped them at a police station where an on-duty career-minded policeman made a full report of their mishap. The report, for no reason, ended up at Avenue Louise, Gestapo headquarters, and so did Fritzi, mother and kitten. Since a truck was just about to leave anyhow, the interrogators were out to lunch or just out, the cells crammed with wall-to-wall people, and Fritzi herself extremely allergic to the mere sound of the word "Gestapo," she chose what she then thought the lesser of two evils, a ride out of there and into Malin.

It wasn't her unusual story, even for these crazy times, that I initially paid much attention to. It was the number they'd put around her neck which made my blood stir. Fritzi's number was: *one thousand seven hundred!* She was the one thousand seven hundredth prisoner in here. As of this moment we were already two hundred more than full house — with more to come. This clearly meant that our time in Camp Malin was borrowed time . . . that the clock had stopped ticking . . . and that the powder keg we had all been sitting on was ready to blow.

It did so just twenty-four hours later, when Mayer ordered us down to the yard, where he informed us that Commander Fränk was about to make a very important announcement. After a thirty-minute wait during which no one uttered a single word, he appeared. With Mayer clearing the way, Commander Fränk marched to the center of the crowded yard, lifted his megaphone, and without the usual *"Achtung!"* announced what we had expected to hear:

TRANSPORT!

Commander Fränk's announcement was more of a speech than an announcement. A well-prepared, deadly serious and extremely convincing speech. Right off, he told us that this time everyone was going. That Malin would be emptied completely, and that included all E numbers, without exceptions. However, on his word, all documents and case files, whether from here, Brussels or any place else, would go with us to our next destination. "Poor Jean," I thought, "whatever is he going to do?" There was a lot of booing from all the E numbers and staff, which Commander Fränk not only ignored but talked right over. He then told us that we were going to a brand-new camp which wasn't quite finished yet, waiting for us to do so. Also, since we would be the first ones there, we not only could make it beautiful but could grab the best jobs. We could even choose our very own mayor, run the camp ourselves. We could plant flowers, grow our own vegetables, and make it the best-looking camp in Europe. Now, *there's* something to look forward to. Of course, everybody would have to work, not only a few. It was, after all, *ein Arbeits Lager,* a work camp, not to be confused with a labor camp, where one labors, toils and sweats, not just works. In our brand-new *Arbeits Lager,* proclaimed an incredibly convincing Commander Fränk, we'd be treated well, get decent food and medical care. We would be going to a much, much better place than old, cramped, primitive Malin.

He hadn't looked at us once. Over us, through us, but not at us. After a short pause, he abruptly lowered the megaphone, letting his eyes wander around as if he were taking inventory of the faces around him. Then he lifted his head, standing tall and very straight, and with the megaphone back he cheerfully informed us that just in case some of us were still thinking of jumping, to go right ahead with it. "Try it, why don't you!" he mocked. It was a challenge — a deliberate, undisguised challenge. He dared us. In fact, he promised the Iron Cross to anyone succeeding in jumping off this transport!

He did not wait for the silence to break, for heads to turn or look away. He did not wait for any reaction at all. "Two hours!" his powerful voice blared over the megaphone. "Get ready! You're leaving in two hours!"

With Mayer again clearing the way to let the Commander pass, the crowd stepped back, and he left.

The chaos started as soon as he was out of sight. The dispersing alone almost caused a riot. Everyone was running every which way, back to their barracks, or else trying to find a family member, a friend, anyone who could tell them why so soon. For us, in spite of Commander Fränk's unsettling invitation to jump, it couldn't be soon enough.

I sat in my pigeonhole for the last time wondering how many last times there were in a lifetime. How could I let my mind walk through the crowded minutes of those last two hours and know which ones to carry with me and which to leave behind? It was like being in a room with a hundred clouded mirrors with clouded images and being told, "Pick one or two or all of them. You can, you know." I had packed my clothes, the ones I thought I should take with me, and unpacked them and just now packed them again. I went to see Jean, who still believed that they wouldn't send him away, and said my good-byes to the group I came with, especially the De Hartogs and baby Erika. How she has grown! She'll be one year next month . . . or will she? Bernie would have liked to jump but of course can't, not with Rebecca and the baby. Millie won't, she says she'll teach school in this brand-new *Arbeits Lager*. And the De Hartogs — Did they have enough wisdom and patience left to make it through the next lie too . . . the next betrayal . . . enough years? They've gotten friendly with Rainer. I'm so glad about that. They're better than a tonic for her. They all want to stay together, with Fritzi, her mother and that cute little kitten, if they'll let them. No one knows for sure.

The Flitzers insist that it will be a numbers game. That we'll be called up by number, not by name. Thus, anyone wanting to stay together better make sure their numbers are not too far apart. Most people know about that anyhow, for nearly everyone has switched numbers already. The one I had was no good, too high a number, thus miles away from my friends. We could have been six railroad cars apart. Werner, in charge of travel arrangements, finally managed to get the right one for me. Now we were close enough to be all together.

I'm watching Jonny steal the Polish tailor's wooden shoes for the last time and noisily clog his way out of the barracks. Jonny thinks there is something fishy about this transport because of the short time between the announcement and the move. They used to give it a couple of days, not a couple of hours. Mainly though because they've never emptied the camp completely before.

I'm still not sure what to do about my clothes. Jonny wants me to forget about them altogether. To him, it isn't even worth thinking about. With his one pair of shorts, his motto, is the less the better. Besides, it's summer and a hot one. Martin wants me to take everything. He says he'll carry them. What's he going to do, jump with both arms holding boxes and suitcases? Heinz thinks I'm better off just wearing whatever I can. Like three pair of undies, a couple sets of this, a couple sets of that. It actually sounds perfectly reasonable in a bizarre sort of way. All I really need is my coat, my money–jewelry–filled coat. Perhaps this time it will get me and my friends to Switzerland.

Two hours later, Boden, over the loudspeaker, orders us back down again and to line up according to numbers. He wants us to leave the larger pieces of luggage, with our number attached to it, upstairs in front of each barracks. How much more he wanted from us after that he never gets to tell us because the loudspeaker goes haywire. Intermingled with ear-splitting sounds, like that of a metal saw or a dentist's drill, Boden's voice can still be heard but not understood. After several attempts to fix the electronic voice-box with no success at all, Mayer switches off the loudspeaker and calls out the numbers himself, one hundred at a time. He calls 1,750 numbers belonging to 1,750 people . . .

My number comes up: 781. Mayer had had to call it twice before I reacted and stepped forward.

⮑

I DID NOT SEE THE TABLES, set up only a few feet away from the gates, until I was standing almost in front of them. Sitting behind them, erect as wooden soldiers, with only their eyes peering down at the stacks of papers in front of them, were the big three. Commander Fränk; the scarface straight from Gestapo headquarters; and Erdman. The three repeated my number in rotation while looking through a pile of files and then asked my name. I didn't know which one to give: my real name or the short-lived one with the fake ID. I had thought of giving them my newly acquired Aryan Hungarian father's name and would have done so if I had known it. So I gave them the one I was born with — no difference. They neither listened to it nor bothered to look at me. All they were interested in was finding the file which had the number 781 stamped on it. How ludicrous. Why ask my name when I'm no more than a number to them? Number 781. Like on a crate. Stamped and ready for shipment, ready to go. Just cross it off the inventory list . . . Next!

Having the big brass there face-to-face, although they never really did face me, was as startling as it was unexpected, not only to me but to everyone. This too had never happened before a transport, or any other time. Trying to figure out why, at least to me, would have made as much sense as asking them who they thought would win the war. Besides, I was much more eager to find Martin, who the last time I saw him was still trying to squeeze money into his half-empty bottle of shaving lotion.

Ahead of me, Heinz and Werner, together with a mass of other people, were pushing and shoving their way through the partially open gates. I didn't even see them disappear, since right behind them, in spite of the guards, other people were all jamming through as though deliverance was waiting for them on the other side.

My first question after maneuvering through myself was, what are those soldiers doing here? Where are the trains, and how are they going to get nearly a thousand more people into this already crammed enclosure that looked more like a place to keep livestock than a railway station?

It was unbearably hot. The hottest time of day, without an iota of shade anywhere. Good day for a sunstroke. If they don't move us out of here soon, we're all going to have one. Right then a wet towel would have helped a lot. Joseph would have known how to get one, but I hadn't seen him or Martin since the two-hour deadline speech.

At last I heard Mayer call out the very last number. The soldiers, armed with big rifles, had to move back to make room for the people still coming through, which gave everyone a little breathing and looking-around space. That's how I found Heinz and Werner, who'd thought for sure that Martin and Joseph were with me, too. "No matter," said Heinz, "they'll show up."

Mayer, who always seemed to be looking for me, did so for the last time. Sweating fiercely and looking completely done in, he suddenly was before us, slipping a key into my hands. "Coal cellar," he whispered, hurried and breathless. "Lock yourself in, I'll get you out. Run — now! No one will know!" To my friends, "You two come with me!" He pushed the three of us forward and promptly lost us in the crowd.

He came back a little later, wiping his sweat-soaked face with a long white scarf. "Too late!" he sighed. "It's already too late! It can't be done anymore." He then told us they were watching the places he used to hide his friends and that in the past Commander Fränk had allowed him to do so with no questions asked and nothing expected in return. Not this time.This time there was Erdman sent by Berlin to find out, once and for all, why the head count in Malin at the beginning of a transport was always so much higher than at the end. Berlin wanted to know why so many kept turning up missing and whether perhaps, as Erdman suspected, Commander Fränk took bribes. Mayer swore he never did. Mayer was also pretty certain that Erdman would travel with us just to make sure we really got there. The Commander and his nervous wife usually went on holiday after a transport. So did Boden, which only left the guards, who then mostly drank, slept, and drank.

We told Mayer that we really didn't mind that he couldn't help us anymore and that we'd rather get on that train and out of here. That's when totally unexpectedly Mayer blurted out, "Martin can stay." I felt a little ill, and it wan't the heat. Heinz and Werner put their arms around me and for a while we just stood there, too perplexed and overcome even to ask why. "It's the dogs," Mayer announced. "The Commander wants Martin to train them." Some idiot, Mayer swore he didn't know who, had told Fränk that Martin was an expert dog trainer. And that's how he got to stay. No, Martin did not think that he was lucky, had tried to get out of it, but the Commander insisted. What a stupid joke! Martin of all people. He had never even considered staying behind, not for a moment, not without us and certainly not so he could teach Fränk's dogs to attack. Like most of us, he was afraid of them. It would have been the very last thing he'd ever volunteer for. Besides, Martin had never trained anything larger than a parrot. Oh, yes! Maggie could stay, too. Someone had to cook. For the dogs?

Mayer had one more piece of information for us. Joseph — poor, lost Joseph. They let him go. Set him free. He didn't have to stay, didn't have to go on transport. All he had to do was go away. Erdman had given him a piece of paper which said that he could leave, was free. I wished that just once I could figure out why fate at the most crucial moments keeps coming up with one more trick, always one more.

⌒

THE SCENERY FOR THE LAST ACT, the grand finale of Camp Malin, like a revolving stage where they don't move the set, just rotate the axis, had been there all along. From where we had been standing, almost around the bend, running parallel to the outside of the buildings on the left, there they were: the tracks. And on the tracks, not trains but cattle cars. For us, the livestock.

The little young soldiers with their big old rifles opened the makeshift enclosure planks and poked us with them, as though the boards were cattle prods. They then picked some men and ordered them to bring down the rest of the luggage and boxes left at the barracks. Hoping for a chance to somehow see and talk to Martin, Heinz and Werner were the first ones to go. For a short while, the place we'd been herded into was empty, making it possible to look farther out to the other side where the street was. A lonely-looking, deserted street. And on this lonely-looking deserted street stood the most lonely, most deserted man on this earth — Joseph.

I wasn't close enough to see his tears or hear him cry, but I could feel them as though they were mine. He stood, clutching my bowl, just like he had done the very first time, but he wasn't running away. He just stood there, trembling. In the sizzling hot afternoon sun, my friend was cold. He must have seen the three of us before and tried to get to us. I could tell by the way he kept watching the soldiers watching him. He tried many more times, but the soldiers kept hustling him away, kept telling him to get lost as if he wasn't already. Didn't he know that he was free, the shouters asked. "Go, get a beer, get drunk, just go," they hollered belligerently, but he just stood there.

I kept watching him until the men brought down the suitcases and boxes from upstairs. They came and went, came and went, many a time. I saw Martin all the way at the end carrying the heaviest loads. He could not come to me to say good-bye, my friend, my lover. He could not hold me one more time, he had to stay inside the open enclosure. Only those riding the cattle cars could carry the belongings all the way into a special wagon. After it was all stored away, except for what we had brought down with us, the soldiers, running alongside the cars, bellowed for us to get on. "Step right up!" one of them blared, sounding suspiciously like a carnival barker.

The cars were high and there was no ramp. We had to climb up. I had no wish to study the interior of these moving stables, not yet. Barely inside, I was already fighting to keep my place by the open door so as not to lose sight of Martin. He too looked terribly lost and alone and sad. While bedlam was going on all around me, I held on to Martin's face, read his lips, his un-spoken "I love you always," and all the sorrow that went with it. I wanted to tell him to look after Joseph, not even realizing that he could not, and tell him to take care.

On the other side from me, Heinz and Werner were helping others into the cattle car, the still open cage. Just then, Mayer came racing by. He stopped, reached for my arms, pulled them and my head down, and with his face right by my ears he cried out, "Jump! You must jump!" and raced on. Right after that, the opening in the middle of the door was shut. I could hear it being bolted from the outside and for a short, stifling minute, everything stopped. The screams, the cursing, the pushing, the loud heavy breathing all stopped. It was heart-stoppingly still. Heinz took my hand and led me to a small window, so I could look out. The window, scarcely larger than a eight by ten photograph, rather high, with bars on the outside, was hardly big enough to crawl through even without the bars. It was the only window and our only air supply.

Through this small opening, I saw Martin one more time. His lips no longer moved, and the expression on his face had changed completely. It showed the shock and disbelief of what he had had to witness, and while he must have tried not to give himself away, the horror of it all was transfixed in his eyes. He didn't show it when first he saw us, but now he did. Now that the cattle cars were shut and bolted with us inside, he did! I could feel his torment, his fear for us, as though he already knew the road that lay ahead, as though he had seen it like some old Gypsy in a scratched and misty crys-tal ball. I could see it too, for it was written in his eyes: "Death is riding with you." I saw him nod, wave, bow his head and walk away.

Farther out in the deserted street stood Joseph. The soldiers who had been trying to chase him away were gone. He was all alone. His shoulders drooped, his head tilted to one side as though he had been hung, but not quite dead yet was waiting for someone to cut him down. He stared into the nothingness around him. He must have heard the whistle blow or seen the train as it began to move, for suddenly he lifted his head and started to run. He ran toward the tracks, those hastily laid tracks, that let the monstrous wheels carry us off. He ran very fast, shouting, "Wait, wait for me! I want to go with you! Tell them I can! Tell them you want me! Want me!"

He had caught up to our wagon, holding on to the bars of the little window with one hand of his outstretched arm, clutching my bowl with the other. The three of us put our hands through the bars, and for a second or two we held on to his. When the train picked up speed, he let himself be dragged along still clinging to our hands. He didn't care that his feet were dangerously close to the tracks and his arm almost torn from his shoulder socket. Once he tried to pull himself up, and for a moment there our faces almost touched. "God," he cried. "Why don't you help me!" And then he let go. He stumbled, fell, got up again, and never moved another inch. I watched him become part of the vacant landscape, part of the vast emptiness that had dominated his life, watched him till I could see him no more, watched Joseph, the forgotten man I can't forget.

⌐ THIRTEEN

SHUT AWAY FROM THE WORLD in a moving boxcar with sobbing, panicky, spooked people doesn't help one's courage stay afloat. They packed us in — the young, the old, the sick, the healthy, the brave and the not so brave.

Involuntary closeness, without the separation of the sexes, was only one of many explosive situations we had to cope with. Whatever belongings we had brought with us, no matter how few, there still was no room for them. Everything was in everyone's way; everyone was in everyone's way! ˙

The heat inside, after they had locked the door, went like a flame from unbearably hot to hotter than hell in one miserable minute.

While the food, which was to last us till who knew when, had to be eaten straightaway or rot, we did not dare touch the water until we absolutely had to, and even then, we were careful not to waste a single drop.

In the middle of the cattle car stood the bucket. The totally non-privy privy, without a lid but lots of straw around it to cover up the misses. With or without the bucket, this kind of cattle car ride, unfit for man or beast, could only have been thought up by beastly men who should have been the ones in there, not us!

But that's not how it was, and all my feeling mad and sick about it could not change one thing. In there, but not for long. I told myself, "It will only be a little while . . ."

I wonder, did Commander Fränk really think that his uncanny verbal postscript inciting us to jump could possibly have made a difference to us? He had been sounding off about the Iron Cross for those who made it. Made what — the jump, the getaway? When did he think he'd be giving it to us — at the spot where we jumped off? Would he be waiting there to catch us like fish in a net and take us back to Malin? Is that what he had found so humorous?

Don't bet on it, Commander, you will not catch us. We're not coming back, and you can keep your Iron Crosses. None for me, thanks, I'll be fine without it. Besides, I really don't like crosses. No crosses at all — just think what happened to Jesus . . .

The sweltering heat inside the cattle car forced even the most bashful ones to drop their prudishness, together with their clothes, down to the barest of bare minimum. Nobody said a word about it, nobody gaped or made the others feel self-conscious.

Amid the almost naked, sweat-covered bodies, there was one woman who never removed a single stich of her clothing. Dressed completely in black, she sat on the bucket with a pillow underneath her. She sat on it as if it were a throne. No matter the choking stench, the stale, stifling air that must have made it difficult for her to breathe — she sat! Whoever came to use it would find her getting up, stepping aside with her back to it, and re-turning when they finished. She looked like a character out of a Strindberg play who still wore the costume but had forgotten her lines.

In barracks or cattle cars, someone always had to be in charge. We luckily had Heinz. Heinz had volunteered and immediately regretted it, realizing that since he was not planning to go all the way, he ran the risk of drawing the wrong kind of attention to himself. But no one else, least of all Werner, wanted the job, and so he got stuck with it. The very first thing Heinz did was to set the time each person could spend by the window, indulging in the luxury of breathing precious fresh air. He had the sick and elderly moved closer to it and farther away from the throne. He then gave a little speech about preserving our strength and oxygen as much as possible, not to let the less than human conditions turn us into less than human too.

Soon after his speech, my friends and I, joined by a fourth jumper — Janosh, a Hungarian professional football player — started work on the spot that needed to be cut, sawn through, and taken out for us to get out. It was a two- by three-foot square, right above where Heinz, Werner and I'd been sitting, where the left side wall leading to the couplers was. We had decided not to jump but to get under the train and lie there until the last one of the cattle cars — too high to crush us, so swore Janosh — had rattled over us and wheeled away.

We had decided, egged on by Janosh, on this way out, instead of jumping, because of all the soldiers with their big rifles and machine guns who were accompanying us. Ending up as their target practice wasn't quite what we had had in mind. Of course, it was possible there weren't as many as they had wanted us to think, that most of them stayed behind in Malin, but who could really tell? Janosh, an ardent collector of smuggled tools, finally convinced me, too. If he, weighing a good two hundred pounds, was not afraid of getting smashed under the train, why should I be?

Jonny was not with us. At the very last moment he got into the car next to ours. I can't imagine why, unless he'd counted every one of them and found that one to be the closest to where he wanted to be. Somehow I felt that this time he would make it, no matter which car he was in.

It was getting dark; I was getting tired, exhausted from the heat and nervous. Not about doing it, but about the dreadful noise the saw made. Standing close to it, that's all I could hear. It drowned out everything, even the rattling-rolling of the train. What if the soldiers heard it, too? Where were they, anyway? Janosh was almost certain they were on the platforms of those special wagons. They and their weapons, some in front, some in the rear and some in the middle. This was a first for Janosh, too; yet, no matter where the soldiers were, it didn't bother him one bit.

How much longer — how many hours before we could get out of here? Werner and Heinz had moved as close as they could to where the opening was going to be so I could stretch out and rest a while. It made me look directly at the woman sitting on the bucket-throne. She now was watching us. Watching my friends sawing away, watching me lying there in my short, low-cut white lace slip, barely covering my bra and scanty briefs. I don't know which of us looked more out of place. She kept moving her hands as if she were washing them, didn't stop even when she had to get up and step aside. Earlier on, I had heard someone say that the lady on the throne had a young son in one of the other cars who was going to jump in spite of her pleading with him not to. "She doesn't want to watch him get shot," explained the one who seemed to know her. "That's why she is in our cattle car. Just a boy . . ."

It got me wondering how many would be jumping, how many altogether and how many from each car. There were only the four of us in ours. I thought for sure there would be many more. Just being stuck inside this stifling, sweat-, urine- and vomit-reeking cage should have made everyone want to break out. How was it that they did not? Hardly able to breathe, they stared at us. Some shook their heads; others offered to help, taking over to give my friends a break, giving their last drop of water to wipe their faces, wet their lips. They wished us luck but did not dare to jump themselves. What if, because of us, their lives were to be threatened; would they betray us?

"Finished — it's done! Let's try it!" Werner went through first. He had no trouble getting out and landing on the couplers. He stayed outside for many heartbeats, breathing the clean evening air while balancing himself and looking around. When he got back in, he was all smiles, beaming. "It works!" he called to us enthusiastically. "It really does! Can you believe it? There's room enough under the train for someone twice Janosh's size! We're almost there! Home free!" He put his arms around the three of us and cried. Then, others came and put their arms around us, also cried, sobbed, sighed, holding us close, not uttering a single word.

I went out next. The fresh air got to me more than the shaking couplers. All I could think of was breathing it, inhaling it, drinking it and letting it flow into me like a freshwater brook. For a short minute, it made me forget why I was out there. I didn't even realize that I was standing, both my hands holding on to the opening on either side, with my head thrown back and my eyes closed. It felt terrific. It was Janosh, shouting to me that his wife and child were expecting him home for dinner, to get on with it, who brought me back. I slowly lowered myself, quickly grabbed the couplers and sat myself down. It was a little like riding a temperamental iron horse, which wasn't the way I was supposed to be doing this. Then quickly I did it right. In reverse! Straight and balanced, one foot in back of the other, I climbed back into the stinking cage.

Heinz too had gotten out and in again. Now it was Janosh's turn. But then the train suddenly stopped, with Janosh still outside. At first we really didn't think much of it. Heinz thought it the perfect opportunity for us to take a nap so we'd be fresh and ready for the big moment, as long as one of us stayed awake. Taking turns, this would be the time to do it.

Around us, the others, huddled together, had already fallen asleep or were about to. Entangled arms, entangled legs, entangled lives . . . a brotherhood of sweat and tears . . . What a strange cargo . . .

⤔

IT WAS LIKE AN EXPLOSION! The *rat-tat-tat* of machine guns together with a barrage of thunderous gunfire, mixed with the shrilling sound of screams and shouts, shattered the silence that had lulled me . . .

The train was moving again. Uphill, very slowly, sluggish, almost reluctantly it puffed along. This was the spot — the one I'd seen in my mind a thousand times before, like old familiar picture slides!

It was dawn. Outside, on the couplers, stood Janosh. He stood for a moment, then lowered himself all the way down and was gone. I could feel Heinz pulling me up, pushing me toward the opening, through it and out. I saw a swarm of people from other cars jumping off, running, running, *rat-tat-tat,* and falling.

I saw Jonny jump. Dodging bullets, racing, rolling down the slope and disappearing into the woods.

It was my turn to go down and not waste another second when what flashed through my mind was that I'd forgotten my coat. I stepped back and at that moment, like the whiplash of an evil wind, I felt something whizzing by me and someone's arm pull me back in.

It rained bullets *rat-tat-tat* leaving footprints soaked in blood.

It rained bullets *rat-tat-tat* on the slopes of liberty.

I stood pressed against the little window with the bars, like a monkey in a zoo, watching our freedom getting shot full of holes and die with those who had died already . . .

The train had stopped again, this time with a harsh, screeching halt. Everyone was thrown about, with the woman on the throne getting the worst of it. She fell right off the toppling bucket, unable to escape the full force of its contents and stench. Whoever could fled as far as possible away from it. Hovering in some corner, we quickly covered our noses, trying not to breathe at all.

Outside, the gunfire had stopped. In its place the blaring voices of angry Germans, racing alongside the cattle cars, cursing and swearing, bounced off the stinking cages. Louder still, much louder than anything we had heard and seen in those last murderous minutes, were the chilling screams of the woman in black. Her voice, a mother fearing for her son, was harrowing to hear. Covered with filth and the indignities of her night on the bucket, she staggered to the window, reached for the bars outside, shaking them and howling: "Swine! Stinking swine! Give me my son! I won't let you have him! He is mine! Take me, take me! I stink as much as you do! Here, here! See — Take this!"

She put her arms all the way through the bars, pushing them as far as they would reach, shaking the excrement and filth from her arms and hands out of the window down at the Germans.

A split second later, Werner and Heinz, in record speed, covered the opening with the board and nailed it shut — like a coffin, with us inside . . .

The door of the cattle car flew open with such force that it bounced back all by itself, stopping, half open, in the middle. Someone must have broken the lock without any of us hearing, it which, with all the goings-on, was hardly surprising. Instinctively, I leaped up and pressed myself against the board. I could feel a part of it that was still loose, heard it bang against the frame like unhinged shutters on a window.

The woman in black had gotten thrown backwards. Werner caught her just in time so she could land in his lap on the floor. But that was not what they were watching anymore, the others in here with us. They all kept staring at the not-quite-nailed-down coffin cover, as though their stare alone could silence it and make it go away.

He was tall, he was ugly and he was mean. They were all tall, ugly and mean. Whatever happened to the little soldiers who did such a good job with their *rat-tat-tat*? I couldn't see a single one. The ones I could see and hear now were the true Hitlerites — brutal, fanatic, iron-heeled executioners. Erdman's men! This time the rumors back in Malin had been right. Erdman was on this train and with him his murder brigade.

They were dealing out the punishment for breaking Erdman's edict: "This time no one escapes." They kept dragging one or two people from every car, no matter who they were, and shooting them dead right in front of us — the old, the young, and if they found a pair of lovers, holding each other, they shot them both together, right through the heart. They then chased others down the slopes, guns in their backs, and had them pick up the jumpers who'd gotten hit but weren't dead yet, only wounded, and made them carry them back up again, one on top of the other, only to throw them like sacks of potatoes into the cattle cars. What madness! So much killing for the handful that had made it, for the few who had gotten away. Or was his outrage not because of them but because against all odds we still had dared?

What an embarrassingly simple plan this man had devised. Right on schedule, he let the train roll along till it had reached the beginning of the uphill slope, and then five counts away from jump, with dusk already gone, no stars in the evening sky and dimness reducing the risk of the jumpers being seen, he had stopped the train. And there it sat all night long. Right time — wrong spot.

I must have slept all through it standing still, not just taking a nap, for it was evening when I'd closed my eyes and morning when the *rat-tat-tat* woke me, when Janosh disappeared, when Heinz pulled me up and out, and when I had stood ready to get under the train at exactly the right spot, at the wrong time.

One of the tall, ugly, mean ones, standing in front of the open door, demanded to know how many in our car were missing, how many had jumped or had tried to. His uniform, spit-polished clean, showed no traces of the desperate mother's reaction to it all. He must have just arrived. Even though it would have been quite impossible not to have seen or smelled the filth, he made no reference to it. All he commanded us to tell him was "How many?" In one voice, sounding like an ill-prepared chorus suffering from stage fright, we told him, "No one."

Once more he shouted, "How many?" And then, without waiting for an answer, he raised his right arm, stretched it straight out, and with his two index fingers pointing at a middle-aged couple on the opposite side from me, he roared, *"Raus! Raus. Mit euch Zwei!"* — Out, out, you two!

The woman sharply turned her head and buried it in her husband's chest. She wept, making little shrieking sounds, until her husband put his arm around her. He kissed her hair and calmly told her to do what the S.S. man had ordered them to do. He helped her up, held her close, put his jacket over her shoulders to cover her near nakedness, walked toward the open door and begged her not to be afraid. "If God wants us now," he said, "we'll go now. It's better anyway. That's no way to live!"

They were within a foot of the door when Heinz jumped right in front of them. With his legs and arms spread wide, he firmly placed himself inside the door frame shielding not only the couple but us as well. He told the S.S. man that he was the elder in this car and that if he wanted to shoot someone, he would have to shoot him. His voice was loud and forceful, without a note of fear. Heinz kept shouting that these people were his responsibility and then repeated that nothing had gone on in here other than the unfortunate accident with the stinking bucket.

"I'm not afraid of you and I'm not afraid of dying!" Heinz screamed. "So go ahead and do your damn killing. See you in hell!" With these chilling words, he leaned forward as if he were ready to jump the man, leaving no doubt that he wasn't bluffing one bit.

We'll never know what made this Hitlerite change his mind. Whether it was Heinz being just as loud, just as commanding, just as furious and just as tall, blond and blue-eyed as the one with the gun, or whether the S.S. man didn't like what he saw inside this cage. Perhaps the stench did finally creep up to him too, for he let Heinz pick out a cleaning crew to get rid of the mess, which meant turning clothes into rags and sweeping it, along with most of the straw, out the door. It wasn't something the officer cared to watch, so he just stepped aside, and for a very short minute, he turned around. We badly needed this time to hide the tools even more thoroughly. The thought of him finding them was unthinkable. When he turned back again, he definitely looked like he himself had had enough of it. He warned Heinz that he would kill us all if he found that he had lied, and if not this time, then next time round.

From way in front, on the outside, someone yelled to shut the doors and be done with it. "Long way to go yet!" another one blared. I was waiting for Heinz to move away, for the tall and ugly one to slam the door shut and lock us in, when quite suddenly, I felt nauseous and weak. My knees were shaking. I tried to hold myself up, to hold till this elite brigade was back in their special compartments and all we'd have to worry about till next time was someone passing out or fighting for their turn at the window.

But I could not. I kept sliding down. And with my back still pressed against the board, I ended up sitting on the ground. At that moment I heard a cutting noise above me. Somebody screamed and from outside, directly behind me, a brash voice yelled: "It's open! They had the whole damn board out! Herr Leutenant, come, take a look!"

I looked up, only to see that where I had been standing, there now was a knife sticking through the board.

In those next seconds, the last ones I might get to count, I thought, "No one will ever know about this, not what they did to us, nor why so many died." But then I thought: "That knife, which had my name on it yet missed me by no more than the echo of a cry, means there is still a chance for us," even though I could not imagine how.

The battle fought for our lives was fought with words sharper than swords. Both Heinz and the officer were like two boxers in a boxing ring, with only one wearing gloves. Heinz neither pleaded nor apologized. He told the lieutenant to step inside and see firsthand that this was how it had been before we came into this shithouse. He told him that it was rotten wood to start with and that all we were trying to do was nail it shut so as not to get blown out. Heinz then stepped aside just far enough to let the lieutenant see the old, the sick and those trembling with fear, which, except for Heinz and Werner, was every one of us.

The brash voice outside, directly behind me, kept calling for the Herr Leutenant to let him see the real proof, but anyhow, who needed proof? Jews always lie and deserve to be shot just for that.

He did shoot, pointing the gun from left to right, around full circle, at every one of us, and then he fired into the air!

Outside, I heard the coffin lid being hammered down, the cattle car door slammed shut, heard whistles blow, shouting, yelling, heard stones, sounding like brittle bones, crack under the heavy boot-clad feet charging along. And then a jolt, the screeching of worn-out wheels, and we were moving again.

The train kept lumbering down the tracks, with us too weary, shook up and overwhelmed by all that had been happening to do or say anything. We needed quiet to sort things out, take stock of all that had come crashing down on us, needed aloneness and comfort both. I know I did. I'd never seen anyone get killed before.

How does one witness so much bloodshed and not go mad? How does one *not* think about it, not keep the picture of those dead bodies forever in one's mind? And how does one say thank-you to this brave friend who kept us all alive . . . ?

Later on, someone remarked that I was really very lucky because my life had been saved twice. Once by Heinz, and once when I sat down just before the knife cut through. This person also said that ours was probably the only car where no one had gotten shot, and that we better keep our wits about us so we can make it to the new *Arbeits Lager* in one piece.

The couple who already had walked the thin line between life and death were on their knees praying. They prayed together, to the same God, but not the same prayer. She asked God why. He did not. Perhaps his faith was impregnable to anything that men could do. After they'd prayed, they went to Heinz, who hadn't left his place by the door since it had been slammed shut. He stood like he'd been rooted to the ground. The woman kissed his hand; the man said that he'd been braver than David who slew Goliath, but not to risk his life for them again.

Werner had somehow managed to have the woman in black compose herself. She seemed resigned or else just didn't have another scream left.

We sat together — Heinz, Werner and I — closer than ever. Perhaps it was the tragedy we had lived through, or the lost chance of the escape we so had believed in, which made the need for one another so much greater. We had our arms around each other and we held hands, the three of us. We talked about Martin and Joseph, thankful that they weren't with us. Being that close to Werner and Heinz made me feel better and stronger. "You can't make it alone. None of us can," Martin had said. "We need to hold each other so we can hold on."

We rode for hours without a clue as to where we were or where we were going. Whoever had their turn by the window was told by Heinz to watch closely: a sign, a name, a railway station, some little named village; a poster with a written word and in which language. But we saw nothing. Nothing but fields and forests, nothing but far-away dots which could have been cows or people, or dogs. We didn't pass a single railroad station, as though the world around us had ceased to exist and all that was left was this train and us.

How many miles we had already put behind us before we stopped again I do not know. The stopping place was on an open road, a straight and level road. The Germans banged and hammered on each car, first checking and double-checking every inch of it, and only then opening the doors. This time there was no *rat-tat-tat*, only their usual brassiness and shouts. They ordered two from every car to empty the buckets and the rest of us to do whatever was necessary under the train. They drove us on with whips and whistles as though this were a bloody game or some sort of a hunt.

And there we were now, 1,750 sweaty, exhausted, unnerved people, minus the dead they had left behind and those who'd gotten away. How many of each?

The wounded and sick we did what we could for. We helped or carried them down. Our provisions were gone and our water bottles empty. We badly needed water. Heinz went up to one of the whistlers and asked him for water but was told there wasn't any. We did our best to stall, without creating suspicion, so we could look around. I looked for Rainer, for the group I had left Holland with, for Fritzi, her mother; I even looked for the little kitten, but couldn't see any of them. Janosh had been right: there was enough room under the train for the whole sorry lot of us, if only we could have made it. I sat there in a squatting position wondering if any of this was real. Was this what all my practicing and waiting back in Malin was for?

In these few minutes while I was out of the cage, out of sight, a thousand crazy thoughts raced through my mind, all dealing with escape. What if I stayed where I was, just didn't come out anymore . . . what then? I quickly turned my head to see who was behind me, and there was Werner whispering, "Not now." Could he have read my mind? I didn't get the chance to ask my friend why not. They drove us back into the cages. Again, *"Mach schnell! Mach schnell!"* with whistles and whips. Then came the slamming of the doors, the jolts, the screeching of the worn-out wheels, and we were off again.

Even those who felt great sympathy for us and our misfortune wanted us to get rid of our tools. "Throw them away before they find them," they urged. "What good are they to you now?" But Heinz and Werner did not want to hear about it; instead, they covered them up yet further. Both were determined to try it one more time, and so was I. We'd do it just as before. Take out the board, wait till dusk and then jump. There would be no one watching anymore, no *rat-tat-tat's*, no one suspecting anything at all. Why should they think that we were fool enough to try it twice, and at some unknown spot at that? And yet we surely would if between now and then we could find out where we were.

Many hardship hours later, the man who'd taken his turn by the window gave up his place before he had to. He'd been there less than a minute when he abruptly turned and gloomily declared, "I think we are in Germany."

He'd seen a little station with a German-sounding name and Germans carrying swastika flags. Right after that we all flocked to that tiny open space, crowding around it for the longest time, looking out, just to make sure.

It was Germany all right, every cursed inch of it. There, suddenly, they were: the small and large railroad stations, the villages and towns, and everywhere we passed people kept staring at the cattle cars and us. They saw there were people in there, not cattle. Only a few turned away; most of them didn't. None of them looked shocked or surprised. If they showed any reaction at all, it was one of unmasked annoyance, as if they were thinking, "Do they have to come through here?"

After it had gotten dark, Heinz took the tools and one by one threw them out — saw, hammer, nails. It made me think of severed limbs, useless limbs.

I slept, woke, slept, and when I awoke again, it was morning. My belongings were packed. Everybody's belongings were packed. Heinz and Werner had been busy dividing our money. Some went into my coat pocket, some into theirs, and bills hidden inside the soap, toothpaste and shaving cream we left where they had always been. Everyone said that we were almost there, but where no one could say.

How much further could it be — we'd already come such a long way?

When I got to the window, the only thing I could make out was a hot, glaring sun in a vast emptiness. There was nothing to see but flat, desertlike stretches of land, leading from nowhere to nowhere. It didn't look like anything belonging to this earth, more like something from another harsh, hostile planet.

There was a lot of pushing going on. Everyone wanted to see for themselves what was out there, admitting afterwards that they were just as unprepared, just as stumped as I was. No one recognized anything or liked what they saw. The major point though, we all agreed, was not where this place was, but who was running it. Were our captors Wehrmacht or S.S.? There wasn't one among us who didn't fully understand the gripping, grave difference. A life or death difference.

By now the train was moving slower than a lame duck. We could count the cracks in the broken, infertile earth. A while later Werner said he'd seen some movement in the distance — shapes, forms, something. When I was able to look out again, the shapes and forms had gotten closer.

Men! A group of striped prison uniform–clad men. They were carrying huge stones on their shoulders. With their heads unprotected from the blazing sun, their backs and shoulders stooped forward, weighed down by their heavy loads, they trudged past us. With them were two of the Third Reich's boys: S.S.! Other S.S. opened the wagons, hollered for us to get out and to line up alongside the train with our belongings next to us. I stood between Heinz and Werner, staring into this boundless forbidding corner of hell . . .

It was morning. It was the birth of a new day and the death of hope.

PART THREE

And All The Gods Went to Find Another World

⌒ FOURTEEN

THE PEOPLE FROM THE FIRST WAGONS were marched forward. They were told to keep going and then ordered to stop. After they had come to a halt, we were told to keep going, ordered to stop, followed by those still behind us. No one was really marching. We were all dragging our feet, just limping along as best we could. Some of our comrades had not made it. They had arrived dead. Others, in spite of having been badly wounded, in spite of shots in the head, bullet-ridden arms and legs, did manage to hang on. They had lost a lot of blood. It had seeped through their makeshift bandages, their ripped clothing; still, they dragged on . . .

And then the cattle cars lay behind us and there, in front of us, in the middle of this sun-scorched road, like a fantastic apparition, stood a tall, impeccably clean, perfectly beautiful man.

Kommandant Rudolf Hoess.

I didn't learn his name till much later, not that it mattered anyhow then or later, not to me, only to historians. Linked to the darkest hours of mankind, Commander Hoess did get his name into the history books.

In full uniform, with all the stripes and medals befitting his rank and position and without a drop of sweat on his unblemished handsome face, he more resembled a matinée idol than a camp commander. He spoke to us quite cordially, saying that those who weren't too tired to walk should line up over there, five to a row, and that the others who didn't want to or couldn't walk could catch a ride on the open trucks waiting on the other side.

The choice of which way to go — left you walk, right you ride — was, for one inexplicable moment, ours to make. Although Hoess made most of the selections himself, left right, left right, passing sentence with the blink of an eye, there was that one incredible split second in which we could choose which way to go.

I went to the left because I'd seen Rainer and Fritzi standing with those wanting to walk and because the trucks were already pretty full, with more and more climbing on. I went to the left because Heinz and Werner had been pulled from my side and told to help with the wounded and because I needed to be close to a friend, have someone I knew hold my hand.

The trucks left long before we did. The people on them called to us that they would see us later, and on the last one, right in the midst of all those weary bodies, stood Fritzi's mother, tall and proud, and with her was the little kitten. She waved to us and smiled until she and the others all disappeared into the white heat of the barren landscape.

"Two miles before we reach the camp," someone said. Two miles to walk under the blazing sun. I wore my coat. What else could I do? I couldn't trudge along half naked in my torn and dirty slip. That's how I felt, too. Torn and dirty. My coat weighed a ton. My rich coat — too heavy to wear, too heavy to carry.

What kind of place is this? Where are we? Who knows about this deserted, dried-out desert, this accursed, godforsaken, hotter than hell hell? If we now all started to scream, could anyone hear us?

We had reached the entrance. It was easy to recognize because it said "Entrance" where the gate was: "EINGANG." I never saw one that said "Exit," though I did look for it.

Above the one we went through, in letters large enough not to miss, stood: "ALBEIT MACHT FREI." Work makes free.

There was barbed wire everywhere. Big signs — "ELECTRIFIED" — let those planning an escape know that getting out was the least they'd have to worry about.

The soldiers and the one female guard accompanying us didn't look much better than we did. The soldiers were grimy and she looked even worse. Her face was full of blotches, like insect bites, and she kept scratching them while yelling at us to get a move on. I asked her where our men were and when we'd see them again, but she was not in a talkative mood, didn't answer. We kept watching out for them every step of the way, but they were nowhere about.

In the far distance, other male prisoners, at least we thought they were male, were picking up something heavy, carrying it away and putting it down somewhere else. It made me think of Devil's Island, the penal colony of French Guiana, a hundred or so years ago.

We were inside the camp. I began to realize this was not a godforsaken little place but a godforsaken enormous place. It would be easy to get lost in here. It all looked the same. Barracks after barracks, loam, dust and dried-out mud. That's all there was, except for some bizarre-looking figures crouched in front. Their clothing consisted of rags and some sort of cloth around their head, tied in a way I hadn't seen before. They stared at us. Actually, it was more like looking right through us. They were everywhere. They and the barracks. We kept on walking and there they were. We turned corners and there they were. I kept trying to catch an expression, guess their ages, but I could not. Their faces were stiff masks. No smiles, no sadness, no tears, no joy.

And still I didn't know where I was.

The first "Halt!" came as we reached a large building. We were pushed through, ordered to undress, drop everything and line up, one behind the other — alphabetically.

The humiliating, nevertheless unequivocal fact of having to undress in front of those pimply, grinning S.S. guards, together with the mad scrambling rush to find someone whose name one knew, did not come easy. Handbags were flying. People kept stepping on someone else's clothes while trying to hide their own nakedness behind their belongings, holding on to some of it, holding on to each other. Mirrors got stepped on, mirrors broke, before they got to see themselves one more time. Seven years bad luck?

The S.S. guards kept kicking and pushing indiscriminately, laughing, laughing their stupid heads off. They had such good fun.

My coat fell off my shoulders, my rich, rich coat with all the money and gems. Gone forever. It never would get to Switzerland now, not in this lifetime. Would I?

We kept stumbling over all that had been discarded, one's very own last pair of shoes, while attempting to find our place alphabetically.

Somebody pushed me, and I landed next to Rainer. She was trembling. My handbag had also landed on the floor, and all I could manage to save from it was my comb. My strong comb. I really needed it. My hair was much too long and thick to get a small one through. One of the guards was playing football with my handbag. It flew through the air, opened, and dropped to the ground right next to me. Two photos, face-up, fell out: one of Herbert, the other of Margit and Toni. They were laughing. Happy pictures, happy smiles, all the way from home . . . The football player kept on playing tackle with my pictures. He kicked them forward and jumped on top of them. He dug his heels into them and marched off. Left behind were bits of paper, without faces, without smiles, all the way from home . . .

Somebody screamed. It sounded like it came from the beginning of the line. Then there were other screams and others still. Not very loud or long ones, resembling, I thought, more the noise of a sudden fright than pain. Chilling to hear. After I had finally gotten close enough, I saw that those in front had left the building and lined up outside. They were still stark naked, with their left arm bent and drawn back to the side.

And then Rainer and I were outside, too. Also stark naked.

The small table with the two S.S. men on either side of it was empty. Behind it, wearing cotton dresses and white aprons, stood two women. Clean women in clean dresses. One of them was holding something in her hand that looked like a pen, except for the pointed end which seemed much longer. Whoever was next was being pulled by one of the S.S. men to the table, grabbed by her left arm and ordered to keep it stretched out. Then the two women took over. While one of them held the arm, the other pierced the pointed end of the pen through the skin and into the flesh.

Tattoo! They were giving us tattoos! Not with one's name but a *number!* Without a name, they can say that we don't exist. Who cares about numbers? Arm after outstretched arm went through the ritual of becoming nameless, nonexistent, canceled out.

When Rainer's turn came, I kept sending her signals not to cry out. She didn't. Her head, turned away from them, looked straight at me. I'd never seen her naked before. Not any woman. I really didn't want to look at her, nor the others, but it was impossible not to. Rainer was beautiful: long slender legs, small hips and waist, a wonderful straight back and shoulders, and then there was her magnificent long golden hair. She had let it fall forward to cover her breasts, wishing I'm sure that it could cover all of her.

My turn. I had made up my mind not to let those halfwitted S.S. guards touch me, so I moved forward and stretched out my arm. I immediately felt the first stab. It felt like a hundred bee stings or a hundred very dull needles, not really sharp but very fast, and it did hurt. When it was over, I was number 51841. There was blood on it, my blood, and underneath the number was a triangle. I did not know what it meant. All I knew was that I could never hide any of it and that all the blood flowing through my body was not enough to cover it . . . Not now, not ever. Branded for life!

The number they gave me is on my left arm just below the elbow. On the outside. It's very large and it won't ever go away. Those pin-pricking moments were the worst of my life, and nothing that came afterwards could ever erase them.

The practical side of it, we all recognized, was that it permanently eliminated any chance of an escape, feasible or not. Also, the changing of one's appearance and documents, so as not to be recognized, had become useless. An illusion no longer worth dreaming of . . . They stripped us naked, stole our clothes, and when there was nothing left to steal, they stole our identity and left us with only a number on our arm.

They had us marching again. Five to a row . . . Why always five? One hundred and twenty of us were in here now. As for the rest, we kept looking for them — and wondered. More barracks! More of those bizzare-looking figures in rags with their empty eyes, their empty faces, stooped over, hanging about. Perhaps they weren't real. Not flesh and blood but lifeless puppets right out of some demented puppetmaker's morose nightmare. Rainer held on to her toothbrush; I kept clutching my comb. Everyone in our nudist parade held on to something.

We were taken to still another building and told we could take a shower. Certainly the best news yet! They had us line up in a very long hallway that was full of people, full of action. Lots of girls were running past us. They wore neat, clean dresses and looked extremely busy. While they kept rushing past us, more S.S. guards lurked by the doors. Their only reason for being there was to stare, to stupidly laugh and to ram into us. Their deliberately lewd behavior made us move closer together, made us want to shield each other. I heard one woman say that there was definitely something going on a bit farther ahead from where I stood. Another one of their unimaginable surprises. There, they took the only thing they hadn't taken yet: *our hair!* Not just a haircut — they wanted it all, every strand of it. Shaven heads; make us completely bald. *Bald women!*

As I watched the first ones move on, I was struck by the way their appearance had changed. They had become terribly clumsy and ugly. Their movements, suddenly shockingly awkward, were grotesque. With their arms dangling as if they no longer belonged to them, their sagging shoulders and bent-forward backs, they were no longer recognizable. They looked like something the demented puppetmaker could have invented, fantastically strange and sad.

The guards even made them pay for having no hair at all and for looking so bad. No longer did they only laugh or ram into them, now they pounded on them with their fists and boots, kicked them out the door, screaming insults and all the filthy names they could come up with. None of the women fought back nor did they protest. They had lost their selfhood, were women no more . . .

The floor was full of hair. It looked pretty — like a colorful carpet. The closer I got, the more I was able to see. There were two chairs in the middle of the otherwise empty room and two women, with hair, behind each one of them. One had a pair of scissors in her hand, the other a straight-edge razor. I had been leaning against the wall wondering whether it was better to go to the one with the scissors or let the razor do the job. The razor was faster. I had watched it all very closely. Had watched those barely able to stand up, yet still standing tall and straight until they slid into the chair, where they surrendered all their dignity along with their hair. That's why they were being abused. Were they, themselves, aware how it had changed them? If so, did they still care?

The carpet got bigger and higher. Already the naked feet stepping on it were completely covered. Among the women who'd already gotten in and out of the chair, only Fritzi held her head high and walked even taller than before. No matter her baldness, which made her head look like an odd-shaped melon. She walked by those guards boldly and unafraid, wearing her nakedness regally and proud, her shiny bald head like a glistening star. The guards gaped and then let her pass without laying a finger on her. She had stood up to them, had held on to her self-esteem and not surrendered anything. And all she had done was walk tall and look them straight in the eye . . .

It made me think of my old acting teacher, Professor Wieland, who once had told me to do just that. I wasn't naked then, nor bald, and those I had to face weren't my enemies either. Just other actors. Grand, legendary ones, still, only actors deciding whether or not to let me pass the Actors State Exam. Not quite the same, I know, but I was afraid then, too. "Look straight at them . . . Think of those great men sitting on a toilet with their pants down . . ." That's what the grand old master had told me to do. I'd done it then and many times since, and it had always worked. Perhaps he had taught Fritzi, too.

Rainer had chosen the razor. She had smiled at me, had made a flippant remark to the girl about to shave her head, had shaken her hair to make it fly every which way, and then suddenly dropped her head forward and down. "Just my neck, please," she mockingly told the girl, batting her eyelashes. "I'd like to keep the rest, if you don't mind." But the girl pulled Rainer's head back, and with one swoop cut right through the middle of her hair all the way from her forehead to the base of her neck. It left a three-inch gap. A long, wide, bald, grotesque-looking gap. The golden strands, up there only moments ago, landed on Rainer's shoulders and then fell to the ground. Now the carpet was covered with gold. When she was done, she jumped off the chair, and laughing hysterically, traipsed off. The chair was empty for only a second before I sat down in it.

The one with the scissors really didn't like having to cut beautiful hair like mine and Rainer's. She thought it was a "crying shame." At least that's what she told the quick-shaving one, who, very much to my surprise, agreed. Watching her could give one the impression she enjoyed her work. She did it so well and so fast. Then, out of the blue, she asked whether I was a nurse, because if I was, I could keep it. Nurses were allowed to wear their hair short. I had to tell her no. It wasn't the sort of job I would have dared to fake. She then wanted to know what it was I did or had done before. That's when someone felt obliged to let her know that I was an actress. Given the circumstances, it certainly was the most ludicrous thing anyone could be. Surprisingly, though, not to the one about to shave my head. Pointing at the S.S. guard closest to the door, she suggested that I talk to him, reason being that he liked artists and was known to occasionally help them. Also, they had an orchestra here, and I perhaps could get into that — make music and keep my hair.

The incredible idea of a real orchestra in such unreal surroundings hadn't quite sunk in when I saw the same S.S. man the girl had pointed out trip a bald, frightened woman before she could get out the door. He tripped every-one not fast enough to get by him. I shook my head and said nothing. The girl did, though. She called me stupid. Even after I'd told her that I didn't play any instruments, another thing one can't fake, she still called me stupid, very stupid, and slashed her straight-edge razor, like a crazed doctor's scalpel, over my head and into my hair. She did it faster than a fast torpedo, and yet it felt like she had shaven every hair off individually.

It fell down all around me. Covered my back, my shoulders, my face — and then joined Rainer's hair with all the rest. My arms pressed against my body, I sat up as straight as I could. My hands were clenched, and I could feel the teeth of my comb cut into the palm of the hand holding it. The pain was a welcome diversion, almost a relief. A strand of hair had gotten tangled up in the part of the comb that stuck out of my fist; it just hung there. A moment later the girl shaving off my hair said, "Next one," and pushed me off the chair. She too was a camp inmate, she and the one with the scissors.

Someone had forced my right fist open. Someone wanted my beautiful green comb. "You don't need it anymore," this woman in her neat skirt and blouse, with short hair, hissed. "Let go of your comb! You hear?" and she swore at me. I'd heard all right, but kept holding it just the same as though it were my ticket out of there. She had to wrestle me for it, pry it out of my hand.

Nothing to hold to hold on to anymore. Not even a small strand of hair! No one had really physically harmed me as yet; nevertheless, I felt violated and overwhelmingly naked. Still, I did not drag my feet, dangle my arms, sag my shoulders or lower my head while walking past those S.S. guards. I let them stare at me and moved into the next confine.

It looked like a bathhouse without dressing rooms, a swim hall without a pool, or a sports arena with spectator benches leading all the way to the top. The same women who only a short while ago had hidden their bodies and shame from their persecutors no longer did so. They were on their own now. By themselves, just sitting around, one here, one there, not doing anything really.

They called her the Queen of the Sauna. She was merciless, hated every one of us and herself most of all. She was fatter than the fattest swine, uglier than the ugliest sin, more vulgar than the most common slut, and escaping the foul lashing of her tongue was as impossible as trying to escape the violent lashes of her whip. In the world outside she had been a *Puff Mutter*, madam of a cheap whorehouse, which she was proud of and had sworn to continue as soon as the Third Reich realized the value of her service to the fatherland and set her free. She was from Hamburg, also a prisoner but definitely not a Jew. She had no number, no tattoo on her fleshy arm. Her job was driving us from the benches into the next place, the shower room.

At last I landed under one of the showers together with other women, but before I had a chance to let the water we all needed so badly refresh me and wash myself, the shower was over. I didn't even get to use the tiny bit of soap we had between us. From there, the Sauna Queen drove us into yet another room. It had a long table stacked high with shabby, tattered, threadbare clothing on it. Behind it sat several girls, wearing black aprons over some sort of uniform, with scarves on their heads, pulled tight in the back. They were handing out what a ragpicker must have left behind, without regard to size, length, shape or season. It only took a couple of minutes, and we were dressed again, all one hundred and twenty of us. The lucky ones came away with something that once definitely had been a dress. The less lucky ones got only an apron.

We were lying on the stone floor of yet another room while the Sauna Queen, busy snoring, took her nap. My eyes, scouting around, were still trying to find other familiar eyes. Close by, I knew no one. Farther away, though, I spotted two odd shapes crawling my way. It was instinct, not recognition, which told me they were Rainer and Fritzi.

Rainer had gotten only an apron. Fortunately, it had a front and a back. The kind one pulls over one's head. The color was an ugly brown, and it was quite short but all in all, not too bad. If nothing else, it was cooler than most of the rejects we had ended up with, and it had pockets. Pockets with nothing to put into them, nothing but Rainer's nervous, fumbling hands. Fritzi, the statuesque opera singer, whose glamorous mother had been riding on the truck with her little kitten, was wearing a sack made of some very coarse material. In spite of her height, it reached all the way down to her ankles, hiding the best part of her figure, her legs. At best it emphasized her overly large, melon-shaped bald head. My outfit wasn't a prizewinner either. It was a dress all right and it was black. It had buttons, pleats, a proper high neck and long sleeves. The sleeves were too narrow, thus very uncomfortable under the arms, the waist far too big and it was much too tight across the chest. The worst of it was that it was one hundred percent wool. In that heat. No, the worst was that they had also handed me a very long, old-fashioned white slip to wear beneath the dress. It hung down like a piece of white bedsheet not properly tucked under. Fritzi had shoes, worn-out slippers that wouldn't last the day through. Rainer and I didn't even get those. We didn't tell each other how absolutely deplorable we looked. We knew it anyhow.

We were all very thirsty, but there was nothing to drink. Nothing to eat, either. The room shook from the noise of the fat madam's snoring. It sounded like a crew of drunken, snoring sailors. When she awoke from her nap, she immediately resumed her yelling, her cursing, and her favorite sport: whip lashing.

From the hall, the Sauna Queen chased us into the *Aufnahme Buros* — Admission and Registration Offices. More little rooms, more desks, more neatly dressed girls sitting behind them asking us more and more dumb questions. They asked our names, who we were, where we came from, what we had done and anything else we wanted to tell them. They wrote it all down and filed it away. Not that any of it served a purpose or made any sense. Still, they had to do it or else they would have lost their cushy jobs. I told them the same old story, why the hell not? It had almost become a game with me. Told them about my Aryan Hungarian father back in Budapest who had no idea what had happened to me. These girls, also inmates, had more than just a cushy job. They had made friends with the S.S. They talked with them, laughed with them, smoked cigarettes together. Who knows what else they did together. They had gotten the jobs Commander Fränk, back in Malin, had promised we'd be getting in that new *Arbeits Lager*. These girls didn't have tattoos, either. All spoke German, most with a very heavy accent which was quite foreign to me.

The girl who had asked me all those questions powdered her nose while going through her little routine. She had had a powder compact in her hand, a pretty one with a real mirror. The only time she had looked up was when I'd told her I was an actress. As to my Aryan father and my being a *Mischling,* that she wrote down automatically. Personally, she'd taken no notice of it. I soon began to realize that everything in the camp that needed to be done was being done by inmates, not by the S.S. or the guards. They only gave the orders. Who then chose the ones carrying them out, and how did one get to be one of them? There was such a difference between us and them! Was it because they had come here before us, had proven themselves? Or was it that they had sold out, had traded their soul for a dress and a cigarette?

We were standing outside again. The sun was so bright that it hurt my eyes. The sun is not a friend here. Ahead of me were those who had gotten through before me. Behind, those who'd finished after me. Five in a row. That much I understood already. Only that much. Rainer and Fritzi stood next to me, and I'd seen Betty all the way in front. Perfect Betty no longer had to worry about being perfect. From what I could make out she looked as crummy as the rest of us. We were forbidden to talk. We were forbidden to move around. We were forbidden to do anything except stand! stand! stand! So we stood, with no one paying attention to us. My lips were dry and cracked, and I could feel the wool of my dress stick to me like hot glue. I envied Rainer for her skimpy apron. The hot ground was burning my feet. My head was throbbing and burning, and as I looked up to the sky, I saw that it was burning too. Flames — grisly red and yellow flames shooting out of gigantic chimneys high into the choking air — were burning up the heavens. And still I didn't know where I was.

The air smelled so strange. It wasn't like anything I'd ever smelled before, and it wasn't just strange. It was nauseating. Like a foul taste.

A young female S.S. guard passing by us was playing with her revolver. She was doing tricks with it like in cowboy movies. Someone behind me asked her about the people on the trucks, where they were and when we would see them again. I knew that voice. It belonged to a Viennese woman whose husband and ten-year-old daughter had climbed on the trucks because the little girl loved riding in cars. The S.S. guard stopped at once. Standing very close, pointing straight to the chimneys, she said stoically: "Up there. That's where they are, the ones from the truck. What the hell is wrong with you? Did you think we're burning coals in there? Jesus — what a terrible stink! Makes one want to vomit!" Then she moved closer. Parting the rows and standing between us, she screamed: "Imbeciles! Don't you know what this place is? It's the last place for Jews! It's the crossroad between heaven and earth. Crossroad — get it? Those up there have already crossed over. Not to worry, your turn will come soon enough. You'll see, there's no waiting list. Before you know it, you'll be gone too!" She laughed a nervous, high-pitched laugh, shot her revolver in the air, and marched off. In the first row someone collapsed. Otherwise it was very still, as though we all had stopped breathing together.

My feet felt like lead. I could not separate them from the burning ground. Inside my head there was a fire raging too, and I couldn't shake the smell, that horrid, choking smell of burned human flesh. And yet, I was unable to believe that what the guard had told us was really true. It must be that what the mind cannot comprehend, cannot grasp, it also cannot believe. "She's just trying to frighten us," I told the mother standing behind me. She didn't answer, almost as if she had turned off all sights and sounds, all smells.

Next to me, Fritzi, looking up to where they were burning the skies, then down to where they were stoking the fires and feeding the flames with Jews, said in a hollow, far-away voice, "My mother's in there," and after that, she never spoke again.

On the other side, on a narrow strip of road, a small group of men were walking by. They were no further than a few arm's lengths away from us, yet unreachable because of the barbed-wire fence between us. It did wake everybody up, though, caused quite a reaction. The women waved and called to them; the men waved and called back. Everybody tried to recognize somebody — a husband, a father, a friend. I was trying to find Werner and Heinz but could not, with all the dust flying around the men, who all wore the same striped prison jackets and caps on their shaven heads. The uniformness made them look identical. Perhaps if they'd stayed a little longer, had walked a little slower, but they were gone before we could make out who they were. Still, there were some among the women who swore they had seen their husband, their father, their brother. Whether or not they had, it did give them a lift, a tiny ray of hope, no matter how self-deluding.

⌐

THERE WAS NO CRASH COURSE that could have taught us survival in this pit of hell. There was no antidote for fear, no substitute for hunger, thirst or disease, no relief from the heat. There were no shelters where one could have hidden from inhumanities — inhumanities which had never existed before in the history of the world. There was nothing but one's own irrevocable will to live. Unless unconquerable, indestructible and above of all predestined, even the Messiah could not have saved one.

To rot here, I told myself a hundred times each day, was not my destiny. Learning to endure beyond endurance was. Learning not to fear, not to feel heat, hunger or thirst was. Learning not to give in to pain, no matter how painful.

It was a decision I had reached consciously when, on my very first day there, for the very first time I saw them — *them*, a caravan of living death moving slowly on the wide camp street toward us. Dots to the eye while they were still far away; limping, crawling, staggering, ghostlike mortals as they came closer; and finally, skeletons as they were near enough to touch. Their eyes were dead already and still they clung to each other, carried and helped one another to make those last few steps to the showers together. One last bath before they became fire too, dust in the wind, ashes on a pile of ashes. It was a group of about two hundred. Malaria and typhoid had done them in. They'd come from the hospital where they had gotten a bed, a sheet, and nothing else. When they didn't get better, they were thrown out to make room for the next disease-riddled expendables.

I think the S.S. wanted us to see this. Letting us know right from the start that there were many ways to die here, not only the chimneys. No one was saying it, but we surely must have asked ourselves how long this caravan of living death had been here. A month, weeks, a few days, hours? Were they young or old when they first came, healthy, or ailing and already spent? How long can one last here anyhow? How long till one looks just like them or like those rag-clad figures ostensibly neither dead nor alive? Perhaps it was because of *them,* because of all the evil and perversity I had seen already, because death and dying was all there was, and life, precious life, had lost all meaning, that I wanted to live more than ever, wanted to know what it's like to grow old. I swore to make it through somehow. More than that, I just couldn't believe that the sole purpose of my being born was to die as a nameless statistic in this subhuman place whose name I still didn't know.

Main Street of the damned! Endlessly it stretches its broken, tired earth from one end of the camp to the other. There never was a street like this before, and if the world comes to its senses, there never will be again. It is a street on which no tree has ever grown, no child has ever played, no prayers have ever been answered, and where no laughter was ever heard. It is a cruel, deadly street, a street that spawns the kind of nightmares Satan himself has come to fear. It's full of diabolic demons and hollow diabolic sounds that follow one everywhere. It's the one they call "The Street Without Mercy." The one that leads to the chimneys where the expendables crowd about until their number is called and their time is up.

I too will have to "live" on this street. I'm certain it will be close to the chimneys, and a long way from the office girls with their clean dresses who powder their noses and smoke cigarettes with the S.S.

THEY FINALLY MARCHED us down to our barracks after too many hours to count; we'd seen enough caravans dragging their bones to last a thousand lifetimes. There we stood again and waited. Waited for water, for bread, and to get out of the broiling sun. The bread, hard and old like this earth, came, but no water and no relief from the burning sun. In front of "the Block," as they call it here, are these barracks, which are neither barracks nor blocks, but stables left behind from some other war, so some say, where the earth is covered with sharp little stones. Standing on them cut our feet like razor-sharp knives. Rainer was the first to sit down. I'd hoped that she wouldn't. I was afraid she might not want to get up anymore, had stopped caring. Rainer was too thirsty to think of anything else. Her lips, cracked and swollen, were bleeding. Her feet were bleeding too, but that didn't bother her, only her thirst.

Around the corner, hovering against one side of our block, half naked women were watching us. Their heads were shaven, too. They had olive skin, were thin like rails, dirty, full of sores, and yet they were beautiful. I think it was their eyes, which were deepset, large and blacker than the blackest onyx, with a glimmer of life still in them. They were holding wooden bowls in their hands, and in those wooden bowls was water they wanted to sell us! Their water for our bread. They spoke in a foreign tongue. Gesturing wildly, they were egging us on to buy their water, to sell our bread. They shoved the bowls right under our noses. I took one look and knew that I would never touch a single drop of it. It was yellow like loam and it stank. Rainer did hand her bread to one of them and took the bowl with that poisonous filth in exchange. I begged her not to drink it, but she wouldn't listen. She was mad with thirst and drank from it before I could knock it out of her hand, swallowing the poison. Not all of it, not enough to quench her thirst, but enough quite possibly to make her very ill. It scared me. One couldn't afford to get ill.

Rainer had given up. She wanted no part of the misery. Not her own, not that all around her. She didn't want to fight. All she wanted was water. Not so Fritzi, though she'd lost the one she was closest to. She had not given up. She hadn't taken a sip. Something about her made me believe that she would do whatever was needed without losing her humanity. Ah, humanity! That was the one thing none of us would have an easy time holding on to.

More and more of those onyx-eyed women were creeping from behind their block over to us. Fights broke out between them, and in the process most of the water spilled. Then other women in shoes and dresses showed up and chased the dirty, half naked ones away. They kicked them, snatched their bowls, and threw water and bowls after them. These women called the others "filthy Greeks!" Lice-ridden, lazy, good-for-nothing Greeks. That's how I found out who they were and where they were from: Salonica, the seaport city of Greece on the Gulf of Salonica. Forty-six thousand of them had been brought to this place.They hadn't been here longer than a couple of weeks and already they were unwashed, sick and starving.

As soon as they had retreated back to their block, I saw a young Greek woman huddled against one of the corners. Completely naked, she was sucking the milk from her breasts. She seemed deliriously happy — and insane. Each time her mouth left her breasts, she sheepishly giggled to herself like someone having outsmarted a mighty enemy. Her eyes kept moving around suspiciously as though she didn't want anyone to know about the white, sweet liquid stored in her breasts. She wanted to have it herself, all of it, now that her baby was gone. I was told that she had smothered the newborn, killed it before they could kill it and throw it into the lime pits with all the other babies.

I could not look away from her, as though each new and shocking sight was meant for me to see, meant to prepare me for the next, bigger and more shocking nightmare:

AUSCHWITZ!

That's the name of these acres of hell. It's in Poland and no more than forty miles from the city of Krakow. It means that civilization is right around the corner, that life outside those electrified barbed wires goes on. And that the world has known all along about the burning and mass murders in here, known about it before the victims did.

That startling information — given to us, the new ones, quite freely and in great detail — was provided by the women already residing in our block. They were what was left of the well-known Bensburger Ghetto. Thirty-one thousand, that's how many had arrived here; less than a thousand were left. They were Poles. The camp was full of them — Jewish Poles, non-Jewish Poles, Poles who had committed crimes against the Third Reich, Poles who hadn't committed crimes. Saboteurs, black marketeers. Poles! Poles! Poles! It was they who had gotten most of the cushy jobs because Germany, eager to get rid of them fast, had brought them here first. They were only liked by other Poles. Not the ragged ones in our block, the others who weren't much better — occasionally worse — than the Germans. These women also told us that the Greek girls were being treated worse than the rest because they were all thieves. And they added that there was a shortage of water, and what little there was carried typhoid and malaria bacilli. "If you drink it, you will die." Will we live if we don't . . . ?

The longest day of my life was almost over. At last the barefaced sun had gone into hiding.

Appell! Assembly, muster, stand straight and be counted. I knew it from Malin, but it wasn't quite the same here. Here we had to stand much longer because none of the female S.S. guards knew how to count. They could shoot, curse, yell, hit, but they couldn't count. The male S.S. guards were rarely seen at this side of the camp, and then they were usually drunk. Which left the counting as well as the running of the Block to the more career-minded prisoners. It meant that my suspicion as to who was running that death camp had been right: *Everything in the entire camp was done by prisoners.*

The S.S. commander gave the orders, but it was the prisoners who carried them out. Voluntary or involuntary.

Our *Blockova* — block elder — was Ilse. As *Blockova,* she could do mostly what she wanted to, and did. Ilse, a twenty-two-year-old blond, blue-eyed lesbian from Berlin, was considered to be one of the better elders. She was tough, loud, but not really cruel. Her ambition, to have as little as possible to do with us, accounted for her spending most of the time in the other camp where the non-Jews and criminals were. There she bought food with our rations, new clothes and new girlfriends. Siestas and nights, however, she did spend in her own private little room to the left of the entrance of the Block. Opposite hers, to the right, was Katja's. Katja was Ilse's assistant, which meant that she did hers and Ilse's job. Katja was absolutely totally mad. She screamed and hit, using a whip indiscriminately whenever she was around, and unfortunately, she was always around. She did everything in a state of uncontrolled frenzy; very frightening. I found out later that Katja's parents, her husband and two-year-old son, were shot in front of her and then shoved into the ovens. They made her watch. It was Katja herself who told me that. Katja was from Slovakia, a former province of Czechoslovakia. She was twenty-six, spoke five languages and had been a university professor.

Two more nicely dressed girls were busy lining us up, one young, the other quite a bit older. Both, though, seemed friendly and were pretty. One was the Block bookkeeper the other the Block housekeeper. Catherine, the older one, was the bookkeeper. Her job was crossing off whoever had died that day. She then reported it to Katja, who reported it to Ilse, who reported it to either a female or a male S.S. guard, depending on which one of them was nearby and sober, who then reported it to the Commandant. *Ordnung muss sein!* — There must be order! There were so many to be crossed off every day; fewer and fewer to be counted.

Catherine was a decent soul. A journalist on the outside, she represented the less than one percent with cushy jobs who hadn't stepped on others to get them. Catherine would have liked to help everyone, but she couldn't. Not enough clout. Hers was only a little job. Besides, she was tired. She couldn't have been more than in her early thirties, yet the couple of inches of hair growing on her head were gray. She'd been here too long, knew too much, for she no longer believed that there still was another life. She would surely die here. Katja would die here too. She wanted to. Moreover, none of those cushy jobs came with a guarantee.

The young one was Simone, and she was French. She was the only French one in our block. There must have been others, but no one here knew where. Hers was a job nobody wanted. She was to see to it that the Block was kept spotless and clean. Quite impossible. There was nothing to clean those stables with. *Blockova* Ilse had stuck it to Simone after she'd refused to sleep with her. Simone was in love with a young French diplomat and afraid that she wouldn't see him again. All she could think and talk about was her love. She longed for him, cried for him, was always sad and very frightened. Everything frightened her, most of all the gas ovens and the burning chimneys. Whenever the chimneys worked overtime burning a hole in the sky like they'd done the night they incinerated the thirty thousand from the Bensburger Ghetto, the little French girl trembled and cried even more. Simon was very young, very pretty and not very strong. Still, I did not think that she would end up food for the chimneys or die of typhoid or malaria. Simone was going to die of a broken heart because she couldn't live without the man she loved . . .

Abtreten — Off with you! It meant that *Appell* was over and that we could go to our block. Not a moment too soon. It was dark inside. Not knowing the layout caused us to bump into each other, stumble and trip over those who'd fallen down. Yet it was a blessing not to be out on the street anymore. Someone had mentioned that it was eight o'clock and *Appell* always started at six. We'd gotten here at 8:00 a.m. That made it twelve hours, standing most of the time. In those twelve hours each of us had lived through a thousand miserable years.

By then the lack of anything to drink had gotten to me, too. I felt that I could not possibly take another step without it. Thirst. Just one more thing one can die of here.

Someone put a bowl into my hand and pushed me forward. I knocked against some sort of barrel. Just then, somebody else took my bowl and put something in it that smelled atrocious. Soup. Hot, foul-tasting soup! It barely covered the bottom of the bowl.

It could never really be light inside the Block because there just weren't enough windows. My eyes, having adjusted, could see that this place which housed about eleven hundred was worse than a stable. They called the sleeping places *kojens* (Polish for cages) and that's exactly what they were. Cages without bars. No matter the season, or whether morning, noon or night, it was always dark, musty and dank.

I was one of the lucky ones. I got myself a space with almost a window. The glass was broken but the frames were still there. The Block had stone floors, and the cages were held together and separated by wooden beams. Three levels of cages, one on top of the other, each cage about four feet long, four to five feet wide. Space, like water, was precious little to be had here. We had no mattresses, no straw sacks — only torn, paper-thin, lice-ridden blankets. One slept on wooden beams, got thrown against wooden beams and hid behind wooden beams.

The cages ran parallel to the Block. One row of cages, a narrow aisle, another and another. Three rows of *kojens* and two aisles. Inside the entrance, where I had bumped into the barrel, was an empty space. It was shorter than the aisles but wider. Those who miraculously still had an ounce of humor left called it "the lobby."

It didn't take a mathematician to figure out that the Block was already overcrowded. Whether one lay down on the stone floor, the second or third level, there wasn't room for more than four in any of the *kojens*. Having been the first one climbing up to my broken window, with Rainer and Fritzi right behind me, I tried my best to defend the tiny bit of space I thought I'd conquered. Yet, when they called lights out — what lights? — we ended up with five more people. Eight altogether. Knowing that there were nine or ten squeezed into most of the other cages was little comfort. I don't know how anyone could have gotten any sleep that way. I couldn't; not sitting pressed against the weather-beaten window frame, with my legs pulled up and my arms around my knees.

What agonizing sounds the night unveiled. What tormenting sobs, moans and whimpers. So full of pain, so full of restless, uneasy movements. Squeezed together — we were much too close — somebody's body was always touching someone else's . . . No room to turn unless we all turned — no room to breathe . . . Arms, legs, entangled limbs, entangled lives. When would I sleep again . . . alone . . . and in peace?

They got us up at 4:00 a.m. for the worst of all reasons, another *Appel.* Since there still wasn't a single S.S. guard around that could count, they had us stand for three wearisome hours on those cold stones, barefoot. After that was finally over, they chased us up an incline, past the Greeks' block, toward the latrines and one water outlet, dripping drops of putrid water. Shivering, we stood some more, waiting endlessly for the communal latrines to become available and for a chance to catch a few drops of the grimy water in our soup bowls. Not to drink but to wash with.

We did pick up bits of information, all bad, learning quickly though that they were all true and that survival here was more than just a game of chance, it was a miracle. Not getting eaten up by lice was a miracle. Not finding one's body covered with pus-infected sores, which did not heal because of lack of vitamins and proper nourishment, was a miracle. Not catching typhoid, malaria or dysentery, not getting beaten or worked to death, was a miracle. Not starving or thirsting to death, not getting shot or gassed when driven to the showers, not keeping the chimneys hot and aflame was a miracle. And beating the odds, twice every day, during *Appell* while they were playing Russian roulette with us, that indeed was some miracle . . .

The game of Russian roulette — a favorite among the illiterate, dense S.S. — was played without a gun at one's head. They simply showed up while we were being counted, stopped in front of this or that prisoner, pointed their finger at the ill-fated one they had chosen and said: "You! You! You! You're dirty — I think you need a shower!" They pulled them out and marched them away. In through the gate they came, out through the chimneys they went. Sometimes they took an entire row or rows. Because we never knew where to stand, we were constantly changing places, musical chairs against Russian roulette, with Lady Luck as the referee.

⌐ FIFTEEN

THE CAMP MY FRIENDS AND I were in was called Birkenau. It was part of Auschwitz, and in an insufferable way, it was the most notorious part. It's where they'd installed the crematoriums, where the lime pits and the gas ovens were, and where Hitler's scheme for a "Final Solution" was being played out. Conceived and hatched in the crazed head of Gestapo's headman Lieutenant Colonel Karl Adolf Eichmann, Birkenau with its death factories was the only mass burial ground that never had a burial or a grave. It wasn't only Jews they wanted to get rid of, but Gypsies, too. There were lots of them in the camp, and with one small exception, they weren't any better off than we were. That small exception was a beautiful, five-year-old Gyspy boy, picked out by Commander Hoess personally to be his very own pet. He had everything a child could want: lots of good food, lots of toys, the best of care and lots of fun. Especially when he was riding with the commander on his motorcycle around the camp in his lovely white fur coat. He had everything — but his mommy and daddy.

Birkenau was also the home of the infamous Dr. Mengele, the Angel of Death, who practiced slaughterhouse butchery in the name of science. Experiments too gruesome to even think about, that's what he was into. This devilish man meant to create a blond and blue-eyed master race, and there was nothing he wouldn't do to bring his Führer such a specimen. Whatever was going on in his torture chambers, healing was no part of it. He found his guinea pigs among the sick, badly in need of medicine, the incurably naive and the trusting ones, and among the not yet sick nor naive or trusting ones. Whoever went or was dragged there never left, or left minus certain vital organs, limbs or eyes. There were those who insisted that Dr. Mengele conducted all his experiments and surgeries without any anesthesia or painkilling drug.

Absurdity after absurdity! They did indeed have an orchestra here, right where the working colonies gathered: the Live from Auschwitz All-Girl Birkenau Marching Band. Every day these women, whose job it was to sing and play idiotic songs, marched in front of us, spurred us on. Always five in a row. Every morning, every night. They helped lift the morale — whose morale? They did not stay with us though. They left as soon as the work of planting grass that didn't grow, of digging squalid water ditches, of building roads and bridges had begun. Day after day after day, we marched . . . they played their fiddles. With shovels and axes, pushcarts and heavy bricks, we marched . . . they sang. These girls lived in a better block, wore better clothes, ate better food than we. Something about them reminded me of clones.

Once they were gone, we were left with a couple of yawning, hungover S.S. guards, the ever-blistering sun, our wounded feet and feverish heads. Every day seemed longer than the one before. The loads heavier, the ditches deeper and the cursed earth harder. None of the work made any sense. It wasn't supposed to. They just didn't want us to hang around the Block all the time. The women who collapsed were left there to rot. I'd been pushing the wheelbarrow for days now. It was full of large squares of artificial grass, which I had to carry to one end of the wasteland, where the barbed wire was, dump out, pick up again, and then carry, piece by piece, to the other side. Ten hours a day with no break . . . and that was one of the better jobs. It really didn't matter what one did. It was all equally exhausting and stupid. I hated having to be that close to the electrified fence with nothing but more wasteland on the other side of it.

Who would have thought that one could indeed sing oneself out of pushing a wheelbarrow? Who would have thought that *Blockova* Ilse loved being sung to almost as much as she loved girls? She said it made her forget everything else. It was about two weeks into the horrifying days and nights already endured that Rainer, who'd never quite bounced back or been herself again, came down with typhoid. For a couple of days, Fritzi and I had managed to keep her hidden inside the Block, but when her fever got too high and she started to hallucinate, we had no choice but to report it. While Fritzi stayed with Rainer, I, being more scared of Katja than of Ilse and even more of catching typhoid, went straight to Ilse. Just returned from one of her frequent excursions to the higher-rent district part of the camp, and apparently well sated from her visit, Ilse was in a pretty good mood. At least she listened. Afraid that our entire block might end up in quarantine, or worse, Ilse, who also wanted to survive, had Rainer instantly transferred to the isolation ward of the hospital. Not to Dr. Mengele's barbaric operating rooms — he didn't get turned on by contagious diseases. It was then that Ilse, surprisingly relieved that I had come to her instead of telling an ambitious Kapo or the S.S. about it, asked me whether I could sing.

What was really weird about that kind of question being asked at that moment, with my friend so ill, was that I no longer thought of it as weird. On the contrary. If a song or two could get me some decent help for Rainer, why not? Ilse, a wizard when it came to calling in favors or promising them, did both. She made it possible for me to see my friend twice, bring her tea and soup that didn't stink and medicine to get her fever down. But it was too late. Rainer did not recognize me anymore. Both times she lay, wrapped in a white sheet, next to a very pale-looking girl who was already dead. Dead and waiting for Rainer to join her. She did so three days later. If there was anything to be grateful for, it was that Rainer was spared the agony of ending up as just another ghost in just another caravan as just another living death.

One didn't mourn a friend who died in the camps, not if their pain and suffering was greater than they could endure. One only wondered where God was in all this, especially for someone like Rainer, who always did believe in Him.

Ilse had tried only once to get me to "see it her way." She really wasn't all that serious about it, more of a let's-test-the-water idea. She actually wanted to hear me sing more than she wanted me. Also, she did believe me when I told her that Katja was not her friend and had been watching her. Katja did not condone amoral behavior, and that was why Ilse did whatever it was she did away from the Block.

I sang for Ilse every afternoon in her tiny room. She sat there like a little child, sometimes laughing, sometimes with tears in her eyes. That tough, aggressive butch was easily moved, and she did make life just a hair easier for me. No more pushing wheelbarrows, no more dumping grass, and no more

Ilse stealing my Sunday ration of one slice of sausage and margarine. I even got her to stop stealing my blockmates' rations, too.

↩

A FEW GOLD PIECES farther from where we were — past the Greeks, the Gypsies and a few other blocks that housed the social misfits and political nonconformists — that's where it could be found: the great secret of Auschwitz. The business center — the market! There they sold diamonds for bread, gold for salt, salt for cigarettes and cigarettes for clothes. All those good citizens had brought with them their jewels, money and furs — at least I wasn't the only one. The fearless Nazis took their possessions away, and so whoever dared stole their own jewels and sold them for the price of another day. If they lived, they stole and sold again. Fifty English pounds for a carrot; rubies and sapphires for a small clove of garlic. There, for a brief moment, the dealers in tomorrow dwelt. They called it "the Street of Filthy Lucre," the street that was paved with deadly gold.

Everybody stole; everybody robbed. We stole from the robbers, the robbers stole from the higher-up robbers, who in turn robbed Germany of everything they had robbed us of. They sent our hair to Berlin to fill their mattresses and coat linings; they sent the gold from the teeth of those they had murdered, their eyeglasses and frames and tons of clothing, tons of valuables. Lots of new stuff came in every day, lots of new stuff went out every day, and lots stayed right in Auschwitz. Everybody stole, everybody robbed. Even Commander Hoess. He stole the little Gypsy boy.

One night, we had entertainment. Not like in Malin with a stage and all the pompous Nazi brass. It was on a much smaller scale, right in one's own block, inside the entrance, in the lobby. That's what they did once in a while. Not only so they could forget where they were but to remember who they were. The Poles were the ones performing. They sang songs from their homeland, their village songs of long ago, songs their grandparents had taught them. None of my group wanted to participate, nor did I or Fritzi, who still hadn't spoken. All it meant to us was a chance to have our *koje* to ourseves for an hour or so. The space around the lobby, where the stinking watery coffee and soup barrel stood, was filled. Everyone wanted to watch or be part of it.

Was it the song or was it the voices I was so intensely drawn to? It made me leave my *koje* and go toward the voices. Was it the song, which I had heard many a time before, or was it the voices that sang the song the way I'd never heard before — I had the record at home. American, "My Yiddishe Mamme," sung in Yiddish by the legendary Sophie Tucker. In it, tribute is being paid to the mother for the bounteous love she gave her children, for her devotion and sacrifices. "Worth more than all the treasures on earth," say the lyrics, "is the love of my Yiddishe Mamme mine." Sophie Tucker's powerful voice and dramatic interpretation gave it that special something which made one want to remember it. Hearing it again in the death camp of Auschwitz made it impossible ever to forget.

Two fifteen-year-old twins stood there with their mother in between them, singing with the voice of angels what their Mamme meant to them. They were frail and thin, wearing only skimpy dresses, with dirty scarves tight around their childlike faces. They were holding hands, mother and twins, looking with their large brown eyes straight ahead out to the cursed street. Every note they sang sounded like the echo of a silver bell. Every word, straight from the heart, indescribably beautiful, indescribably moving. Spellbound, I'd stood and listened with everyone else in the Block. Then, just before the gripping climax, a smug S.S. guard came marching in. Without a moment's hesitation, she went directly up to them, pulled the mother away from the children and marched her out. No force was used. The mother went willingly, her face betraying no emotion, as if she'd known this was going to happen and had prepared herself and her girls. The twins watched her go. Moving closer together and holding hands, they sang the last bars of "My Yiddishe Mamme" just as their mother disappeared into the relentness darkness.

The next day, our kind and gentle bookkeeper Catherine told me that all blocks had received the order to get rid of every woman over forty. "It was her birthday yesterday," Catherine said. "That's all I know. Her fortieth," and she crossed her off the list.

Unable to sleep, I'd spend nights looking out my narrow window and listening to the sounds of the street. The street never sleeps. It only waits till all the limping shadows are back in their wooden horse stables before it dumps its dirty secrets out. Wide awake the night the twins sang and said Kaddish, the prayer for the dead, for their mother, I watched the empty street. Watched as a phantom moon appeared in a phantom sky. There were no stars. The moon turned on her yellow flashbulbs and threw a joyless light down on the street. That's when, from far away, the sound of moving trucks invaded the stillness. It might have been two hours past the time of dreaming; whatever time it was, the danse macabre had begun. Another load of human freight moved slowly through the silent street. It carried many little boys and girls. They were born in Warsaw, and this was where their journey ended. Right on this street, beyond the stables, where giant chimneys spat out their ghastly yellow flames to celebrate the ultimate achievement of human cataclysm. The trucks had stopped, and all the little ones were stumbling to the ground. Each child a refuge for the trembling body of another. They did not understand — and yet they knew — it was their turn to feed the monster. Their screams, much louder than the sound of cannons, hurtled through the grisly night, while panic-stricken children, in agony of pain to come, ran, fell and crawled, crying to a distorted moon that they were only children.

Help us! We're only children! Jewish children! Help us! The fiery, greedy dragon tongues have swallowed all the children. What a fantastic holocaust . . .

The memory of it will always haunt me. The hollow echo of their voices, swept by the wind to every corner of this earth, was never heard. Charred souls keep searching but could find no reason for their death. And while a disastrous harvest has been reaped, no one stopped the foul, malignant seeds from spreading. So crushed by the gigantic wheels of time are we, so dazed by the enormous pace of history, that we have wrapped a blanket of forgetfulness around the ghosts of yesterday and stored them in a warehouse filled with latent nightmares. I heard that the graveyards in this world were getting bigger every day and soon there will be no one left to pray. But God still loves us . . . Will He Say Kaddish for us all?

IT WAS SIX WEEKS INTO THIS WRETCHED EXISTENCE, during morning *Appell,* that Betty (whom I hadn't spoken to since Malin) and I were approached by a female S.S guard and ordered to follow her. Mixed feelings or not, we went. She led us to another block, a fair distance away, handed us over to a cotton-clad female and took off. Apart from not having a clue as to the reason for it, she'd never said a word. This definitely was the wrong time, at least for me, to be singled out. For over a week now, I'd been plagued by sores, those dreaded, pus-infected, spreading-like-wildfire sores. Just when I'd thought that I was fortunately immune to them, they appeared. Between my breasts! First one, then three more. Painfully aware of the possible consequences of this ugly disease, I hid them and told no one.

There was a healing ointment — not a cure — right here in Auschwitz, but I had not dared to ask Ilse for it; I didn't trust her that much. So I had done nothing — nothing except try to stay out of sight. Now, though, someone was sure to find out. My attempt to stow away in some dark corner of the new Block didn't work. I was assigned a bunk, not a *koje,* right in the middle, given clean bedding and bedclothes, permitted to bathe alone with soap, washrag and towel, was able to exchange my outlandish clothes for a dress that fit, fed soup that didn't stink and given bread I could actually chew rather than the usual leftover crust. All of which was very welcome and most appreciated. I even considered asking someone there for help, but not knowing why these unexpected niceties were happening made me think better of it. As time dragged on, with no one to tell either me or Betty anything, I found myself wishing for my old lice-infested block.

Twenty-four hours passed. It was morning again. Another *Appell,* but not for us anymore. We were finally told why they had brought us here.

Transport! They were shipping us off to another camp — Betty, me, and seventy-eight other women! If I had dared to scream and jump for joy, I would have. All eighty of us would have. Only those who'd been there could possibly have known what getting out of that hellhole meant to us. I felt stupid with relief and did not spend another second worrying about my sores.

They put us on a canvas-covered truck, and we were off. Eighty impatient, giddy with excitement, chattering women. Like going on a picnic. They'd kept the rear of the truck open, which gave those of us sitting there a chance to see where we were going. We had no armed guards with us, which made us twice as giddy. No guards at all.

We'd driven for a little while, with our heads in the clouds, with the jubilant sensation of just being alive . . . incredibly alive, when the driver slammed on the brakes and stopped.

At that precise instant one of the girls yelled: "We're at the ovens! Dear God! *They're going to kill us!*"

My heart stopped — Literally. With the roar of thunder in my ears, a pounding in my chest and the ominous sensation of falling into a black, bottomless pit — I died. Fright — that's what I died of — only a few heartbeats away from the "Final Solution." It's the worst way to die, and I don't ever want to go through it again. All that blackness with not a shimmer of light coming toward me from the other side.

The panic stayed with us till after the electrified barbed-wire fences were behind us. Then for a while I wasn't sure I'd ever breathe normally again. They let us out in the middle of nowhere right in front of a railroad track. A few German soldiers with dusty uniforms and dusty rifles were standing around. They looked tired and bored.

It was morning. It was the birth of a new day . . . and the resurrection of hope.

It wasn't the Orient Express, but neither were they cattle cars. What finally came to take us to wherever they were sending us next was a half empty passenger train carrying civilians. With us were the soldiers we'd seen by the tracks. With their rifles in firing position, they had stationed themselves on the platforms at both ends of the cars. Four per wagon. If their goal was to prevent us from trying to escape, it seemed a foolish waste of manpower. What were we going to do? Attack those leering, uptight people and then escape with our shaven heads and the numbers on our arms? They wouldn't let us sit together, nor next to those shameless gawking passengers. It was ironic, but that's what I had wished for all along: a window seat, with no one nearby, so that, undisturbed, I could get some perspective on those past twenty-four hours. Apart from that, and apart from wanting the train to fly with mercurial speed as far away from Auschwitz as possible, I felt extremely good, remarkably unconnected and blissfully calm. Very much like an uninvolved spectator strictly along for the ride.

The train did anything but fly. It crawled, stopped, and when it did continue, it did so on shaky wheels. The reason: bombs. The Germans had gotten a taste of their own medicine. Finally! Entire parts of towns and cities gone. Derailed trains next to wrecked railway tracks, demolished buildings on deserted streets. Empty farms with burned tractors left behind. What a sight — what beautiful rubble! What magnificent destruction! It made me want to shout for joy.

While languishing in the abyss, I'd never once thought of the big war being fought in the world outside. I had my own war to fight. Moreover, we were completely cut off. No news at all, not even rumors, reached us; the roar of war seemed many thousand miles away. I'd never seen or even heard a plane fly through the dismal somber skies of Auschwitz. I knew nothing. Now, though, I saw! Hour after hour after hour, detour after detour after detour, I saw the ruin and rejoiced!

It went like this all day long. Passengers, looking weary-eyed and gaunt, boarded the train, or got off, speaking the language I had learned to hate: German. Hitler's German, which used to be my mother tongue. It didn't even sound the same.

We were somewhere in Germany and spent the night on the stationary train. That night the Allies bombed again — sweet music to my ears, this symphony of blaring sirens, of crashing structures, of shattered earth. It was quite marvelous. The possibility of us or the train also getting hit never entered my mind.

We weren't hit, and shortly after daybreak we started moving again. This time with no more stops before we were let off. From there, wherever that place was, our soldier escorts had us march — what else but five to a row? — on country roads, through fields and lovely, peaceful fir tree woods. How very odd to come upon such tranquility amid this raging war.

↬

WE STOOD BEFORE A MONUMENTAL IRON GATE, which was closed. The towering gate was all that separated the outside world from whatever was going on inside. Two soldiers, parading back and forth, were guarding it. After a short exchange with the head of our guards, they opened the imposing entrance and marched us through.

On September 15, 1943, on a beautiful midmorning, the gates of still another concentration camp, Ravensbrück, closed behind me. Far away from Auschwitz, I thought of the friends I'd left there. Far away from home, I tried remembering the voices of those I loved. While learning, once again, to adapt to yet another life, the evil I had just come from, the good I once had known, seemed very far away. Everything seemed far away, although none as far as the end of the war.

"Do you play bridge?"

The one asking the question had her right index finger pointed straight at me. She stood in the exaggerated pose of a fashion model, in striped prison uniform, shamelessly staring at me while sounding deadly serious. "Nuts," I thought, "they've taken us to a nut house!" It wasn't just the peculiarity of the question or the girl's demeanor that made me think so, though they were the first words anyone had spoken so far. It was all of it.

There we were, standing in front of the bathhouse waiting for the longest time, being gawked at by a procession of the oddest-looking female populace I'd ever been exposed to. The ones who won my vote for most obnoxious were the unfortunately much too well represented Jehovah's Witnesses. They snuck around us like evil witches, round and round with their arms up in the air, blaring in their nasal singsong voices, prophesying this to be the last day on earth.

Singsong sisters aside, for reasons we couldn't figure out then, our arrival in Ravensbrück caused quite a stir. Up and down the camp streets, from behind the blocks, everywhere I looked, prisoners were eyeing us. We undoubtedly were the main event of the day.

Before the sun went down, we finally got to take a shower, got to exchange our travel clothes for the regular prison getup, got to eat raw potato peels swimming in water, called soup, and were then led to our latest accommodation, our new home-away-from-home: Block 27.

According to those already there, the next thirty days was settling-in time. Exact translation: quarantine. We found out later that having come from Auschwitz was why they kept us isolated. Who knew what strange diseases we had brought with us? Guards and prisoners alike were as curious about us as they were apprehensive.

Whatever they had heard about that place, they did not dare to speak its name. I think they were afraid that the word alone could cause them to be sent there — prisoners as well as guards. Guards, so I was told, were transferred to Auschwitz from other camps as punishment for improper conduct or lack of conviction.

My first impression of having landed in a nut house was, if not completely true, not completely false either. Even without the characters I had met so far, the acquaintance of my bunkmate alone was grounds enough to think so. She, Ollie was her name, was by her own admission a murderess. She killed three husbands (I think that's all she had), bludgeoned them with an ax, buried the hatchet, so to speak, right in their skulls. To hear her say it, it was only men that she'd killed, husbands to be precise, never strangers. Her looks made one wonder how she ever got one man, let alone three. She was short, pudgy, with a huge swollen stomach, beady eyes and a puffed-up face. Her hairless head, like a full moon, was completely round and shiny.

Naturally I asked first myself, then others, what is a husband slayer doing in a concentration camp? Answer: Being rehabilitated. Not quite the same as the ordinary enemies of the Reich I had met so far. I soon learned that Ollie wasn't the only one here with such an indelicate background. There were many others. One might say the camp was full of them. They weren't all murderesses, at least not confessed ones, but there were plenty with a long list of criminal activities and arrests to their credit. The majority of the asocial element, though, were merely ladies with a shady past — prostitutes. Anyway, someone was getting a good rest here.

As quarantines go, the one in Ravensbrück was a bit of a farce. They kept us in most but not all of the time. Perhaps they thought that diseases only spread at certain hours. Dawn and dusk must have been pretty safe because that's when they let us out for assembly, to be counted again and again just like in Auschwitz. We never were allowed to venture farther out than the front of the Block, not for the first thirty days, and the guards who came to count us either couldn't, or just wouldn't, count. What they did do with great diligence was smoke cigarette after cigarette.

Our block, capacity seven hundred, was entirely full. There wasn't a foot of empty space anywhere. None of the other six hundred twenty residents in Block 27 were new arrivals. Most of them had been here a while. In spite of that, they all had to go through the mock quarantine with us.

Our sleeping places were divided — half bunked on one side, half on the other. In between, perfect for running into each other, was a circular-shaped dirt hallway with a useless old potbelly stove. All the way in the rear was the washroom. It had many broken sinks and a lot of leaky faucets, which sometimes had cold water, never hot water and sometimes no water at all. There were also loos — always occupied, rarely functional, disgustingly smelly loos.

The occupations of the women in Block 27 were as varied as their nationalities. We had everything from common street walkers (all German) to black marketeers (German, Czech, French, and others) to thieves (multinationalities), to journalists and women whose own families or closest friends had turned them in. At the top of the list were women whose relatives were suspected — only suspected — of having been involved in adverse political activities.

Lowlife and decent people living together in unhealthy closeness with nothing in common. Nothing to say to each other, nothing to share but the long, long days and nights and the waiting.

Ravensbrück, the largest women's concentration camp (capacity 25,000) not just in Germany but in all of Europe, is only ninety-six kilometers north of Berlin. One practically can smell the sauerkraut. It is not a Jewish camp.

Still, I'm certain I am not the only Jew here. The ones I suspect of also being descendants of the Hebrew people, the Chosen Ones with two thousand years of misery as their credentials, are a few Czech girls. One of them is Lydia, the lunatic who wanted to know whether I played bridge; and another, a very attractive, clever and gutsy girl, Eva.

Meanwhile we go on pretending that we are *Mischlings*, half Jewish, half not. It is the "not" we hope we'll never have to prove. They give numbers here too, but they aren't tattoos. It's just a piece of cloth sewn to the left upper sleeve of the prison dress. At least this one I can get rid of someday. I don't think I'll ever wear stripes again. Shoes — that's what I'll wear, lots of shoes. They didn't give me any here either. I bet they have plenty. I bet they have plenty of everything. They also left me without underwear. All I have is that scratchy dress.

My number is 23,177. It makes little difference what it is. All it does is tell others how long one has been here. It's the color and shape of the patch which tell the story or the lie: *red,* political; *black,* asocial and criminals (Ollie should have gotten three); *green,* Jehovah's Witnesses.

Outside the camp, inside the camp, the doomsday sisters are as popular as the plague. Dauntless, they keep preaching their gospel, keep promising the end of the world every day. They could go home, those nasty little witches, could give us a rest from their whining singsongs, if they would sign an official paper and swear that they'll shut up. But they don't want to do that; they won't even admit that Hitler exists. Their stubbornness hurts us, not them. While everyone in the camp wants the stand-and-be-counted assembly nonsense to be over with quickly, they don't care how long it takes. They're not standing at attention, we are. They're not standing at all. Cross-legged, in their costomary yoga position, they sit in front of their blocks, still singing and praising Jesus. The guards yell at them, nudge and poke them, but they won't budge. After enough time has been wasted, the guards pick them up and carry them, in their yoga position, to where the other twenty-three thousand plus camp inmates, all lined up and waiting, stand. There, without any change of expression, they continue their ritual singsongs, and sitting cross-legged.

Not that it isn't farcical to watch them being carried, like wooden mummies, through the camp to the "plaza." They have enough annoying habits to alienate even the most tolerant. They have it made. They all work in the clothing room, and it is they who decide who gets which clothes. They have a lot of power. None of them wears prison uniforms, and they all have their hair. They wear the clothes the other prisoners have brought with them. As for the rest of the booty piled up in the stockroom, rumor has it that they're conducting a thriving business there.

⤳ Sixteen

A BIRTHDAY IN A CONCENTRATION CAMP, especially the first time around, is pretty tough to get through. Mine came two weeks into the quarantine, and all I could think of to wish for was not having to spend another one in here. On such a day one cannot help but think of birthdays past, the parties and gifts, the friends, the laughter . . . and home.

Birthdays when we were still all together. October 1, my seventh birthday, will always be the one I'll think of most. Papa had asked for us. We three girls rushed immediately to his side. Papa was in good spirits, but ever so sorry that he couldn't celebrate this special day with us. But he did promise to make up for it next Sunday, when we could have another party with him. Two birthdays in a week. How wonderful!

I was awakened by a scream — a long, agonizing scream. A woman's outcry piercing the early morning stillness with harrowing despair. Terrified, I sat up in bed, and moments later, my twin sister Elly was at my side. She was trembling. The screams continued, shrill and uncontrolled, as if someone had suddenly gone mad. I had never before been that frightened. Not even the closed double door could dampen the cries that came from my parents' bedroom. A nightmare, surely, I must be having a nightmare. But then Marie, our housekeeper, came staggering in, disheveled, a flood of tears streaming down her face. She stumbled to our bed, fell on her knees, and stammered, "Your father is dead!"

Her voice echoing through the room jolted my ears mercilessly. Elly instantly pulled the covers over her head. I clutched my Teddy bear and stared at that door. It looked the same. The screams, now muffled, were aberrant and ominous. Apprehensively, I asked my favorite toys: "What did she say?" But the rocking horse only grinned and the dolls sat in their doll house undisturbed and unseemly pretty. Even the big stuffed clown and the hairy monkey on his shoulder stood smirking in their corner, not caring at all. These were my friends, my playmates: Why didn't they do something to drive away this fearful morning?

Marie, still sobbing, gently pulled the covers from Elly's head. Her big hands, touching ours, were clammy. "Did you hear me? Your papa, he is dead!" She wiped her nose without a handkerchief. "Dead" — I did not understand the meaning of it at all, just felt a crippling, icy fear creep within me. Marie literally had to drag us from our bed to that door, and quickly shoved us inside. We crossed the threshold that led from our happy nursery into a world of antiseptic odors mixed with the sickly smell of chloroform.

The shutters of my parents' bedroom were wide open. All the lamps were lit as if the night had not yet ended. Elly and I stood barefoot in our nightgowns. The parquet floor was cold. Pressed against the wall near a window was Kate. She did not look like Kate, more like a clay statue. Elly and I clung to Marie's shawl, our shield against an unknown enemy. "Papa, Mama, where are you?" It was such a big room.

Finally, I did let go of the shawl, and with shaking knees, went to Papa's bed. I could not see him, but I knew he was there. Mama was hiding him. She was lying on his bed, facedown, her body spread all over Papa, as though she were a human blanket. His blanket. Mother's long, loose hair had tumbled down, tousled, a shimmering, golden-red pillow for Papa to rest on. It was such a dazzling sight. In this wan, hovering light, my mother's body appeared to swell and expand. It kept moving up and down in a rhythm all its own. Her face never left Papa's face. She kissed him, over and over again, calling his name, calling . . . calling. But Papa didn't answer. He was asleep, a deep, deep sleep.

I did not hear the doorbell ring, but Marie must have. She left and returned with two solemn-looking men wearing black frock coats, each of them carrying a black bag. I'd seen one of them before, just a few days ago. Void of emotion, they walked directly to my father's bed. Mama did not notice them. She had buried herself in Papa's body, crying little wailing cries,

"Berty, Berty." It tore me apart. The black-frocked men seemed to be in a hurry. One of them attempted to unclench Mama's arms, to lift her up, away from Papa, but he could not do it. Then both men grabbed her, but Mama lashed out. She pushed and kicked, desperately fighting the inevitable, groping for air while thin, hoarse screams escaped her tired throat. At last, those bloodless men caught Mama's feet and dragged her off the bed. She sat on the floor, pale and helpless, shrouded in grief, very still now. Her eyes, wandering around the room, looked at Kate, Elly, and me without seeing us.

For the first time since that wretched day began, the house was silent. Somewhere far away, a churchbell rang. A plane zoomed through the gray skies, and on the street below, people went to work, or sat in their coffeehouses having breakfast and reading the morning papers. And all over the city, little girls went to school. Nothing had changed — not for them. For a moment before those hollow men covered Papa's face with a white sheet, I could see my beautiful father. His eyes were closed, and his strong, gentle hands folded over his tummy. He was sleeping peacefully. Somehow, Mama had gotten up again. Suddenly, she stood tall. With all the anguish still left in her, fists clenched, arms threatening the mighty heavens, Mama cried out: "There is no God! No God at all! What God would take my husband, my love? Why him? *Why?*"

But the Almighty did not hear her — no sign, no hope. And so she renounced Him, "God, God! Damn you!" Then, with a gurgling sound, she collapsed. There she lay, at the foot of my father's bed, not my mother but a pitiable, broken doll that someone had thrown away. Alone. I wanted to cover her, as she had done with Papa, but Marie pulled me back, quickly took hold of Elly, and pushed us both into our room. Marie had become hysterical. She yelled, "Too much, it's all too much. Get out of here! Get out! Go to the park, and don't come back till it's dark. Hurry. Don't just stand there! Get out!"

She had never yelled at us before. She helped us dress, filled our little lunch boxes, and we left. I wondered about Kate, the clay statue. Why wasn't she sent away? But I didn't ask. I don't know how long it was that we weren't allowed near Mama, but I do know that I never saw my father again.

We didn't slide down the banister, nor did we take three steps at a time. Stiffly and mechanically, we walked as we were told, out of the house. Without a word between us, we crossed the square, the busy intersection, till we reached the park. I felt lost, and yet each step reminded me of how often my parents had come here with us, always remarking how lovely it was. Together we would listen to those dreamy outdoor concerts, with the smell of lilac and jasmine all around us. Papa called it "the garden where all romantic souls of Vienna have their rendezvous." Perhaps the dolefulness that filled my parents' bedroom had traveled with us, for it was not the same. We walked and walked, meeting no one. Only the storks in the small lake stood as always, and a few swans swam unruffled in the still pond.

Trotting along, we reached our playground. It too was curiously empty. Around us, yellow-reddish leaves fluttered to the ground. Last year at this time, and the year before, and every year, we'd all go to the Vienna Woods and watch them change into a carpet of brilliant colors covering everything, farther than the eye could see. Knee-deep, we'd wade through it, giggling and dazzled. "Who paints these leaves?" I'd ask Papa, and he would say: "Nature does. She is the greatest painter of them all." Without Papa, we are no longer a family and never would be again . . .

At last, we spotted two women on a bench. We sat down next to them, very close. It seemed less lonely. The ladies, elderly, were facing each other and much too busy talking to pay any attention to us. I listened to them, glad to hear a human voice that wasn't screaming or crying. They spoke about some close relative who had just died, and what a shock it had been to everyone. The words "dead" and "dying" rang through loud and clear.

"Yes, I know. My father just died!" I blurted out.

The woman turned to me, startled but enraged. "How dare you make fun! Have you no shame? You are disgusting!" They immediately got up and shuffled away. I cried after them, "Please, ladies, please, my papa, he is really dead. I'm sorry!"

But they had gone, and I felt more confused than ever. "Dead" — I actually had said the word out loud, but still I did not understand. Elly never uttered a word, kept staring at the slide, watching invisible children at play, looking forsaken. We did not cry. We did not touch or comfort one another. We sat together, each struggling with our first loneliness.

"Don't come back till it's dark," Marie had said. How long is a day that never ends? Slowly my mind began to concentrate on the last few weeks. I sorted out each day, retracing each moment that had preceded this gelid, leaden morning. We had returned from our summer vacation, the villa, the lake; everything was fine. The first week of September, we had entered second grade. One week before our seventh birthday, Papa had missed dinner. He retired early, and Mama asked us not to disturb him. Papa was tired, and "needed a little rest." After a few days of tiptoeing, we wanted to know whether Papa was sick. "Your father? Of course not! He's never been sick a day in his life. He's been working too hard; a little rest, that's all." We believed her. Papa had never even had a cold.

When Papa had asked for us on our birthday, his voice sounded a little weak, but otherwise I thought he looked fine. I didn't notice any change, not till he reached for Kate's hand without finding it. And as he tried to kiss us, he moved his head in a strange fashion, as though he needed to pin down the direction our voices came from. He looked at our faces, but could not see them. Papa was blind! My heart skipped a beat. My papa, blind? Not he! Not like the men I'd seen carrying a white stick. I used to watch them waiting at a curb until some stranger would come along and help them across the street. I couldn't imagine my papa could ever be like them. We cried and carried on, but Papa wanted no pity. "Hush, now! No tears, you hear? In a few days I'll be as good as new, and, of course, I'll see again. Now go to your party. Happy Birthday, sweethearts!"

We didn't want to leave him, but Mama came in and told us that Papa "needed a little rest," and we had to go. We went to the party, but it wasn't any fun. I kept on seeing Papa who couldn't see me anymore. Papa who wasn't really ill, just blind. "Just blind." Ever since he had come home to "rest a little," the door to his room had been locked. Dark thoughts raced through my head. What if he were never to see again? What then? Would all his days be just one black night? I even practiced "blindness" with the same fervor I used when rehearsing a new role. Then, one restless night, I suddenly knew. It was so simple: I would be his eyes, his white stick. I would give up my career and stay with Papa always.

Four days after our birthday, I found their bedroom door unlocked. I opened it just enough to peek through. That's when I first saw those black-frocked men, three of them. Two were talking intently with each other, while the third one had put something very long into Papa's arm — it looked like a thin, brownish snake. Mama stood on the other side, holding Papa's hand and stroking his hair: there was a big washbasin on my father's bed, and it was full of dark red blood. Papa's blood. It came from his arm, and from some other hidden place under his blanket. It was dreadul to watch Papa laying there so patiently, so brave, while those vampires took his blood away.

If only the door had been locked. Why did Mama let them do it? How could this help Papa?

I had run out of the apartment and sat gagging on the impassive stairs. "Blood . . . blind," and my father wasn't sick. Sunday, he had said, next Sunday! On October 8, Papa didn't wake up anymore. He was forty-one years young.

◡

THE FUNERAL looked like some obscure scene from a movie, except I was in it. The long procession of big, black limousines moved slowly out of the city. Far out, to the periphery where everything ends and nothing begins.

Three gates, three cemeteries. As we passed the first one, someone said, "That's for the Catholics." It must have been very large, for it was quite some time before we reached the second gate. The same voice informed us that this was only for Protestants, and on we went to the third and last gate: the Jewish cemetery. It was the smallest. That's how I first came to realize that we were Jewish. I did not ponder over it, not at that moment nor for many years to come. There was no reason to — then. I did wonder about the walls and gates that separated Catholics, Protestants, and Jews. Why weren't they all together, as people should be? Were there three heavens?

Only once did I visit my father's grave, when the headstone was put on. I remember wanting to bring pansies, but it wasn't the season. I recall the inscription on the dark gray marble tombstone: "Here rests Berthold Grohs, beloved husband and father," his birthdate, and "Rest in Peace." I refused then, and have ever since, to believe that he was really in there.

No one had bothered to explain to us the plunging mystery of death. No one had mentioned funerals and cemeteries. Perhaps they tried to spare us the traumatic experience of seeing our father in a coffin. But it was wrong. Without the last good-bye, nothing ever ends. My mother's heart was broken, and in many ways she died with him. But Papa's little girl who loved too deeply too soon kept on believing that he was alive — sleeping, but alive.

I missed him terribly, but never faltered in my conviction that one day he would be with me again. How and where, I didn't know. I was right. When I needed him most, he came to me. Not that I've ever been able to unravel the mysticism of it all, but I don't think it matters. It's one more secret he shared with me, the last and most miraculous one.

Actually, my father was killed. Not by a knife or gun, just by some irresponsible, ignorant doctors. Their consensus had been that Papa's body was producing too much blood. That's why they took it from him. By the time a famous professor discovered that one of his kidneys was not working properly, it was too late. So, at the age of seven, I had already learned to stay away from doctors; and that there were three heavens — but no God.

⌇

TO GET TO BE A SMART, experienced Ravensbrück inmate takes longer than thirty days in quarantine, though one does find out a thing or two quickly and learns some of the rules. It isn't because most of what one hears is rumors or lies but because no one really knows everything.

Among the few things I did find out was that one can take a shower every two weeks and exchange one's dirty scratchy prison dress for a clean scratchy prison dress. No guarantee, though, when it comes to underwear or shoes. Then there is the good news that one can let one's hair grow a whole three inches. The bad news is that when it has grown three inches, they shave it off again. They claim that three inches of hair are enough to make us look a little bit more human yet too short to be invaded by lice. While the little bit more human look is strictly for the benefit of visiting Nazi VIP's who do occasionally come to Ravensbrück for propaganda purposes (pictures and such), it's doubtful that the issue has ever been discussed with a single louse. They have made their happy home in anything that even looks like a hair. What I haven't been able to find out about is my patch. It's a red and yellow six-pointed star. Although I know that the star is the symbol of Judaism, I don't know what the two different colors mean. Do they mean that I'm two different people, one Jewish, one not? One good, one not? Each time I ask someone, I get the same answer — guess.

It's fall and getting colder. The air is crisp and clear. My feet are full of blisters from walking barefoot, and if I don't get shoes soon, I'll get frostbite. The sores on my breasts haven't gotten any bigger, but they haven't gone away either.

I'm beginning to think that they have the same chef here as they had in Auschwitz, or else they went to the same cooking school: the how to cook with garbage school. The house specialty is their half-raw, half-cooked potato peel soup with beans. Not a real potato in sight anywhere. Their Sunday rations, with the famous slice of sausage, margarine and bread, are something, just like at Auschwitz, that we mostly hear about but rarely see.

These rations often end up in the mouth of those who can get their hands on them first, or are sold for cigarettes and other luxuries, with soap and toilet paper at the top of the list. This is not called "stealing," the word for it is "organizing." Learning how to organize, and get real good at it, is an essential part of one's existence here.

The first day out of quarantine they shoved me into a work detail: digging up potato fields — extremely serious business. After they handed out the equipment, the detail — about two hundred, with me in the midst of it — marched through the big gate, out of the camp, up a winding road into the wide-open, completely deserted fields. With us were a forewoman and two sleepy guards, one in front, one in the rear. The forewoman, a resident inmate of Ravensbrück, insisted that we really march and at the same time sing those nauseating Nazi marching songs. Marching barefoot, asleep, with a perpetually empty stomach could not possibly boost my potato-digging career, but what could I do? Worse still was the huge, heavy shovel I had to schlepp. Instead of resting on my shoulder, it kept flipping backwards, doing a great deal more than just tapping the one behind me on the head. From her I got a kick in the rear and foul curses, and from the forewoman an outraged, *"Zum Teufel, was haben sie denn draussen gemacht!"* — What the devil did you do on the outside? You can't even carry a shovel! Soon she discovered I wasn't any good at digging either. Regrettably, it took another three weeks and several near-miss head injuries before she decided that I and my shovel weren't helping future potato crops a bit.

After this, I gave up farming altogether, doing most of my slave labor indoors. I didn't win any prizes there either. I learned other things, though — important things. I learned how Ravensbrück differed from the other camps and who was running the show here. I learned about the astonishing diversity of characters, social as well as philosophical. The saints and sinners, the rich and poor, all stuck together, all caught in the same giant, snarling net of the Third Reich . . . Heil Hitler!

Ravensbrück has no gas chambers, no wholesale murder factories and no typhus and malaria. After Auschwitz, it almost sounds like a country club. What it is is a different kind of hell. Instead of typhus or malaria, one can die slowly, or not so slowly, of hunger, being kicked to death, or both. The actual killings, however, the ones without any witnesses, take place outside the camp in the surrounding woods at night. The murder weapon: a gun.

Hardly a night goes by that we don't hear gunfire shattering the silence. Who is getting shot? We don't know. Who is doing the shooting? We don't know. We do know that what we can hear isn't firecrackers and what they're doing isn't target practice. Will anyone be able to prove that these killings really happened? Anyone? Probably not . . .

One of the major things I've found out is that the hospital here, with Dr. Rosenthal as its guiding force, is not a good place to go to if you're ill. The problem is not that one can't get any treatment, the problem is that the treatment one gets isn't the treatment one needs. Furthermore, it's no secret that the good doctor charges a lot. Medication alone, like for instance the salve I need for my sores, could end up costing me an arm and a leg. Literally. No wonder no one stands in line to get to him.

Among other things, I was told that Dr. Rosenthal likes his patients young, pretty and Polish. His German girlfriend Gerda, also a prisoner, doesn't like them young, pretty or Polish, so she sends them to the good doctor for a "cure," whether or not something ails them. One might say they make a perfect couple. The ones Gerda dislikes the most get a little card from camp headquarters ordering them to appear promptly at the hospital for an examination. All this is done quite officially.

To no one's surprise, these girls are then either never seen again, in which case they are deemed missing in action (his), or they are seen again, in which case they're just missing a kidney, a lung, or other indispensables. He's been described as overzealous, especially when operating. The man loves to cut. Rumor has it that he loves cutting even more than he loves Gerda. His secret passion, loudly whispered, is his notorious injections. He pricks them out like on an assembly line — not to eliminate pain but to study its effects. Only he knows what's in the injections and how much.

What this all means to me is the burdensome fact that I can't afford to get sick here either. And I also can't afford to make the personal aquaintance of the other swell-headed brass in here. I'm absolutely certain their names will one day appear in the black pages of history, an honor they well deserve. They spend much time and energy practicing cruelty, doing everything contemptible just to prove they indeed are worthy to take their place among the Führer's henchmen.

The one one must never get too close to is the pretty, blond, blue-eyed Oberaufseherin Binz — Overseer, supervisor. Only twenty-four, the little miss from hell shows a remarkable talent for her job. She always finds time for something extra. Extra brutalities. Extra punishments. Her unconditional power over the entire camp, which she uses unconditionally, makes her the most feared and the most hated enforcer in Ravensbrück. Binz is a sadist — there is no doubt about that. She forces the sick and the elderly into work details from which no one returns. Using her boots like a sledgehammer, she batters and crushes whoever happens to be close by. The pretty sadist has two great passions. One is her little dog, who has never seen a potato peel in his life, let alone eaten one, whom she showers with love, feeds ice cream and cookies. The other is lampshades. Human skin lampshades. Now *there* is something straight out of a horror film. Only a psychopath could think that one up. Oberaufseherin Binz not only makes them, she also paints them. Many a story keeps going the rounds about her terrifying passion, which some call a hobby. There is talk of her robbing the dead of their skin, talk of her killing them first and then flaying them, of her selecting the ones with uncommon skin texture and pigmentation, and a whole lot of other ghoulish tales. The grisly details differ, but not the reality of the actual occurrence.

Sometimes at night, with my eyes closed, I see her sitting in her room with all the lights on . . . painting lampshades.

The other ranking Nazi guard here, assigned to watch over the prisoners slaving in those heavy machinery textile factories, has her own unconscionable methods of brutality. Who knows, one day, Fritz Rühren, the Commandant, might let her be Oberaufseherin Binz's assistant. Not that she doesn't have one anyhow. Louise Brunner: This one too deserves a special dishonorable mention.

On our side, to even up the odds just a bit, there is a large group of prisoners who also will not yield, bow or bend to their captors. They do not pray like the Jehovah's Witnesses, do not predict the end of the world, and they do not have to be carried to assembly. They wage their war differently. Self-controlled and disciplined, they do what they are ordered to do, showing neither contempt nor indignation. Standing or marching all day or all night, they refuse to give up, refuse to give in. Hungry or ill, they work like mules and never complain. They are immune to everything — to the harshness of the seasons and to the tyranny of their aggressors. They are strong and silent: they are Russian parachutists, courageous peasants from the Ukraine.

They do not mix with us; they don't even bother to look at us. Still, I think they're wonderful. Proud and invincible. Far, far away from their homeland, much farther than any of us, with no one speaking their language, isolated, they most likely don't even know where they are. Their blocks are at the far end of the camp, and they are constantly watched by special guards with special training. Everyone knows that these women are genuine soldiers, soldiers who know how to fight. There must be a reason that they aren't in a prisoner-of-war camp like their male counterparts, and the only reason I can think of is that there aren't any for women. I guess the Germans never thought of Russian women dropping from the sky.

Whenever they're being marched around just for the fun of it, or to show them who is boss, they do so with their heads held high, singing their Russian war songs and smiling.

↩

SOMETHING EXTRAORDINARY HAS HAPPENED. A miracle — a card from home! It's censored, of course, and most of it is inked out, but at least I know that they are alive and know where I am. I don't have a clue how they know, I just know that they do, and that makes my bruised and blistered feet want to dance. Mama writes that a few weeks ago my sister Kate gave birth to a son, Mario. Fanny was right, and now Mama is a grandmother.

I do wish though that my grandmother was still around so that Mario could get to know her too. Oma: Mama's mother; we were all crazy about her and would turn her weekly visit into a big event. Oma was deaf. Grandpa had passed away a long time ago, and still Oma would always wear black. She was strikingly beautiful, with her snow white hair and fiery black eyes. She always carried a big, black *beutel*, like a pouch, and in it were the presents she brought us. Each week, we played the same game. We sat patiently, watching Oma open her bag and take out her little belongings, one by one, ever so slowly, till it was almost empty. We knew what she had brought us, and Oma knew that we knew, but she had such fun teasing us. Not until her deep, melodious voice announced: *"Zucker bleibt am Grund"* (For the good things, you got to wait) did we get our reward — rock candy! We would bite into the hard sweet crystal, loving the crunching noise as much as the candy.

Sometimes we would visit Oma in her small, cozy flat. The grand old lady spent days cooking and baking especially for us. The food she served was strange and had funny names: gefilte fish, matzoh dumplings, stuff that quivered in aspic. I thought it tasted awful, but Mama said it was superb and

I had to eat it. Afterwards, I always threw up. But I did love my grandma. I used to wonder what it was like to be deaf, as she was, and whether she was lonely. Without the sound of music and laughter, how cheerless her life must have been. And yet I knew her heart could always hear us.

Oma died at seventy-six when I was fifteen. I never thought that she would leave us. How strange, I didn't even know she was ill. Perhaps she wasn't ill, just old. Seventy-six is very old to someone who is just fifteen.

❧ Seventeen

It is Christmas 1943: and I have never seen a taller or more beautifully decorated tree. It is right in the middle of the camp, in the square, the plaza, all by itself. Snow has been falling, and that makes everything look very peaceful and serene. From our protectors' quarters the radio is playing "Silent Night, Holy Night," only it isn't night and there is nothing holy about any of it. What it is is a deception meant to impress Heinrich Himmler, chief of the Gestapo, whose announced visit was the reason for this idyllic picture postcard scene. But Himmler did not show. The brass is furious and that's why we in Block 27 and the Russians have been standing barefoot, without warm clothing or food, all day long.

It is these cold-hearted hours that make me remember the lessons of Auschwitz. Make me remember to let my mind fly me away so I won't feel the pain. My mind has taken me many places, places I've never been to before. And more than once it's taken me home, to the home of my childhood — with Papa, Mama, my sisters, Oma, Marie, in a room full of presents. We had goose and roasted chestnuts, drank hot chocolate by the crackling fire till I fell asleep in Papa's lap all cozy and warm . . . all happy and safe.

Christmas — and then New Year's. We had a tradition at home: my parents always spent New Year's Eve with us, and we were allowed to stay up till midnight. That's when the whole family gathered eagerly around our big tile stove, to prepare for the most important event of the year — the pouring of lead. We each got a soup spoon, a bowl of cold water, and a piece of lead. Precisely at the stroke of twelve, Papa opened the oven door, and we quickly scooped the lead on the spoons and held them over the hot, glowing coals. A few seconds later, we dumped our spoons of molten lead into the ice-cold water. The sizzling lead miraculously changed into mystifying shapes and forms, each enormously significant, for it revealed our future, predicted what lay ahead.

"Mine first! I want you to look at mine first!"

"What does it say, Papa?"

"Mama, which is the best?"

My parents examined them, one by one, playing their role as fortune-tellers to the hilt, and always telling us exactly what we wanted to hear: Kate is going to marry a beautiful prince; Elly will become a great scholar; and Silvie, naturally, is going to be the most famous actress in the world. We never doubted the authenticity of their prophecies. How could we? Papa and Mama knew everything.

Afterwards, with the flames of the crackling fire dancing like glowworms, playful and mysterious, we all ate the traditional *fashing krapfen,* something like doughnuts, filled with a delicious marmalade with lots of powdered sugar on top. Sweet and powdery like snow, but the snow I'm standing on this Christmas is not sweet . . .

They had gotten us up, out and lined up before 5:00 a.m. They dismissed us, "Back to the Block," just after 7:00 p.m. Not all of us were still standing. Hunger, cold, and the long, merciless hours had taken their toll. There would be more room in the Block now, and more skin for Oberaufseherin Binz's lampshades. Icy-cold skin for the icewater-veined pretty lady.

It isn't always easy to get one's mind back into one's head. The mind, as a safeguard, needs to make sure that it is safe to return. It also must have a rest from the dangerous minute-by-minute mind games being played out here . . .

I have only a vague recollection of how I got back to the Block and up to my bunk. My feet, imbedded in snow, did not want to move at all. The rest of me, numb, stiff and strangely lightheaded, just wanted to go back to sleep. I think the two Czech girls, Lydia and Eva, were the ones dragging me away, but I'm not really sure.

In the early spring of 1944, Heinrich Himmler did come to Ravensbrück, twice. I remember his visit because of the crazy cleaning up we all had to do, because of the one million flowers planted in the square for him and because of the only boiled potato I ever got to eat there.

Things changed for the better for me after that Christmas in 1943. I got three invaluable presents: a small piece of real soap, a few pieces of real toilet paper, and one whole raw potato. A great treasure! A potato works quite well in case of diarrhea but also has great buying power when exchanged for something else. The generous gifts came from homicidal Ollie, bridge-playing crazy Lydia and gutsy Eva. Of the three, only Eva had also been in Auschwitz, and like me, she too was one of the lucky eighty who got out of there. Eva spent more time in Auschwitz than I did, worked as a nurse and says she remembers seeing me in the hospital when I visited Rainer. She swears that she's seen more dead women in that place in a week than there are in all the cemeteries in the world collectively.

Eva is brainy, has the energy of a dynamo, the quickness of a runaway train and the wit, humor and humanity of a Scarlet Pimpernel. A survivor herself, she is always ready to help others survive, if she can. In her early twenties, tall, broad-shouldered, with a headful of two-inch-long blondish brown curls to match her brandy-colored eyes, she is mentally and physically strong and can roll with the punches. I trust her and would go with her all the way. As the saying goes: *Mit ihr kann man Pferde stehlen* — One can steal horses with her.

Eva's wealthy parents were killed in an accident and left everything to her and her brother. Everything was quite a lot: a fine house, a country estate, factories and a fat bank account. Always in a hurry, she married at seventeen, with a baby to follow. Eva was young, rich and beautiful; the man she married, beautiful — a coward and a turncoat. He turned Eva in. With the Nazis on their doorstep, Eva's brother fled to Australia, and baby Ruth wrapped in a blanket was taken to safety by the couple managing her country estate. Eva was also taken, though not to safety. As far as she knows, her dapper, dashing husband is now marching with the Nazis to victory and glory. Eva doesn't know if anything is left, after he stole all he could from her.

Lydia has made friends with Eva, which is actually strange since Eva doesn't play bridge either. But she speaks her language, Czech. Lydia had had a ritzy fashion boutique, ladies only, and the only thing left of that are the ladies . . . the ones here. I have finally figured out what this bridge crazy-ness is all about. It's Lydia's way of judging the other prisoners' social status and intellect. A bit eccentric, I'd say. Well, it could be worse. What she and Eva talk about in their native tongue, I don't know. When they talk German, though, they mostly talk about food. Food! That's what everyone else talks about. They talk about it, think about it, dream about it and even graphically depict the look, smell and taste of it. They say it's better than talking about hunger. Frankly, I think it is perverse and masochistic. Anyway, no fantasy has ever made my hunger go away. It's a real battle. Mine is with those fabulous Belgian waffles drowning in hot chocolate sauce with mountains of whipped cream. I still remember where I had them last. In Holland, in Scheveningen. Me, and every fat woman on the beach. I wasn't even hungry then, and I didn't know that hunger could hurt, nor that one could live with so much hunger. It feels like someone punching holes in one's stomach, someone with heavy hands wearing boxing gloves. The worst thing about it is that one can't just say, "It'll get better." It doesn't — only worse.

Once a month we can get a package from home; we can write and also get mail. It's the one day I don't mind waking up in the morning, the one day I can say, "Look what I got from home!" Red longjohns, that's what I got just before New Year's, as well as a pair of flannel pajamas, slippers — still no shoes — a pair of mittens, and soap. A whole bar of soap that smells of chocolate and a bar of chocolate that tastes like soap. It's all messed up. The wrappers are broken and so is the jar with marmalade, most of it stuck to my longjohns.

I'm singing again! I'm not sure who coaxed me into doing it, I think it was Lydia. She is so damn curious about me. It's all right, though, I'm not singing for the guards or the Nazi brass, like in Malin. Here it's for my blockmates only. I gave my first concert New Year's Eve, right in the circle-shaped dirt hallway. The response was overwhelming: They cried, they laughed, applauded, wanting to hear more and more. Afterwards, Eva went around and collected my fee. They gave of their meager possessions whatever they could. Even Ollie was overjoyed. She offered me anything of hers that I wanted and what I wanted was for her to change places with Eva. She pouted a little, but did so anyway.

Lydia and Eva are convinced that I'm not a day over sixteen. They insist that I need protection from the lesbian element here, which targets the young. The lesbians' extensive presence is just as aggravating as that of the Jehovah's Witnesses, only much more personal. Most of them have also been sent here for rehabilitation, which isn't quite the way it seems to be working out. Too often a comforting arm around a frightened, lonely girl is all it takes.

I'M ABOUT TO START ANOTHER JOB. All I know of this one is that it is something very secret. Some new invention whispered to have been masterminded especially for the Führer and his cronies. Something for their fast getaway maybe?

From one breath to the next, twenty-one buildings, or rather halls, have gone up. They must have put them up in triple time when nobody was looking. But we couldn't have seen them even if we had been looking. They're not inside the camp; they're on the other side of it. Farther than the empty fields, farther than the silent woods with their deadly secrets and farther still than the little cottages where the elite guards live. They could be warehouses or hangars or rows of wooden blocks, but in fact they're Siemens factories — completely equipped, makeshift factories. They are not part of the camp, do not belong to the camp, and their only connection to it is us. Two thousand prisoners, including Eva and me, make up the workforce. I don't have a clue what is being manufactured there, and from what Eva tells me, I won't know when it's right in front of me either.

Eva started before me, saying that whatever it was would be better than shoveling coals in the freezing cold — who could argue with that? So, in spite of my aversion to factory work in general and assembly-line drudgery in particular, I got in line with the rest to find out whether it indeed was better than shoveling coals.

The first good news was that I finally got shoes. They were heavy mountain climbing shoes, which hurt my feet — already blistering, cut and swollen — so I gave them to Ollie, who in return gave me an IOU for toilet paper. They didn't give us shoes so we would have shoes, but to spare the German civilians at Siemens the embarrassment of having to look at our dirty feet. To accommodate them, I wore slippers.

The one who instantly gained prominence as the most swinish brute was the Kommandoführerin Holthöfer, commando leader, especially assigned to Siemens. While she didn't have the authority to interfere with the work in the factories, she found other ways to show us, in her customary physical fashion — large-scale beatings — who was master. This overweight

forty-year-old brunette, just like pretty Fraülein Binz, has tyranny and dic-
tatorial fiendishness down pat. Holthöfer is a true National Socialist (Nazi,
anti-Semite) but she does not discriminate against foreigners. She hates us
all equally.

Hers is a big job. She is responsible for the female guards under her, and
for us: responsible that we leave the camp on time at 6:00 a.m., take our two
breaks, ten minutes each for a run to the six latrines, responsible that there
is no hanky-panky going on between us and the male civilians, and responsible that we leave the factory together, all present and accounted for at 6:00
p.m., and get back to the camp on time.

When it comes to Holthöfer, there is no disagreement between us and the
guards on duty inside the factory. They don't like her either and wouldn't
tell her a thing about anything. That's why she has lots of spies working for
her — at least one in every Siemens hall. Most of them are prisoners earning
their keep with their ridiculous spying. We've known from the start that
they were among us, but not who they are. At first we did not know that
Holthöfer, with her group of little spies, was really working for Criminal
Commissioner Randolph, the present chief of the Gestapo, formerly Berlin's
very own chief of police in charge of vice. The prostitutes here, who ought
to know, say that Randolph's career switch was due to Hitler's shutting
down the brothels and putting all the pimps and whores in jail or into
camps like Ravensbrück for moral rehabilitation.

While working for Siemens I learned how to sleep while standing up,
how to sleep while sitting down and how to sleep even when marching. It is
the only activity here that makes sense. Besides, there really is no other way
to make it through those endless hours. Not with a day that starts at night
and ends at night, day after day after day, from 4:00 a.m. till 10:00 p.m. I
hardly remember daylight anymore.

They shout us awake at four. We then have thirty minutes to get dressed,
push through the mass of other prisoners who are also pushing through the
mass of other prisoners, trying to get first to the loos, then to the broken
sinks, just in case there is water so we can wash. Then, perhaps, to get some
cold, thin coffee with the daily crust of moldy bread they call breakfast.

Eva keeps bouncing around the factory hall we're working in like she be-
longs there and knows what she is doing. Could be she does. Already she's
been promoted to be assistant to Herr Stöber, the civilian boss who is one
step away from cracking up. Except for having gotten me a sitting-down job

with a very nice civilian man who is taking great pains to teach me what it is I should do and how to do it, I can't see what her promotion is good for. It doesn't get her more or better food, shorter hours or even an extra few minutes to get to the latrines. Eva disagrees. She thinks it is essential to let the civilians here know that just because we all look dreadful does not mean we're nothing more than low-grade, worthless idiots. Otherwise, she says, we'll never get them to loosen up and talk to us about matters such as how goes the war.

She is right again, of course, but it isn't all that easy. Our presence makes the civilians feel downright uncomfortable. I think they feel guilty. Maybe they don't feel anything. I'm sure the boss, Herr Stöber, does not. He is a hysterical screamer who blows up every hour on the hour, shouting that he can't meet the deadline with a bunch of undernourished, overtired, unskilled morons. This skinny, unattractive man is the kind of person who was never young but always a German. Not someone I'll ever miss should he be sent to the front. Luckily, I have nothing to do with him. I'm not in his department. My boss is that nice, tall, good-looking man, Herr Bahls. Herr Bahls is an electrical engineer and an inventor, as is Stöber. Both had a lot to do with what is being made here now. What they do in Eva's department is too complicated to even think about; what I and about fifty other girls are doing is soldering. I didn't know what soldering was before I got to Siemens. I do know now, but that's about all I know of what's going on here.

What we are working with isn't ordinary tin or lead but silver and platinum. I think that's why they're making such a big deal of it. That stuff must be worth a pretty penny. Each piece is smaller than my little finger and is called *Heissleiter* ("electro-head conductor" is as close a translation as I can come up with). It's to go into a specific part of a plane. Near the factory entrance is a huge oven, big enough to hide a dozen people, with a special kind of timer and all sorts of other gadgets, waiting for those odd-shaped, platinum little things. That's where the *Heissleiters* go after we're finished with them, and that's where they bake all through the night.

If not for Herr Bahls, who thought it necessary for someone besides himself to know and handle the exact procedure in case he fell ill, and who wanted it to be me, I wouldn't have known even that much. As long as it gave me a chance to thaw out in the huge oven after the predawn morning drill, I didn't care. To me, it was the warmest and best place. It also was the place where, once Herr Bahls dared talk to me about more than *Heissleiters*, he would hide the little packages of food he'd brought. Not very much and never anything fancy, but food just the same, and once in a while a flower. Because no unauthorized personnel, including guards, were permitted to go inside this heating device and because I was kind of authorized, I felt safe there. The only place where sometimes for a rare few minutes I could still be alone with myself. This too had become a luxury one could only wish for and dream about.

Herr Bahls, like all the civilians here, was sent from Berlin as an old and loyal Siemens employee to get things done. A man of conscience, he was appalled by what he saw, shocked at the subhuman, foul conditions we had to endure, and embarrassed at having to be a party to it. He had difficulty pretending that what we were doing six days a week, twelve hours a day, for the Third Reich and for Siemens wasn't slave labor. He had not known that he would be working outside a concentration camp with prisoners from a concentration camp, and only women at that. He wasn't a hero, yet he did take chances talking to me as much as he did and bringing me what he could. He was a good German whose only crime was that he didn't ask questions soon enough.

This man did not hate Jews, did not hate foreigners. What he hated was war and the price of victory, no matter whose. "The human cost," he said, "is much too high." Dear Herr Bahls, what does he know about the human cost? He has lived with the Hitler lunacy, like all the Germans, for ten blood-soaked years. And only now that he has seen hungry women in prison clothes, watched their degradation and even met a Jew, only now is he beginning to wonder why he never wondered about any of it before. This German is one of the better ones, perhaps even one of the best, but by no means the exception. He too, like all the other scientists, has been hiding behind his scientific cloak, inventing clever things for what he hates the most: the war. How does he reconcile himself to such a contradiction?

The girls working in his department are mostly French and German. He hardly ever talks to any of them. The French are doing a great job sabotaging this important invention by working at a snail's pace. Of course Herr Bahls knows about it but keeps looking the other way. Besides, he doesn't speak French. The German prisoners can't do their work fast enough, well enough or enough of it. They volunteered and are doing it all for the fatherland — their fatherland, which sent them here.

There is one more civilian here from Berlin and Siemens: Frau Linke. She is the office manager in our hall, in charge of all the secretaries, of whom there isn't a single one. So she has to do it all. Frau Linke, whose husband is somewhere on the Russian front, does, remembering Stalingrad, worry a lot. She'd rather have him fight the Americans, the English or the French; she'd rather have him fight anyone but the Russians. It's interesting how terrified the Germans are of them. The mere mention of it makes them shudder, because they know what their soldiers did to the Russians. The stories of their brutalities, their looting, burning, the raping of women and the wholesale murder of innocent people have come back to them with every returning soldier. They are no longer proud of it. Now they are convinced that the Russians will do the same to them, and they are petrified, especially Frau Linke.

Kommandoführerin Holthöfer, whose husband is also on the Russian front, spends her days thundering through the halls with the fury of a tornado. She is constantly in a rage, constantly on the verge of breaking everything in sight, including someone's head. I think she has too much energy. Holthöfer is also in charge of the shoveling of coal, which is stacked up outside the Siemens halls and guarded as if it were gold. It's not to warm us, but for the stuff that's being made here. For us they wouldn't burn a single coal.

Anyone working the coal detail is doing so as punishment. The sins they have committed might be anything from talking to staying too long in the latrine and other such major crimes. Whatever it is, the punishment is much too backbreaking for women. Their hands, half frozen, can hardly lift the shovel. But that's only part of it. After they have dumped the coal into the carts, they also have to haul it away, like horses. All that's missing is the harness and the reins.

I can't get any accurate information about how the war is really going because the only ones who know the truth are the German generals, and I don't know a single one. Neither does Herr Bahls. He'd love to get his family out of Berlin before Allied bombs turn the city into a pile of rubble. Herr Bahls thinks this is where the final battle will be fought.

Each day lasts forever; each hour another sixty miserable minutes to cope with and bear, and I just can't understand why Roosevelt and Churchill don't put an end to it. Doesn't anyone care? Eva says she'd give a lot not to hear me ask every day at four in the morning, "How much longer?" She says it's too gloomy and depressing. So is waking up in a block that's so cold even the lice are complaining. Broken windows (I'm right next to one), a dilapidated potbelly stove, constant hunger, and the dismal never-ending darkness.

↝

THE WINTER OF 1943–44 was the longest of my life. While the rumors about Germany losing on all fronts and the war being as good as over could be heard throughout the camp, what we didn't hear enough of were Allied planes over German skies. Some, yes, but hardly enough for the last hurrah. Whenever air-raid sirens did go off at Siemens, the civilians hurried to the shelters built for them. We had to stay, weren't even allowed to dodge under a table. Not that we paid much attention to that rule. Who was to know? The spy they had stuck in with us? If nothing else, we were stuck together. For better or worse . . . till a bomb do us part. There was a kind of perverse satisfaction in knowing that.

I often wondered if the pilots who flew over the wooden Siemens factories knew who and what was down there. If one day they had to make a choice between bombing it all to bits with us, the two thousand prisoners, in it, or passing it up because of us, which would they choose?

Besides Holthöfer — who would have liked to have twenty-one pairs of feet so she could be in every one of the twenty-one halls at the same time all the time — there were twenty-one more guards, all female. One for each hall. Without a doubt they had the most boring job. They had absolutely nothing to do. They could not talk to anyone except about their duties. Thus, all that was left for them was to walk around and around the hall and peer over our shoulders so we wouldn't goof off. These guards changed quite often. Boredom, I think.

Frau Linke's request for an assistant was finally granted. She was told she could pick one of us. Naturally, she wanted someone with experience, which also, naturally, got her me. What a quirk of fate that Frau Linke was a real movie buff, a great fan of the theater and crazy about actors. All she ever talked about, when she didn't talk about how scared she was of the Russians, was the movies, the theater and actors. I think it kept her from going batty. So the moment Eva, with considerable exaggeration, let it slip what a famous actress I was, her pick was clear. Herr Bahls got someone else to solder, and I moved into Frau Linke's glass-enclosed office, where I did little else but tell her about the silver screen and the stage. She was thrilled. In order to keep the appearance up, I did some filing. Herr Bahls was kind enough to let me keep the time-setting job at the oven, so I could continue to slip inside for warmth and stolen moments of meditation. Under the circumstances, it probably was the best I could have hoped for. Yet I never spent a single minute unaware of the subhuman conditions and the precarious ways that governed our lives.

My unplanned one-on-one encounter with Holthöfer occurred shortly after I had become Frau Linke's storyteller. The confrontation had nothing to do with telling tales instead of secretarying, but ridiculously with Eva's and my hairdos, all three inches of them. Holthöfer didn't go berserk because we dared to look almost human, human-looking women, at that, in a place where there were also men, but because our hair was curly. Even a moron like her should have been able to figure out the reason for that. Our hair was naturally curly. Did Holthöfer think we had gone to a salon, perhaps in the town of Fürstenberg, next to Ravensbrück?

One day around noon after she had finished her miserable rounds, she burst into the office, took one look at me and exploded, "What do you think this is? A factory or a place to show off your *Locken Kopf,* curly head. Don't think because you are sitting in an office [I was standing] you can show up here the way you want. Your hair has to be straight, completely straight! Everyone's hair has to be straight! You're a goddamn prisoner, and you're here to work, not to show off!"

Just then her eyes caught Eva's, ready to duck out of sight, and without stopping to take a breath, she continued her blowup. She finished her sermon, which was loud enough to be heard in England, by promising us the most severe punishment if by tomorrow we hadn't "done away with those repulsive curls." With this she stormed out.

Silence . . . complete silence . . . The machines stopped . . . Everything stopped. There wasn't a sound to be heard in the entire hall. Because I was standing in the middle of the glass-enclosed office, everyone was looking at me. Like being on display in a store window. It was embarrassing, humiliating, infuriating and worst of all, impossible to do a thing about it.

Later that day, I found a lovely poetic note beside the oven timer. It was from Herr Bahls. In it he wrote that after many months of gray and somber days, the sun had finally come out and that he'd watched it illuminate my hair as I stood near the window. "It made your hair look golden," he wrote, "only more beautiful." He then went on to say that even though he knew

Holthöfer's unresponsive heart was colder than the winter chill and her eyes blind to beauty because of her black soul, he would talk to her and set things right, and please not to be frightened or worried. I was very moved. It almost made me forget that he was a German. I would have liked to keep the note but didn't dare. So I just memorized it to recite it to Eva.

Frau Linke never said a word, but she seemed a little shaken and more than a bit flustered. At that moment I think she was ashamed of being one of them. Before we shut down for the day, she took a hairbrush from her handbag, put it in my lap, whispered, "Try that," and left.

Eva's reaction to my recitation was, "The Schmock is infatuated with you. Golden, my foot. You look like a blown-up pink chicken!" She had called me a pink chicken before; blown-up was a first. I knew it was her way of getting back at me for my daily "How much longer?" Besides, she was probably right. Carrot red brows and lashes in a face full of freckles with flaming red, very short locks could remind one of a chicken — especially when hungry. "Blown-up" was pretty much on target, too. Blown-up not as in full of hot air, but rather full of water, or water retention, as they would call it in the outside world. In the kitchen, following orders from camp headquarters, they kept putting something fed to horses into our slop, which made us look meatier, bigger, better and so much healthier. That, just like the Christmas tree and the flower planting, was strictly for propaganda purposes to show the neutral countries how well we looked. I don't know about horses, but the success rate with us was at best a partial one. Those who, a war ago, had been thin like me, blew up like me; those who, like Eva, had been more zaftig, became thin. Skin and bones or heavy, inside Hitler's boxing ring we were all featherweights . . .

Eva and I didn't sleep a wink all night. We brushed and brushed our pathetic three inches of hair, trying to uncurl it. All we ended up with was sore arms. We kept wetting our hair till the water dripped down on us, well aware that the only lasting result would be icicles on our head or pneumonia.

It did not go the way we had planned it. We'd leaned more toward organizing (stealing) a couple of headscarves to hide our hair. No go! Those in possession of such luxurious accessories simply never took them off. Moreover, we couldn't have found them at night anyhow. Thus, after exhausting all other possibilities and ourselves, and remembering the enormous sums of money women all over the world spent to get their hair curled, we decided to hell with it.

It was not a day I looked forward to. Not that any of them was. Nothing short of Holthöfer's dropping dead could have saved that morning. But she had no such intention. She didn't even wait till after her rounds. She flew in like a wind-whipped powerhouse and didn't stop until she stood in front of me, her purplish-red face only a nose-length away from mine, looked like an overripe pomegranate. For a couple of seconds she stared at my hair. Then her hand landed a blow to the right side of my face, making my head spin. The pain momentarily blinded me, and I lost my balance. The sound of the stroke was still ringing in my ears when, an instant later, my fist struck her face.

It was an instinctive reaction, which had nothing to do with whatever went on in my conscious mind — as though my arm had taken over, guiding my fist, completely independent of me. I realized what I had done but couldn't believe I had done it. By the time I'd gotten my composure back, she was still struggling with hers. Stunned, and totally bewildered, she glared at me. Her face had changed from purplish-red to sickly white. Her mouth was half open and she was sucking in air. It made her look as if she had swallowed a fish hook. She never took her eyes off me, not even when she reached for her gun. She clutched the holster, waited, stiffened, then threw back her shoulders, turned and strode out.

I kept seeing her clutching the holster for a long time afterwards. She never took the weapon out, but she sure came close. I guessed she was going to do the next best thing: report me to the Commandant and let his shooters do the shooting . . . in the silent woods . . . at night.

My fellow prisoners stifled their disbelief. Many racing heartbeats later, when I sat down, I saw that Frau Linke was sobbing. Tears streamed down her painted cheeks, while Herr Stöber, mad as hatter, had another one of his fits. This time it was the disciplinary rules imposed on us, the camp inmates, which he objected to. He wanted them to be kept out of his factory. As for my poetic boss Herr Bahls, who always kept his distance from Holthöfer, he looked as if he'd been attending his best friend's funeral. The ones who had missed this morning duel totally were Eva and the guard assigned to the hall. They were in the supply room — Eva to get supplies, the guard to see that that was all she got.

Holthöfer did not return that day. Each time the door opened, my heart sank. I did not see her again until the next morning. She was standing next to a group of women waiting their turn at the latrines. There were at least twenty feet and a hundred prisoners between us. Nevertheless, she saw me as clearly as I saw her. Her expression was strangely blank, almost as though she was running on empty. Still, she kept her eyes fixed on me and me only until, pretending to be unconcerned, I turned around.

Holthöfer did not report me. Not that day, nor any day. And she never bothered me again.

I did not think it would have a happy ending. Neither did Eva. Nobody did! But wasn't standing up to them the greatest lesson Auschwitz had taught me? Deliberate or not, planned or not, it was the one thing that worked.

⌒

HE HAD BEEN IN THE HALL when my clash with the malicious Holthöfer occurred. He had been here before, and I had seen him before but had never paid any attention to him. There was no reason why I should. As far as I knew, he was only another engineer from one of the other Siemens halls. A visitor. Nothing unusual about that. They dropped in all the time, talked to each other, but never to us. This one though, according to Eva, appeared to be considerably more interested in us than in his colleagues. He had approached her before the curls incident, had asked her questions: How long she'd been in Ravensbrück and at Siemens, and what kind of prisoners were in this concentration camp.

Since Eva's position as Stöber's assistant allowed her to move around without creating suspicion and since most guards took frequent siestas, he, the curious one, could get acquainted with Eva without too much trouble. Yet it took my getting hit and returning the favor before he trusted us enough to tell us who he was. Six feet three inches, raven black, curly-haired Teddy — that, so he said, was his name — was by his own proud admission a Communist. For Siemens he worked as an inspector, inspecting the production in the twenty-one halls; for the Communists as an inquirer, getting and giving information. His weight, over two hundred pounds, he carried quite well. All in all, he looked like a man who was more at home on a mountain than in a factory or lab. He did seem a bit clumsy. His feet kept getting in his way. His eyes, as black as his hair, were alert and forever scouting about. Not devious, but on guard. He was young, mid-twenties, and whether or not Teddy was his real name, it suited him — a big, wee bit klutzy Teddy bear.

He knew there was a spy among us. He knew there was one in every hall. Unfortunately, he didn't know who was the one we were cursed with. His assignment now — not the inspecting but the one his conscience had led him to — was to find out the names of relatives of high-ranking political VIPs or important persons here. For this, he needed a couple of nervy, spunky, dauntless girls who knew their way around, a couple of idiots — us! He told us that he belonged to the German underground and not to underestimate its importance. Why it was so important he didn't say, only that it was. He also didn't tell us how to go about finding these VIP relatives, only that we must. We did believe it to be of major seriousnes — why else would he ask? He also said that Germany was losing the war and that just about everyone knew it, especially the military. Most of the generals didn't want to go on; only crazy Hitler did. Teddy kept us up to date about the real state of affairs of the war, bits of news he didn't get from German radio or propaganda papers. I think he understood that this was what kept us going.

It was the first week of April 1944 when Teddy recruited us. Before the month was over, we had a network of a dozen girls in our employ. They all got paid the same: free entrance to my Sunday night concerts, discharging their contributions to me. Most of the girls were Czech, with a fierce hatred for the Germans that I really admired. Eva and Lydia enlisted them. The girls, all fairly fluent in German but refusing to speak it, did a lot of listening and snooping around. It led them all the way to the front offices where the prison clerks and secretaries, the real clerks and secretaries, worked.

Whenever they encountered a problem in the form of an overly conscientious inmate, they would invite her to my concert, which in no time at all brought me such a crowd that I had to give matinées as well. News of my singing traveled fast, and before I knew it, fights broke out, just to get in. More than once I saw other uniforms next to our striped ones in the audience, and more than once it was they who stood watch. Still, afraid I might end up having to perform for the big Nazi brass, like in Malin, and well aware that Teddy did not want us to make any waves, I curtailed my performances, using lack of time and tiredness as honest reasons.

By probing around for Teddy, we ourselves learned that there indeed were some big fish swimming in this Nazi pond. Most of them were French and Belgians. Their names, except for one, meant little to me. That name was de Gaulle. No, General de Gaulle wasn't in Ravensbrüick, but his niece was, and so we were told was his sister, plus perhaps half a dozen other close family members. The ones who knew about it talked of them as "the de Gaulle Clique." There would come a time when I myself stood face to face with them, although no formal introduction ever took place. By then I also knew that they were really who we had been told they were.

Eva and I didn't think it was too much of a dangerous game we were playing. More frustrating than dangerous, we thought. Frustrating because of being kept in the dark about it.

Toward the end of April, on a rainy Sunday afternoon, my matinée was moved outside, with everyone attending and the occupants of several other blocks, too. It was showtime again, though not like any I'd d ever taken part in or attended before.

There we were, nicely lined up like chorus girls, told to put our best face forward and smile, and there they were, three spitting-clean German officers, looking for volunteers — many volunteers for their whorehouses. The thought alone was something that took some getting used to. While standing there, I thought, "They've come to the right place. We have squadrons of whores here! High time those lazy girls came out of retirement and went back to work. Pick up where they left off. For the sake of their fatherland and those poor sex-starved German officers." It was to be a six-month engagement, and such a good deal. Six months of getting fed, clothed and unclothed, six months of getting soap and toilet paper and letting one's hair grow. Six months of sleeping in a bed, bathing in a tub. And no standing around for hours for assembly. That's what the mouthpiece kept telling us.

It sounded so good that I was almost sorry I wasn't one of them. Not that they specifically asked for prostitutes. Anyone could participate! All they wanted was enough volunteers. The mouthpiece also said that those who'd put everything into it might be released afterwards. The others would be returned to Ravensbrück, no worse for wear. Before he invited those ready to go to raise their hands, he stressed that they did not want the same crop of whores they had had before. No used-up rejects in their brothels.

I was certain there would be more than enough volunteers. I was wrong. Too many hands stayed down. The three officers kept pushing the benefits of this fun job like their promotion depended on it. Walking from row to row, they looked us over as though we were pieces of meat, headless carcasses ready to be feasted on. It went on and on, on and on, until their patience ran out and they threatened to pick out the merchandise themselves.

And suddenly it wasn't a far-fetched silly bit one could laugh and gossip about. Suddenly I understood that everyone here was fair game and that any one of us could be chosen. I came within an inch of finding out firsthand what it was like to be the whore for a whole regiment of German officers. So did Eva and Lydia. The mouthpiece had pulled us out, remarking that we would make a nice trio. My knees shaking, I quickly opened the top buttons of my dress and showed him the ugly sores above my breasts. That's all I had to do. He pushed me back and with rapid strides marched down the line to the next row. It all ended there with newly found volunteers from yet another block.

Why did they have such difficulties filling these enticing posts? Because of the stories those who'd been there had brought back with them. Stories of incredible perversities, unimaginable cruelty and shameless orgies that went on day after day, night after night. Only after those dapper officers would sink into a drunken stupor could the girls get some rest. But it wasn't their tales alone. It was the way they looked after that six months, sick and frightful, as though each moment of their sordid life there had etched itself into their faces, their blurred eyes and badly bruised flesh. Quite a few had killed themselves or just died there. Non-professionals mostly. So much for morality in the Third Reich.

⇝ EIGHTEEN

IT WAS TUESDAY. Not just any Tuesday but the one history would record as the day Allied forces invaded France: D-Day, June 6, 1944.

It was Teddy who told us. We weren't certain what it meant, but since everyone in our hall was running around like they didn't know which way was which, and since the guards in the camp were very jumpy, it had to be good news. How much longer till the Allied forces would get inside the gates of Ravensbrück and set us free? There really ought to be many more letters in the word "free" to better express its profoundness. Only those who aren't free can understand this.

June 6 was also the day when those in command put men and machines on a twenty-four-hour schedule. Someone in the Third Reich must have decided that they needed more of the stuff we were manufacturing, and faster. And Siemens was only too happy to comply. Teddy said in the world of inventors and industrial engineering, Siemens, a German family business, was a giant of international reputation, like Krupp (German manufacturers of steel and ordnance). And like Krupp, Siemens had joined the ranks of unscrupulous war profiteers. Do they ever think of us or the wages we aren't getting while they are putting billions into their pockets? I would like to meet one of those Siemens boys after the war any place he cannot hide behind his corporate seal and ask him: What about compensation? What about paying an unchallengeable debt?

I found myself doing the night shift before I even had a chance to think about it. The switch from day to night must have happened rather fast, which, looking back on it, was just as well. What was absolutely terrific was that I could miss the "wake up, you lazy bastards" morning calls and assembly. Another definite plus was not having to worry about Holthöfer dropping in on me. And in the almost empty block, just for once, there was no bumping, no pushing — no one was trying to manhandle me. I had space, precious space all to myself. Space to stretch out . . . and sleep.

The night shift at Siemens was as different as night from day. Not because it was night but because there was less authoritarianism, less tension. Also, not all of the halls were working at full capacity; mine, for one, was not. Eva's department wasn't working at all. Neither was Eva. She was stuck with Boss Stöber, who couldn't do without her.

I was supposed to be confidential secretary to the mastermind radio engineer. It was another secret project. So secret that only he, or an even greater genius, could decipher the notes — notes I was to type neatly. The first time I peeked at them, I knew this wasn't such a good idea. Teddy's idea, of course. Teddy, though, had his reasons. I discovered the main one the first time I walked into that tiny office in the back of the hall the genius used.

There it was, on the desk with the typewriter, next to the desk lamp. Just standing there . . . in this place . . . at this time . . . A working shortwave radio. If I should dare, I could turn on the BBC and hear England. I felt all funny and strange just looking at it. For a few nights, that's all I did do — look. It was as if the genius wanted me to listen, the way he didn't show for nights on end, leaving me alone with this link to the outside, the real world, leaving it up to me whether or not I'd tune in and find the channel of truth. He was the silent type, this genius engineer, whose real name I never did get to know. He was a balding man in his forties, with deepset grayish eyes and huge, thick glasses that covered nearly his entire face.

He handed me the keys to his office door the very first night. I became an expert in how to handle and listen to a shortwave radio, and at the same time typed the nights away without knowing how to type. The latter, a superb exercise for two of my fingers, introduced me to the basic functions of a typewriter. The engineer's handwritten notes were full of symbols, numbers and signs, half of which I couldn't find on the machine because they weren't there. It took a little bit of inventiveness on my part — and a lot of luck.

I had other duties, too. There still was some filing to be done for Frau Linke and a promise to be kept for Herr Bahls to turn the oven off before leaving in the early morning. The rest of the night I mostly sat in the front office trying not to think of the consequences of being caught listening while attempting to interpret what it was they were really saying over the radio. They did talk a lot about the invasion of France and about Rommel who, no longer in Africa, was now in France. I'm sitting in Germany! What about right here?

⌐

THEY CAME IN ALL SIZES, all shapes and forms. Blondes, brunettes, the young and the not so young. It must have been the uniform that made them look so uniform, the guards of the night shift. They switched them around more often than I got to go to the latrine. They asked the same question — What do I do now? — sat in the same chair, dozed off at the same time and marched up and down the hall, up and down, precisely as often as the ones who'd been here before. Sisters of regimen — all brainwashed by the same master.

It was not surprising then that I was a bit astounded by the latest newcomer's, "How do you do." She did not ask, "What do I do now?" but marched straight into Frau Linke's office, pulled up a chair, sat down and immediately quizzed me about what I was doing. To get her off my back, I exaggerated the difficult, confidential work I had to do for the good genius and all the other immense responsibilities the day bosses had laid on me. I didn't get her off my back, but she was very impressed, telling me that she knew instantly that I was a very intelligent girl. She then invited me to sit down next to her and tell her all about my life. She said she wanted us to be friends, explaining that she'd been transferred from another camp and that she hoped to stay in Ravensbrück. She said she resided in one of those lovely little cottages outside the camp. She hinted that she carried a lot of weight. She didn't have to, I could tell. Before the night was over, we'd talked our way from famous Dutch painters to great Italian composers, outstanding German writers and eminent philosophers, all the way through to renowned psychoanalysts, without ever mentioning Sigmund Freud, the Jew.

For the next few nights, nothing much changed. Once or twice she did try following me to the back office, but each time she strode along the engineer happened to be there too, and so she quickly retreated to the glass-enclosed office. From there, she had a perfect view and was able to watch the girls work without being observed herself. She was in her late thirties, would never win a beauty contest, was unmarried and not at all anxious to change that. She brought me sandwiches and home-baked cookies which wouldn't win a contest either, but did make time go fast. So fast that I twice forgot to turn the oven off. I knew that Herr Bahls would take the blame for it. If detected, he'd have to pay the price. They send men to the Russian front for less. Besides, there was too much at stake. It wasn't just because of the radio that Teddy had wanted me to switch to the night shift. What he'd really wanted was to get me away from the snitch. Sooner or later she'd have to come up with someone to keep on earning her Judas bread. It was my chummy relationship with the German civilians and my calamitous run-in with Holthöfer that had worried Teddy. "You've pushed your luck far enough," he'd told me. "Got to get you out of harm's way."

I didn't get it. I know I should have, but I didn't. The friendly night guard's intimations were just too subtle. Innuendo after innuendo, cleverly disguised words and phrases resembling a monologue or the perplexing prologue to some enigmatic play. She had waited a week before she'd started on this play on words with all its hidden meanings. Surprised at my lack of response, and not certain whether I hadn't caught on or just pretended I hadn't, she decided to risk it and ask the question straight out: "Do you know what I am talking about?" It wasn't her simple query that made a signal in my head go off. It was her suddenly moving closer and planting her hand firmly on my thigh that did it. That's when I understood what I had never wished to understand. What this genial Fraülein, this night shift guard, was after was my body. My undernourished, blown-up, strained and aching body. What an upside-down, cockeyed world this had become. And what was I supposed to do? Say, I don't understand what you're talking about so please don't talk about it?

I managed to rescue my thigh by pulling my leg away from her, and said nothing. She said, "I can help you, help you all the way. You can trust me." Sure, all the way to the firing squad. Her hand had gotten hold of my thigh again. It felt like the grip of a man. I hated it.

She then went on to tell me that she knew what she was doing and only wanted what was best for me. She had a plan to get me out of the camp so we could spend time together in her lovely cottage. We'd listen to Mozart —

not worth the firing squad — have tea and cookies, and enjoy each other. Not each other's company but each other. She also felt obliged to tell me that she had had some nice little friends in the other camp and knew exactly how to go about it. "Nothing wrong with gratifying one's needs for physical pleasure," she went on. "We all have desires. After all, we're all just human."

The woman with the wrong hormones felt obliged to tell me in detail how she planned to go about having this little rendezvous in her enchanted cottage. First, she would get me a uniform — my size, not hers — which I could put on in the morning after everyone had left and the camp was practically empty. Second, I would put it on behind the Block where she would be waiting for me. Third, the two of us would walk through the camp, and through the gate, out together. According to her, no reason in the world why anyone should stop us. According to me, no reason in the world why I should want to do this unless I could walk out and keep going . . . going with lots of money in my pockets, ration cards, travel permits and brilliantly forged IDs. And that's exactly what I told her. She replied that we ought to take it easy and start with the no problem one first, namely, tea for two. She implied that I could think about it for a few days. When I told Eva, she laughed, certain the whole thing was a joke, and then wanted to know whether she could come too. "Not too," I told her. "Instead!" She declined.

We put our heads together, Eva, Lydia and I, trying to find a way out of this unsavory predicament. What could I really do? She had all the power, and this liberated Fraülein could make my miserable life a lot more miserable should I refuse her. She could report me and blame it all on me. Could say that it was I who'd made a pass at her. Of course I could object, which wouldn't do me a bit of good. I really wasn't anxious to find out what the punishment was for corrupting the morals of an overweight Third Reich night shift guard with private cottage. Giving in and getting caught before something happens; giving in and getting caught after my visit to the enchanted cottage; or not getting caught. What choices! Not a one I could have lived with, not a one I'd risk my life for, not a one indeed that would take me out of Ravensbrück, far, far away . . .

I decided to stall and tell her I needed time to think about it. I would also mention the spy who, as everyone knew, had been roaming around the factory during the day, and according to the latest talk, was now doing her spying at night. Why not tell her who this creature really works for? That should do it! That should frighten even her enough to keep her wandering hands in her lap.

I told her about it the following night. Her response was total indignation, not directed at me but at the spy, the Gestapo and anyone else using such despicable tactics. The mere idea of someone maybe watching us distressed her immensely. In the end she said, "We have to be careful."

In the nights that followed she did keep her hands to herself but didn't stop her orations of love — the love she felt for me and the love we two were meant to share. She showed up outside the Block on a Sunday morning, called in asking for me and then waited for me to come out. Eva and I had just finished making up the bunk when she appeared. She said she came to see where I slept, who my sleeping partner was and to check that I was all right. Everyone inside the Block witnessing this embarrassing scene naturally would never stop talking about it. I asked her not to come anymore; she did anyway. Always on Sunday, every Sunday. Because Eva's place was next to mine, she determined that Eva must be the reason that I was playing hard to get. I didn't bother setting her straight on that, but was grateful for her totally unfounded, persistent belief that Eva and I were a pair. We would spread some gossip about it ourselves, preventing any reoccurrence of that kind of unpleasantness, not only with the guards but with the other prisoners.

~

AS UNEXPECTEDLY AS I HAD FOUND MYSELF on the night shift, I was back on the day shift. It was summer now. Hitler boots were still marching over the European map; bombs were still missing military targets, hitting civilians instead, thus solving the problem of overpopulation; and innocent people were still being arrested, deported and murdered. The killing spree — like the war — was far from over.

The routine in the Siemens factories hadn't changed, either. Herr Bahls was still doing the *Heissleiter* stuff, and Frau Linke, though worried about her husband because of the Russians, nevertheless still wanted to hear tales of the silver screen. And, yes, the spy, so I was told, was also still with us. But Teddy had disappeared and wasn't heard from again. Eva said that Teddy thought he was being watched. I chose to believe that he hadn't ended up in a concentration camp or gotten himself shot but had gotten away and was safe. He seemed too much of a pro to get caught.

My lovesick friend kept up her weekly visits to my block, and just when I was almost convinced that her interest in me was a humane one, not only sex, she disappeared too. Word of her sexual preference had preceded her from the previous camp, which was why she had been transferred to Ravensbrück in the first place. I later learned that she'd been on the moral hot seat for quite some time, not only for advocating homosexuality but for practicing it openly.

They eliminated the night shift altogether. Poor engineer genius, I never finished transcribing any of his notes. Perhaps he'll be lucky and they'll get him a real secretary.

New rumors are floating around again. One never knows who starts them, and now, without the radio and Teddy, there is little chance to confirm any of it. The latest is that a group of high-ranking German officers and even generals have tried to assassinate Hitler. Unfortunately, it all went wrong, and the evil one is still alive. The one about Hitler made the rounds in July 1944. A month later, the French in my block came up with the next rumor. They swear that France has been liberated and that their beloved Paris is free. If it is true, I'm certainly happy for them, but I can't help but wonder what good that does us stuck in here. France is free! What about Holland? I haven't heard from home for ever so long. No packages, not even half empty ones, and no censored mail, either. Is my family still there. "Alive and well." Is anyone still alive and well? Am I to spend yet another birthday in here and still remain optimistic and sane? I hate this harrowing existence, this balancing act on the tightrope of life. When will it end? How much longer . . . ?

What isn't a rumor are the brand-new blocks they've recently put up in the midst of the forest no more than five minutes away from the factories. There are ten of them, ten for the two thousand women working there. They were much smaller than the ones in the camp and are not divided. The latrines are outside, testing one's hardiness in the winter soon to come, but at least the sinks and faucets aren't broken. And for the time being, the heater inside the Block also works. We are moved out of the camp and into this completely secluded new housing. The road leading to Siemens is only a stone's throw away, and yet from the road the blocks are undetectable. Why this hideout with the factories out in the open for the whole world and every half-blind pilot to see?

We have a live-in house mother (guard) now. Every block has one. What a fabulous job that would have been for my liberated, misbehaving night shift guard at Siemens. The one we have in our block resembles her in size but otherwise is an exact copy of all the other crazy Hitler Fraüleins. After a while, it's hard to tell them apart, as if they all came out of the same dragon's womb. All sisters of the abyss bought and paid for by demented Adolf.

Except for having to start earlier and finishing later, nothing is different. The time we save getting there we now spend working more. Is it better, easier? As the French say, *"le même, le même,"* it's the same thing.

My birthday came and went — again. I'll never get used to it. I'll never believe that what is happening to me is really happening. I've been marching hand-in-hand with misery and fear, on the edge of death, for almost one and a half years now. Each day an eternity, each week a forever, each month like one more one and a half years.

⸎

WINTER CAME EARLY THIS YEAR, as though it couldn't wait to cover the earth with its virgin white blanket and hide the blood-drenched earth. It looks so peaceful. Will it bring peace? Snow has been falling since early November, and the majestic tall pine trees have all changed into marmoreal statues. It's quite a sight. The air smells clean, fresh — unspoiled, newborn. It's all part of the great deception. Nature's joining in the game of make-believe. We make-believe this tranquil landscape is just what it appears to be. Serene and still. Yet we know better, all of us! We leave our footprints in the snow as we march through the woods to the road and up to Siemens in the shadowy darkness before dawn. They are all snowed over or blown away by the wind by the time we march back again, down the road, through the woods, in the shadowy darkness of night. How much snow does it take to hide the crimes of a nation?

The little girl they've sent up with a group of other new prisoners from the camp down below won't leave many footprints. It is written in her sorrowful face, her feverish, shimmering, large dark eyes and her thin, trembling body. She won't make it to Christmas. We do what we can for her, Eva and I. Marching, we hold her up so she won't fall. We drag her along with her feet trailing behind. There are tracks where her tiny feet have touched the ground, tracks like from a child's sled. At Siemens, she sits bent over the *Heissleiters* and dreams of home. Herr Bahls is very kind and shields her from the bully guard who's constantly on her case. She is only fourteen and the only Pole they've sent up. The others are Germans with a questionable past. The world she comes from is as small as she — a mama, a twin sister.

The town she comes from is just as small, a dot on a map. She's never been away from home, never been separated from the two people she loves most.

She is the little sparrow that's fallen from the nest, the baby doe caught in a hunter's trap. She is every frightened, suffering child and every lost and tormented soul that makes one's heart weep. Her name is Esther. Esther neither knows how she got here nor where she is nor why. She is very tired from the many days and nights she's been made to travel from place to place . . . and from crying so much. She doesn't know where her mother and twin sister are and doesn't understand why she is all alone. Esther keeps telling Eva and me that she is a good girl and can't comprehend why God should want to punish her. Eva got her a bunk right next to ours so we can keep an eye on her, and whenever I hear her cry out at night, I move closer and hold her in my arms. She weighs less than a feather. Before long there won't be anything left to hold, and all there will be left to see of her will be her eyes. Her beautiful, soulful, questioning eyes . . .

It's Christmastime — another goddamned unholy and not at all silent night Christmas! A workday like any other — for us and for the Germans in the factories. Everyone is depressed and wants to be with their families and forget everything else. Around noon, Frau Linke asks me to sing "Silent Night" not only for her but for the entire hall. The bully agrees and so do all the others. I do think it a strange request but sing anyway. There was no announcement. The moment I start, the machines, as by silent command, stop. It is very still. No movement, no sound, only my voice singing the song of heavenly peace to this sorry group, these casualties of Hitler's war. As my voice rings through the hall, leaving an echo that lingers on, I watch their faces and know that in their minds they were going home. That for the three blessed minutes of the song, they were home, were celebrating Christmas . . . in heavenly peace.

Christmas Eve. No presents under the tree. No tree. No roasted chestnuts, no children singing Christmas carols, no holly wreath on the door. Nothing but stale memories and an aching heart. The mood in the Block is subdued and somber. There shouldn't be any Christmases while carnage consumes the world. It's such a melancholy time. Underneath the snow, the earth is a mantle of frozen limbs.

Even our house mother is subdued, turned inward. Eva and I put Esther to bed, with a cold rag on her forehead. She's ice-cold and burning up at the same time, but at least she knows nothing about this holy night. Esther is Jewish Orthodox and very religious. Not a good thing to be these days. The little girl's voice has gotten very weak, yet she keeps on praying as loud as she can.

The guard wants me to sing "Silent Night" again and whatever else I might like to sing. She's taken her uniform off for tonight.

With special holidays comes a special kind of loneliness. Like a great thirst or hunger, it's full of gnawing anguish, relentless and continuous as a bottomless well. If they would only let us sleep through them . . .

The soldier boy standing watch outside the Block looked as miserable and lonely as the rest of us — another Resnick? He wasn't much older than Esther and seemed as much out of place there as the big rifle he carried. I'd first noticed him looking out the window while singing the evening blues away. I had never seen any soldier up here before. Why were they guarding us instead of the factories?

It was one of those unforgiving, freezing nights that chills the bones and turns one's breath to ice. The boy soldier's boot-clad feet were buried in snow and so were half of his legs. His gloveless hands clutching his rifle were frostbitten. His adolescent face, looking up to the cloudy heavens, was as blue as the cold that enfolded him. He had such a young, forlorn, sad face. Watching him through the closed window, I thought of the beautiful song by Oskar Strauss from *The Chocolate Soldier*. So I sang it. Sang of the lonely soldier standing watch, alone at night, at the Volga strand. He asks for one angel to be sent down to him, only one from the One up there who has so many. Could he hear some of it through the drafty cracks underneath the window, the boy I shall call Resnick too? He's just like the one guarding me in my theater way back and like the one in the guardhouse at the Belgian border.

Christmas Day: We're one person short this morning. One pair of footprints less, one less child on this earth. Esther is no longer with us. She left us last night. She may have waited till everyone was asleep. It would have been typical of her to slip away in the dark so as not to bother anyone. I do think night is a good time to leave this merciless planet . . .

Our house mother guard, back to wearing her normal uniform, and acting accordingly, tried to wake Esther. Standing in front of the little girl's bunk, she grabbed her by the shoulders, shaking and hitting the frail, lifeless body while screaming for that lazy Pole to "get your stinking bones out of bed!" Like a madwoman completely out of control, she kept pounding and pounding the motionless girl. It was a frightful, freakish display and blood-curdling to watch. Finally, Eva stepped in. Making it look accidental, she rammed into the guard and said, "She is dead." The woman immediately dropped Esther's limp body, screaming, "I didn't kill her! I didn't do nothing to her! Why isn't she moving? Tell her to move!" Once more Eva told her that Esther was dead. Then Eva bent down and closed the little girl's wide-open, lost-forever eyes. One of the girls in the Block said a prayer.

It's Christmas Day . . . and a Jewish child has gone to heaven. Merry Christmas . . .

⌐

IN THE MIDDLE OF JANUARY 1945, two concentration camp veterans, by then both experts in survival techniques, landed up in "the bunker." Neither had had any experience there. Until the gate slammed shut behind them, they hadn't really been sure that a bunker existed. There had been whispers, of course, and not all of them had been hushed or repressed.

Eva and I were the two seasoned inmates, immune to any new tribulations, or so we thought. As for the bunker, to our mutual dismay, and as the world would also come to know, it did exist.

The bunker, inside the camp, a distance away from the blocks and everything else that made up the camp, was a fortified two-story stone prison, built deep into the earth. Like all other prisons, it had many cells with walkways outside. It did not have common indoor or outdoor facilities. All the accommodations were strictly private. And so was what went on inside.

When Eva and I were told by the guard who took us out of Siemens that we were under arrest, all that came to mind was that the spy in our hall had finally earned her traitor's loaf of bread. It had only taken her nine months. The guard escorting us into the bunker assured us, when we asked what the charges were, that we would find out all in good time. What was wrong with that little statement was that time just isn't good. It moves too fast, it moves too slow, and while imprisoned, it doesn't move at all. Thus, there is no such thing as "all in good time."

A cell is a cell . . . or is it? Not in this place. It's altogether different here. In here a cell is a dungeon — a cold, dark, impregnable tomb. An eight- by five-foot open casket with a ceiling instead of a lid. It's deep inside thick walls of stone they dont want anyone to find or know about. A place where savagery and torture are not the exception but the rule. Savagery and torture! What a splendid way to procure a confession, whether or not there is anything to confess.

"Persuasion" — that's what they call it. In this era of enlightenment, this wondrous twentieth century, here in this bunker they have revived the dark Middle Ages.

The cell Eva and I were in was on the side of the bunker that faced Berlin. We were almost all the way in the back. Above us were the German soldiers who allegedly had done all sorts of nasty things to irritate their Führer, like for instance not wanting to die for their fatherland anymore. Not wanting to fight, period — those who kept marching in the wrong direction, away from the battlefields. The cells on top and nearer the exit were reserved for — and occupied by — high-profile anti-Hitler government people of various countries, as well as political adversaries of influence, including Germans. In time I learned some of their names and the reason they were being kept there. I also learned the reason why they, and only they, stayed in cells very close to the exit. It had to do with planes and bombs — Russian planes, to be precise. They flew right over us on their way to bombing Berlin, all winter long, day and night, night and day, with us directly in their path. It didn't take a seasoned combat pilot to realize that, as locations go, we weren't very safe. Not from the Russians missing targets or losing bombs, not from the German antiaircraft firing. They may have known there was a concentration camp down there and not wanted to hit it, but what about us, way down in the depths of the bunker, who knew about *us*?

The Gestapo in Berlin, that's who. It was their bunker, their operation, they made the arrests. Sure, the facility was inside the camp, but it had nothing to do with the camp. Whatever took place in the bunker took place independent of the camp, with the Gestapo as the only law. And it was they who didn't want to lose those VIPs to bombs, no matter whose. For they were the Gestapo's bargaining chips, to be cashed in when their glory days were over and their whole army started marching the other way. They were here so the Gestapo could move them out fast.

They didn't hand out brochures recounting interesting facts about this bunker at check-in time. Whatever information we gathered came, in dribs and drabs, from many sources, mainly from listening to the talking walls . . .

The cell that the old watchman with the constant grin took us to already had a tenant. Its size and generous furnishings — one army bed with a straw sack and one chair — seemed to suggest that one was all it was meant for. Nevertheless, Eva and I were shown in and told to make ourselves comfortable. The girl sitting on the chair, a spitting image of a human mouse, with voice to match, was glad for the company. She immediately got up, offered us her bed and chair, and, most important, the half broken commode in the corner. It didn't even take three seconds to see what else was there: the usual closed opening in the door for food to be pushed through; a dirty light bulb on a thin cord hanging from the casket lid ceiling; a naked stone floor and naked stone walls. No marks on the floor, no names on the walls. Nothing else.

The girl, Renata, from somewhere near Frankfurt, wasted no time telling us that she too was a concentration camp inmate. Her crime, as she called it, was trading with a male guard the cigarettes she'd gotten from home for the clothing she now wore. The guard, she said, was now upstairs with the other naughty boys. With her hat, coat and snowboots on, she looked like she was on her way out to go shopping.

"They want me to say that I was trying to escape," mousy Renata complained, "and that there was something between Hans and me. What shall I tell them?" She then went on to say she'd been told that if she were to confess, they wouldn't hurt her. Before we could think of a response, Renata asked what crime we had committed. We told her that we had done nothing and didn't know why we were here.

But Renata kept first begging, then insisting that we tell her, because after all, how else was she going to know that she could trust us? She needed to pour her heart out, or so she said, and she wanted us to do no less. By the time supper had been served through the door slot, she had used the words "trust me" at least a hundred times.

The dingy light bulb was turned off in the late evening, leaving us to spend the first night sleeping on the icy floor of this wretched place — groping in the dark.

Renata waited till the second day before giving us a detailed account of the torture chambers which, she swore, she had seen with her own two eyes. It reminded me of some horror tale straight out of the Tower of London. Starting with the crucifixion chamber, where one got tied to a large wooden cross hanging on the wall; next, the water-tread room, where the choices were treading water or drowning; the truth bed, where truth serum injections were administered; and finally the whipping table. There, stark naked, facedown, they gave you, with a braided pigskin whip, your special share of lashes.

What Renata didn't tell us was that these amusing hobbies of theirs weren't what they started one out with but rather finished one off with. There was also the short, certainly less painful, firing squad. Unfortunately, not always instead of torture but after . . .

Renata left us the next morning. She was moved to another cell, our for-ever smirking watchman told us. He said that we should be glad she was gone. "She's not your friend," the old man muttered while pushing the tray with its watery coffee and slice of dried-out bread through. He also said that she was working for "them" and that getting us to confide in her and tell our wrongdoings was what she was down here for. "They think prisoners tell other prisoners everything," he added, kind of amused. "Well, some do and some don't. Some are easy, some are not, and some will sell their own mother for a warm coat. This one would have sold you for less. Be glad she's gone."

We weren't really surprised about Renata. Girls like Renata and those at Siemens, having frequently broken the rules themselves, were only Gestapo pawns. Not that they ever did anything of vital consequence; they only broke the silly little rules like stealing a cigarette or a sock. When they got caught, they were offered a trade, a chance to redeem themselves. Forgive-ness in exchange for spying on their comrades — and a hat and coat.

I was never quite convinced that either got their money's worth — the informers because they did have to invent a lot of stuff just to come up with something, and the others, Gestapo and such, because they didn't believe half of it anyhow. They had a saying, this hunting secret police of the Führer. They'd say: *Wir lieben den Verrat aber nicht den Verräter!*" — We love trea-son but not the traitor! Which meant that after a while the Renatas in their employ didn't fare all that well either.

That same afternoon they also took Eva out. The guard who came for her was a lot younger than our watchman and less talkative. A silent come-on gesture was all he managed. I listened to the *thump, thump* of his boots and the clumping of Eva's wooden shoes as they marched off, until I couldn't hear them anymore.

⤳ Nineteen

I WAS ALONE. For the first time in more than twenty and a half months, I was alone. Left by myself, to myself, with practically no one knowing where I was. It made me feel extremely vulnerable, alarmingly isolated and strangely forgotten. And yet, aloneness was what I had wished for every day of those twenty and a half months. I had wished for it in Malin, in Auschwitz, but most of all here in Ravensbrück, where the forever crowding masses of prisoners had been driving me absolutely mad. I guess I'd gotten my wish. Lydia would have said, "Whom the gods love, they grant their wish." Did I wish the wrong wish or did the wrong gods hear me? Eva keeps insisting that it is a great time. "Think of all the stories we can tell our grandchildren," she says. Sometimes she makes me positively crazy with her cheerful outlook. I wonder what joyful predictions she would come up with if she were here now.

Just before dark they came for me too and took me to a cell all the way in the front. There, two uniformed S.S. men playing good policeman, bad policeman told me that my very best friend had already confessed. They naturally advised me to do the same. What an old trick! As a prison newcomer, I might have fallen for it, but not after all that time. Not now, not when I had already learned a few prison-smart tricks of my own. Frankly, I thought it dumb that they even tried. Much dumber than putting us in with Renata. They wanted us to give them all the names of all the people we had had contact with at Siemens. Seemed a bit odd as they knew them anyway, kept files on them. Everyone knew that's what they did. Apparently, though, a few of them had turned up missing — files as well as people — with Teddy heading the list. They had been looking for him and the civilians he had had contact with. The two S.S. men never mentioned Resistance, which, according to them, didn't exist, but that was surely what they meant.

They wanted to know everything we had told Teddy. They were especially anxious to find out the names of prisoners in our camp related to foreign dignitaries, names of Socialists, names of Communists. I told them nothing. What I would have liked to say was that if my very best friend had already confessed, what the hell did they need me for? But of course, I didn't. Couldn't let them know that I was wise to their game. Also, after more than an hour of that grueling nonsense, I really wanted to get out of there. By then, even my bleak and lonely cell was beginning to look good to me.

With warnings and promises of very unpleasant consequences should I not cooperate next time around, they let me go.

The only positive thing about that entire day was that Eva had come back too. I was never so glad to see anyone. She'd gone through the same charade as I had, with only a slight variation. For the first few hours she was left all alone. When the same pair finally did show up, they told her the same rubbish they had told me, "Your friend has already confessed," wanting her to think that the hours she'd been alone were when they'd gotten to me. She never believed it either and told them exactly what I had. Nothing.

Is sitting in a pitch dark underground cell, shut away from the world, the right place to talk about the future? Of course not! But that's precisely what Eva did right in the middle of this freezing night. Above us the AWOL or otherwise disgraced German soldiers, as usual, cheered the Russian flyers on with: *"Hurrah! es kommen schon wieder die Russischen Flieger!* [the Russian flyers are here again]." While I was trying to decide whether I was suffering more from hunger than from the cold, Eva insisted on talking about our just-around-the-corner future. Hers even had a name. In fact, three names: Britta, Tore — and Summer. Britta and Tore Warren were Eva's friends, and luckily for them, came from a land that didn't have a war, a land called Sweden.

They had met on a summer cruise of the Greek Islands and had instantly become friends. The couple had invited her to spent all of next summer on their beautiful island, not far from Stockholm, but as it turned out, Eva had spent it in Auschwitz instead.

Devoid of all logic, she somehow managed to make the impossible seem possible. She did admit that she hadn't heard from them for a very long time, but was certain that they hadn't forgotten her or the invitation to their lovely island. Ah yes, they were millionaires! With yachts, many cars, lots of servants and a young son by the name of Charles. Listed in *Who's Who*, Britta and Tore Warren were, best of all, my best friend's friends.

Eva kept talking and talking about them until, in some hard to define way, they became real to me, as if I also knew them. "We'll go there the moment we're free. We'll spend all summer there. Lie in the sun, swim, sleep and eat. That's what we'll do! Swim, sleep and eat, sleep and eat! Eat! Eat! Eat, till we bust . . ."

For a while, Eva and I thought that we had contracted some unknown wretched disease just from being down there. A cell disease! We thought so because we hadn't been shivering all the next morning. On the contrary, we felt unusually warm, like we were running a fever, but neither our foreheads nor our hands were hot, and we hadn't been sweating. We felt cozy and warm. We didn't know what to make of it until our watchman, armed with another army bed and blankets, disclosed that he had been ordered to bring them to us and to warm the cell up. "You see," he beamed, "they're not so bad. Give them what they want and they let you be." With this he wandered off.

They let us be till late afternoon after which, in reverse order, we went through the same game, same results. They didn't believe us, and they knew that we knew that too. We also knew that having gotten away twice with no more than threats was not the end of it.

Twenty-four hours later, Eva was taken out once more and not brought back. Neither the two army beds with blankets, the hot soup (which actually was soup), the no more than a week old bread, nor the warm cell could dispel the creepy feeling I had as to what lay ahead. It wasn't my certainty that the worst was yet to come and that all else had merely been a prelude that troubled me, but that I had to go through it alone, without Eva. It made me feel extremely unprotected, like going into battle without a shield.

They came for me past midnight. Down the long walkway to where the stairs were leading up, out and into the night, I followed the soldier. A sliver of moon shining down on the frozen earth and the flashlight in the soldier's hand were our only light. The icy wind and wintry air hit me full force. It bit my face, whipped through my flimsy prison dress and wrapped itself around my bare legs. It felt like someone had thrown buckets of ice at me. It hurt and took my breath away. I left no footprints in the frozen snow. Nothing to tell that I had been here. I listened for sounds. There were none. None but the crunching noise underneath my feet, sounding like someone's moaning.

We crossed a road and walked through the wintry forest, stopping at the foot of a steep mountain. In front of us, innumerable primitively cut, narrow wooden steps and a jiggly handrail led straight to the top. When the soldier came for me, I had been tempted to ask where he was taking me but pretty certain that he wasn't going to answer anyhow. Now, though, with what was looming before me, I did ask him and he did answer, "Up there," raising his arm and pointing all the way up.

A lot went through my mind while climbing those dangerously ramshackle steps. I'd thought of counting them but after the first two hundred gave up. I thought of Eva, where she could be and whether she too had had to make that climb. Most of all, though, I thought of the mysterious shots. The ones we could hear inside the camp night after night after night with none of us knowing where they came from or who was getting shot.

I managed to climb the seemingly endless hundreds of steps with only a few slips along the way. I knew that we had reached the top when instead of steps and a handrail, my feet touched flat ground. After about twenty feet, we reached a house. What with the elements fighting their own little war, fog against wind, wind against fog, and the moon having disappeared altogether, there could have been a whole town up there and I wouldn't have seen it. The soldier opened what probably was the front door of the house, led me into a small, poorly lit hall, and immediately left. I barely had time to look around when a thunderous voice bellowed, "Come in."

He stood behind an enormous desk. On both sides of it and on the floor were heaps of papers, all in folders stacked up high. The man's eyes were fixed on an open file right in front of him. I noticed as he bent over it that his reddish-blond hair was thinning at the top and that the skin underneath it was shiny and pink.

The huge desk took up most of the room. There was no rug on the wooden floor. no pictures on the walls, not even one of the Führer. There was nothing but the man, his legion files and a thick, double-braided whip spread across the desk. He wore a S.S. uniform full of ribbons and medals. No matter what he or the room looked like, I knew that this was the place many had come to but few had left.

"Come closer!" he yelled. "Don't keep standing by the door! I am Criminal

Commissar Randolph. Does the name mean anything to you? Have you heard of me before?"

The word "Yes" got stuck in my throat. I did try to speak but nothing came out.

He had stopped looking at the file and, looking at me instead, he asked again. This time I managed a nod. He then said: "I see you were in Auschwitz. *Da bist du ja den Totengräber von der Shaufel gehüpft* [You must have jumped off the gravedigger's shovel]." His tone had changed. I even thought I detected a certain admiration and respect in his voice, as if my having survived the death camp had made me a worthier adversary. "All right," he added. "Now we both know that you are tough."

My being alone with him petrified me. His reputation as the most depraved and despicable monster had assured that fear. The police inspector in charge of vice from Berlin, Holthöfer's boss. How does one stand up to a man with unlimited power and no accountability? Being fully aware that he could rape and torture me, beat me to death with his whip, and with no witnesses ever to accuse him of anything would get away with it, was what made this entire situation so very hard to deal with. I'd thought that after Auschwitz I would never be afraid of anything or anyone again. But standing face to face with this man, trapped and totally helpless, with no way to defend myself, I was terrified.

Criminal Commissar Randolph, of average height, in his middle thirties, pushed back his chair, picked up his whip, walked around his desk and stopped right in front of me. Three times the whip swished by my face no more than a couple of inches away. I could hear the hissing sound it made, could feel the air rushing by me like a sudden burst of wind. Three times I held my breath but did not blink or close my eyes, and never moved an inch. I kept looking straight at him . . .

Throughout the entire interrogation, the whip — pigskin, he proudly informed me — was never out of his hand and only occasionally at rest. Mostly he kept swishing and swinging it by me with hair-raising accuracy and speed, while at the same time hurling questions at me. He too wanted names. The names of those he claimed I had gotten information from and given information to.

The questioning continued all through the night. He never took his watery blue eyes off me and was never more than a foot away from me. He kept screaming that it was all in my file (the one lying open on his desk), and that if it took as many hours as there were hours, and as many nights as there were nights, he would get the answers. He did not say how.

At one point he showed me an official paper with a swastika stamp at the top and bottom. He made me read it. It said: DEATH BY FIRING SQUAD. The names on it were Eva's, mine, and two other names unknown to me. In it we were accused of: one, belonging to an underground cell involved in sabotage; two, the deliberate withholding of vital information crucial to the security of the Third Reich. It was signed Heinrich Himmler. I did not respond. I was numb, too weary to respond. Besides, I wasn't absolutely sure that the whole thing was real. I was no expert on Himmler's signature. The paper, typed in big fat letters, looked a bit like a telegram. Either way, I did think it was kind of flattering to bring such a major player as Himmler himself into it.

He called it a night when he himself had had enough. The soldier, appearing out of nowhere, took me down the mountain and back to my cell. He must have carried me more than I walked. I sank down on the bed and immediately plunged into a deep dreamless sleep. In the weeks that followed, my perserverance and willpower were taxed and tested every day. The launching of this methodical ritual, routinely orchestrated by the Man of the Mountain to break me, began the very next night.

It started with our watchman, who came and took out the army beds. The straw sacks were next, and after that the blankets, the heat in the cell and finally the damn dangling light.

For more than two weeks I sat, stood, paced and slept on the hard, cold floor of this unlit, freezing cell alone, waiting for pneumonia to put me out of my misery. I didn't get pneumonia.

I think I understood early on that giving Randolph the names he wanted would be signing my own death sentence. Once he had them, I was no longer any good to him. Thus, my only chance of staying alive, barely, but alive, was to remain silent. As I was weighing the odds of survival under the present conditions, they took my food away — not all, but almost all of it. Three weeks into this not dead, not alive existence, they rationed the already rationed ration. Instead of giving me my daily bread daily, they only fed me every fourth day. The old watchman referred to this latest privation as something they were doing to help me see it their way. He also assured me that it had been tried and tested with terrific results.

After Eva and I were separated, I tried to find out about her from the old watchman. I asked him every time he came. But he refused to give me any information. Pretty certain that she was alive for the very same reason I was still alive, nevertheless I was anxious to know how she was coping. Where Eva was concerned, the old man told me nothing.

In my dark cell, day and night had become one and the same. Everything had became one and the same. The same few steps I'd taken a thousand times already, a few steps forward, a few steps back, the same hunger and cold as my only companions, the same twilight sleep whether awake or asleep, and the same state of confusion about what was going on.

The steps up to the mountain continued. There seemed to be more of them each time I went, and they got harder and harder to climb. Often the soldier had to pull me part of the way, and even then I needed to rest in between. My legs couldn't follow anymore, and I was having dizzy spells. I was getting weaker. How many times did I creep up that mountain, how many whip-swishing probes and inquisitions by Criminal Commissar Randolph did I suffer through? After the fourth one, I stopped counting.

If it hadn't been for the roaring of the Russian planes flying over us and the German soldiers in the bunker cheering them on, I would have fallen into a deep well of despair, probably lost touch with the rest of the world altogether. But that made me hold on. It truly was like a breath of life — that, and the knocks that came from the other side of my wall. The knocking did not start until much later, not till I had already lost track of time and anything else there was to lose track of. Frustrated at first, for I no longer remembered the Morse Code from my Girl Scout days, it did cause me to wake up my mind and to revive old memories again. I never managed to understand all of what my neighbor was trying to communicate to me, but it really didn't matter. What mattered was that I wasn't the only one left down there and that, though still alone, I no longer felt alone.

They always came for me at night. Never once in the morning, never once in broad daylight. I could tell by the darkness outside. Also, whenever I'd ask the soldier with me what time it was, he'd say, "Two or three o'clock a.m."

THE GUARD WHO OPENED MY CELL DOOR to take me to yet one more interrogation was neither the old watchman nor the regular soldier I had had before. Whoever he was, he showed absolutely no interest in me, his job, nor did he appear to be in any particular hurry. As we made our way down the dim-lit walkway, I saw that quite a few cells on the opposite side from me were wide open. Even though I made no effort to hide my surprise and curiosity, the guard paid no attention to that either. Some of the cells were empty; others were occupied by male prisoners. One to a cell, some of them wore German uniforms, the others civilian street clothes. Looking to find a familiar face among the civilians, I shamelessly stared at each of them. Most of them stared back, nodded, and smiled. As I passed by them in slow motion, I thought I had seen one of those faces before. So I stopped in front of his open cell door and stared some more.

The man inside was very old and frail and seemed preoccupied with his thoughts. He had a blanket wrapped around his shoulders and a book in his hands. The more I looked at him, the more certain I was that I had seen him many a time. Still, I could not place him. Every open cell had beds and bedding and empty food trays on the floor, and even though I could never figure out why their doors had been left open, I came away convinced that all these men were important prisoners. Notable enemies of Hitler's Third Reich. The Elite.

It was the toughest climb yet. Icy, stormy, and every step more treacherous than the one just taken. While hanging on to the soldier's coat with cramped hands, my legs kept giving way under me. I was more lying on the slippery ground than standing, more crawling than climbing, more wheezing than breathing. I had started exercising right after the knocking on my wall had begun, telling myself that I just had to stay mentally and physically healthy. The truth was that both my body and my mind were definitely running on empty, which only made me silently ask the same old question: How much longer?

The man sitting behind Randolph's enomous desk was not Randolph. He was younger, much taller and more muscular. He too had my file in front of him. Reading from it and without looking up, he announced: "Playtime is over. You either tell us what we want to know or you get what your friend got."

Two thoughts crashed simultanously in my mind. One, something has happened to Eva; the other, he must be Dutch. His accent was very pronounced. Without responding to his puzzling and disturbing announcement, and trying my utmost to sound engaging, I said, "You're from Holland! That's great. Where are you from? Amsterdam is my home." I had spoken Dutch, and it startled him. For a short minute there he interrupted whatever it was he'd planned to threaten me with. Then he picked up where he'd left off with much of the same old menacing warnings Randolph had used, only far louder, but without a whip. It made me realize that he didn't get to sit in Randolph's chair because he was nice. He wasn't! He was mean, contemptible and shockingly vulgar, yet not altogether sure of himself. I had a hunch that he was kind of new at this.

While speaking Dutch to him got me no more than his screaming back at me in Dutch, and when I asked about my friend no more than a *"Halt's Maul!"* (Hold your trap) in German, he did not pester me half as long as Randolph used to. "Forty-eight hours!" he hollered before letting me go. "You either talk then, or join your friend."

Stumbling, slipping, falling down the mountain again, with the disgruntled soldier in front of me, did not prevent me from agonizing over Eva. I don't know how I knew that the Dutchman wasn't lying, I just knew! I never once thought about his forty-eight-hour threat, or much else for that matter. All I did think about was that I had to find out what they'd done to Eva. Back in my cell I waited a while and then, with no other option available, I started banging on the door. I banged and kicked, banged and kicked, and when I took a rest from that, I screamed. They finally came, the guard on duty and the old watcman. They yelled at me and I yelled back. I yelled that I couldn't take it anymore and that they might as well give me what my friend got and get it over with. Crying out as loud as I could, I accused them of having killed her. Well aware that I was sure to attract an audience, if not from the entire bunker then certainly from the men inside their unlocked cells, I gave it all I had left to give.

The guard, convinced that I had flipped, wanted to get the doctor, but the watchman, not quite so easily taken in, told him to get me some water instead. While he was gone, the old man whispered, "Your friend is alive. They gave her twenty-five lashes! She'll be all right except for her kidneys. They won't be no good anymore." I asked him whether he was sure that she was alive, and he said that she was. I also wanted to ask about the new man and Randolph, but the guard had returned with the water. Not wishing any real trouble for myself or the old man, I drank the water, said I was feeling much better, and went back into my cell.

Forty-eight hours later, I was back in the camp.

⌐

THE FIRST PERSON I saw after my eyes had gotten used to daylight again was Eva. She was standing inside the small, almost invisible gate that connected the bunker with the grounds of the camp, waiting for me. We were ever so glad to see each other, but the watchman who had let us out did not give us time for a reunion. He insisted that we report at once to the main office and have one of the girls there assign us to a block. Off the record, he told us that the bunker was being shut down and that was why we were being returned to the camp. When we asked him why they were shutting it down, he murmured, "The Russians are coming," sighed, and walked back to his bunker.

I knew most of the girls working there. They used to come to my evening concerts before Eva and I were moved up to Siemens and before our three-month lockup in solitary confinement. The girls running the offices were prisoners, too; privileged prisoners with access to privileged information. I wasn't sure whether they remembered me. The watchman had given us a piece of paper to turn in to the office. It only said our names and released from bunker. Still, for reasons I could not have explained, I would have preferred to remain anonymous.

Something was not right. The camp looked different. Not the way I recalled it at all. What had changed were the people. There were more of them than ever before, and they all just stood around. Women — so many women! Some of them wore prison dresses, others their own clothes. All ages. All looking weary, worn-out and confused.

The girls in the offices, though, hadn't changed. They were still the same, only a lot busier and also confused. We handed the release paper to the very first girl in the very first office; she acknowledged it with a slight nod, but, as we soon came to realize, that was all she acknowledged. Listening to them pecking away on their typewriters and their constant chatter, I thought that it was almost like real life, almost like having a regular job in a regular business, with them believing that was just what it was.

At last one of the girls working there, Fredericke, with fond memories of me and my songs, did tell us where to go, but also warned us to stay out of sight and not do anything to attract attention. She claimed we were "goddamn lucky" to be alive but now would have been better off staying in the bunker. "They've all gone nuts.They're in a panic! Nobody knows who to listen to anymore!" She went on to explain that all these women outside were prisoners from other concentration camps, evacuees. Her theory was that the Germans, not wanting the Allied forces that were closing in to find them, had rounded them up, and off to Ravensbrück they were sent. Some by truck, some made to walk for days on end. "We'll be the last ones" she continued. "They'll get to us at the very end. That's why they bring them here. It's awful how they keep dumping them on us as if we weren't crowded enough already. Where are we going to put them all? Lay them out in the camp streets like one big carpet? And who's going to feed them? With what? The barrels are empty, there's nothing left. Furthermore, who even gives a damn!" Her need to blow off steam and vent her frustration couldn't have come at a better time for Eva and me. News-starved but shockproof, we clung to every word, giving her our undivided attention.

Before we left, we made her promise that she would keep us informed of any changes, especially bad ones. It was then that I asked her quite casually whether she had heard anything about Criminal Commissar Randolph. She had, and for a song she wanted me to sing just for her, she would tell all she knew. Facts, she swore, not rumors.

Behind the offices in the supply room, I sang her the song she wanted to hear. My voice was weak, shaky, with lots of tremors, but Fredericke didn't mind. She took us to an empty office, and over tea she brewed herself, and toast with a hint of marmalade, she told us about the war. Not the big Hitler war being fought in half of the world but the little one between Randolph and Rühren, the Commandant of Ravensbrück. This one too, just like any other war, was about power: the power to rule, the power of unaccountability. That there wasn't any love lost between the Commandant and Randolph was understandable. Rühren didn't like the Gestapo — no one but the Gestapo liked the Gestapo. And Randolph didn't like being observed by the Commandant. Since both wanted to get rid of the other, instead of killing each other, they investigated each other. Whoever could dig up more dirt, pin more on his foe, was bound to win. Fredericke said it had been going on for a long time and finally, despite Randolph's battalion of spies, Rühren, the Commandant, had won. Mighty Randolph, believing that he was invincible, had allowed himself to get caught. Not only was he more than once found in the arms of a woman prisoner, but his pockets and drawers were full of costly goodies slated for the Third Reich. In other words, he stole. According to Fredericke, enough for many rainy days. Since everything was stolen from us, the prisoners, first, one could argue that all he really did was steal it again. Not being a stupid man, he probably did argue that. Apparently, though, it did him no good.

On the way out, we met another girl working there who also remembered me, and she, obviously assuming that I knew more than I did, asked me straight out whether it was true that Field Marshal Erwin von Witzleben and Carl Goerdeler, mayor of Leipzig, both instrumental in the plot against Hitler, were still being held in the bunker and whether I personally had seen them. Not wanting to admit that I knew absolutely nothing, I told her I had seen quite a few Germans in uniform there. But since I couldn't tell one uniform from the other, and didn't know them by sight, I couldn't be sure who they were. She then said, "Well, I'm sure they were there. If they aren't anymore, they probably shot them." That's when Eva blurted out, "It was them, I'm certain! I heard others talk about it. Karl Seitz was there too!" Karl Seitz was a social Social Democrat, former president of Austria and mayor of Vienna when I was a little girl.

Karl Seitz was there — of course he was! He was the one I thought I knew but couldn't place. The old, frail man in the open cell with the blanket over his shoulder and the book in his lap, that was him. I had met him twice, as a child. The occasion was a big affair at which my dance group was invited to perform. After the performance, when he came backstage, we were all introduced to him. I remember that I curtsied, that he smiled and that he was nice. Being reminded of those free lighthearted days of my early childhood, these happy moments of my past, made me doubly aware how perilous and heavy-hearted the present was for me and for him, the once beloved mayor of my city — Karl Seitz.

Awaiting us at our assigned block were two inmates. Acting as self-appointed guards, they informed us that we were definitely not welcome. They told us, with obnoxious presumptuousness, that they were not taking anymore dirty, lice-ridden criminals in, they already had too many. Since these two looked pretty messy and unwashed themselves, and since some of the others standing around in the doorway didn't look any better and everything around them smelled like a garbage dump anyway, Eva and I didn't think it worthwhile to assert ourselves. We left them standing there and went to the next block, and the next ... and the next ... and the next.

It was more or less the same wherever we went. Wall-to-wall women, wall-to-wall sick, vomiting smells, wall-to-wall lumped-together misery. We had made the rounds from one end of the camp to the other, only to find that they either weren't willing to make a place for us or it was some tucked-away corner with no breathing space at all. We were on our way back to Fredericke's office hoping that she could tell us what to do and where to go when I saw a big girl beating up an elderly, wispy little woman. She had her down on the ground, trying to rip her jacket off. The poor woman could not

fend her off. Getting into a fight was the very last thing I wanted. I had neither the strength nor the inclination for it, yet there was something about
that small, defenseless, gray-haired woman that made me jump in. I kicked
the big girl in the groin, and before she knew what hit her, Eva attacked her
from behind. The girl let go of the jacket, threw off Eva and fled, screaming.
Surprised that we still had it in us, we sent a dozen or so warnings after that
miserable coward, promising her fatal injuries should she ever come near
that frightened woman again.

The little woman, whose name was Gemma Glück, insisting that I had
saved her life, embraced and kissed me, repeating over and over what a
brave thing I had done and that God would bless and protect me and my
family for it. That's when it came to me, the reason why I had wanted to help
her: She reminded me of my mother. Not that they looked alike; they didn't,
not at all, still, she could have been my mother. Mama. I had not heard from
her for many months, didn't know where she was or whether she was safe.
She could be anywhere, and if she was . . . Good heavens, if she really was in
one of those hellish places, perhaps some young girl there would look out
for her, be by her side when she needed help.

Mama certainly had had no help — or very little — after Papa died. With
him gone, our home had become an island of sorrow. He'd taken every bit
of happiness with him. And if this wasn't depressing enough, there also was
the practical matter of maintaining Papa's business. Both his furniture factory and store needed supervision, and Mama did try to run them. But her
mind was not on furniture. Unable to accept her immutable fate, Mama ne-
glected the business and fled into the spirit world. In her pursuit of this
other place, she went from séance and medium to more séances and medi-
ums. Relentlessly, she followed them. Driven by her own agony and the im-
ponderable quest to "reach" Papa, her days and evenings were spent in
foreign regions, far removed from us. We needed our mother; she needed
deliverance from her grief. With Mama spending more and more time trying to "make contact," and practically none tending the business, the only al-
ternative was to let someone else manage it.

A Mr. Kurzberg was put in charge of Papa's business. A logical choice; not
only did he know a lot about furniture but, more important, he had been
Papa's closest business friend. A man in his forties, single, good-looking,
with a most disarming smile, Mr. Kurzberg took his new position very seriously. Mama was greatly pleased and soon made him a full partner. Out of

gratitude, the new partner offered to handle all of Mama's affairs. She accepted, thankful and relieved. Mama liked him because he was not a stranger. We liked him because he had a terrific motorcycle and took us for rides through the city. In those days of constant sadness, the rides were a welcome distraction. He was good to us, and he was good to Mama. He brought us presents, and never bothered Mama with such demeaning details as to where the money went.

Mr. Kurzberg was a crook. Stealing from Mama was a piece of cake, and Papa's friend took every piece of the cake. One day, the business was gone, and a very wealthy Mr. Kurzberg left Mama, us, and the country. This rather catastrophic occurrence was not mentioned at home at all. Only a fleeting remark that Mama had "sold" the business.

Mama's pride was tremendous and she kept up the facade. We stayed in our expensive apartment; it never occurred to me that cutting expenses might be the reason. That our grand piano was gone and our lessons stopped gave me no clue. Mama tried to make a living, but in spite of her earnest efforts, my none too great earnings as a child actress became the major source of income for my family. In those days, women hardly worked, and ladies of her breeding certainly did not, and Mama was a lady. She held on to her armor of pride, no matter what, following upper-middle-class doctrine with the obedience of a well-trained dog. It was her salvation, and her pandemonium. It was this irrevocable class distinction which made a snob out of me, and drove Mama into that forbidden territory of the working class. There, her unprofitable exploits raised no eyebrows, for no one knew about them. Her fancy acquaintances would never chance to leave their world of drawing rooms and heavy curtains. And we, her children, what possible reason could we have to be on the wrong side of the tracks?

I was almost ten, had just left a gymnastics event and was naturally out of bounds, when, on my way to a tram stop, I spotted Mama outside a doorway. It was so unexpected that for a moment I thought my vision had gone haywire. There was something about her that wasn't like Mama at all. A different mother, but damn it, it *was* my mother. She was selling ice cream out of a barrel right on the street. Next to her, on a little folding table, stacks of cones were piled up. Dumbfounded, I watched her peddle the ice cream for a penny a scoop with cone — stopping pedestrians and waving it in front of them as though it were the national flag. Such a pathetic sight! I desperately wanted to erase that picture from my mind, erase her; but I never could. Mama looked awful. So plaintive. There were new wrinkles on her face; her lips, once so lovely, had changed into two thin lines, without shape or color. Standing there in her faded flowery cotton dress, she no longer was the lady I used to see with Papa. Papa's lady wore chiffons and silks with pretty parasols to shield her from the sun. Papa's lady gave parties and was a queen, beautiful, loved by all.

Mama suddenly saw me, too. She was so stunned that her penny ice-cream cone dropped out of her hand and splashed on the pavement, vanilla and chocolate. Her tired eyes, painfully apologetic, kept begging forgiveness for having found no other way to feed her children. I could not bear her sorry expression. She gaped at me for only a few seconds. Then her eyes abruptly changed from sad to hard and impregnable. She looked away without a word, reached into the barrel, dug out another scoop, and rigidly continued her odious task.

Papa's lady had a lot of guts, but I didn't think so at the time.

GUTS! That's what my new camp mama, Gemma Glück, needed. She was American, born and bred in the USA. When I first heard her say that, I thought perhaps my hearing had gone bad. So, then I wanted to ask her what she was doing in Germany in a German concentration camp, but before I got around to it, Mrs. Glück disclosed that she was married to a Hungarian living in Budapest and that her husband was the Hungarian police president. Her maiden name, she said, was LaGuardia. As if that wasn't amazing enough, she added that the mayor of New York was her twin brother, Fiorella LaGuardia.

Gemma Glück had been brought here from Budapest together with hundreds, possibly thousands, of other Hungarian women a couple of weeks ago. Jews, all of them! Why only now, why not before when they first started deporting and killing Jews? That, the sweet lady explained, had to do with Hitler reneging on the deal he had made with the Hungarian government in the early days of the war. The deal called for Hitler and his hangmen not to harm one single Jew in exchange for unrestricted passage for his arms and troops. Hungary, said Gemma, was strategically of great importance to the Germans, and so they did leave the Jews alone. *Was* of great importance, but now it wasn't anymore. And that was why they had come for them, too. She also said that the end of the war was near and that everyone, including the

Germans, knew it. The question was, could we hold out? Gemma Glück did not have the answer.

Fredericke had left. Everyone in that building had left. The offices were closed, and suddenly it was dark. Not night yet, but evening, and still Eva and I hadn't found a place. It must have been sheer desperation that made us return to the almost hidden gate behind which lay the bunker. We rang the little bell, knocked on the gate and called for the old watchman to please, please let us in. It sure was a wacky thing to do. Wackier yet was that we didn't think of it as wacky. All we thought about was how much space they had in there and that it had to be better than bedding down, without bedding, on one of the camp streets next to one of the blocks where someone was bound to chase us away or worse. Besides, neither of us had an ounce of strength or a clear thought left. "Enough already!" said Eva, pounding on the gate and ringing the bell.

After a while the old watchman did show up. This time his smile was frozen and he looked utterly perplexed. We told him why we had come back, which he had a problem comprehending. He kept shaking his head, mumbling, "You want to come back, you want to come back?" We tried to assure him that it was only that night and that he just had to let us in, but he didn't appear to get that either. Very frustrating. There it was, within our reach, only a few feet away: an entire bunker, empty. An empty cell with beds, blankets and pillows. But he did not see it that way. He said it was out of his hands, wished us luck and walked away.

It had started to rain, the kind of rain that doesn't stop until it has turned all the camp streets into a muddy river. This forced us to take immediate action, no matter how practical or wise. After no deliberation at all we decided to head for the *Kleider Kammer,* the clothing supply room, and try to sneak in through a window. Closed all night and hopefully uninhabited during those hours, it made sense, especially when one considered the whole assortment of clean, dry clothes. We needed a change of clothing as much as we needed food and sleep. The only drawback was the location: it stood to the right of the block the Jehovah's Witnesses were in. With their never-ending nasal singsongs, which never predicted the end of Hitler, only the end of the world, they were the last people we wanted to run into.

There was a six-foot wall separating the *Kleider Kammer* from the Block on the left. We really had been looking for a window when we discovered the wall. It was quite baffling. Never having been dealt any fresh clothes from the clothing supply room before, never having even been there before, we didn't know when the wall was put up. More important still, why? The supply room windows were bolted from the inside and the door was triple-locked. Not so the walled-in Block. A flimsy latch-lock, like on some picket-fence gates, was all there was. Drenched to the skin, with darkness already moved in for the night, we felt our way along the wall, then along the Block till we found the door. We pushed it open and went in. We didn't know where we were, nor did we care.

We had come to the right block at the right time because they were just dishing out their famous watery potato peel soup with the customary slice of stale bread and because they didn't throw us out. We barely got to tell the one in charge of the evening meal where we came from before she instructed the girl next to her, Alice, to get us soup bowls, spoons and dry clothes. We, of course, expressed our gratitude for her kindness, telling her that she wouldn't regret it, to which she replied that *she* wouldn't, but we probably would. She then filled our bowls to the rim, gave us two slices of bread twice as stale, and showed us to our bunks.

They were not upstairs and not together. Mine was in the middle of the Block, on the outside, Eva's almost all the way in front. I had only one neighbor, Eva had two. We were too exhausted to do much looking around. I ate while half asleep, undressed with my eyes closed and was fast asleep before lights out.

The next morning my clothes were gone! Not only the wet ones but the dry ones, too. So were my shoes. I was told that I was lucky to still have my panties and that I would be wise to glue them on or else I would find them missing. One of the girls wanted to draw me a picture of my clothes, so I at least would have a momento. I soon discovered that they served up these little surprises here every morning, instead of breakfast.

I also found out that mornings here were not being wasted on assembly nonsense like in the rest of the camp. Here it meant: Let's bring out the crazies, let's have some fun.

They gathered every dawn after sunrise whether or not the sun rose, whether the ground was full of puddles and mud or snow. They came in full uniform, troop leaders with their shiny medals and buttons and their pompous grins. They came to watch a play about madness by those who had gone mad . . .

The program never changed, nor did the players. It was the same every day. It had to be because that was part of the plot. It didn't change and it didn't end. It took place outside, and the first ones out were always the blind runners who were neither blind nor could they run: they were blindfolded so they could not see and their feet were tied together so they could not run. It was the Nazis' favorite part watching them hop-hop-hop along. Watching them smash into each other, fall, and try to get up again. Winning the race, that's what it was all about. Making it to the farthest corner of the wall without touching the wall. The winner would get the biggest sausage in Germany . . . with sauerkraut! Nobody won — nobody could have. The moment someone, miraculously, did break loose and get halfway, a Nazi would stretch out his leg and trip her.

Next came the wrestlers. Kicking and punching was not only permitted but highly recommended. Screaming, too, the louder the better. Each one screamed when they got hurt, and they had to scream when they hurt the other. Cheered on by those who had put them there, it was not wrestling but a bloody mess. Every morning blood gushed from their mouths and noses, every morning they punched each other silly all over again. The one who walked away whole would get the biggest sausage in Germany . . . with sauerkraut. Nobody won. Nobody walked away.

These women reduced to the level of sideshow freaks had lost more than their families and possessions. They had lost their minds, here in Ravensbrück. Before they came, they were fine. Who knows what they saw and had to endure that caused their mind switch to turn off completely?

The show had two solo acts. One was the Stripper, the other Cinderella. That's what they were called: the Stripper and Cinderella. The Stripper was a thief, and a very good one at that. She stripped off the clothes she'd stolen the previous night from her fellow inmates. She did so because she was told by those sadistic Third Reich imbeciles, roaring with laughter, that she could keep all of the clothes and wear them one on top of the other — as long as there were six of each. Of course she had to show them: they wanted proof every morning, again and again; and so, looking like a blown-up balloon ready to burst, she stripped down. Then, naked and shivering, she stood in the raw morning glare while the pleasure boys kept poking her, accompanied by lewd remarks, never failing to remind her that tomorrow she just had to do better.

She was from Poland, this thieving lunatic, and she had the bunk next to mine. Well, at least I knew what had happened to my clothes — the wet and the dry ones.

Cinderella, I was told, was from somewhere outside Warsaw. She wasn't cunning like the Stripper, but sweet, shy, polite, a mere child. She — Teresa was her name — spent her days walking up and down the aisles in the Block, asking everyone for a pair of shoes. Shoes that fit. "They said that if I have nice shoes, I can go home," she told everyone endlessly. "Please, won't you let me have your shoes so I can walk home? They won't let me go without them. Please!"

Teresa and her shoes were the finale for the morning's entertainment: Walking all the way back to Poland. Every morning, she showed them another pair, walked in them whether they fit or not. Whether the shoes fell off her poor little feet or pinched her, the Nazis made her walk, often for hours because Poland is very far away and she better make sure that they are right. "Wrong again," she is told no matter what she wears. "Strong shoes, Cinderella, strong and pretty! Pretty shoes for a pretty girl! Got to try again, try harder."

Alice, the hospitable girl from the evening before, educated us about the other side of the Block, named the *StrafBlock* — punishment or Penalty Block. There, the prisoners are all either unlucky lesbians, unlucky thieves, or both. In any case, unlucky because they've gotten caught. Since there wouldn't have been any place for us anyhow, we didn't need to worry which side would have been better. Just as well, one problem less.

Eva's bunk, so Alice felt compelled to reveal, had just been vacated and could possibly still be warm. Alice maintained that its occupant would still be there if she hadn't refused to walk on her hands and knees as the guards had ordered her to do. They furthermore wanted the former occupant to bark and growl like a mad dog, which she also refused. Instead, she bit one of them on his right cheek. So they took her out into the woods and shot her dead, like a mad dog.

After that shocking report we left the Block for a while and went to see Fredericke to let her know our whereabouts. More important still, we badly needed the miracle salve for Eva's badly bruised back and the lesions on my feet, which were increasingly getting worse — without going anywhere near the hospital.

The last twenty-four hours had been so erratic that I did not see the results of Eva's beating, nor hear her account of it, till later that morning. What agonizing pain she must have endured! They had stripped her naked, tied her with leather straps facedown to a table, and savagely beaten her twenty-five times with a thick pigskin whip. Very slowly, very hard. Even more incredible, they examined her first. Checked her heart, her blood pressure, everything. Probably making sure she didn't drop dead before their eyes. That worthy task was the responsibility of Dr. Gebhart. He had decided how much the accused could take and it was he who was present from start to finish. There also were witnesses. Two Gestapo gents, a female guard and, of course, the lasher himself.

My breast lesions had wondrously healed by themselves, leaving me with one bad left foot and an even worse left lower calf to worry about. The sore on my calf had grown and grown and become an ugly, badly infected, very painful deep hole. It had been there for a very long time; while we were at Siemens, it had been treated by Eva with stolen dirty and oily machine rags — there were no clean ones. There probably were better treatments, none though had been available to us. Most likely they still weren't available to us; nevertheless, we had to try, without coming within sight or sound of the hospital.

We found Fredericke sitting behind her desk, looking flabbergasted and rattled. She was speechless, at least for some very puzzling moments. Then she got up, paced a few times, faced us, stopped, and barely breathing, whispered, "Roosevelt died."

My heart stopped. Eva's response was a piercing, sirenlike sounding "No!" She wasn't stunned or upset, she was angry! Eva did not believe Fredericke, nor would she have believed the gods themselves if they had told her. I didn't believe her, either. It was too impossible, too unexpected. We never even considered the possibility. It just couldn't be — not Roosevelt! Not the greatest president of the greatest country on earth! How could the war be ending if he was dead? How could there be an Allied victory if he was dead and how could we now thank him for wanting to save us? Didn't he know how much we counted on him? Not only we, the Jews, but the downtrodden, the downhearted everywhere.

Before we left Fredericke, we told her that that the only place they would let us stay was the crazy Block, to which she responded, "You must be nuts!"

She then advised us to be extra careful because someone might think it a good idea to torch it all. When we asked whether that someone could be a crazy prisoner or a crazy German, she thought for a while and then said, "Probably both!" After that cheerful comment, figuring that we had had enough upsetting news for one morning, we got out of there and went to look for Gemma Glück.

We found her at the same place we had left her the day before, with her jacket still intact and no bullies nearby. We didn't have to be the bearer of bad news. She knew already. Someone from the camp command had told her last night, and, yes, it was true. Franklin D. Roosevelt died on April 12, 1945, and on that day the world lost a great leader.

Gemma Glück was inconsolable. She had known him personally, thus to her his untimely death was especially tragic. Feeling as bad as we did ourselves, we didn't do too well comforting her.

With heavy hearts, we returned to our block. There we sat and brooded. We hadn't gotten any medication, hadn't even asked Fredericke's help in getting us some, hadn't done anything except think about Roosevelt and the possible consequences his untimely death might have.

Gemma and I became very good friends. I really liked her. She was so sweet, so vulnerable, so motherly, and yet it was Eva and I who looked out for her. She wasn't very strong and she wasn't very prison-wise, and she and I both knew she couldn't possibly hold out for too long a time. But that we never talked about. Once she showed me a picture of her twin brother she kept hidden in the pocket of her jacket. I remember staring at it and staring at it because I just couldn't believe how very much alike they looked. Short and chubby, with dark eyes and complexion, they made me think of two sweet milk chocolate puddings. I asked her whether the officials knew who her brother was, because if so, they surely would want her to stay in good health so they could exchange her for one of theirs. She said she hadn't told anyone, nor did she know what they knew. What was very clear to me was that my new friend was as afraid of them finding out as she was of them not finding out. Either way, she had been hoping for her American brothers to liberate her.

Twelve more days passed. Twelve more days of dawn entertainment for the Hitler boys with the runners and the wrestlers, the Stripper, and little Cinderella still looking for the right shoes to walk home in. Twelve more nights of getting our clothes swiped, of strange-sounding moans and laments breaking an uneasy silence and of dreaming, while wide awake, that the Russians were really coming, that it was all over and that we all, with or without shoes, were going home.

On the twenty-fourth morning of our stay in this walled-in block with its pathetic, deranged inmates, a messenger from Fredericke's office brought a note telling us to "get out of there at once and stay out." We didn't need to read it twice. Without completing our daily search for the Stripper's hiding place — she never hid the clothes in the same place twice — we left immediately.

By now the camp streets were so crowded that one could hardly move ahead without someone obstructing the way. Newcomers, arriving daily by the truckload, were unloaded and then left in the middle of the camp without a place to rest or lay their weary heads. Nobody knew how many had come. Nobody knew or cared how many there were altogether. The talk was anything from 80,000 to 100,000 — in a place with room for only 25,000.

Whenever we'd tried to talk to Fredericke about the increasingly appalling conditions, she'd shrug her shoulders and say, "What can I do about it?" Lately, though, they handled the newcomers in a different way. They still brought them in by truck or on foot, still unloaded them, but then just lined them up again and marched them out of the camp into the woods where they shot them, hundreds and hundreds at a time.

"There just wasn't any place for them," an apologetic guard said.

Fredericke might not have known what to do about a lot of things, but she also knew about a lot of things. Working in the front office, especially toward the end, gave her access to invaluable information which she, being something of a blabbermouth, gladly shared with us and others. I shudder to think what might have happened if Fredericke had not sent that note. For on that morning the runners and the wrestlers, the Stripper, and little Cinderella, wearing a brand-new pair of shiny red pumps to walk home in, as well as all the other pitiful souls from our block were taken for a springtime picnic into the pretty forest. They were laughing, singing, waving.

They were never seen again . . . it wasn't a picnic.

PART FOUR

Twenty Kilometers to Lübeck

⌐ TWENTY

THE NEWS THAT BROKE those next few days swept through the camp in such rapid succession that we could barely keep up with it. While Eva and I were still frantically trying to find a place, unfortunately with zero success, the reports that "The Russians are coming! The Russians are coming!" were now being treated as fact. The only one not pleased about it was Fredericke, who saw the liberation of Ravensbrück not as the end of a horrible time but as just one more disaster waiting to happen. She was certain that when the time came, a legion of uncontrollable women would storm the gate just as the Russian military troops were charging in. Predicting the worst chaos ever, she had already figured out that with a hundred thousand women running amok, at least half of them were going to get trampled to death.

Fredericke actually thought of exchanging uniforms with some low-ranking guard, walking out of here all the way back to Berlin. That's where she came from. Despite the round-the-clock bombing of Hitler's favorite city, with mountains of rubble probably all that was left, she still thought it safer than the camp.

That same morning, I found myself being escorted by a new male guard to a stone building that I had never seen before, situated behind the bunker. Like a good little prisoner, I followed the staid guard up the three flights of stairs, down a long hallway, straight into an office, without even wondering why. The man behind the desk was jovial-looking, and better yet, he was not wearing the hated black Nazi uniform. Still, he did have his share of pretty-colored ribbons on his chest, with just one lonely medal and enough papers spread out all around to make him look important in a congenial sort of way. In his right hand he held a large manila envelope. It was larger than an eight by ten.

He motioned for me to come closer, smiled, and told me that he had wonderful news for me. With this amazing statement, he handed the envelope to me, saying that, coming direct from Berlin, it was now official. Not really expecting a response, yet sounding every bit as agreeable as he looked, he continued his little speech with, "We know that these documents are authentic, we checked. Take them and don't let them out of your sight. They may still save your life."

He chuckled, leaned forward, and with the kind of familiarity usually reserved for intimate friends, chortled, "Came through for you, did he now, your old man, your father? Did the right thing, didn't he? Born out of wedlock, what?" Then, with his mouth practically in my ear, he whispered, "Never you mind, still better than being born a Jew."

There wasn't an ounce of saliva left in my mouth. I couldn't even swallow. My tongue, suddenly strangely attracted to the roof of my mouth, stuck to it like glue, making any reaction or reply on my part impossible. Luckily the guard, witness to this curious encounter, saved the situation. *"Komm,"* he said with great astuteness, while firmly taking my arm and leading me out.

Once alone, I opened the envelope and took the documents out. There it was, all of it, the original papers. They had traveled from Hungary through Germany to Holland, then followed me first from Holland, hand-carried by my intrepid friend Margit, to Malin, Belgium; Auschwitz, Poland; and finally Ravensbrück, Germany. They had sure gotten around. I had the original in original Hungarian, the original translated into German, the stamp of the Hungarian king's notary, the swastika stamp with the falcon insignia, the who, what, when and where, all delivered to me.

Only, two years too late. I never did let it get out of my sight, and it is with me now, too many other wars later. What was good about all that? I didn't have to bother learning his name: Karl Hagymasi.

Eva almost fell backwards when I showed her the documents and told her what had transpired. Her mouth stood open for a long time and then, with nothing better to do, she started to laugh. The irony of this whim of fate reached its climax when, for the first time ever, American Red Cross pack-ages were let into the camp and distributed among the Jews. Jews only.

Thanks to my new status (Aryan fathers bought or real were not part of the deal), I got nothing, and Eva stopped laughing when she got nothing too. There wasn't enough to go around, they said. What else there wasn't enough of to go around were Jews. Live ones! President Roosevelt had de-manded an accounting of how many were left, and that was what the mur-derous master race, no longer cocky or victorious, had a hell of a time trying to come up with. Why now, with Roosevelt already dead, or why at all?

Imagine that — Jews, indispensable! Alive and kicking, however barely, they suddenly mattered. Those damned to get shot merely a sigh ago were now getting fed and treated humanely. They were given showers, fresh clothing and the closest to a real bed we here had seen in years. I bet some of them even thought they had died and gone to heaven.

Who benefited from this last, frenzied effort to tip the scale just before Judgment Day? Only the new arrivals. Not Eva. Not I . . .

Some of the rats were leaving the sinking ship and running away. They were taking whatever they could lay their thieving hands on. Except their swastika and uniform — those they left behind. As a keepsake and special souvenir, several of the female guards helped themselves to our attractive prison clothes, put them on and left them on. It suited them, as if the uni-forms were meant for them.

One who didn't run, hide or pretend to be one of us was a young female guard who, instead of leaving her post like those other Fraüleins, stayed, not to play watchdog but to help. She was tireless, dedicated and remarkably un-affected by the fact that her glory days were all but over with. "Time to pay the piper," she said, when asked why stick around when she could play it safe like the rest of them.

I remember her not because she took Eva and me to a block with real bunks and bedding (formerly used only by guards) and let us stay there. Not because she spent hours trying to treat my worsening leg — regrettably still without any medication — nor for the food she stole for us. I remem-ber her because whatever her name and wherever she came from, among all those Nazi bitches I'd met in those never to be forgotten hellish years, she was the only one ready, in her words, "to pay for her sins." The only one! Sometimes, while watching her going about her business, I got the feeling that she did not look for salvation, only retribution. Perhaps retribution *was* her salvation. She was so unlike the others. Withdrawn and strange and yet so easy to talk to.

"How did you get to become one of them?" I asked without the slightest fear of reprimand. She managed a pensive smile on her pleasant, otherwise expressionless face. Then a few lines showed on her forehead, faint lines as though they had been especially penciled in to give her face more character and distinction. She thought a while, letting her pale blue eyes wander away from where the two of us were standing. Finally, with neither sadness nor fabricated remorse in her throaty voice, she said, "I don't know."

I had just finished making up my bunk when she suddenly reached for me. Clutching my hand, she cried out, "You must never forgive me! You must never forgive Germany, nor those who stood idly by and let it happen! You must tell the world, everyone must know what we have done. You must!"

Imprisoned by her own conscience, she was a captive already. Poor Fraülein. She'll find no solace — not in her future, not in her past. I couldn't have known then when my nightmares would end; I did know though that hers, barely beginning, would last forever.

Gemma Glück was gone! She'd disappeared in the middle of the night. According to Fredericke, they'd shipped her off to God only knows where for safety reasons. They planned to trade her for a handful of their butchers. I wasn't really all that surprised. As Fiorella LaGuardia's twin sister, my dear friend and camp mama had become a valuable bargaining chip.

IT WAS THE FOURTH TIME that the same announcement had come over the loudspeaker. The fourth time that I had heard it and the fourth time that I had failed to understand it. The important part, anyway. Too much else was going on. Too many other deafening noises, unrivaled commotion and ear-splitting shouts kept drowning the announcement out. I did hear the words "French, Dutch and Belgian" repeated over and over, but not what they meant. I couldn't even figure out whether it was good for the French, Dutch and Belgians or not.

Eva, with no connection to these countries, did a very sensible thing. She didn't listen at all. She didn't, Fredericke didn't, our guard, *Dass gute Fraülein,* the good miss, didn't. Only Renie, a bouncy, all-ears Dutch girl, did. In fact, Renie had listened to it all along from when it was merely a rumor. Though I didn't know Renie, she knew me from the good old days in my theater, a leftover fan.

I had decided to forget the entire loudspeaker affair and return with Eva to our block when Renie came up from behind, hollering, "You're going the wrong way! It's over there!" With this, ignoring Eva completely, she swung me around and insisted that I follow her. Noticing my hesitation and confusion, nevertheless bouncing around as though she was a ball, Renie yelled: "Don't you understand? You can get out of here! Now! You're Dutch! If not, pretend. You're an actress — you know how!"

With, "I'll explain later," ready to run a hundred-mile race and win it, she pulled me along, with Eva not far behind, and did not stop until we had reached the other side of the *Lager Platz*. We weren't the first ones there. Not the first ones and not the only ones.

They had come by the hundreds. Just standing around talking. Talking French, Dutch, Belgian-French, or Flemish — talking, talking to their hearts' content. Not a single one spoke a single word of German.

Most of them already knew what this gathering of foreigners was all about. Those who didn't found out the same way I did: someone finally told them. Eva and I didn't know because when these rumors began to surface, we were too busy staying alive, first in the bunker and then in the loony bin.

What should one call a truly unbelievable rumor that one day does come true? Truly unbelievable, that's what! And what should one call the one who made it come true? *Bernadotte: Count Folke Bernadotte!* A good name to remember, a good man never to forget. A Swede from a neutral country, a Swede who cared, from a country that cared. Not just a rich, influential count, not just an internationalist and nephew of King Gustave V, Sweden's reigning monarch, but a man with a mission. In the early days of the war, it was he who arranged the evacuation of all Scandinavians from detention centers and other such unpleasant places, and it was he who conveyed a peace offer to Heinrich Himmler from Britain and the United States.

None of that, though, would have done us any good if it hadn't been for his strong involvement and the important role he played in the Swedish Red Cross. While procuring freedom for his own people, he wanted to free also every imprisoned French, Dutch and Belgian person. That deal was to be carried out in the form of an exchange. Us for German prisoners. Unfortunately, he did not succeed. Not then. No matter how apparent the Third Reich's defeat was to the rest of the world, Himmler was not yet ready to concede. Thus, no trade. Count Bernadotte did not give up. He kept on negotiating behind whosoever's doors until finally Hilter and Himmler, with no cards left to play, agreed.

The magic number? Seven hundred! That's how many the Swedish Red Cross were going to take out first. Seven hundred women today, seven hundred tomorrow, and after that, many more seven hundreds until the last ones were out. They'll be taking us to Sweden, so goes the word, Eva's Sweden where her friends — and freedom — live. It was indeed a miracle, and not just a little one, either.

They did not call up names alphabetically, nor did they care how many of each nationality. It was strictly on a first-come, first-go basis. All one needed was some outrageous pretext to get from the rear of the crowd to the front. No one wanted to be left behind. No one wanted to wait anymore, not even until tomorrow.

The wooden tables with the folding chairs reminded me of Malin. The German officers sitting on the chairs reminded me of Malin. It reminded me of the day they packed us into boxcars and shipped us off to the hell of Auschwitz.

With much help from bouncy Renie and a great deal of chutzpah from Eva and myself, we got a pretty good place right in the middle of the line. While waiting, it occurred to me that I wasn't really Dutch and that speaking it and having lived there might not be enough. However, it also occurred to me the chance of anyone here possessing an actual birth certificate was not only unlikely but quite impossible. Thus, I convinced myself that I actually need not worry about a thing, not for myself. As for Eva, that was a whole different matter. Czech accents, like Hungarian, sift through, no matter what language Czechs or Hungarians speak, and even the dumbest German can pick up on it.

While drumming my Amsterdam address into Eva's head and reminding her that we were cousins, I once more took advantage of Renie's compulsion to help me by borrowing her headscarf, which I quickly tied around Eva's neck. Using laryngitis as the best possible excuse to keep her from talking and them from asking questions, we slowly kept moving closer and closer to the dreaded wooden tables.

They, just like the ones in Malin, never looked up from their list. They asked my nationality (Dutch, of course), the city I'd lived in and the street address. That was it! Considering what was at stake, I found them treating the importance of such an event awfully mechanically. But thanks to their lack of interest, I got Eva past them by quickly pointing at her throat while telling them without a breath in between that she had laryngitis, was family, and that we lived together.

We had gotten through! It was almost scary how easy it was. They either believed what we had told them, or didn't care. Could be that all they had to make sure of was that there were seven hundred of us. Not one more, not one less. Whatever the real reason, on that day the word "Next" had a special glorious ring to it.

It was only a short walk on an uphill winding road that took us from our camp to another much smaller one. I never even knew that there was one up there. We soon learned that we really weren't meant to stop there. What we were meant to do was leave Ravensbrück and wait for the comfortable, brand-new Swedish Red Cross buses — that's what we were told — outside the gate of Ravensbrück. We were also told we'd be leaving as soon as the buses got here, which would be any moment. Not so! After seconds had turned into minutes and minutes into hours, and there still was no sign of them, they marched us up to this totally deserted, ghostlike camp. There, they took us to the last block at the far end of the camp, told us to go in, to relax — and wait.

We did go in and we did wait, none of us though could relax. A thousand questions, with not a single answer, kept swarming like countless flocks of nervous, twittering birds, back and forth, round and round the Block. The only one not saying a word was Eva. Afraid she might be found out by someone whose sister or friend had to stay behind because she'd stolen their place, she kept her neckscarf on and her mouth shut. The guards who'd come with us left. They went back down again assuring us that we, in fact, were as good as free.

As good as — And free to do what? — Free to go where? — It wasn't the way free was supposed to be.

After waiting had become something the more restless among us could no longer bear, a handful of the as-good-as-free ones, with Renie in the lead and Eva and me tagging along, went to have ourselves a good look around. Not much to see though. A miniature copy of what was down below, nothing that stuck in one's mind except that whatever was left behind in the empty blocks was men's stuff. Men's torn prison shirts and trousers, men's bandanas and an occasional piece of an American Red Cross carton still smelling of chocolate and soap. And in the empty guardhouse by the entrance, a calendar full of naked girl pictures.

A concentration camp for men, that's what this place was. And where were they, the men? Had they been let go, let go home or let go just as far as the next forest? Lying there still in the melting, blood-drenched snow next to pansies like those I'd once found in the so long ago forest of my childhood with Papa. Blood-soaked earth, blood-soaked flowers; what a way to welcome freedom.

Around noon, they brought us soup and the same stale bread we had had before we had become "as good as free."

The day dragged on. The tension in the Block went from hardly bearable to completely unbearable. Rampant speculations spawning suspicions of the wildest sort made trying to keep hope alive a travesty. It was this sitting on the edge of a communal nervous breakdown which made us leave the Block again, determined to wait it out somewhere else.

We had walked the length of the camp several times when we were joined, first, by a small group of men in ill-fitting shabby civilian clothes, and later, by men walking alone. They all were prisoners of other concentration camps — camps about to be liberated, camps deserted by their captors, camps these men had fled before their send-off into the next world. Most of them were Czechs or Poles, and every one of them was attempting to get home. They did not know which direction to go or how far. All they knew and cared about was that they, at last, were free! They would fight forever to stay free, fight to live and die free. They were hungry, cold and exhausted, but their spirits weren't broken. One of them kept asking if we knew his wife. He thought that she too had been sent to Auschwitz. Had we seen her? Had we seen the pretty brunette with the pretty chestnut hair and the irresistible smile? He had been to many camps already looking for her and would go on looking.

I kept trying to remember did I ever see anybody smile in Auschwitz.

The man who walked into the camp long after the others had moved on would have much preferred not to be seen by anyone. If he could have made himself invisible, he would have done it. He later admitted he made it a point to stay out of sight. He'd been on the road longer than those who'd been through here before, had come much farther, and only he knew how much farther he still had to go. Young, muscular, cockier than a prize rooster, he did not wish to call to mind where he had been, nor where his real home was or what he'd suffered and lost. "What's past is past," he'd say, shrugging off whatever memories had traveled with him. "It's all about to-morrow, not about yesterday." His right hand was buried in the pocket of, I am certain, someone else's coat. After several deliberating minutes, he took out his hand, and grinning sheepishly, showed us the largest, brightest dia-mond I had ever seen. It nearly covered the palm of his hand. He showed us what he had not shown to anyone before: his rich future, his stolen dia-mond. Except he didn't think of it as such. He thought of it as just a little compensation, a payback for what they owed him. He swore he'd get the rest of these plundered spoils of war later on because he knew where those Nazi *Dummkopfs* had hidden it. "I'll be rich!" he kept telling us, over and over. "I'll be the richest man around!"

We hadn't bothered about the Block close to the guardhouse when we had first looked around the camp because of the bolted windows, nailed shut with wooden boards. The likelihood of anybody still being in there had never occurred to us. Yet, there they were: two Czech men. Not forgotten or left behind, but in charge of whatever was now happening or was still going to happen. They showed up only seconds after "the richest man around" had put his precious booty, wrapped in a torn hankerchief, back into his pocket. He never took it out again, nor the hand which held it. I'm certain he would have had his hand cut off before he would have let it become separated from that diamond. Not eager to make new acquaintances or answer questions, the confident stranger left. He'd wait for peace in a less in-habited place.

The two Czechs, Sascha and Daniel, were thrilled to meet a couple of females who, so they jokingly said, from not too close a distance actually resembled real girls. Doubly thrilled when they found out that Eva was also Czech, they at once invited us to spend the evening with them in their "private" quarters. They had been ordered to volunteer to stay behind to look after the sick who were also forced to stay behind. The irony was that these prisoners had all been well until the day the Red Cross packages from America arrived. Starved, the men didn't ration the food but gulped everything down at once. Too much too soon; or rather, not soon enough. The tragic result: diarrhea, dysentery. What a way to embrace the end. What a way to greet a new beginning. What a price to pay for a stick of butter.

While Eva enthusiastically accepted their invitation, I, still counting on being far away by then, told them, "Thank you, but we won't be here anymore." They said they hoped that I was right, but just in case I wasn't, to come anyway, and most important, to make it after dark and not to tell anyone. "We'll celebrate," they whispered, even though there was no one around, making the invitation sound very secretive and mysterious. We chatted some more, or rather, Eva did, forgetting all about her laryngitis, glad she could speak again, especially in her mother tongue.

I didn't want to hear it — none of us did. We didn't want to, but we heard it anyway: the Swedish Red Cross was nowhere about. "Tomorrow," they told us. "Most likely they will show up tomorrow." And what about tonight?

"Tonight," they said, "you'll stay here. Bundle up and go to sleep. We'll let you know when they come."

If strangling the one who'd brought us the upsetting news had been a solution, we would have done so, unanimously.

Sascha and Daniel weren't a bit sorry that we hadn't left. With only the sick men for company, they too were in the market for a little cheering up. They had turned the block with the bolted windows, the former medical quarters, into rooms for themselves. Thanks to their own ingenuity and the generous supplies the Nazis had left behind, their quarters were pleasant, well stocked and very private. The first thing they did was offer us a drink, a very large drink. A whole water glass full of something colorless and also tasteless. I drank it as if it were water. So did Eva. I had no reaction to it at all, not even after the third glass. Remembering my normal embarrassing inability to drink more than a couple of anything ever, this inability to feel different, or at least to feel something, was even more amazing to me than the bizarre circumstances of this, our first date. We had nibbled on some cheese crackers which had made the long journey all the way from America pretty well, but otherwise, keeping in mind those poor wretched men and the reason for their dysentery, we ate nothing.

Fifty toasts and five glasses of this tasteless stuff later, a very sober German guard (he and I were the only sober ones) rushed in, informing us in an alarmed voice that "Control" was on its way. Eva, obviously less immune to the one hundred percent alcoholic content of this colorless stuff than I, greeted the German guard with: "Heil Hitler! Let's have a drink," while Sasha and Daniel kept yelling at the frightened guard, "Stall them a couple of minutes or you'll never get booze from us again."

Eva and her two countrymen had been dancing just before the guard barged in. They'd been dancing, having fun, not too staid, though — and were actually quite drunk.

The word "Control" worked better than an icy-cold shower. It still was one of the most sobering words in whatever language was being spoken. One of the two grabbed Eva, the other me, and before another minute had fled, the pleasant room, the pleasant company and the empty glasses were already a thing of the past. Out of one door, down a short dark corridor, and into another, we went. I found myself being picked up by either Sascha or Daniel and lifted onto what could have been a surgeon's operating table or a steel slab. Just before he covered me with what felt like a sheet, my host for the evening whispered, "Don't make a sound, don't move, don't breathe," and left.

I realized instantly that Eva wasn't with me and, even more disturbing, that I was not alone in this freezing dark. My instincts told me that there were others in here too, others not making a sound, not moving and not breathing. At that moment I really wished that I could have gotten drunk, drunk enough to pass out so I wouldn't ever have to find out what was going on. What almost did make me stop breathing was this distinct awareness of another body next to mine. It was barely seconds later when the distressing sensation of physical contact with a silent, non-moving, non-breathing, naked male, sharing the same sheet with me, nearly stopped my heart. A dead man — a corpse! Stone-dead and as cold as the table we were laid on. I was in a morgue.

Shortly after I had figured out where I was, the door opened. There were footsteps, then I saw a stream of light sweep over the sheet, while at the same time I heard brisk male voices demanding to know who was in there. The two Czechs answered at once, "Corpses." Then casually, "They're all dead. We're just waiting for someone to tell us what to do with them."

"Get rid of them," one of the Germans calmly said. And then they were gone. They never came all the way in, but stood by the door talking. It was nearly daylight when Sascha, more sober than he had ever been in his life, finally came for me. I shall never quite know how I managed to survive the night in the morgue, nor how I managed to get back to the Block. Eva had just gotten there herself. She had been in another room, also a morgue, but had had her own table, and slept through it all. "Go, sleep it off," Daniel had told her. "I promise you won't be disturbed." And whether or not they had looked in on her too, she remembered nothing!

As for the Germans responsible for that unforgettable night, they never really came to check on anyone, not on the living or the dead. They had come because some loudmouth told them there was booze to be had. And so they had it. All of it! Drank till the last drop had been drunk, until they too were good and drunk.

⸎

WE STOOD OUTSIDE THE GATE of Ravensbrück, all seven hundred of us. At least we had made it that far. I had hardly had time to slip back into the Block and think about whether or not I should ever tell anyone about my weird and ghoulish night, when the guards came and marched us back down again. And there I was less than a couple of weeks short of the two years I had left Amsterdam. It was spring and the promise of freedom was in the air then. It was spring and the promise of freedom was in the air now.

Around me the women were indulging in never-ending chatter. They sounded like flocks of geese at a family reunion. A happy reunion. They were talking about old memories and new hopes, about yesterday's perils and tomorrow's bliss. They were talking about everything they hadn't dared talk about before.

While they were gabbing, I kept my eyes fixed on the road our rescuers had to be coming on. All morning I stood there watching, waiting. I kept my eyes fixed on the road until late afternoon. By then, the chatter of my comrades had subsided. Restless and nervous, they kept walking about. Those Swedes and their Red Cross did take their good time getting to us, and waiting had become a real problem for all of us. I had to remind myself that at least this time we were waiting for something worth waiting for. Besides, what else could we do? One thing we all had agreed on was that we would not go back. Not into the jammed women's camp, not into the empty men's camp. No matter what, we would stay outside. Stay till they came for us.

The last light of day brought them to us. Ten old trucks driven by ten very tired men. Good thing that we were sapped out too by then; otherwise we might have incapacitated our rescuers with all that unreleased frustration and stored-up desire to show our gratitude. Even so, the women stormed the buses, surrounding the drivers and those in charge like they had been planning an attack, not a welcome. It nearly turned into a stampede. Eva and I did not join the charge. Eva, because we still thought it best to avoid a run-in with some of the others, and I because my wooden workmman's shoes, two sizes too large and weighing me down, made it impossible for me to keep up. So, we observed the frenzy from the sideline, at the edge of the road, itching just the same to get close to one of them.

"Does anyone here speak English?" I had seen his O.D. green bill cap before I'd heard him speak. Not him, just his cap. Encircled by too many excited women, although much taller than any of them, he was having trouble escaping the outpouring of gratitude. Meanwhile, aghast and totally astounded, I kept rubbing my eyes, wanting to make sure that they weren't deceiving me. They were not!

No matter how far-fetched, considering the date and the place, what I had seen and recognized was an American. In uniform — an American soldier!

Right here outside a German concentration camp, almost two weeks before the war would officially be over, with German guards still guarding us, with bombing and fighting still going strong and the blaring of "Sieg Heil!" not yet snuffed out, the mere sight of a bit of America made me want to shout. I wanted to, but thought better of it.

Instead, after he had asked again and no one had answered, I raised my hand and called out, "I do, I speak English!"

That's when the circle around him parted and the women let him through. He was gorgeous! Tanned, broad-shouldered, handsome, with a strong, determined face but unable to conceal his dismay over our wretched appearance. We were the first women from concentration camps he had seen.

His name was John D. Jackson, of Bossier City, Louisiana. He was the first American man I had ever met and the only hero I have ever known. Without him, this book could never have been written. Without him, the true account, and all that needed to be said, could never have been told. Without him, I now could not be living the rest of my life, for without him, I wouldn't be alive.

John asked me to tell the others that there was no time to lose. The situation was not very good. It had taken them thirty-six hours to get through to us. Most bridges had been blown up, and there were only a few passable roads left to travel on. Our rescuers did not dare to rest. We then were introduced to the Swedish Red Cross officer in charge and his assistant. Both were young, blond, dedicated, very kind and absolutely set on getting us out. The word was that we had to leave at once. No time for questions and answers, no time for who was going to be on which truck. It was, "Hurry! Go, go, go!"

First stop: Lübeck. We were to rest there for a night and then proceed to Denmark, before reaching our ultimate destination, Sweden. Lübeck, a German town close to the Danish border, was an open city. Under international law, any city undefended against enemy capture is considered an open city, gaining immunity from bombardments and attacks.

There were about seventy of us in each of the ten trucks. The two Swedish officers and those who were ill sat next to the drivers; the others in the back of the truck. The heavy canvas roofs of our vehicles, covered with large red crosses, were easily visible from the air and ground. With only a shimmer of daylight remaining, we started rolling, moving out. Away from Ravensbrück, away from all that we had had to endure, away from that damnable pit. I watched the gate until it disappeared completely, swallowed up by the night or, perhaps, swallowed by fiery dragon tongues like those in Auschwitz which had swallowed the children of Warsaw.

We had driven for approximately two hours when out of nowhere German tanks, jeeps and foot soldiers appeared. Their convoy, covered with more red crosses than we had, cut in between us hoping to realize safe-conduct for their retreat, zigzagging all over the place. We naturally tried to shake them, but they were obviously waiting for us. When we couldn't get rid of them, we left the road, turned into a thick forest, and stopped. There, an angry and worried Swedish officer told us that we would have to spend the night in the woods and to find ourselves a place to rest. It was his decision, but not according to plan. Our leader's calculation was that the "German bastards" couldn't afford to hang around, that they had to keep on moving. Thus, staying here was our best chance to lose them. And lose them we must.

It was no secret that the Red Cross transports were not to be attacked. Nor was it a secret that the Geneva Convention, signed in 1864, established a code for the protection of the sick and wounded, and prisoners, during wartime. In other words, no bombing, no fighting, no interference in any way, whether en route or stationary. How did they know, then? How did the German military know where we came from, where we were going and which roads we'd be traveling and how? Our camp commander had told them! He'd broadcast it. Told everyone who wanted to listen, and the German military sure listened. Ironically, it wasn't even the camp commander's fault. He only did what he was supposed to do — that is, make the announcement of our departure over the radio. "*Achtung! Achtung!* Seven hundred female prisoners are now leaving Ravensbrück. They are under the protection of the Swedish Red Cross and will be traveling on . . ." And he named the roads. Perhaps no announcement would have been better.

It was a very unusual night. Not bizarre like the previous one, just not quite real. I had found myself a place under a tree not too far from the road. Eva had settled down under another one and had instantly fallen asleep. Lucky her! The roar of not too distant fighting kept echoing all through the night, while next to me an American soldier broke down the barriers of war with words like "Home . . . United States . . . Freedom."

He talked to me about the war he had fought in Africa, his capture, and how through a prisoner-of-war exchange sponsored by Count Bernadotte, he came to be released. From then on he had driven for them, helping to keep the thin thread of humanity alive. He talked to me about his home, his mother, and how it was to live in America. He said that over there one did not need to register with the police, to ask for permission to do this or that, because one was free — really free. He also said that nearly everyone in the USA owned a car. Not just the very rich but everyone. He then asked about me, my home, my native country, how long I had been in the camps and why. He seemed eager to find out all about it and yet he never asked, "How bad was it really?" or "What did they do to you?" Maybe he sensed what I'd been through without quite comprehending it. Maybe the way I looked, we all looked, said it better, said it all.

It suddenly occurred to me that I hadn't seen myself in a mirror, or even seen one since my compact was stolen in Malin and Boden humiliated me with the flour. Worse yet, I hadn't even thought of it. There, in that German forest so close to the end of this colossal nightmare, spending the night with friend and enemy alike under a dark and sinister sky, I wished not for food or rest but to be beautiful again. Beautiful for him, this greathearted man.

We talked all night. With his arm around me and his heavy soldier's coat over my shoulder to keep me warm, I understood that whatever I looked like, it didn't matter. He didn't pity me. He only wanted me to feel his concern and to know that I was safe with him. With every passing minute, a long-forgotten need for closeness, to share with another human being all that had been locked away for such an endless, dreadful time, arose as from eternal sleep to claim its place once more. Awake, old faded memories gave way to brand-new wistful yearnings, to brand-new hopes and brand-new quests. The stranger at my side from oh so far away, in this oh so strange and starless night, had held my hand, had kept me safe, and, with each picture-painted word, had brought America to me.

John had been in it from the start. He'd seen a lot and grown up fast. He hated war and what it did to people, what they did to each other. This one, he said, had to be fought for the sake of all mankind. I never asked his rank. I did think though that he was much more than just an ordinary soldier. He was so wise, so fully in command, and, in the ways of many battle-scarred soldiers, already very old. He had met different people, among them lots of women, but no ladies, he contended, not until he met me. Nothing he said was trite or superficial; nor was his touch meant to make me feel uncomfortable or frighten me. He was caring, warm, strong and reassuring. A God-send and everything a hero should be.

Before continuing our journey at dawn, John asked me to forget about going to Sweden and to stay with him in Lübeck until the war was over, then go to the States with him. "Just a few more days," he kept saying. "Just a few more days."

Back on the trucks, a very tired but exuberant group was on its way again. Laughing, singing, joking, intensely aware that we were free at last, we turned each breath of this new freedom into a celebration of life. We certainly were the happiest convoy ever to travel through a war.

And then it happened: We drove straight through the last stronghold of the Germans. The road, well protected on either side by heavy woods, was very narrow. We did not see them until we were practically on top of them. High-ranking officers and generals were frantically waving at us, shouting for us to get out of the way, but it was too late. British planes, dropping bombs from a height of fifty meters, hit the target area at the precise moment we were coming through.

It was one big explosion. The earth trembled. I heard screams coming from the burning trucks, saw severed arms and legs separated from limp torsos tossed into the air like broken toys, landing on the ground and like one huge fantastic blanket covering the blood-drenched earth. The macabre sound of moaning women, buried beneath overturned vehicles with their wheels still spinning, was everywhere. Soldiers, drowning in their own river of blood, grotesquely clutched their rifles, while German generals kept on commanding: "Fire! Fire!"

I was thrown from my truck and landed about fifty feet away in a sand hole. I felt no pain. I have no recollection of how long I sat there before John found me. He looked awful! Black and dirty — like he had crawled out of a chimney. He wanted to know whether I was all right. It was a question, but it sounded like an order. I couldn't find my voice, and when it finally came out, it came out in a stutter, "Yes, I . . . think . . . so." Stuttering even more, I heard myself ask John what had happened and how many. He didn't know. "No one does yet!" he cried. He jerked me to my feet, his outstretched arm pointing toward the woods across the road. "Run! Run! I can't stay with you! I've got to find out who is left — I've got to help . . . Run!" With this he led me to the other side and left.

Because the immensity of the disaster had not yet penetrated, I continued wandering without any clear thought of where I was going or why. I was neither afraid nor hysterical. I felt absolutely nothing. Suspended, as though I no longer was part of anything, I kept on going with the lightness of air. Time stopped for me when the bombs dropped and didn't resume its timeless task of moving forward again until the first flash of reality returned.

I was sitting under a tree with my wounded leg stretched out, wondering why I had only one shoe. At that moment, that was all that concerned me. Recognition and recollection came slowly. While staring at the flow of ugly yellow fluid running from the wound down my leg, I wondered whether perhaps Eva could have my other shoe and where the dirty rag which had been tied around my wound could be. I also wondered where she was, why I hadn't missed her before, and when I had last seen her.

In retrospect, I'm positive that I did not believe I was still alive, at least not at first. Perhaps it was the total lack of discomfort or pain, and the light-headedness. Or else this most peculiar sense of being weightless, of almost floating like an illusionist's assistant through midair, made me think so. Strangest of all, I'm certain that it didn't worry me a bit. It was so easy to be dead. Much easier than being alive. I'm sure that while I thought of having died, I didn't fret for one brief moment about life or living. While still alive, though, I had spent a lot of time thinking about death and dying.

Consciousness gradually came back to me. My ears became aware of sounds like that of rustling leaves caught by the wind. My eyes began to see bushes move, twigs and branches swaying back and forth in a playful dance, and then the forest came alive.

Behind each tree and bush were German soldiers. A military unit of anti-aircraft ground troops, perfectly camouflaged to blend in with the colors of the forest, had taken up their positions there. And in the midst of them was I, a sitting duck in a shooting gallery! They must have been waiting for the next attack. With their weapons pointed upward, ready to shoot the British out of the sky, they paid no attention to me, or rather, never took their eyes off the for the moment silent heavens. It was too shocking a reality to come back to. The chances, increasing with each pounding heartbeat, of my now actually getting killed — whether from a friendly Allied bomb or a nervous, not so friendly German soldier — made my head spin. For a time I watched the swaying leaf-covered branches rising from their helmets dancing their dance of death, until I realized that it was solely up to me to get out of this forest of deception. After a muted "Please not now, not here, it just can't be," I crawled on my belly, inch by inch, out of the forest.

Back on the road, chaos awaited me. Rivers of blood, oceans of tears, burning tires, smoke-covered trees, and wherever I looked lifeless bodies with their dead, open eyes full of sand and dust. It was hell! Through the maze of confusion I started looking for Eva and John. I found him bent over his best friend, who was alive but blind. The German generals kept clicking their heels together, saluting our surviving GIS, and apologizing. "What a tragedy." They ordered their remaining troops to aid our wounded, clear the road and get the still usable trucks out of their ditches. Through all that upset, German civilians, who had fled their homes before the Russians could get to them, calmly walked over our dead, kicked and stepped on the wounded, stealing our American Red Cross packages and whatever else they could find.

A short while later, I saw Eva. She was having a wrestling match with a sniveling German Fraülein who'd stolen a food parcel. Eva was all right, or as all right as anyone after such an disaster could be.

Our medical supplies were destroyed, and among the Germans there was not one doctor, not even a medic. The Germans themselves had suffered se-vere losses. We were all trapped, and time was running out for all of us. We had to get out of there and we had to get help. The British planes were certain to return and attack this last strategic point again and again until there was no one left, not even a heel-clicking, saluting, "ever so sorry" German general.

We were only twenty kilometers from Lübeck. Doctors, supplies, transportation, and help were waiting for us there. Distressingly, we no longer had enough transportation. Eight of our trucks had been a total loss, and the other two — one of them John's — were in only fair operating condition. It made it impossible to get everyone out. Someone made the decision to leave our dead and badly wounded behind and to fill the trucks with only those still able to move. No time for grieving over those still left there, no time for promising those still alive that we'd send others back for them. It was now or never!

The drivers were yelling, "Let's get them in! Let's get them in!" Women rushing about like a herd of frightened beasts were piled into the trucks, while I, not too calm or collected myself, kept trying to understand the instructions John was calling out to me — something to do with telling the others that at the first noise of planes, they should jump and run for cover. I did my best to communicate it to them, though very few paid any attention.

Eva and I were the last ones on. There were too many of us on the truck. Overcrowded, with barely enough room to breathe, Eva and I hung on for dear life. At last, with other drivers sitting on the hood as lookouts, we drove away.

The road to Lübeck was a dusty old country road with potato fields on either side. It was sizzling hot, and the women crammed together under the canvas roof were restless. Everywhere in Europe, not only on highways but also on side roads, there are markers to indicate the distances. One white marker for each kilometer — letting one know how far one has come, how far one still has to go. These twenty kilometers were the longest I have ever traveled.

The two trucks, in as bad shape as we were, screeching, rumbling and rattling, kept bouncing us around as if we were rubber balls, yet moved no faster than lazy snails. With only the edge of the truck to hold on to, we had quite a time of it trying not to fall out. The sun was merciless. Its fiery rays hurt my eyes, burned my face, scorched the earth. Clouds of dust, whipped by a hot and unforgiving wind, kept thrashing us every step of the way.

The road itself looked like the entire war had been fought right there. Nothing but overturned tanks, with dead soldiers still pinned inside. The ditches were full of broken-down equipment, weapons and lifeless bodies. Dead soldiers, covered with dirt and dried blood, slumped over their machine guns; dead horses, their big eyes wide open, staring into nothingness with their mouths agape and their teeth showing as though they were laughing at men's insanity. Not a sign of life anywhere — mayhem and ruin. It looked almost staged. Like someone had choreographed the scene.

Nineteen kilometers: The truck kept groaning and puffing, blowing smoke like an old locomotive. Inside, some of the women were getting sick and vomited. There was no air to reach them, and the darkness made them feel trapped.

Eighteen kilometers: I wished that I still had that dirty rag that was tied around my bad leg. Nothing to cover it with anymore. The pus kept running down my leg. It hurt like hell, and where was my other shoe anyway?

Seventeen kilometers: My lips, cracked and dry, felt like parchment. My tongue was swollen, and I had difficulty swallowing. There was also something wrong with the roof of my mouth. It felt raw and full of blisters. Eva kept yelling that someone was kicking her and trying to throw her off the truck.

Sixteen kilometers: More dead soldiers. It made me think of the song Herbert had written for me. The one about the unknown soldier, "What did you fight for ... what did you die for ... nobody gives a damn ... nobody knows your name ... " How appropriate. They should have covered them up or buried them. Somebody should have.

Fifteen kilometers: I was being kicked, too! The women inside, fighting for every inch of space, kept pushing and clawing. They kept screaming, "I can't stand it! Stop the truck! Let me out — Let me out!" They got their wish. I heard the planes the same time I heard the squeaking of the brakes, and jumped before I was pushed out. Everybody jumped and instantly stumbled in all directions. John grabbed me, and moments later we were both lying facedown in a potato field, his body covering mine completely. "Don't move," he whispered. Move? I didn't even dare to gasp.

I got a mouthful of the good ole German earth while the planes zooming over us like noisy flocks of birds went back to the same target area. "Good God," John murmured, "there won't be anybody left." He had lifted his head up for only a moment, and when he lowered it again, his face was next to mine. We were lying spreadeagled, like two crosses melted into one. I could see the sweat on his forehead, the pulsating veins on his temple, feel his breath, feel all of him. We stayed like this for a long, long time. A man, a woman, pretending to be dead yet so very much alive and so very close.

We didn't get back to the trucks until the planes, after returning a second time around, were out of sight and sound. Did as many return as had left? What about their losses — at fifty meters they must have been an easy target, too.

Some of the women were actually fighting; they didn't want to get back into the trucks. Incomprehensible, perhaps, but they no longer cared. They had reached their limit.

Fourteen kilometers: We were passing a figure on the road — an old man with a white beard and cane, wearing a sign around his chest: "BLIND." He looked so pitiful and lost. For one split second I wanted to yell, "Stop, let's take him with us!" But then this moment of humanity was gone, and all that was left inside me was rage and uncontrollable hate. "German, lousy rotten German. Die, die." He looked pathetically absurd trotting alone along death row.

Thirteen kilometers: The road was getting bumpier, and I felt dizzier by the minute, as if I were riding a roller coaster upside down. I couldn't stop shaking, but not because of the ride. My throat was on fire and so was my face and the deep, pus-filled hole in my leg. Several of the women were pushing me aside and jumping out. I got hit and knocked around. My vision became blurred . . . I no longer could see the markers on the road. All I remember of those last twelve kilometers is the glaring sun and the pain . . .

Lübeck! We had made it! We were greeted with enormous joy and an equal amount of confusion. They all came running toward us at once. Doctors, nurses, Red Cross women carrying heavy barrels of hot soup, their eager arms reaching for us and helping us off the trucks. From inside our truck the remaining women were boxing their way out of the darkness and into the light.

I got thrown out. Caught in the arms of one of the Red Cross women, a mere twinkling before landing in the boiling soup, I managed to escape the worst. But my prison dress got soaked, and I lost my remaining shoe.

John always seemed to find me. He looked so tired and exhausted as though he, single-handed, had fought all the wars by himself since time began. He picked me up and took me to a nearby bench. There he told me that the plans already had been changed: we could no longer stay in Lübeck. News of our dreadful disaster must have traveled faster than we, and Lübeck, open city, was expected to be bombed that night. By whom, he didn't know. No time for us to spend together, not even one more day, not one more night. We had no say in the matter. I had to move on; he had to stay. Johnny (I'd heard his friend call him that), while scribbling my address on a piece of paper, urged me not to stay in Sweden but to go home to Amsterdam so he would know where to find me. "I'll see you there," he said, smiling just a little.

Outside the town in a nearby forest, close to the Danish border, Danish drivers were waiting to take us to Copenhagen.

I could no longer walk. Johnny carried me like a sick child in his arms for eight kilometers through the town into the forest where the buses were. There, slowly resting my head on a pillow by the window, he put me on a seat and sat down next to me. Neither of us had any strength left. For some precious moments we just looked at each other. In his bloodshed eyes I saw the agony of every human being who had suffered the cruel ruthlessness of war. I saw the hurt he felt for having to let go of our moments together with no chance of ever reclaiming a single one of them, and I saw the sadness deep inside him, the sorrow of the irreplaceable years the war had stolen from us both.

Kneeling in front of me, he took a chain with a tag from his neck and put it around mine. It was his dog tag, his I.D. Not the metal but the plastic one. Same name, though, same address, same everything. "It's who I am," he said. "Don't lose it. And don't let anyone take it from you, keep it always." He then told me that if I didn't hear from him, to write to his mother. For a magical few seconds he held me in his arms, stroked my sunburned face, and, with a gentle, tender tiredness, he kissed my torn lips.

I never saw or heard from him again. Deep in my heart I've always known that he did not make it through the last night in Lübeck . . .

Was it "friendly" fire that killed my hero? And if so, was death less deadly because of it? Less permanent? And did his mother, when she was told, cry fewer tears?

⸻

WHEN LIFE FOR ME HAD STARTED all over again, at another time in another place, I wrote to Johnny. I wrote to his mother and to the War Department in Washington, D.C., but I never received an answer from anyone. I kept his tag and have it still, this extraordinary keepsake from this extraordinary man who kept me safe. Sometimes, when I'm alone, I look at it.

I touch it, read the address, think of him and say his name: *John D. Jackson of Bossier City, Louisiana* . . . Johnny, for that is who he was . . .

The disastrous outcome of our transport was broadcast all over Europe. Denmark, still under German occupation, had its flags at half-mast, as did Sweden. In London, my twin sister Elly was listening to the BBC when they announced the names of all the survivors safe in Sweden. She was the first one to hear that I was alive. It must have been quite a shock. From the day that I left Amsterdam to the day of the broadcast, she never knew where I was or what had happened to me.

↜ Casualty Count

Dead:

One Swedish Red Cross officer and his assistant
Three American drivers
Two hundred and forty freed concentration camp prisoners

Wounded:

One American soldier missing one arm
One American soldier blinded
One American soldier bleeding badly from stomach wounds
Two hundred and sixty women prisoners seriously wounded
Eighty women prisoners slightly injured, able to walk
One hundred and twenty women prisoners miraculously unharmed

↜

After the disaster, many people in other countries mourned with us. We were the first Red Cross transport ever to get out of a concentration camp before the war ended. The first, the last, the only one.

⤳ Epilogue

ON MAY 8, 1945, the church bells in Göteborg, Sweden, our final destination, rang louder and longer than ever before. They rang everywhere in the land, everywhere in the world. On that day, the planes flying over the city were not bombers but messengers of peace:

⤳

THE WAR IS OVER
the skywriters wrote
THE WORLD IS FREE

⤳

I made it through! Destiny was on my side. It wanted me to live so I could not only tell others about the immeasurable worth of life and of every human being, but also to speak for those who never got to speak at all.

I did not learn this right away. After the war, all I wanted was to get far away. So, I moved to America. At the time, I believed that the more distance I put between me and my past, the harder it would be for my past to find me. That, of course, was never true. It has always been with me, for I am the past, and everything I think and do is because of the past. I am its memory and its reminder.

Returning to Amsterdam and my theater, the Schouwburg, almost thirty years ago, meant that I at last had come full circle and finally could write about myself and those who were no more: those close to me and those I never knew.

It is estimated that for approximately seventy thousand Jews, this theater was their last place of residence.

ᓚ

AFTER THE WAR, the theater under the name Picadilly, had been restored. However, the announcement of a gala opening caused a shocking reaction. Furious Amsterdamers, led by the remaining Dutch underground, threatened to blow it up. Queen Juliana sent her minister, who immediately canceled all performances. The Schouwburg was never to open as a theater again.

For the next ten years, while countless civic groups argued about what to do with the ill-fated building, it just stood there.

Not until 1962 did my theater meet its final destiny. In memory of those seventy thousand Jews who were taken from it by the Nazis, a shrine of extraordinary simplicity has been erected.

There are no comfortable chairs where once the audience sat so comfortably. It is just one big lawn. Soothing to the anxious heart, it stretches all the way across to — the stage?

There are no colorful stained-glass windows, no sculptural art effects to dazzle visitors. There is only the gripping presence of realistic symbols to tell the story. That, and the silence. In here, the silence speaks. Perhaps not everyone could hear it. I could. It spoke to me from every corner of this visionary temple, this quiet, holy place.

At one side of the old foyer, three tombstones, representing a father, mother, child, who left here never to return, cry out a warning to the young. Seventy thousand warnings to all the young. They are the past.

Fresh new plants and baby mosslike seedlings sent from Israel are on the other side. They represent the future. Embracing hope, they weave a new beginning for those who dare to hope.

On a narrow brick wall behind the tombstones, the eternal flame keeps vigil. It will do so always, and forever, for they, always and forever, are dead.

On a plateau of stones, resting on a Star of David–shaped base, stands the obelisk. It is covered with wreaths and flowers. A black plaque reads:

⤸

IN MEMORY OF THOSE
SENT AWAY FROM HERE 1940–1945

⤸

This sacred shrine has no roof; the sky above is its roof. No man-made cover veils its somber secrets. It seems incredibly right to have the heavens look down upon it.

Out of my theater's grand, and joyous, yet devastating past, out of its rubble and ruins, bricks from the original walls have been salvaged to form walls again. They're centered around both sides of the old stage. Ascending unevenly like timeworn steps, these bricks, alas, are the most crushing symbol of all the broken lives.

Yet in spite of the sadness, grief is not the leitmotif here. Remembrance is. Peace and serenity is. Life not yet lived is . . .

Did it take thirty years for me to write about all this? Or did I just not write about it for thirty years? Both. Time never entered into it. Not then. It does now, though.

Why now? Why after almost half a century do I want every living creature to hear my story? Because, in spite of my racing through life like a runaway train to make up for the years the Nazis stole from me, time has caught up with me, too. I don't know how much I have left. I do know there aren't many of us — the survivors — left.

People used to say I belonged to a lost generation, and they were right. Well, it seems that I have graduated. I now belong to the last generation. The last of those who have lived the murderous years and kept them alive. What will happen when we are no more? Who will continue the fight against the Nazi heirs then? Our heirs, anyone? How far have we come with NEVER AGAIN. How much farther do we still have to go? Is anyone even listening any more?

With the twilight years upon me, it is time for recollection. That doesn't mean I'm closing the book on this fantastic journey destiny has sent me on nor that I am rocking chair bound. I will never be oblivious to what the world allows, nor, having had my day, will I fade out. I shall not miss a single heartbeat due to me, a single chance to tell my tale in memory of those whose anguished cries still echo within my soul.

Above all, I will not ever take life for granted; nor will I ever forget how lucky I am to be alive.

◡

In Memory of Those Never to Be Forgotten

Margit Heinrich,
my valiant friend

In the last days of the war, Margit was sent to Auschwitz for having saved the lives of many Jews. There she contracted tuberculosis. She died in a sanatorium in Davos, Switzerland, in the winter of 1947, and is buried there.

Ferry Nagy,
my knight in shining armor

In the same week that Margit died, I received a telegram from the Red Cross: "Shot while trying to escape."

Eva Aman,
my buddy always

In the worst and best of times, our friendship remained impregnable. Eva died unexpectedly in Frankfurt, Germany, in May 1993.

Herbert Nelson,
my friend, my husband

Shortly after we emigrated to America, Herbert began work as as writer for the Voice of America, where he had a brilliant career until he died in New York City in 1991.

John D. Jackson — Johnny,
my American soldier

My family

Mama died in Vienna, Austria, at the age of eighty-seven.

Elly, my twin, died unexpectedly in London on October 2, 1992, one day after our birthday, which we were to celebrate together for the first time in fifty-six years.

Kate, my older sister, lives in Montreal. She celebrated her eightieth birthday on February 19, 1994.

❧

IN MEMORY OF THOSE NEVER TO BE FORGIVEN

The Third Reich,

its murderers and
those who knew and looked the other way — wherever they may be.

Index

⌐ INDEX

A

Actors State Exam, 11
Admission and Registration Offices,
236
air hunger
during transport, 213, 215
air-raids
at Siemens, 280
Alice (at Penalty Block), 318, 320
Aman, Eva, 292, 310
in Ravensbrück, 257, 273
and hair confrontation, 281
in solitary confinement, 298–310
removed from bunker, 301
returned to bunker, 303
removed from bunker again, 304
examination and beating, 321
and Swedish Red Cross rescue, 333
after bombing raid, 344
death of, 354
work detail, 284
America
move to, 351
Americans arrival, 339

Amsterdam
move to, 34
bombing of, 98
return to, 1
annexation
Austria, 14
appell (counting off), 207
at Auschwitz, 242, 245
at Ravensbrück, 256
Russian roulette at, 245
appropriation, 47. *See also* confiscation;
jewelry
Stern's factory, 78
arrest and confinement, 298–310
arrivals
in Camp Malin, 187
in Ravensbrück, 311
artists
exit from Austria, 14
and restrictions, 47
and the list, 82
in Camp Malin, 170
orchestra, 233, 247
Aryan father story, 110, 191, 236
Asscher, Mr. (Jewish Committee), 72

attacks on Sylvie
    Boden's in rain, 192–196
    Boden's with flour, 174–177
    Holthöfer's, 281–284
Aunt Shari, 17
Auschwitz
    All-Girl Birkenau Marching Band, 247
    arrival, 223
    first night, 243
    Sylvie in, 223–251
Austria
    Third Reich annexation of, 44
Austrian people, 11
    anti-Semitism of, 13
    attitude toward Germans, 14
Avenue Louise, 177

B

Bahls, Herr, 291
    at Siemens, 277–278
    support from, 281
band concerts, 247
barracks
    assignment, 167
    in Camp Malin, 170, 171
    at Auschwitz, 229
bartering
    importance of, 117
Beatrix Theater, 35
Belgian Jews, 169
Belgium, 22, 132–135, 143–153
    escape to, 117
    first night, 137–140
    first morning, 140
    departure from, 204–211
    resistance in, 102
Bensburger Ghetto prisoners, 241

Berlin
    Ravensbrück proximity to, 256
Bernadotte, Count Folke, 331
Bernhardt, Sarah, 39
Bernie and Rebecca (Roosendaal escape companions), 130
    imprisoned, 158
Bert, 68
Betty
    and Rainer, 113–117
    at Camp Malin, 167
    at Auschwitz, 237
Oberaufseherin Binz, 268
Birkenau, 246
birthday
    in Utrecht, 34
    first in Ravensbrück, 259
    second in Ravensbrück, 295
    seventh, memory of, 259–265
black marketeers, 79
    in Auschwitz, 249
    at Ravensbrück, 256
Black Shirts, 35
Block 28
    at Ravensbrück, 255
The Block, 240
block construction
    near Siemens, 294
Blockova (elders)
    at Auschwitz, 242
'blown-up' condition, 282
Blue Lantern Café
    meeting-place, 121, 125
Blumethal, 36
Unterscharführer Boden, 162
    attack in rain on Sylvie, 192–196
    flour attack on Sylvie, 174–176
    hatred of beauty, 174
body check, 166
    Auschwitz, 229–230

bombing raids, 280
  orphanage, 97
  German countryside, 254
  Russian, 308
  on Red Cross transport, 342–343
border crossing, 133–135, 136
  Germany, 222
bounty hunters, 60, 75, 80
boy guard
  at Christmas, 297
bridge question, 254
Brown Shirts, 35
Brunner, Louise, 268
Brussels
  Jews in, 169–170
Brussels trip
  hayride, 141–142
  train ride, 142–145
Budapest
  trip to, 16–17
  last trip to, 20
bunker
  confinement in, 298–310
  release from, 310
  voluntary return to, 317
Burg Theater, 12
business center
  in Auschwitz, 249

C

Cabaret International (Utrecht), 32
cages
  at Auschwitz, 244
Camp Malin, 162–211
  arrival, 162
  departure, 204–211
capture by Nazis, 156

career, 22
  first film break, 6
  New Vienna Playhouse contract, 9
  A Clever Lad, 10
  in Budapest, 18
  in Switzerland, 12, 20
  Belgium, 21
  Jewish Theater, 43
casualty count, 350
Catherine (bookkeeper), 242–243
cattle cars, 212. *See also* transport
cell confinement, 298–310
censorship, 44
censorship soldier, 44, 52
Chamberlain, Neville, 29
chambres separées, 18
childhood, 5
children's death, 251
child rescue. *See* Mission Frieda
chimneys. *See also* crematorium
  at Auschwitz, 237
China
  and Austrian Jews, 13
Christmas presents 1943, 272
Christmas tree
  in Ravensbrück, 271
Cinderella, 320
citizenship loss, 45
clothing assignment, 235
clothing supply room
  attempted refuge in, 317–318
coal detail
  at Siemens, 279
coat, gem-filled, 122, 171–172
code for escape, 121
De Cohen, Mr. (Jewish Committee), 72
Cohen family, 56
  Papa's Marcus Stern story, 77–79
cold, 280
  after solitary confinement, 304–305

concert
  in Auschwitz, 249
  in Ravensbrück, 274, *285*
confiscation
  jewelry, 45
  radios, 44
congregation
  forbidden, 50
contributions for freedom, 120
convoy, German
  on road to Lübeck, 340
costumes and gowns, 120
counting off
  at Auschwitz, *242*, 245
  at Ravensbrück, 256
  Russian roulette at, 245
couple on train, 218, 220–221
'crazies' block
  refuge in, 318–319
crematorium. *See also* chimneys
  first sight of victims, 239
criminals
  at Ravensbrück, 255–256
crowding
  at Ravensbrück, 323
crucifixion chamber, 300
curly hair confrontation, 281–284
Czechoslovakia
  Germans in, 21
Czech women, 285
  at Ravensbrück, 257

D

Daniel, 336
darkness, 280
Davids, Henriette, 41, 49, 67

D-Day
  news of, 288
death
  accounting for, 242
  of children, 250–251
  of Esther, 298
  of Father, 259–265
  of Rainer, 248
death papers, 307
deGaulle sister, 286
demons and fear, 168–169
departure. *See also* liberation
  from Camp Malin, 204–211
  from Ravensbrück, 332
deportation center takeover
  second day, 63
  third day, 64
  fourth day, 65
  fifth day, 67
  sixth day, 72
  Sylvie taken to, 81
detachment
  need for, 272
detention camps. *See also*
  Auschwitz; Camp Malin;
  Ravensbrück
  label, 170
  south of Holland, 31
diamond man, 335
doctors
  fear of, 265
documents
  arrival, two years late, 328
  Aryan Father story, 191, 236
donations for freedom, 120
Dürer, Otto, 14
  and Budapest contract, 18
  reunion in Utrecht, 34
Duschinski Theater, 37

Dutch Jews, 169–170

Dutch Nazi Party, 36. *See also* bounty
hunters

Dutch people. *See also* Holland
under siege, 24
Utrecht, 33
and yellow star requirement, 49–
50

Dutch prisoners
release of, 330–331

Dutch Resistance. *See* Resistance

Dutch Theater. *See* Hollandsche
Schouwburg

E

E barracks, 167

E designee, 162–163
revocation of, 184

Eichmann, Lt. Col. Karl Adolf, 246

elders
at Auschwitz, 242
in Camp Malin, 171, 179

Elly (Sylvie's twin), 5, 23, 259
hears news of Sylvie, 349
death of, 354

emigration, 19
England, 25
America, 29

end-of-war confusion, 311

end-of-war rumors, 294, 327

endurance, 239. *See also* will to live

engineer at Siemens
Sylvie's work for, 289

England escape attempt, 26

Enschede evacuation, 31

entertainment night
Polish twins, 249

Entscheidung, 163

Erdman, 217
Margit's visit to, 188
at transport table, 207

Erika (Roosendaal escape baby), 131
good-bye to Belgian farmer, 142

Erlholz, Kate, 37

escapees
murder of, 216

escape from theater, 88–91

escape hole
cattle car, 213, 217
discovery by Germans, 219

escape plan. *See also* postcards
Betty and Rainers, 117
Camp Malin, 200
during transport, 214–215

escape to Belgium, 132–135

escape to Roosendaal, 125–135

Esther (Polish child), 296
death, 298

evacuation, 30

exemption certificate, 76

exercise, morning, 174

exercise classes (Utrecht), 32

experiments
"medical," 246–247

eyeglasses
German theft of, 249

F

factory construction
near Ravensbrück, 275

Fall of France, 33

Fall of Yugoslavia, 41

family life
New Year's, 271

family life (*continued*)
  after Papa's death, 314–316
farmhouse in Belgium, 137–139
Father story. *See* Aryan father story
Father (Sylvie's father), 5
  at Prater park, 150
  illness and death of, 259–265
  burial, 8
fear and demons, 168–169
Ferry. *See* Nagy, Ferry
film break, 6
firing squad papers, 307
Flitzers, 200
flour attack, 174–176
food
  during transport, 212
  at Ravensbrück, 265–266
  fantasy of, 274
  gifts from Herr Bahls, 278
France, Fall of, 33
Commander Fränk, 163, 206, 213
  and Margit's visit, 189
  and transport announcement,
    204
Fredericke, *312, 317, 321, 323*
freedom, 333
French prisoners
  at Siemens, 278
Frieda, 96. *See also* Mission Frieda
friendships
  in camp, 173
Fritz (Camp Malin civilian), 163,
  169
Fritzi, 203, *235, 240, 249*
  in shower room, 235
  stops speaking, 238
funeral of Father, 264–265
future talk
  Eva in bunker, 303
  with Johnny, 348

G

Dr. Gebhart, 321
Geneva Convention, 340
Gerda (Dr.'s girlfriend), 267–268
German convoy. *See also* Third Reich
  on road to Lübeck, 340
German people
  in Holland, 29
  attitude toward Russians, 279
German prisoners
  at Siemens, 278
  in bunker, 308
Germany
  seen from transport train, 222, 253
  spread of control, 22
Gerron, Kurt, 64, 68–69
Gestapo, 299, 301
  in Amsterdam, 35
  at theatrical event, 183
ghettoization, 43
Glücke, Gemma, 314, 316, 322
  disappearance of, 330
Goerdeler, Carl (Mayor of Leipzig),
  313
gold teeth
  German theft of, 249
Göteberg, Sweden
  bells of peace in, 351
gowns and costumes, 120
Greek prisoners, 240, 241
Greta and Gus
  Utrecht hosts, 32
guards, 290–293
  at Siemens, 280
  at Ravensbrück, 328
  regret felt by one, 329–330
'the guessing room'
  in Camp Malin, 170
gymnastic classes (Utrecht), 32

gypsies
    at Birkenau, 246

H

The Hague, Holland, 19
    family in, 23
hair
    German theft of, 249
hair confrontation, 281–284
hair shaving, 231–234
    at Ravensbrück, 265
Harry (underground contact), 117–118
    escape with, 121
    escape to Roosendaal, 126–135
De Hartog, Mr. and Mrs., 131, 147, 205
    imprisoned, 158
hayride to Brussels, 141–142
head shaving, 231–234
heat
    at Auschwitz, 236–237
    during transport, 213
Heinrich, Margit, 63
    first meetings, 53–55
    in hiding, 73–74
    rescue by, 111
    visits Camp Malin, 187–190
    and Aryan father story, 191
    death of, 354
Heinz (elder in Camp Malin), 178
    at transport, 207, 210
    during transport, 213
    saves couple on train, 218–219
Helm, Hugo, 19
    and Operation Schouwburg, 69–70
hiding place
    Mama's apartment, 120
    Margit's, 73–74
    morgue, 337

Himmler, Heinrich, 272–273
    firing squad papers, 307
Hitler, Adolf, 11, 22, 312
    rumor of assassination, 294
Hoess, Kommandant Rudolf, 227, 246
    sorting prisoners, 228
Holland. *See also* Dutch people
    refuge in, 22
    under siege, 23
Hollandsche Schouwburg, 2, 35. *See
        also* deportation center takeover;
        Jewish Theater
    legend of, 38, 39
    return to, 352
    memorial site of, 352–354
Holthöfer, Kommandoführerin, 275,
        276, 279
    confrontation with, 281
home in Vienna, 5
hope
    preservation and return of, 341–342
hospital
    at Ravensbrück, 267
house mother
    in new block, 294–295
humanity, 240
    preservation of, *213, 238*, 341–342
human skin lampshades, 268
humiliation
    physical, 166, 229
Hungarian Jews, 316
hunger, 280
    at Ravensbrück, 266

I

ID cards. *See* identification cards
identification cards, 45
    Toni and Margit's, 79

identification cards (*continued*)

    and escape to Roosendaal, 126

illegitimacy. *See* Aryan Father story

Ilse (elder), 242

infirmary

    at Ravensbrück, 267

Inquart, Seyss, 35

Inspector Bull, 78

intellectuals

    and the list, 82

interrogations

    by Criminal Commissar Randolph,

        305–307

    by Dutch general, 309–310

    during solitary confinement, 302–303

invasion of France

    news of, 288

J

Jackson, John D., 339

    night with, 341–342

    good-by in Lübeck, 347–348

    death of, 354

Janosh, 213–214

Jean (pigeon-hole neighbor), 172–173, 202

Jehovah's Witnesses

    at Ravensbrück, 255, 257

jewelry

    for barter, 117

    gem-filled coat retained, 171–172

    in Auschwitz, 249

jewelry appropriation, 163, 164

Jewish children

    saved from deportation, 95–96,

        99–103

Jewish Committee

    and deportation center takeover, 72

    Sylvie's detainment and escape, 83–85

Jewish ghetto

    and theater restrictions, 42

Jewishness

    first awareness of, 264

Jewish people

    in Amsterdam, 34–35, 79

    in Brussels, 169

    in Holland, 33

Jewish Poles

    at Auschwitz, 241

Jewish Theater, 39, 40–44. *See also* Hollandsche Schouwburg

    appropriation, 58–61

    Sylvie's detainment, 82

John (Belgian connection), 128, 131, 177

    disappearance of, 147–152

Jonny (pigeon-hole neighbor), 186, 214, 216

    and escape plans, 201

    and transport preparation, 206

Joodsche Schouwburg. *See* Jewish Theater

Joseph

    soup bowl incident, 198

    at transport time, 210

jumping practice, 201

K

Karl (and Margit), 190

Kate (Sylvie's sister), 5, 14, 19, 122, 262

    in Amsterdam, 50–52

    and Julius, 31, 36

    birth of Mario, 269

    death of, 355

Katja (assistant elder), 242

Kennedy, Ambassador Joseph, 30

Kleider Kammer, 317

Kneidiger, Karl, 10

kojens (cages)
  at Auschwitz, 244
Krakow, 241
Kurt, 24
  escape and career, 28
Kurzberg (Papa's business manager), 315

L

lampshades of human skin, 268
Van Leer Foundation, 41
lesbians
  in Ravensbrück, 274–275
  guard, in Ravensbrück, 290–293
Levie, Dr. J., 41
liberation, 334
liberation of France, 294
Linke, Frau
  at Siemens, 279
  Sylvie works for, 280–281
the list, 82
loneliness
  at Christmas, 297
Lou's help, 82–86
Lübeck
  trip to, 339–349
  arrival, 347
lucky eighty, 273
  transport from Auschwitz, 252
Lydia, 292
  prisoner at Ravensbrück, 257
  in Ravensbrück, 273–274

M

Madame Zeker, 177
madness of prisoners, 319–320

mail privilege, 169
  from home, 269
  no package penalty, 196
  Sylvie's first package, 197
Main Street, 239
Malin (first camp), 161–211
Mama (Sylvie's mother), 5
  and Sylvie's career, 9
  leaves Vienna, 19
  reaction to escape plans, 118–119
  receipt of postcard, 190
  at Father's death, 260
  as widow, 314–316
  death of, 354
Margit. *See* Heinrich, Margit
Marie (family housekeeper), 259
Mario's birth (nephew), 269
market
  in Auschwitz, 249
marriages
  forbidden by Germany, 48
Martin (elder in Camp Malin), 68
  becomes lover, 179
  at transport time, 208, 209
Mausner, Toni, 55–57, 79, 121
Max, 177
  departure from villa, 154
Mayer (Camp Malin civilian), 163, 168, 197
  attention from, 174
  and Margit's visit, 189
  at transport, 206
Medea role, 10
medical profession
  fear of, 265
Dr. Mengele, 246–247
Millie (Roosendaal escape companion), 131, 205
  imprisoned, 158
Mischlings, 257

Mission Frieda, 101, 103–107
  abrupt ending of, 108
morning exercise, 174
Moskowitz family, 61–63
Mother Superior, 92
Moulin Rouge contract, 18
Munich Pact, 29
murder of escapees, 216
murder of random passengers,
  217
murders
  at Ravensbrück, 255–256
My Yiddishe Mamme, 250

N

Nagy, Ferry (cousin Ference)
  first meeting, 14–15
  second meeting, 16–17
  separation from, 21
  separation from, 33–34
  last letter from, 111
  death of, 355
Nazism
  in Austria, 13–14
  and Austrian Jews, 7
  spread, 22
Nelson, Herbert
  relationship with, 36–37
  reaction to escape plans, 118–119
  death of, 355
Nelson, Rudolf, 37, 41
Nelson Revue, 35
New Vienna Playhouse
  contract, 9
New Year's Eve 1941, in Holland, 46
  family traditions at, 271–272
night in morgue, 337
nighttime attack on Sylvie, 192–196

non-Jewish people
  and restrictions, 47
  theatergoers, 44
no package penalty, 196
NSP. *See* Dutch Nazi Party
number at Ravensbrück, 256
number call, 207. *See also* appell

O

old people
  and deportation center takeover, 66,
    67
Ollie
  Ravensbrück bunkmate, 255
Oma (Sylvie's grandmother), 5
Operation Schouwburg, 65. *See also* de-
    portation center takeover
  release from, 72–73
operetta productions, 19
optimism
  preservation and return of, 341–342
orchestra
  at Auschwitz, 233, 247
'organizing' (stealing)
  at Ravensbrück, 266
orphanage job, 85, 92–107
  Sister Agnes disappearance, 94
over-40 rule, 250

P

packages from home, 169
  in Ravensbrück, 274
Packeten Sperre, 196
Papa (Sylvie's father), 150–152
papers
  arrival, two years late, 328

parachutists (Russian)
    at Ravensbrück, 268–269
patch color
    at Ravensbrück, 257, 265
peace, 351
Pearl Harbor, 45
Penalty Block, 320
perfume confiscation
    resistance to, 160
'persuasion,' 299
Peters, Dr., 64–65
photos
    loss of, 230
Piet (baker), 79
Piet (Camp Malin watchmaker), 169
"pigeonholes"
    in Camp Malin, 171
    move, in Camp Malin, 184–185
    neighbors, 184–185
Poland, 241
    Germans in, 21
Poles
    at Auschwitz, 241
Polese, Kate/Mrs. Julius. See Kate
    (Sylvie's sister)
Polish twins
    concert by, 249
Poons, Sylvain, 67
Population Registry: National Identifi-
    cation Center, 35, 102
postcards
    as code, 118
    message from Belgium, 142
    warning to family mailed, 161
    from home, 269
pouring of lead
    New Year's Eve tradition, 272
Prater memory of Father, 150
Preger, Kurt, 23
Princess Operetta Theater, 19

prison administrators, 220, 236, 242
prisoner-of-war camps
    south of Holland, 31
professionals
    and the list, 82
prostitutes
    at Ravensbrück, 256
prostitution recruitment
    by German officers, 286–287

Q

quarantine
    at Ravensbrück, 255

R

rabbi (pigeonhole neighbor), 185–186
radio
    discovery at Siemens, 289
    false news on, 23
Rainer, 177–178, 205
    and Betty, 113–117
    at Camp Malin, 164
    Auschwitz arrival, 229
    at head shaving table, 233
    in shower room, 235
    arrival at The Block, 240
    illness and death, 247–248
Randolph, Criminal Commissar, 276, 312
    interrogates Sylvie, 305–307
Ravensbrück
    arrival, 254
    compared to Auschwitz, 266
    prisoner in, 254–332
    rescue from, 332–349
Red Cross transport. See Swedish Red
    Cross

Renata (bunker spy), 300
Renie (fan at Ravensbrück), 330–331, 332
rescue
    Swedish Red Cross, 332–349
Resistance. *See also* Mission Frieda
    in Amsterdam, 35
    in Belgium, 102–103
    and bombing raid, 97
    and escape plans, 202–203
Soldier Resnick, 86, 87–89
restrictions, 50
        marriages, 48
    public spaces, 46
    public transport, 47
    radios, 44
    social calls, 47, 80
    stage utterances, 44
    theater, 42
reunion
    with Margit, 187–191
    with Otto, 34
reviews
    Zurich, 13
Roosendaal
    trip to, 125–135
Roosevelt, Franklin Delano
    death of, 321
Dr. Rosenthal
    at Ravensbrück, 267
Rotterdam, 24
rue Lincoln no. 14, 154
Rühren, Commandant, 268, 312
rumors, 280
    assassination of Hitler, 294
    in Belgium, 22
    end-of-war, *294,* 327
Russian parachutists
    at Ravensbrück, 268–269
Russian roulette
    at counting off, 245

Russians
    German attitude toward, 279
    rumored arrival of, 327
Ruth, 24
    escape and career, 28

S

Salonica prisoners, *241*
Sascha, 336
Sauna Queen, 234
saving the children, 99–103
Scheveningen, Holland, 23, 25–28
Schouwburg Theater. *See* Hollandsche
        Schouwburg
scientists
    and the list, 82
Seitz, Karl (mayor of Vienna),
        313
    spotted by Sylvie, 309
sewing efforts, 76
Shanghai
    and Austrian Jews, 13
shoes
    for work detail at Siemens,
        275
shootings
    Ravensbrück, 323
shower
    at Auschwitz, 231
    at Ravensbrück, 255, 265
siege of Holland, 24
Siemens factory, 275
    as bombing target, 280
    importance of, 288
    spy at, 276
silence
    importance of, 307
Simone (housekeeper), 243

singing
  for Ilse, 248–249
  at Ravensbrück, *274, 285*
smell
  at Auschwitz, 237
solitary confinement, 298–310
solitude
  in bunker, 302, 308
  wish for, 278
sores on body, 251, *287, 321*
soup bowl incident
  and Joseph, 198
spring
  always finding it, 150–152
spy at Siemens, 276
Star of David requirement, 48
State Exam, Actors, 11
Stella, 8
Sterkenberg, Bonnie and George,
  61
Stern, Marcus, 76–79
Stöber, Herr, 283
  at Siemens, 276
stork pen
  Magrit's gift gone, 165
stormtroopers, 35
stranger on train, 143, 178
Strauss, Dr. Leo, 9
Strauss, Oska and Johann, 9
the Street Without Mercy,
  239
the Stripper, 319
Stubenältester (elder)
  in Camp Malin, 171
Sturm Abteilung, 35
suicide, 65
Swedish Red Cross
  Geneva Convention protection of,
    340
  rescue by, 332–349

Switzerland
  escape to, 117
  escape attempt, 154–155
  neutral policy effects, 22

T

tattooing, 229–231
Teddy (Communist visitor), 284
  disappearance, 293
theater
  in Camp Malin, 170, 181–184
  Frau Linke's love for, 280
theater takeover. *See* deportation center
    takeover
The Chocolate Soldier song, 297
theft
  in Auschwitz, 249
  of clothing, 319–320
  at Ravensbrück, 256
Third Reich, 28
  annexation of Austria, 14
  appropriation of factories, 47,
    78
  permanent memory of, 355
thirst, 221–222, 236, 244
toilet facilities
  during transport, 213
  in Camp Malin, 170
  at Ravensbrück, 256
Toni. *See* Mausner, Toni
tools, 201
  kept on train, 222
  discarded from train, 223
torture rooms, 300
train boarding
  at transport time, 209
train trip
  from Auschwitz, 253

train trip (*continued*)
  to Brussels, 142
transport, 212
  check-in table, 206–207
  from Auschwitz, 253
  fear of, 169, 200, 204
  murders during, 216
trucks arrival, 338
truth serum injection, 300
twins, Polish
  concert by, 249

U

underground
  recruited by Teddy, 284–
    285
United States
  and declaration of war, 45
Utrecht
  evacuation of, 31
  theater in, 32

V

valuables. *See also* jewelry
  in Auschwitz, 249
Van Raal, Gerda (Sylvie's escape
    name), 126
Viennese people, 5
villa
  stay, 144–146
  garden, 148
  departure, 153
VIP prisoners
  bunker, 299
Vogel, Blauer, 39

W

Walburg, Otto, 63–64, 68
Walter, 24
  escape and hiding, 28–29
war
  news of, 279
  reminder of, 253
Warren, Britta and Tore (Eva's friends),
    303
watchman in bunker, 299, 301
water
  during transport, 212
  need during transport, 221–222
  lack of, 236
water retention, 282
water-tread room, 300
Werner (elder in Camp Malin), 179, 221,
    222
  at transport, 207, 210
  on transport, 213
wheelbarrow work
  Sylvie's at Auschwitz, 247
whipping table, 300
Wieland advice, 232–233
Wilhelm, 114
will-to-live, 239. *See also*
    endurance
  preservation and return
    of, 341
winter of 1942–3, 295
winter of 1943–4, 280
winter of 1944–5, 295
witnessing bloodshed, 220
von Witzleben, Field Marshal Erwin,
    312–313
woman in black
  during transport, 213, 214, 216
work camp destination, 204

work detail, 281
  Sylvie's at Auschwitz,
    247
  at Ravensbrück, 266
  at Siemens, *276, 277*
  night shift, 289
  change back to daytime,
    293
  Eva, at Siemens, 284

Y

yellow star requirement, 48
Yugoslavia, Fall of, 41

Z

Madame Zeker, 145, 147